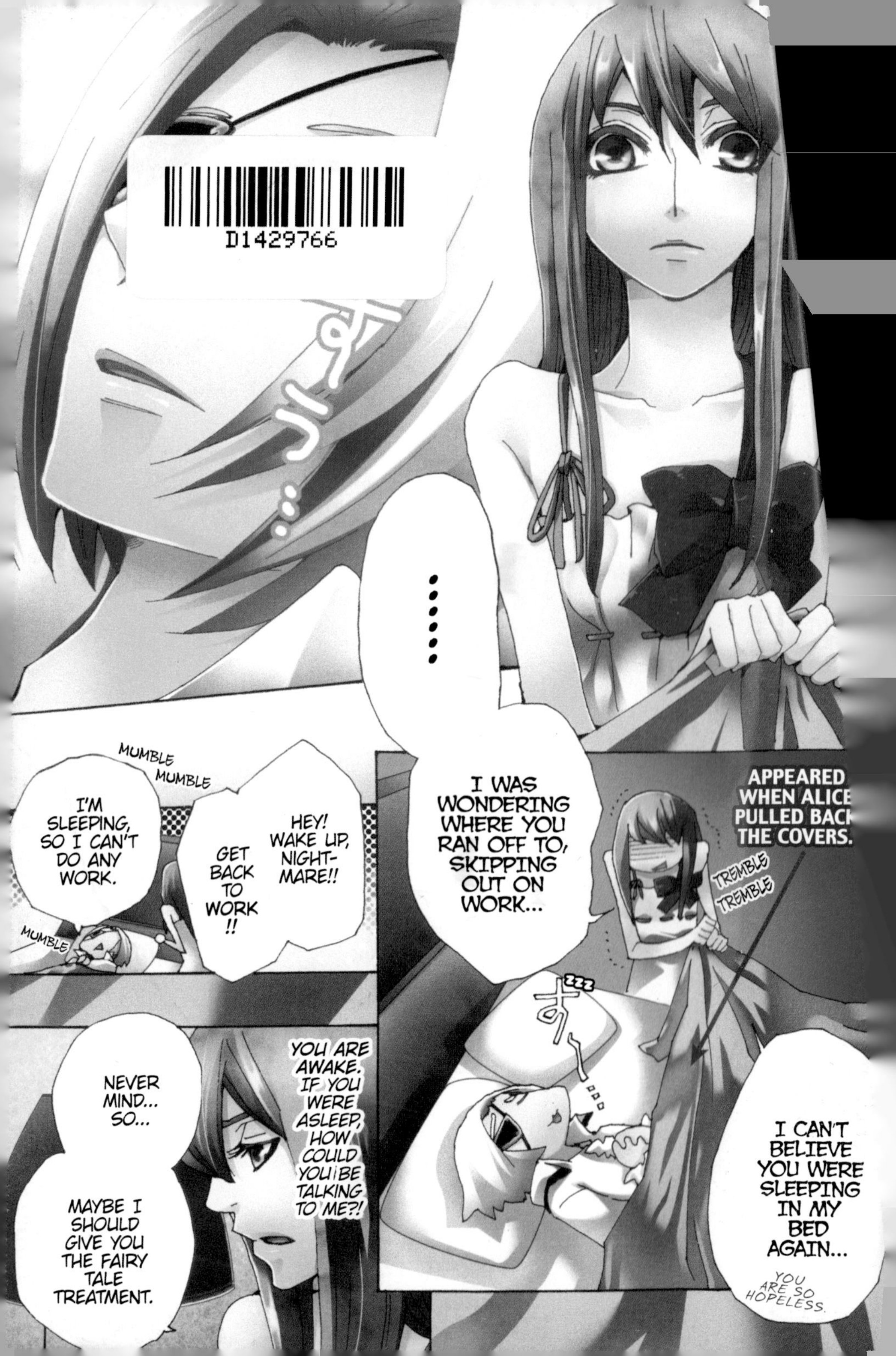
……
APPEARED WHEN ALICE PULLED BACK THE COVERS.
TREMBLE TREMBLE
I WAS WONDERING WHERE YOU RAN OFF TO, SKIPPING OUT ON WORK...
ZZZ
I CAN'T BELIEVE YOU WERE SLEEPING IN MY BED AGAIN...
YOU ARE SO HOPELESS.
HEY! WAKE UP, NIGHTMARE!!
GET BACK TO WORK!!
MUMBLE
MUMBLE
I'M SLEEPING, SO I CAN'T DO ANY WORK.
MUMBLE
YOU ARE AWAKE. IF YOU WERE ASLEEP, HOW COULD YOU BE TALKING TO ME?!
NEVER MIND... SO...
MAYBE I SHOULD GIVE YOU THE FAIRY TALE TREATMENT.

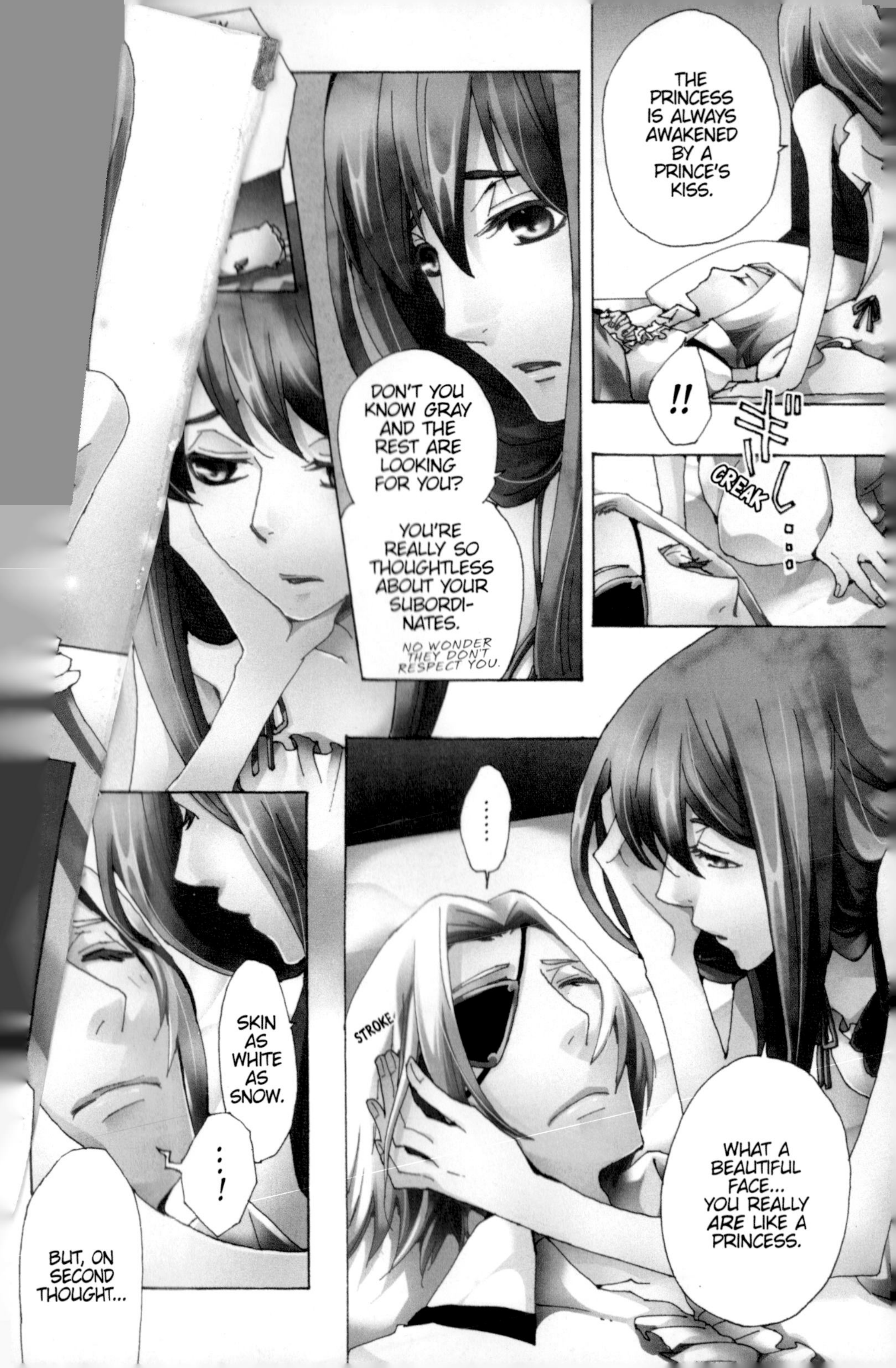
THE PRINCESS IS ALWAYS AWAKENED BY A PRINCE'S KISS.
!!
CREAK
DON'T YOU KNOW GRAY AND THE REST ARE LOOKING FOR YOU?
YOU'RE REALLY SO THOUGHTLESS ABOUT YOUR SUBORDI-NATES.
NO WONDER THEY DON'T RESPECT YOU.
......
STROKE
WHAT A BEAUTIFUL FACE... YOU REALLY ARE LIKE A PRINCESS.
SKIN AS WHITE AS SNOW.
...!
BUT, ON SECOND THOUGHT...

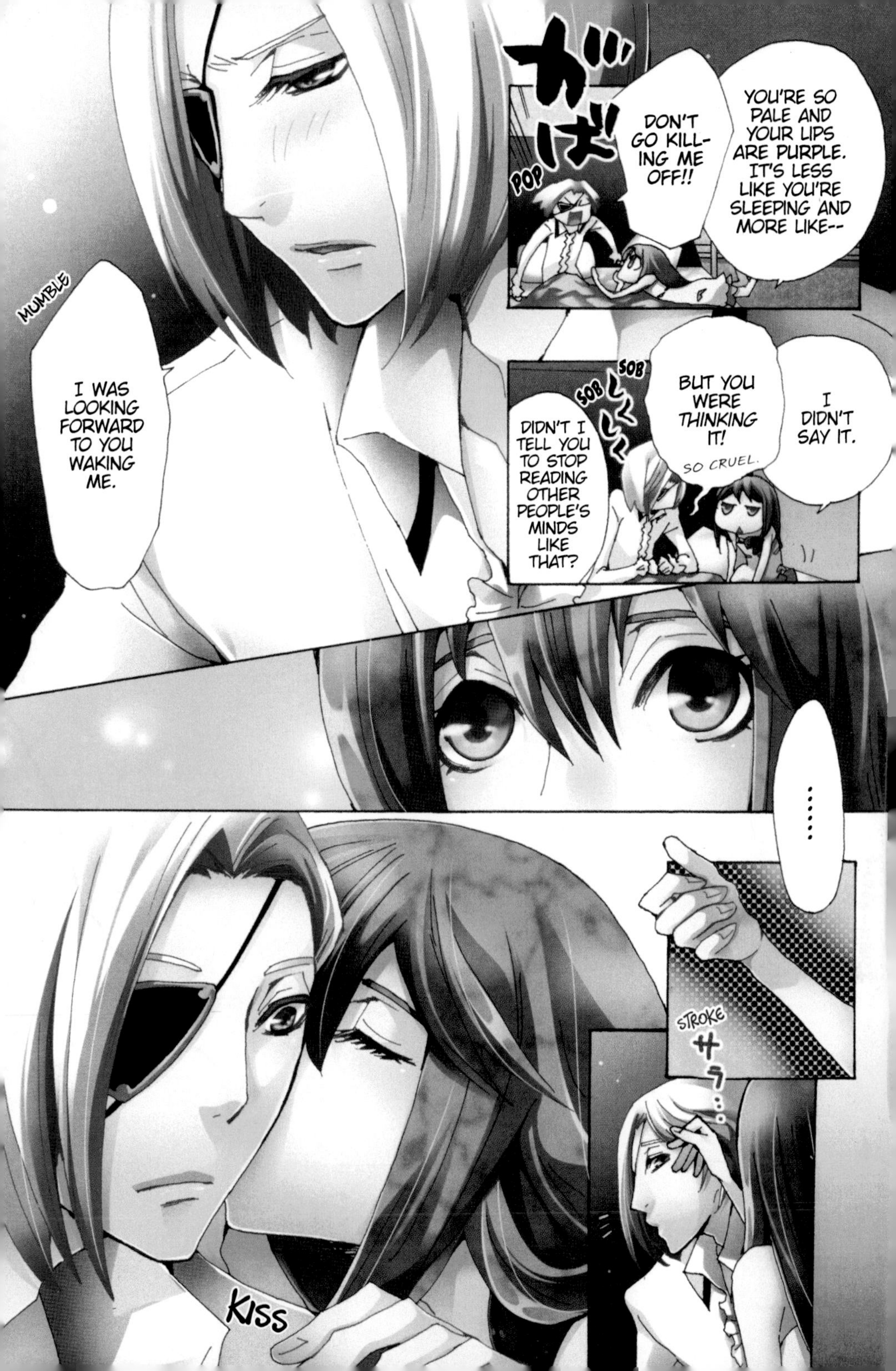

YOU'RE SO PALE AND YOUR LIPS ARE PURPLE. IT'S LESS LIKE YOU'RE SLEEPING AND MORE LIKE--
がばっ
POP
DON'T GO KILL-ING ME OFF!!
I DIDN'T SAY IT.
BUT YOU WERE THINKING IT!
SO CRUEL.
しくしく
SOB SOB
DIDN'T I TELL YOU TO STOP READING OTHER PEOPLE'S MINDS LIKE THAT?
MUMBLE
I WAS LOOKING FORWARD TO YOU WAKING ME.
......
サラ…
STROKE
KISS

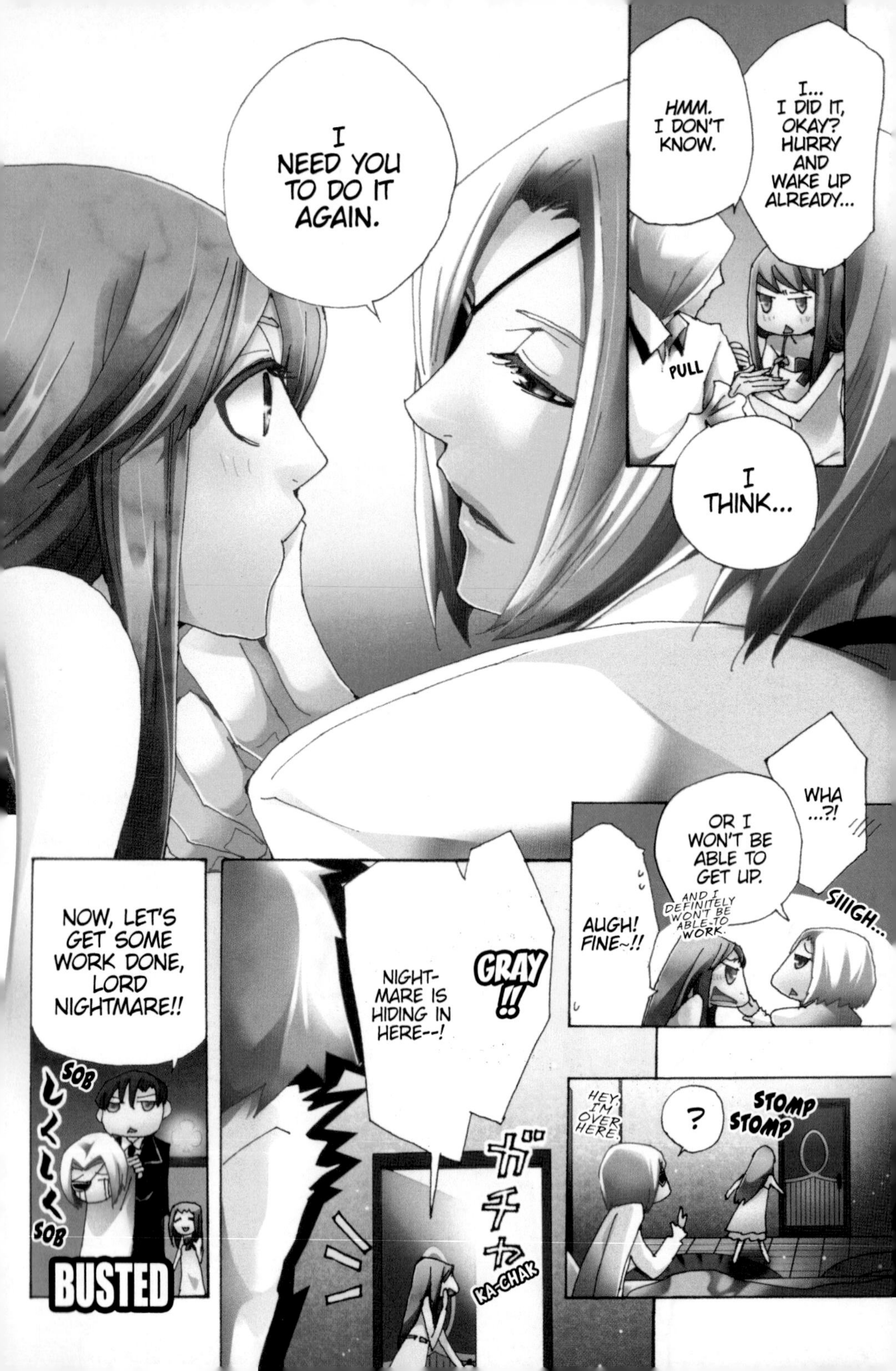
I... I DID IT, OKAY? HURRY AND WAKE UP ALREADY...
HMM. I DON'T KNOW.
PULL
I THINK...
I NEED YOU TO DO IT AGAIN.
WHA...?!
SIIIGH...
OR I WON'T BE ABLE TO GET UP.
AND I DEFINITELY WON'T BE ABLE TO WORK.
AUGH! FINE~!!
STOMP STOMP
?
HEY, I'M OVER HERE.
GRAY!!
NIGHTMARE IS HIDING IN HERE--!
ガチャ
KA-CHAK
NOW, LET'S GET SOME WORK DONE, LORD NIGHTMARE!!
SOB
しくしく
SOB
BUSTED

ALICE IN THE COUNTRY OF CLOVER
~Nightmare~

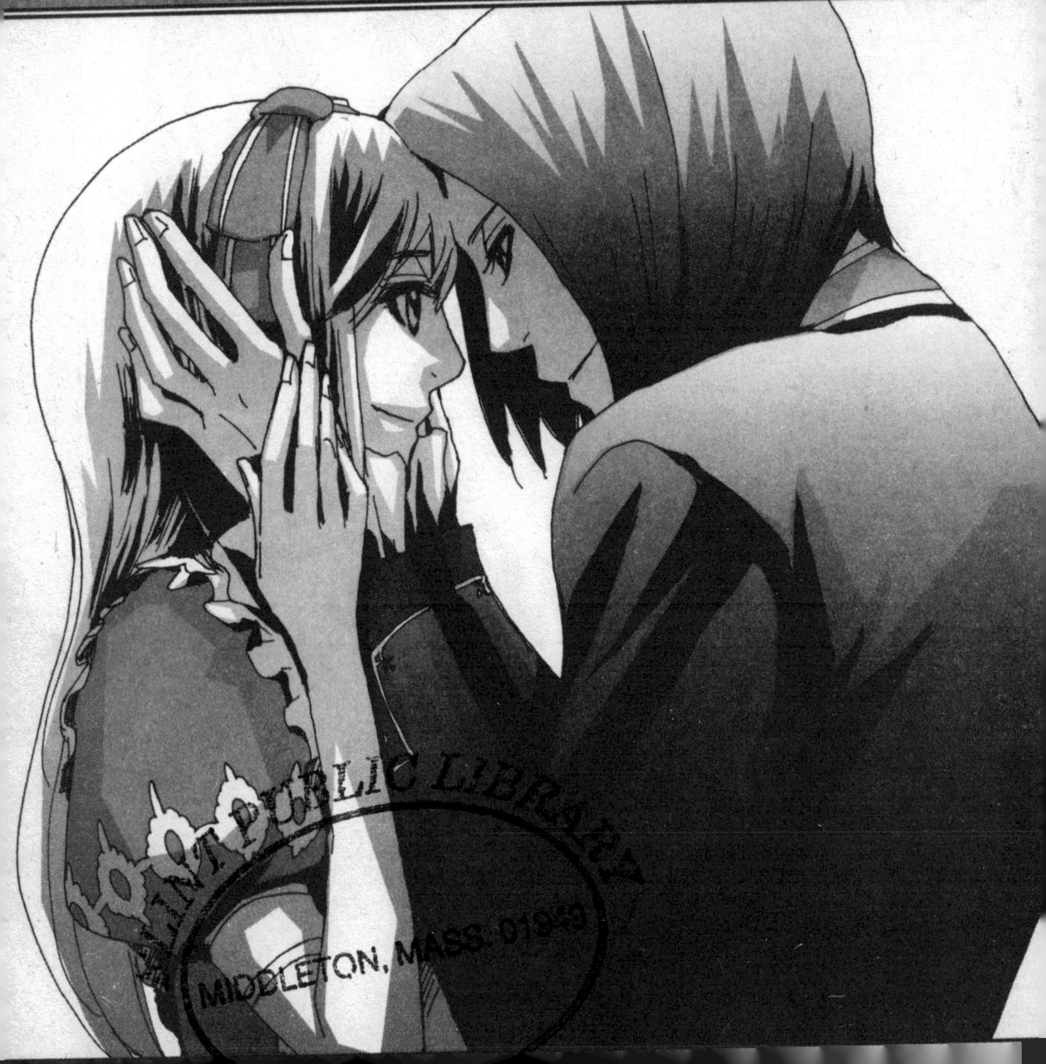

SEVEN SEAS ENTERTAINMENT PRESENTS

Alice in the Country of Clover

NIGHTMARE

art by JOB / story by QUINROSE

TRANSLATION
Angela Liu

ADAPTATION
Shanti Whitesides

LETTERING AND LAYOUT
Laura Scoville

LOGO DESIGN
Courtney Williams

COVER DESIGN
Nicky Lim

PROOFREADER
Lianne Sentar
Conner Crooks

MANAGING EDITOR
Adam Arnold

PUBLISHER
Jason DeAngelis

First published in Japan in 2010 by ICHIJINSHA Inc., Tokyo.
English translation rights arranged with ICHIJINSHA Inc., Tokyo, Japan.

ISBN: 978-1-626920-53-8

Printed in Canada

First Printing: April 2014

10 9 8 7 6 5 4 3 2 1

READING DIRECTIONS

This book reads from ***right to left***, Japanese style. If this is your first time reading manga, you start reading from the top right panel on each page and take it from there. If you get lost, just follow the numbered diagram here. It may seem backwards at first, but you□ll get the hang of it! Have fun!!

1
2
3
4
5
6
7
8
9

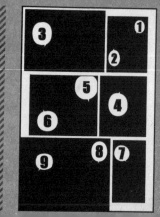

Alice in the Country of Clover
クローバーの国の
アリス
~Wonderful Wonder World~

- STORY -

In *Alice in the Country of Clover*, the game starts with Alice having not fallen in love, but still deciding to stay in Wonderland.

She's acquainted with all the characters from the previous game, *Alice in the Country of Hearts*.

Since love would now start from a place of friendship rather than passion with a new stranger, she can experience a different type of romance from that in the previous game. Her dynamic with the characters is different through this friendship—characters can't always be forceful with her, and in many ways it's more comfortable to grow intimate. The relationships *between* the Ones With Duties have also become more of a factor.

In this game, the story focuses on the mafia. Alice attends the suited meetings (forcefully) and gets involved in various gunfights (forcefully), among other things.

Land fluctuations, sea creatures in the forest, and whispering doors—it's a game more fantastic and more eerie than the first.

Will our everywoman Alice be able to have a romantic relationship in a world devoid of common sense?

Alice in the Country of Clover
Character Information

Elliot March
VA: Tsuguo Mogami

Blood's right-hand man has a criminal past... and a temperamental present. But he's not as bad as he used to be, so that's something. Joining Blood has been good(?) for him.

Blood Dupre
VA: Katsuyuki Konishi

The head of the mafia Hatter Family, Blood is a cunning yet moody puppet-master. Alice now has the pleasure of having him for a landlord.

Alice Liddell
VA: Rie Kugimiya

A normal girl with a bit of a chip on her shoulder. Deciding to stay in the Wonderland she was carried to, she's adapted to her strange new lifestyle.

Vivaldi
VA: Yuuko Kaida

The beautiful Queen of Hearts has an unrivaled temper—which is really saying something in Wonderland. Although a picture-perfect Mad Queen, she cares for Alice as if Alice were her little sister...or a very interesting plaything.

Tweedle Dum
VA: Jun Fukuyama

The second "Bloody Twin" is equally cute and equally scary. In *Clover*, Dum can also turn into an adult.

Tweedle Dee
VA: Jun Fukuyama

One of the "Bloody Twin" gatekeepers of the Hatter territory, Dee can be cute when he's not being terrifying. In *Clover*, he sometimes turns into an adult.

Boris Airay
VA: Noriaki Sugiyama

This riddle-loving cat has a signature smirk— and in *Clover*, a new toy. One of his favorite pastimes is giving the Sleepy Mouse a hard time.

Ace
VA: Daisuke Hirakawa

The unlucky knight of Hearts was a former subordi- nate of Vivaldi and is perpetually lost. Even though he's depressed to be separated from his friend and boss Julius, he stays positive and tries to overcome it with a smile. He seems like a classic nice guy... or is he?

Peter White
VA: Kouki Miyata

The Prime Minister of Heart Castle—who has rabbit ears growing out of his head—invited (kidnapped) Alice to Wonderland. He loves Alice and hates everything else. His cruel, irrational actions are disturbing, but he acts like a completely different person (rabbit?) when in the throes of his love for Alice.

Gray Ringmarc
VA: Kazuya Nakai

Nightmare's subordinate in *Clover*. He used to have strong social ambition and considered assassinating Nightmare... but since Nightmare was such a useless boss, Gray couldn't help but feel sorry for him and ended up a dedicated assistant. He's a sound thinker with a strong work ethic. He's also highly skilled with his blades, rivaling even Ace.

Nightmare Gottschalk
VA: Tomokazu Sugita

A sickly nightmare who hates the hospital and needles. He has the power to read people's thoughts and enter dreams. Even though he likes to shut himself away in dreams, Gray drags him out to sulk from time to time. He technically holds a high position and has many subordinates, but since he can't even take care of his own health, he leaves most things to Gray.

Pierce Villiers
VA: Souichirou Hoshi

New to *Clover*, Pierce is an insomniac mouse who drinks too much coffee. He loves Nightmare (who can help him sleep) and hates Boris (who terrifies him). He dislikes Blood and Vivaldi for discarding coffee in favor of tea. He likes Elliot and Peter well enough, since rabbits aren't natural predators of mice.

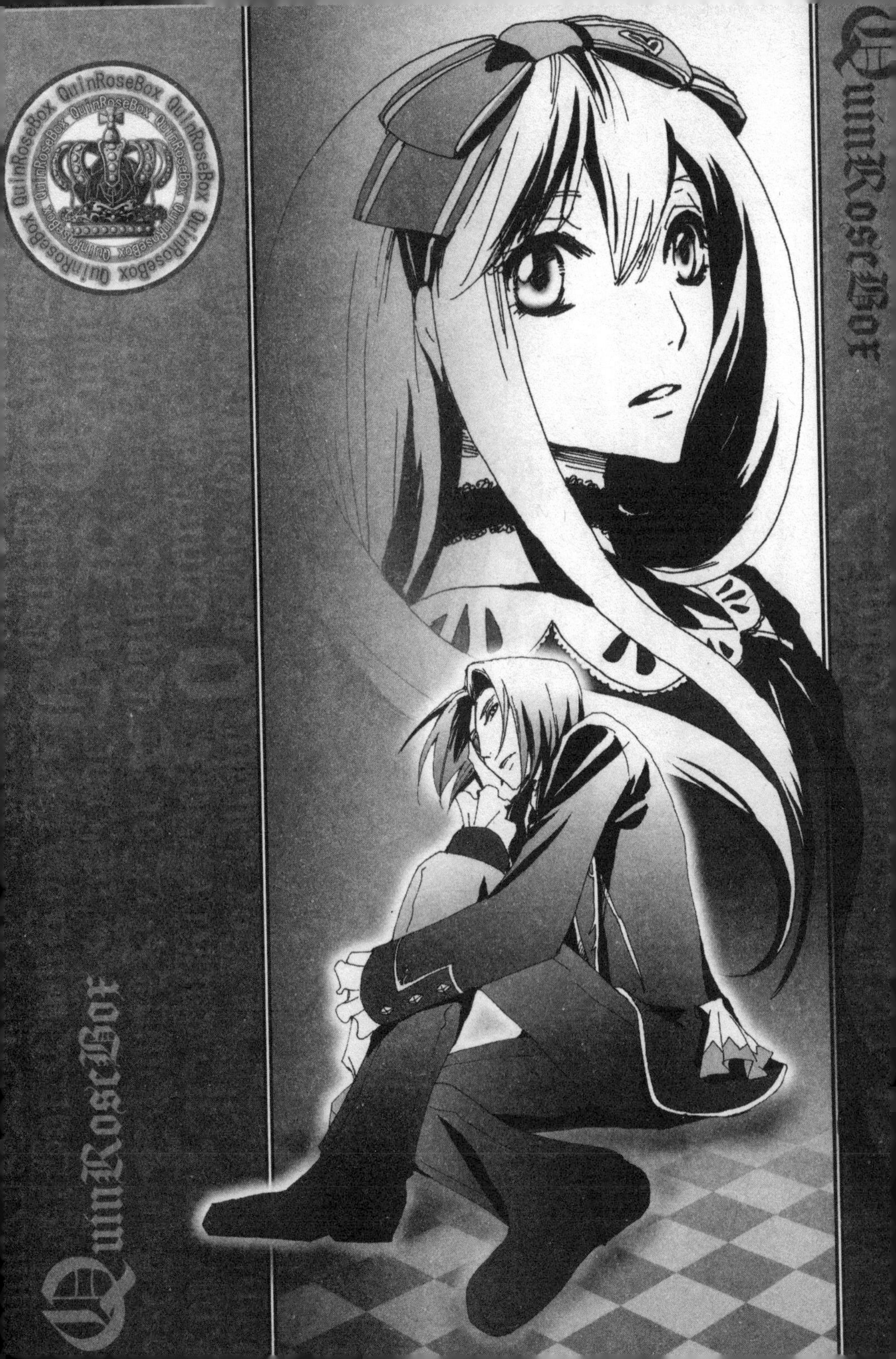
QuinRoseBox

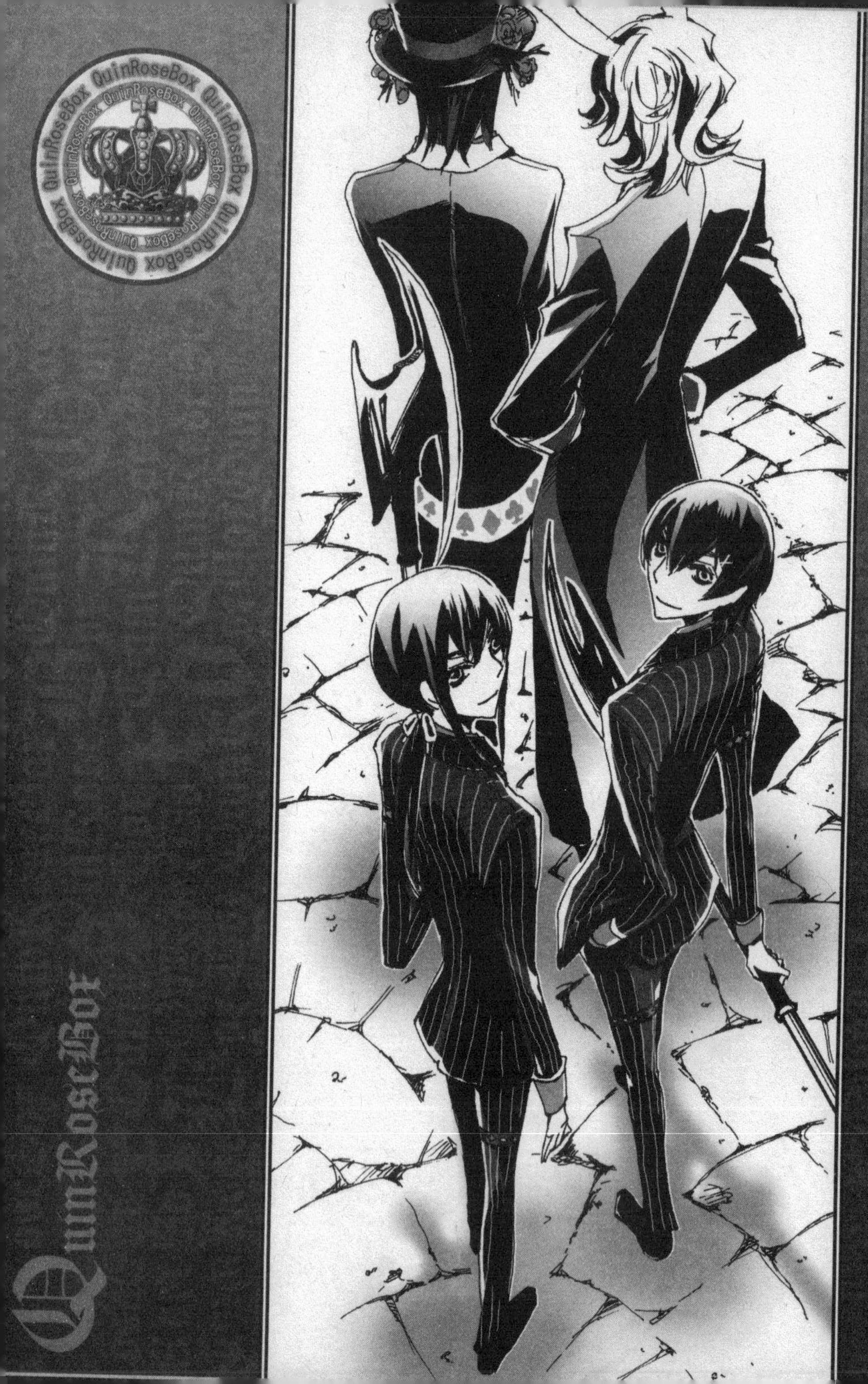

QuinRoseBox

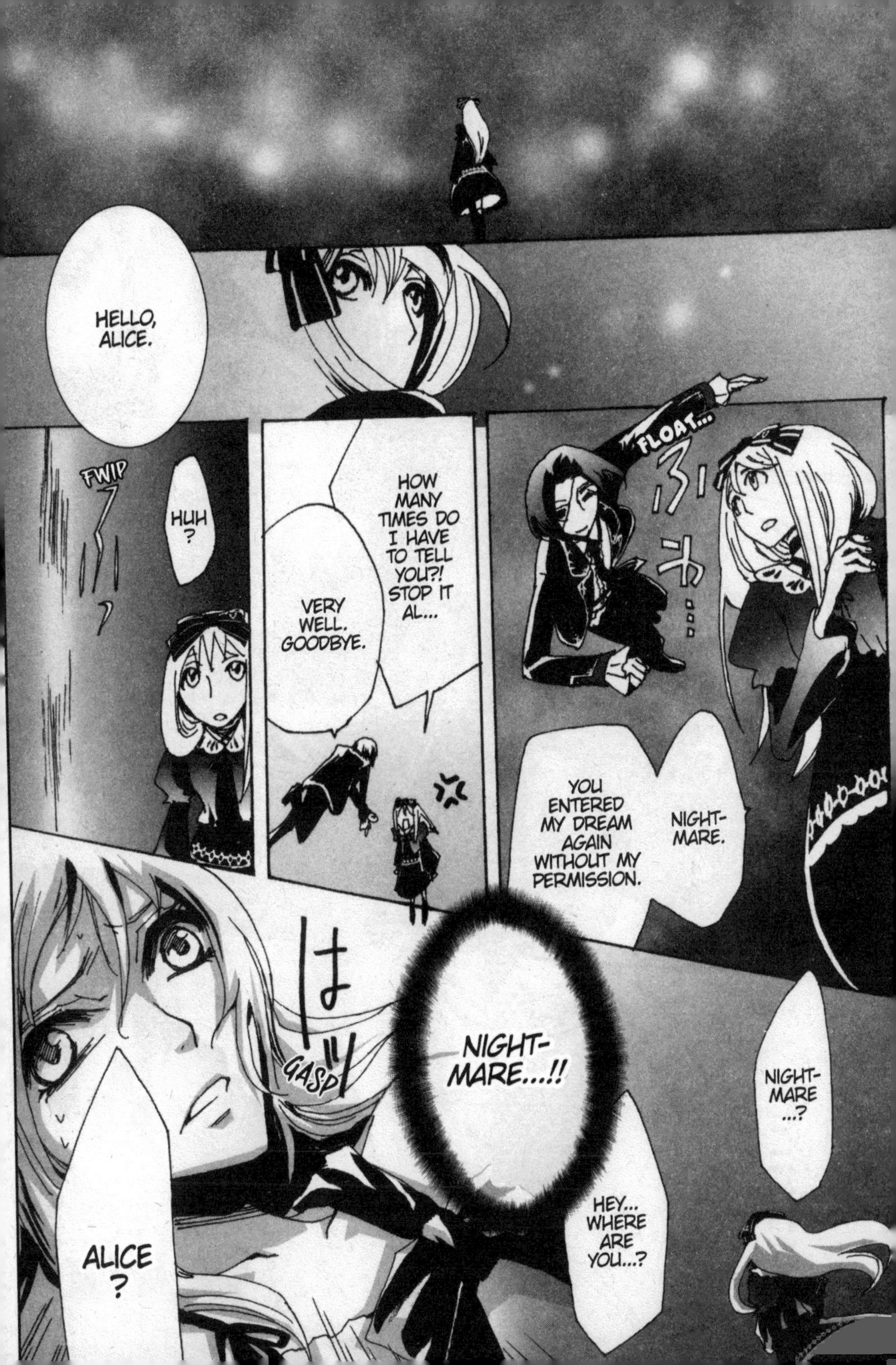

HELLO, ALICE.
FLOAT...
ふわ...
NIGHT-MARE.
YOU ENTERED MY DREAM AGAIN WITHOUT MY PERMISSION.
HOW MANY TIMES DO I HAVE TO TELL YOU?! STOP IT AL...
VERY WELL. GOODBYE.
FWIP
HUH?
NIGHT-MARE...?
HEY... WHERE ARE YOU...?
NIGHT-MARE...!!
GASP
は
ALICE?

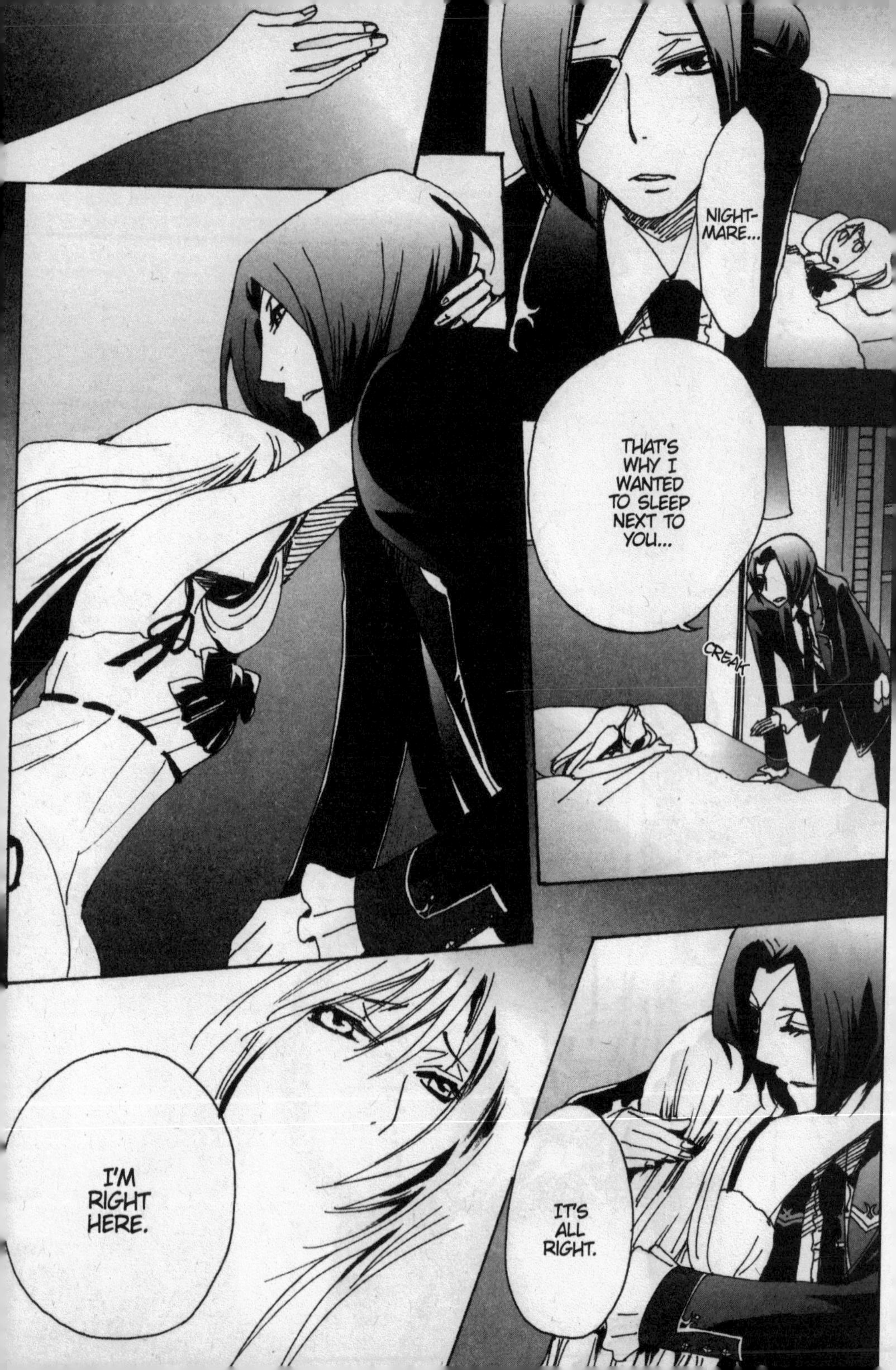
NIGHT-MARE...
THAT'S WHY I WANTED TO SLEEP NEXT TO YOU...
CREAK
IT'S ALL RIGHT.
I'M RIGHT HERE.

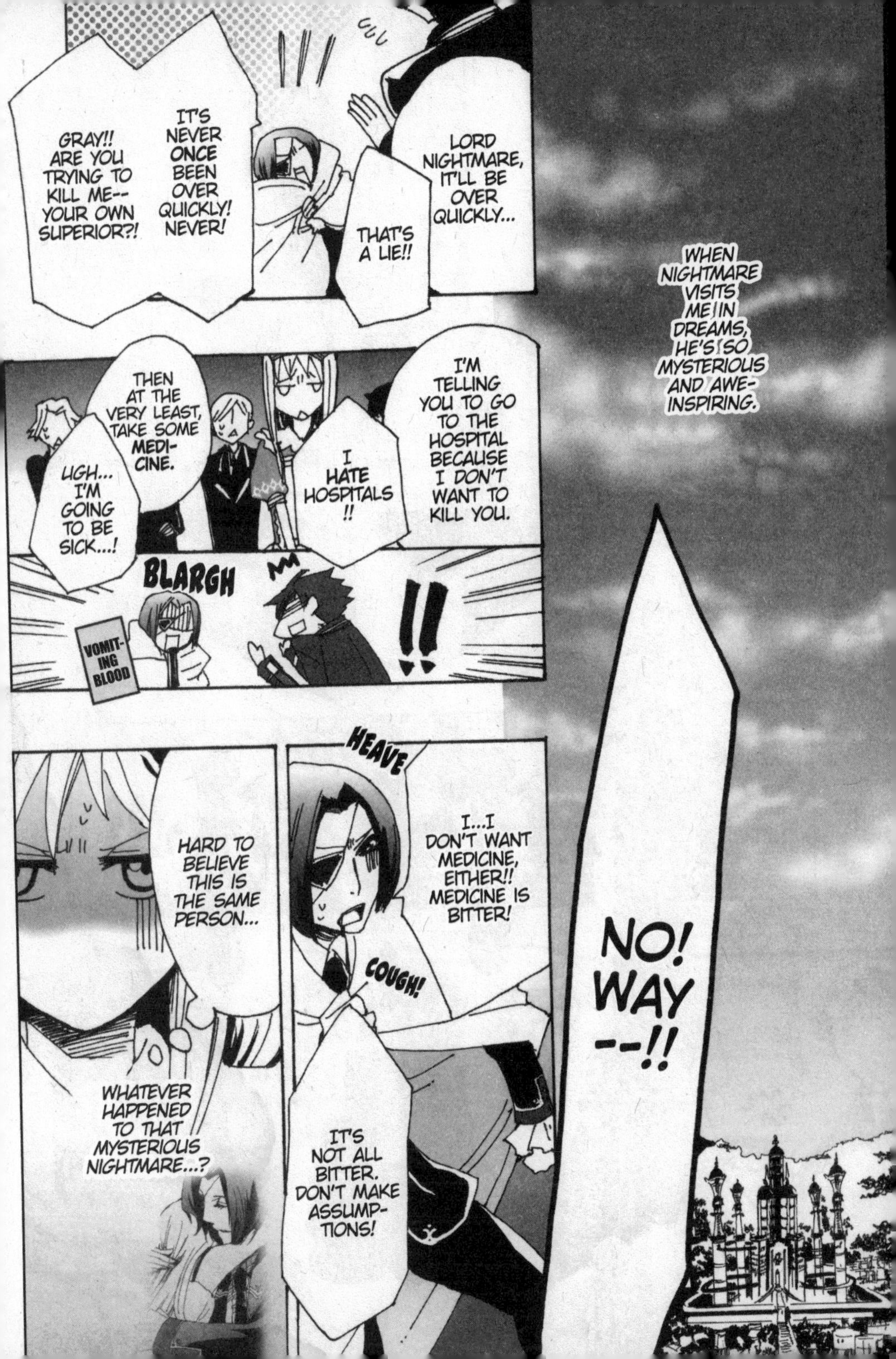

WHEN NIGHTMARE VISITS ME IN DREAMS, HE'S SO MYSTERIOUS AND AWE-INSPIRING.
NO! WAY--!!
LORD NIGHTMARE, IT'LL BE OVER QUICKLY...
THAT'S A LIE!!
IT'S NEVER ONCE BEEN OVER QUICKLY! NEVER!
GRAY!! ARE YOU TRYING TO KILL ME-- YOUR OWN SUPERIOR?!
I'M TELLING YOU TO GO TO THE HOSPITAL BECAUSE I DON'T WANT TO KILL YOU.
I HATE HOSPITALS!!
THEN AT THE VERY LEAST, TAKE SOME MEDICINE.
UGH... I'M GOING TO BE SICK...!
!!
BLARGH
VOMITING BLOOD
HEAVE
I...I DON'T WANT MEDICINE, EITHER!! MEDICINE IS BITTER!
COUGH!
IT'S NOT ALL BITTER. DON'T MAKE ASSUMPTIONS!
HARD TO BELIEVE THIS IS THE SAME PERSON...
WHATEVER HAPPENED TO THAT MYSTERIOUS NIGHTMARE...?

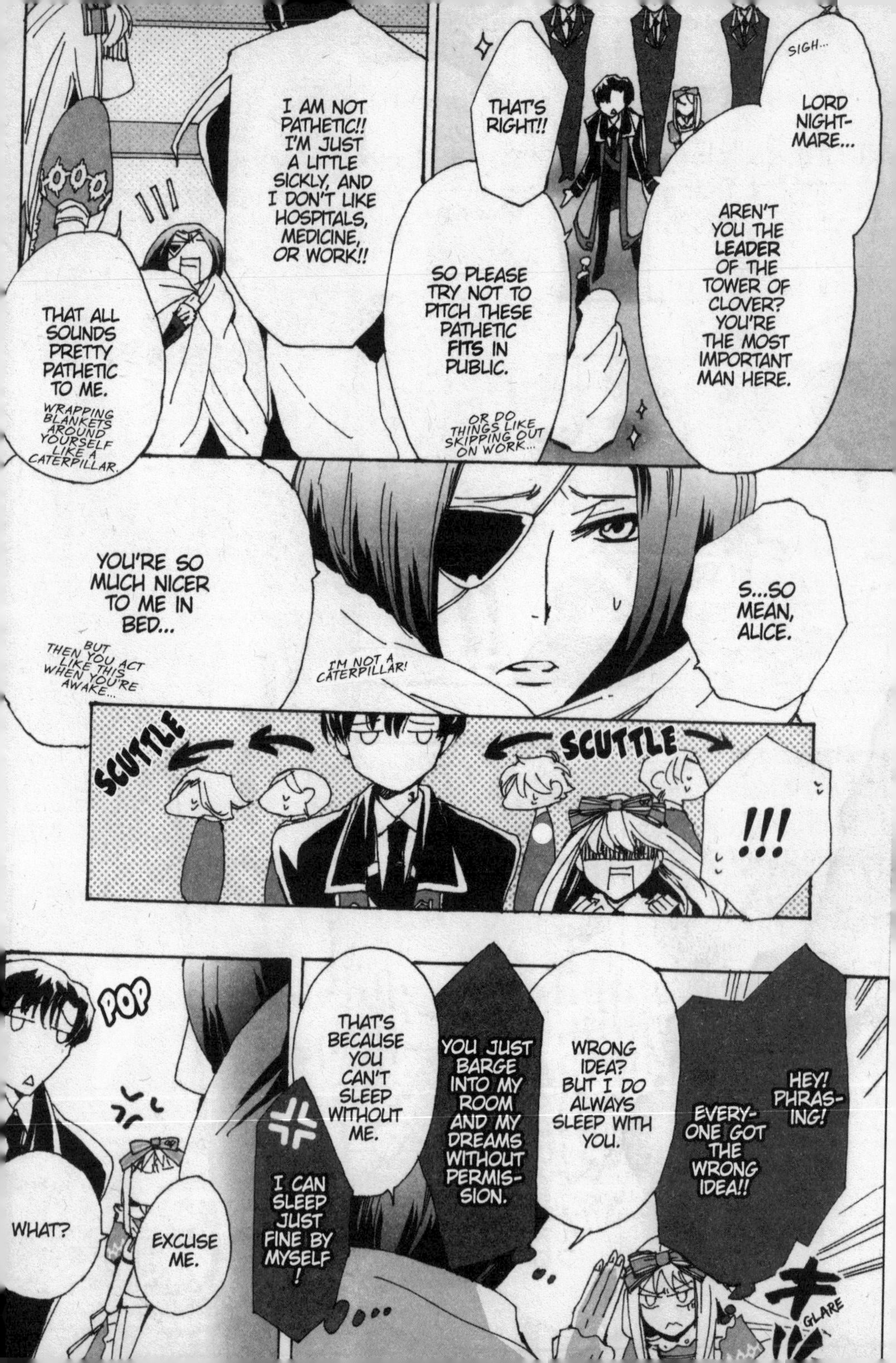
SIGH...
LORD NIGHTMARE...
AREN'T YOU THE LEADER OF THE TOWER OF CLOVER? YOU'RE THE MOST IMPORTANT MAN HERE.
THAT'S RIGHT!!
SO PLEASE TRY NOT TO PITCH THESE PATHETIC FITS IN PUBLIC.
OR DO THINGS LIKE SKIPPING OUT ON WORK...
I AM NOT PATHETIC!! I'M JUST A LITTLE SICKLY, AND I DON'T LIKE HOSPITALS, MEDICINE, OR WORK!!
THAT ALL SOUNDS PRETTY PATHETIC TO ME.
WRAPPING BLANKETS AROUND YOURSELF LIKE A CATERPILLAR.
S...SO MEAN, ALICE.
I'M NOT A CATERPILLAR!
YOU'RE SO MUCH NICER TO ME IN BED...
BUT THEN YOU ACT LIKE THIS WHEN YOU'RE AWAKE...
SCUTTLE
!!!
SCUTTLE
HEY! PHRASING!
EVERYONE GOT THE WRONG IDEA!!
GLARE
WRONG IDEA? BUT I DO ALWAYS SLEEP WITH YOU.
YOU JUST BARGE INTO MY ROOM AND MY DREAMS WITHOUT PERMISSION.
THAT'S BECAUSE YOU CAN'T SLEEP WITHOUT ME.
I CAN SLEEP JUST FINE BY MYSELF!
...
POP
EXCUSE ME.
WHAT?

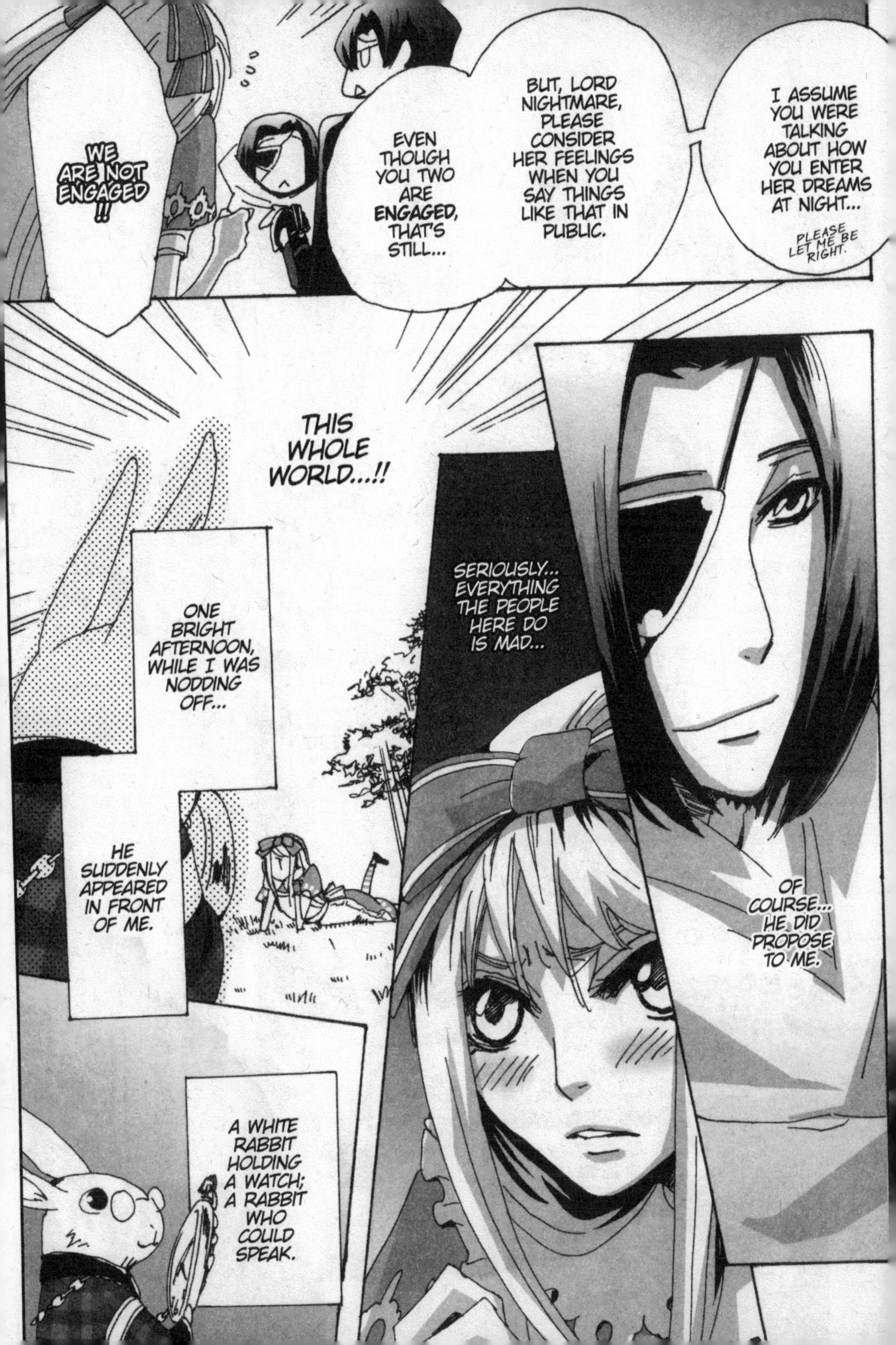
I ASSUME YOU WERE TALKING ABOUT HOW YOU ENTER HER DREAMS AT NIGHT...
PLEASE LET ME BE RIGHT.
BUT, LORD NIGHTMARE, PLEASE CONSIDER HER FEELINGS WHEN YOU SAY THINGS LIKE THAT IN PUBLIC.
EVEN THOUGH YOU TWO ARE ENGAGED, THAT'S STILL...
WE ARE NOT ENGAGED!!
THIS WHOLE WORLD...!!
SERIOUSLY... EVERYTHING THE PEOPLE HERE DO IS MAD...
OF COURSE... HE DID PROPOSE TO ME.
ONE BRIGHT AFTERNOON, WHILE I WAS NODDING OFF...
HE SUDDENLY APPEARED IN FRONT OF ME.
A WHITE RABBIT HOLDING A WATCH; A RABBIT WHO COULD SPEAK.

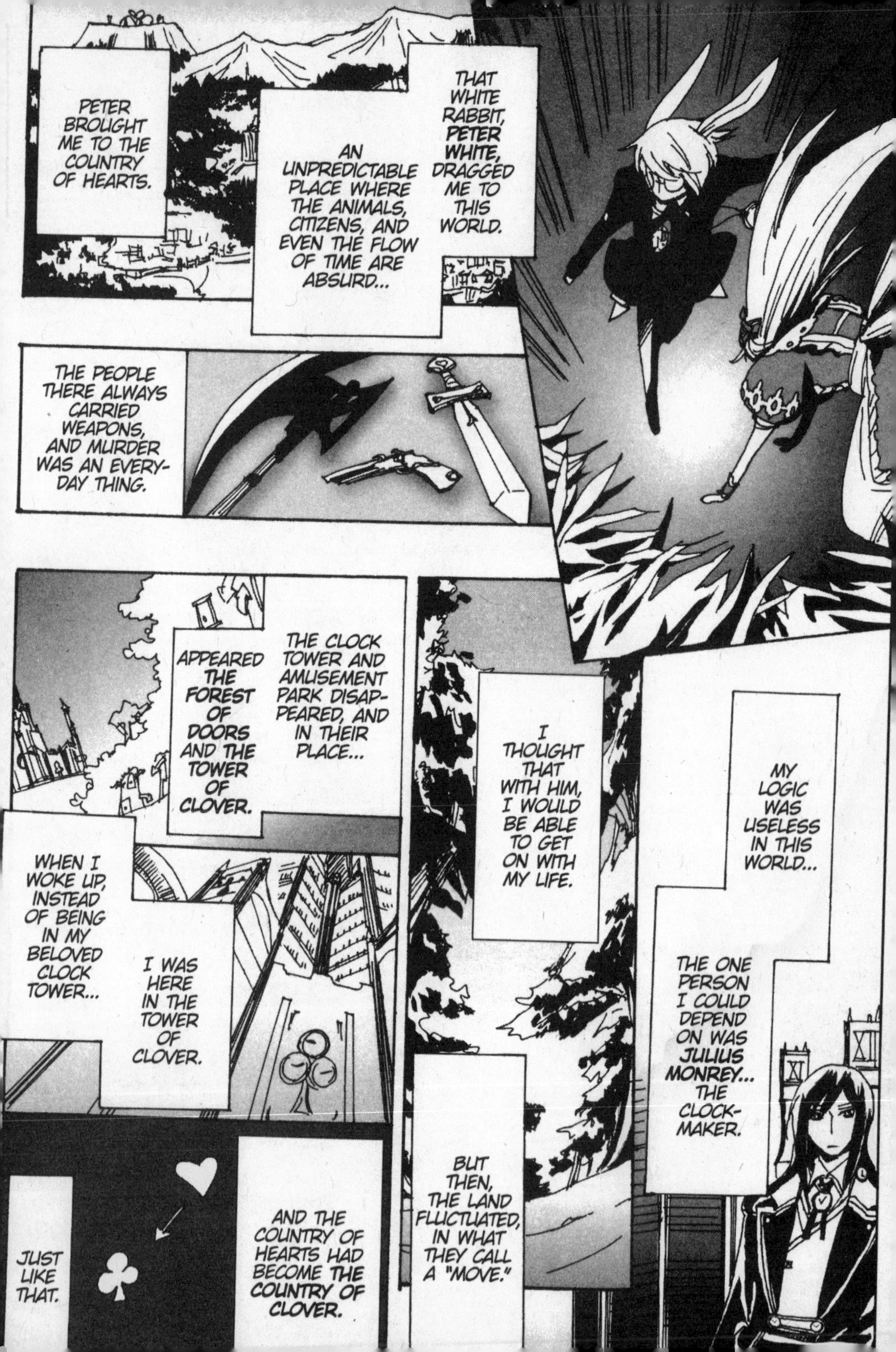
THAT WHITE RABBIT, PETER WHITE, DRAGGED ME TO THIS WORLD.
AN UNPREDICTABLE PLACE WHERE THE ANIMALS, CITIZENS, AND EVEN THE FLOW OF TIME ARE ABSURD...
PETER BROUGHT ME TO THE COUNTRY OF HEARTS.
THE PEOPLE THERE ALWAYS CARRIED WEAPONS, AND MURDER WAS AN EVERY-DAY THING.
MY LOGIC WAS USELESS IN THIS WORLD...
THE ONE PERSON I COULD DEPEND ON WAS JULIUS MONREY... THE CLOCK-MAKER.
I THOUGHT THAT WITH HIM, I WOULD BE ABLE TO GET ON WITH MY LIFE.
BUT THEN, THE LAND FLUCTUATED, IN WHAT THEY CALL A "MOVE."
THE CLOCK TOWER AND AMUSEMENT PARK DISAP-PEARED, AND IN THEIR PLACE...
APPEARED THE FOREST OF DOORS AND THE TOWER OF CLOVER.
WHEN I WOKE UP, INSTEAD OF BEING IN MY BELOVED CLOCK TOWER...
I WAS HERE IN THE TOWER OF CLOVER.
AND THE COUNTRY OF HEARTS HAD BECOME THE COUNTRY OF CLOVER.
JUST LIKE THAT.

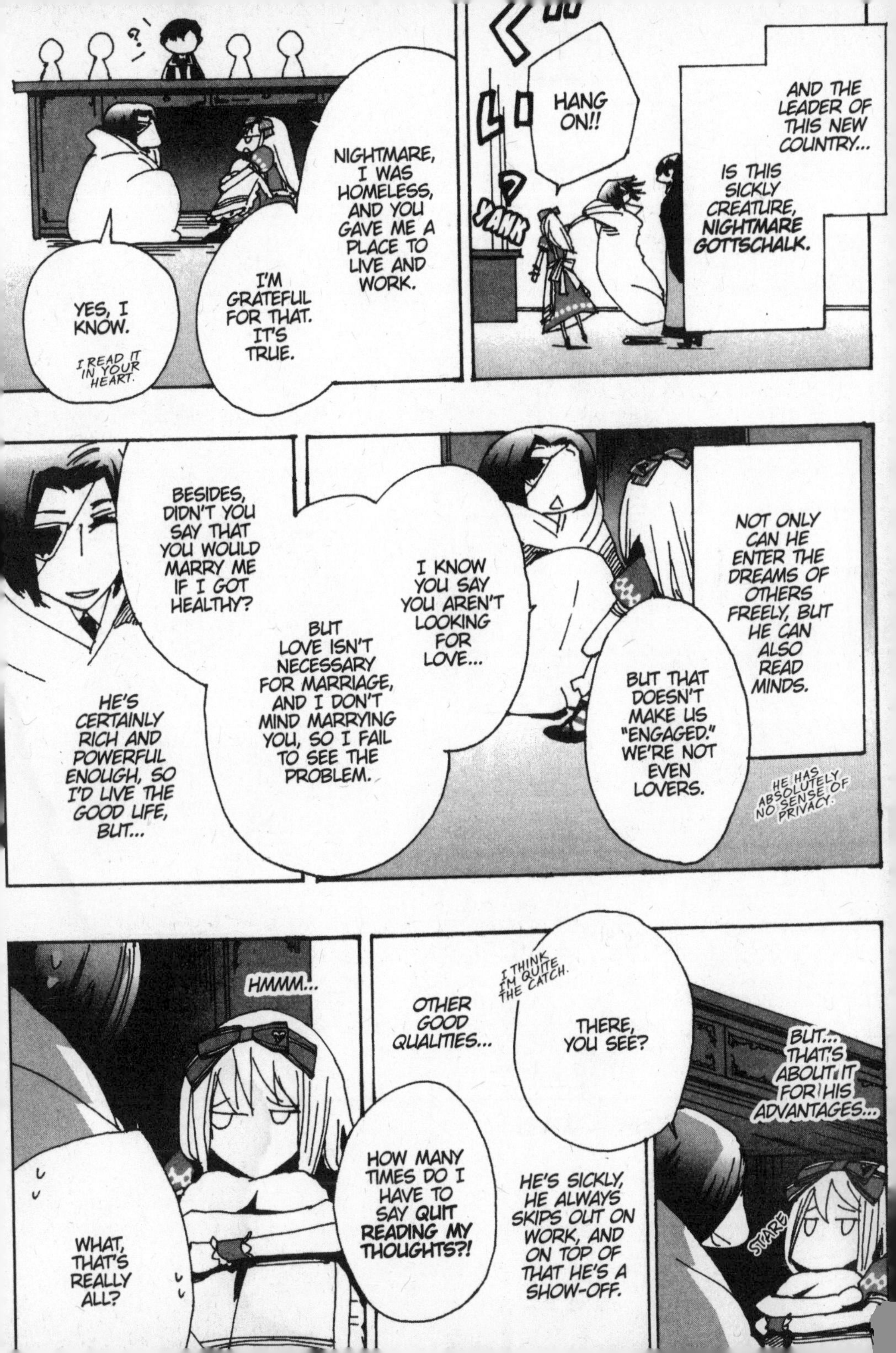
AND THE LEADER OF THIS NEW COUNTRY...
IS THIS SICKLY CREATURE, NIGHTMARE GOTTSCHALK.
HANG ON!!
YANK
NIGHTMARE, I WAS HOMELESS, AND YOU GAVE ME A PLACE TO LIVE AND WORK.
I'M GRATEFUL FOR THAT. IT'S TRUE.
YES, I KNOW.
I READ IT IN YOUR HEART.
NOT ONLY CAN HE ENTER THE DREAMS OF OTHERS FREELY, BUT HE CAN ALSO READ MINDS.
HE HAS ABSOLUTELY NO SENSE OF PRIVACY.
BUT THAT DOESN'T MAKE US "ENGAGED." WE'RE NOT EVEN LOVERS.
I KNOW YOU SAY YOU AREN'T LOOKING FOR LOVE...
BUT LOVE ISN'T NECESSARY FOR MARRIAGE, AND I DON'T MIND MARRYING YOU, SO I FAIL TO SEE THE PROBLEM.
BESIDES, DIDN'T YOU SAY THAT YOU WOULD MARRY ME IF I GOT HEALTHY?
HE'S CERTAINLY RICH AND POWERFUL ENOUGH, SO I'D LIVE THE GOOD LIFE, BUT...
BUT... THAT'S ABOUT IT FOR HIS ADVANTAGES...
STARE
HE'S SICKLY, HE ALWAYS SKIPS OUT ON WORK, AND ON TOP OF THAT HE'S A SHOW-OFF.
THERE, YOU SEE?
I THINK I'M QUITE THE CATCH.
OTHER GOOD QUALITIES...
HOW MANY TIMES DO I HAVE TO SAY QUIT READING MY THOUGHTS?!
HMMM...
WHAT, THAT'S REALLY ALL?

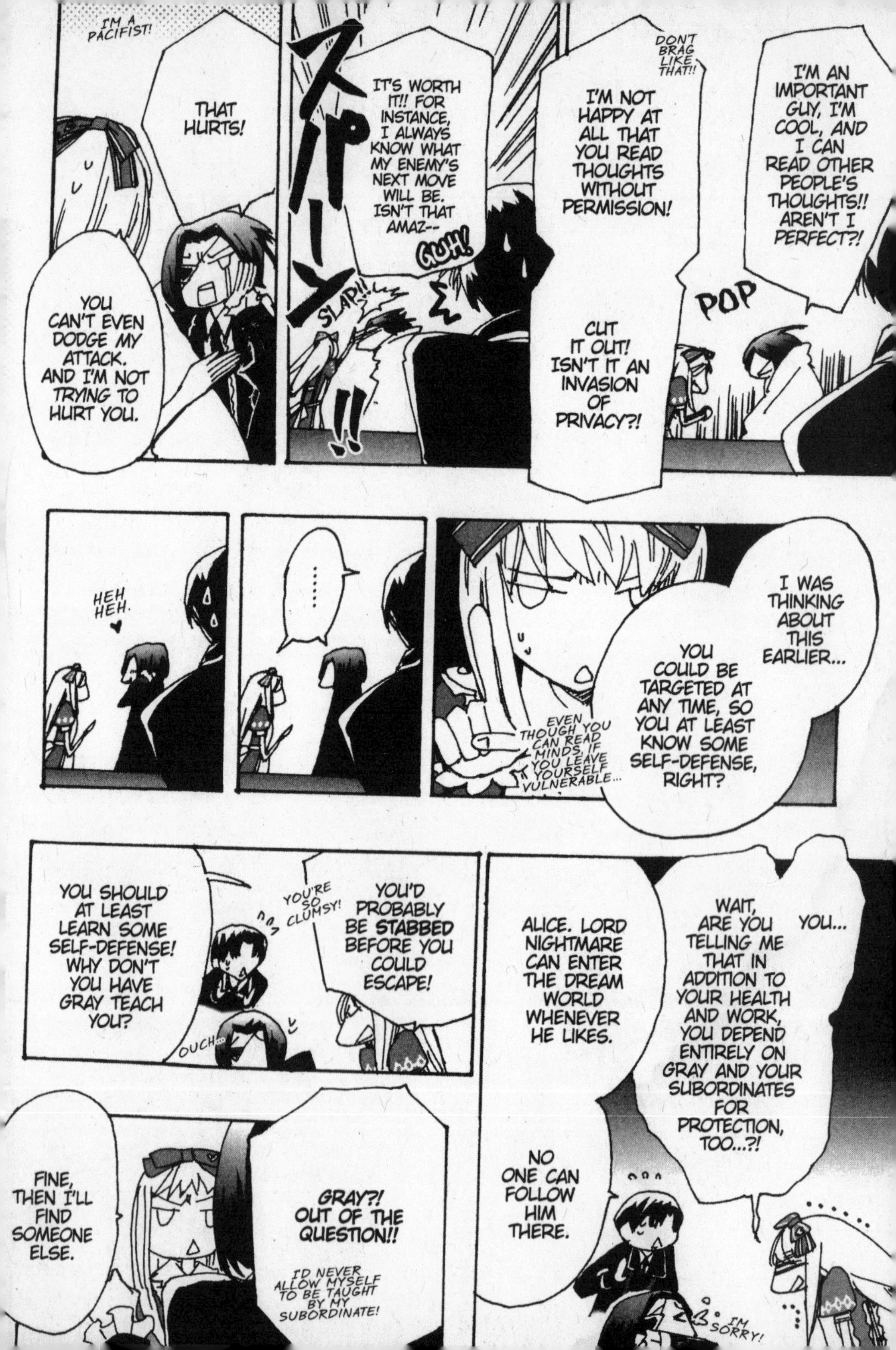
I'M AN IMPORTANT GUY, I'M COOL, AND I CAN READ OTHER PEOPLE'S THOUGHTS!! AREN'T I PERFECT?!
POP
DON'T BRAG LIKE THAT!!
I'M NOT HAPPY AT ALL THAT YOU READ THOUGHTS WITHOUT PERMISSION!
CUT IT OUT! ISN'T IT AN INVASION OF PRIVACY?!
IT'S WORTH IT!! FOR INSTANCE, I ALWAYS KNOW WHAT MY ENEMY'S NEXT MOVE WILL BE. ISN'T THAT AMAZ--
GUH!
SLAP!!
I'M A PACIFIST!
THAT HURTS!
YOU CAN'T EVEN DODGE MY ATTACK. AND I'M NOT TRYING TO HURT YOU.
I WAS THINKING ABOUT THIS EARLIER...
YOU COULD BE TARGETED AT ANY TIME, SO YOU AT LEAST KNOW SOME SELF-DEFENSE, RIGHT?
EVEN THOUGH YOU CAN READ MINDS, IF YOU LEAVE YOURSELF VULNERABLE...
......
HEH HEH.
YOU...
WAIT, ARE YOU TELLING ME THAT IN ADDITION TO YOUR HEALTH AND WORK, YOU DEPEND ENTIRELY ON GRAY AND YOUR SUBORDINATES FOR PROTECTION, TOO...?!
ALICE. LORD NIGHTMARE CAN ENTER THE DREAM WORLD WHENEVER HE LIKES.
NO ONE CAN FOLLOW HIM THERE.
I'M SORRY!
YOU'D PROBABLY BE STABBED BEFORE YOU COULD ESCAPE!
YOU'RE SO CLUMSY!
YOU SHOULD AT LEAST LEARN SOME SELF-DEFENSE! WHY DON'T YOU HAVE GRAY TEACH YOU?
OUCH...
GRAY?! OUT OF THE QUESTION!!
I'D NEVER ALLOW MYSELF TO BE TAUGHT BY MY SUBORDINATE!
FINE, THEN I'LL FIND SOMEONE ELSE.

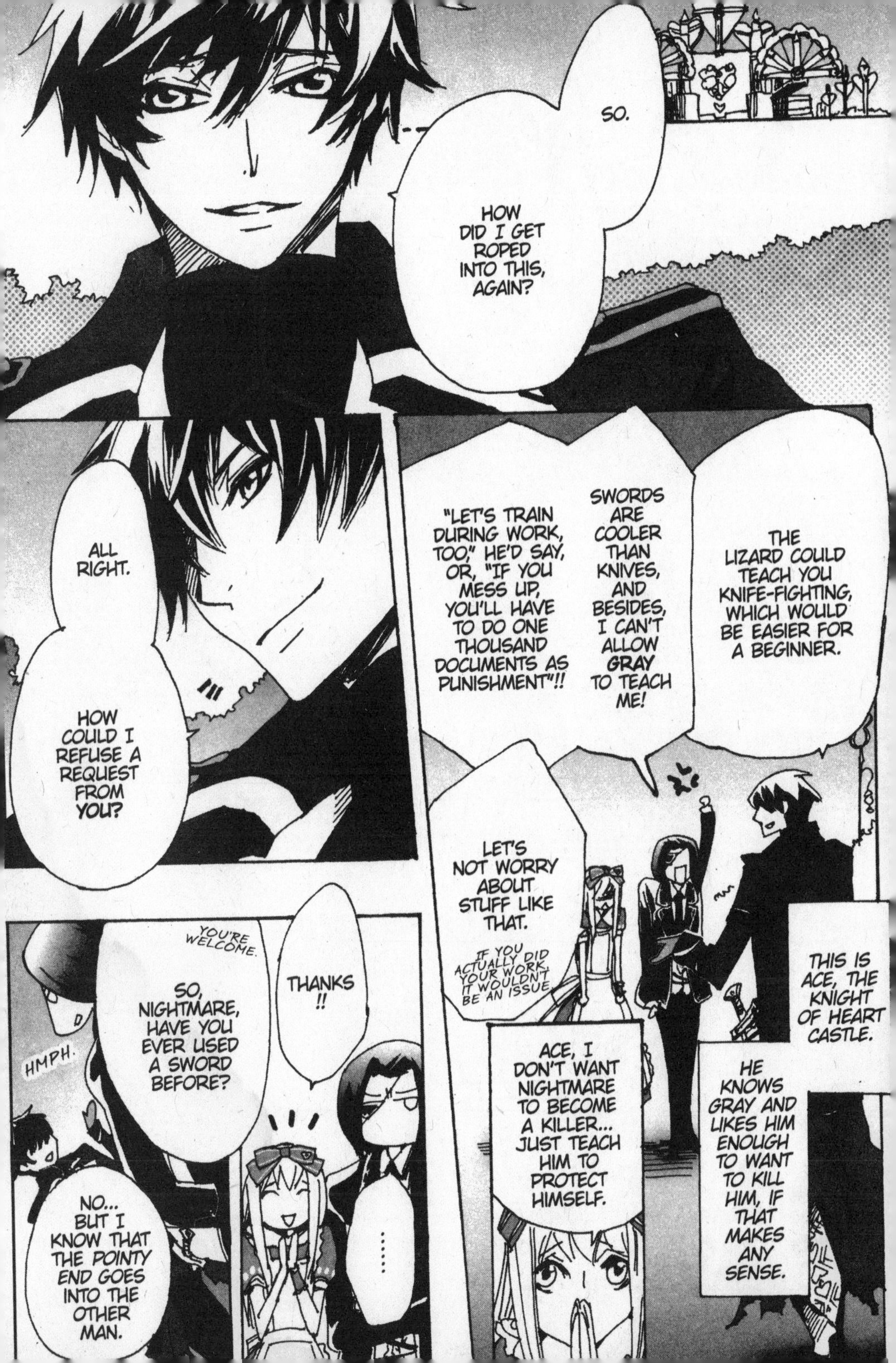
SO.
HOW DID I GET ROPED INTO THIS, AGAIN?
THE LIZARD COULD TEACH YOU KNIFE-FIGHTING, WHICH WOULD BE EASIER FOR A BEGINNER.
SWORDS ARE COOLER THAN KNIVES, AND BESIDES, I CAN'T ALLOW **GRAY** TO TEACH ME!
"LET'S TRAIN DURING WORK, TOO," HE'D SAY, OR, "IF YOU MESS UP, YOU'LL HAVE TO DO ONE THOUSAND DOCUMENTS AS PUNISHMENT"!!
LET'S NOT WORRY ABOUT STUFF LIKE THAT.
IF YOU ACTUALLY DID YOUR WORK, IT WOULDN'T BE AN ISSUE.
THIS IS ACE, THE KNIGHT OF HEART CASTLE.
ALL RIGHT.
HOW COULD I REFUSE A REQUEST FROM YOU?
HE KNOWS GRAY AND LIKES HIM ENOUGH TO WANT TO KILL HIM, IF THAT MAKES ANY SENSE.
ACE, I DON'T WANT NIGHTMARE TO BECOME A KILLER... JUST TEACH HIM TO PROTECT HIMSELF.
THANKS!!
YOU'RE WELCOME.
SO, NIGHTMARE, HAVE YOU EVER USED A SWORD BEFORE?
HMPH.
......
NO... BUT I KNOW THAT THE POINTY END GOES INTO THE OTHER MAN.

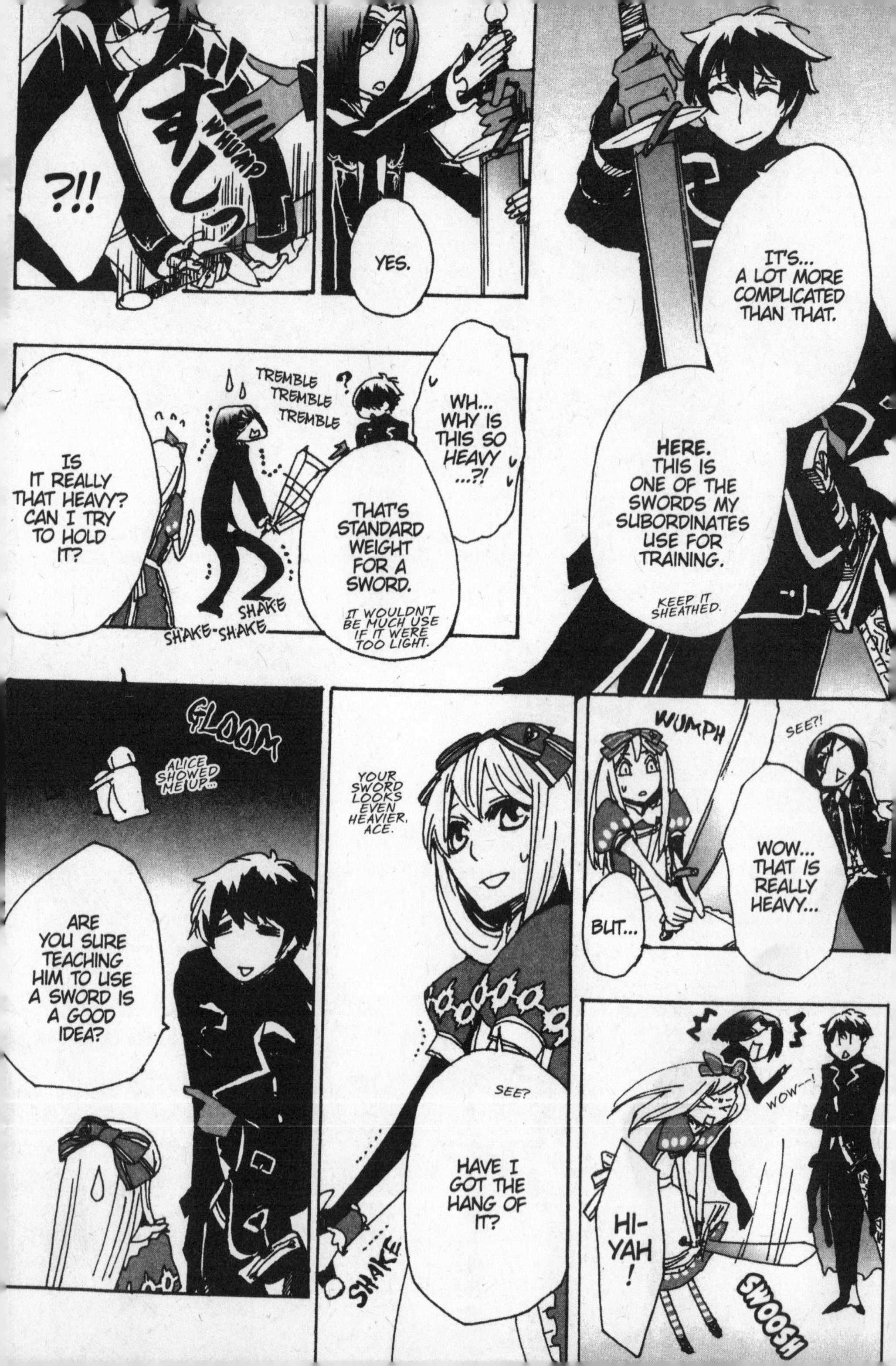
IT'S... A LOT MORE COMPLICATED THAN THAT.
HERE. THIS IS ONE OF THE SWORDS MY SUBORDINATES USE FOR TRAINING.
KEEP IT SHEATHED.
YES.
WHUMP
?!!
WH... WHY IS THIS SO HEAVY ...?!
THAT'S STANDARD WEIGHT FOR A SWORD.
IT WOULDN'T BE MUCH USE IF IT WERE TOO LIGHT.
TREMBLE TREMBLE TREMBLE
SHAKE SHAKE-SHAKE
IS IT REALLY THAT HEAVY? CAN I TRY TO HOLD IT?
WUMPH
SEE?!
WOW... THAT IS REALLY HEAVY...
BUT...
WOW--!
HI-YAH!
SWOOSH
YOUR SWORD LOOKS EVEN HEAVIER, ACE.
SEE?
HAVE I GOT THE HANG OF IT?
SHAKE
GLOOM
ALICE SHOWED ME UP...
ARE YOU SURE TEACHING HIM TO USE A SWORD IS A GOOD IDEA?

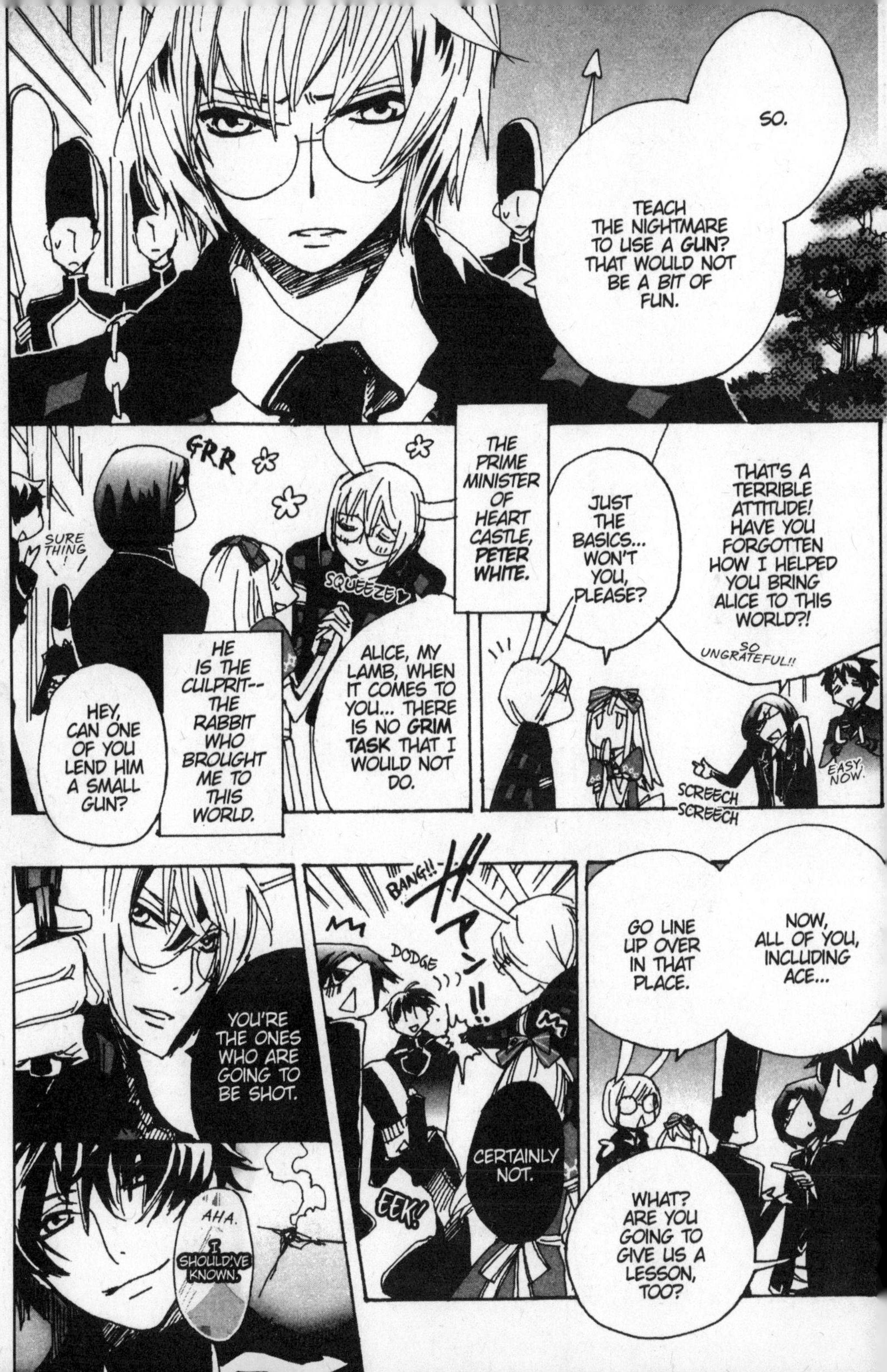
SO.
TEACH THE NIGHTMARE TO USE A GUN? THAT WOULD NOT BE A BIT OF FUN.
THAT'S A TERRIBLE ATTITUDE! HAVE YOU FORGOTTEN HOW I HELPED YOU BRING ALICE TO THIS WORLD?!
JUST THE BASICS... WON'T YOU, PLEASE?
SO UNGRATEFUL!!
EASY NOW.
SCREECH SCREECH
THE PRIME MINISTER OF HEART CASTLE, PETER WHITE.
GRR
SQUEEZE♥
ALICE, MY LAMB, WHEN IT COMES TO YOU... THERE IS NO GRIM TASK THAT I WOULD NOT DO.
HE IS THE CULPRIT--THE RABBIT WHO BROUGHT ME TO THIS WORLD.
SURE THING!
HEY, CAN ONE OF YOU LEND HIM A SMALL GUN?
NOW, ALL OF YOU, INCLUDING ACE...
GO LINE UP OVER IN THAT PLACE.
WHAT? ARE YOU GOING TO GIVE US A LESSON, TOO?
BANG!!
DODGE
CERTAINLY NOT.
EEK!
YOU'RE THE ONES WHO ARE GOING TO BE SHOT.
AHA.
I SHOULD'VE KNOWN.

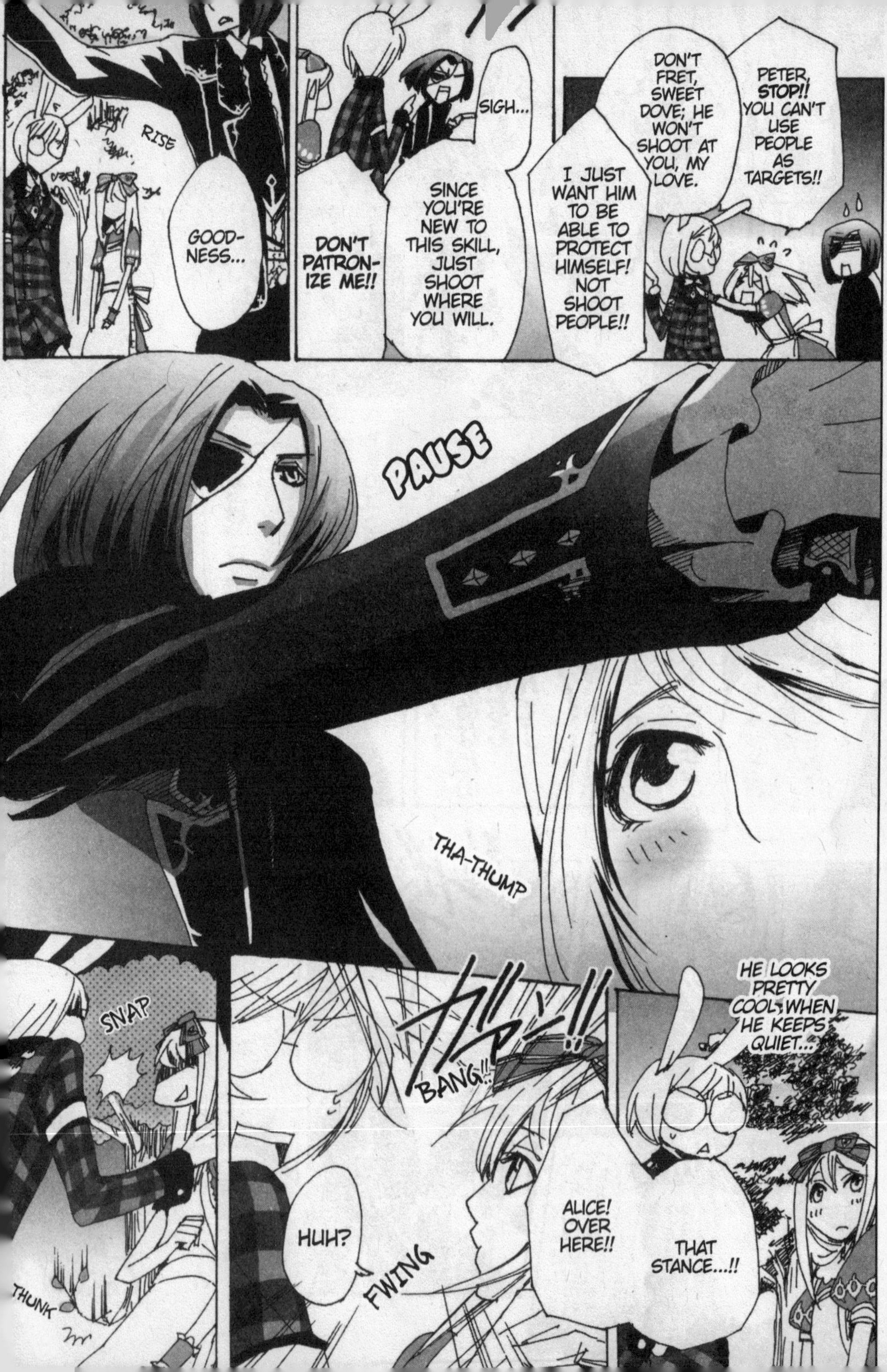
PETER, STOP!! YOU CAN'T USE PEOPLE AS TARGETS!!
DON'T FRET, SWEET DOVE; HE WON'T SHOOT AT YOU, MY LOVE.
I JUST WANT HIM TO BE ABLE TO PROTECT HIMSELF! NOT SHOOT PEOPLE!!
SIGH...
SINCE YOU'RE NEW TO THIS SKILL, JUST SHOOT WHERE YOU WILL.
DON'T PATRON-IZE ME!!
RISE
GOOD-NESS...
PAUSE
THA-THUMP
HE LOOKS PRETTY COOL WHEN HE KEEPS QUIET...
THAT STANCE...!!
BANG!!
ALICE! OVER HERE!!
HUH?
FWING
SNAP
THUNK

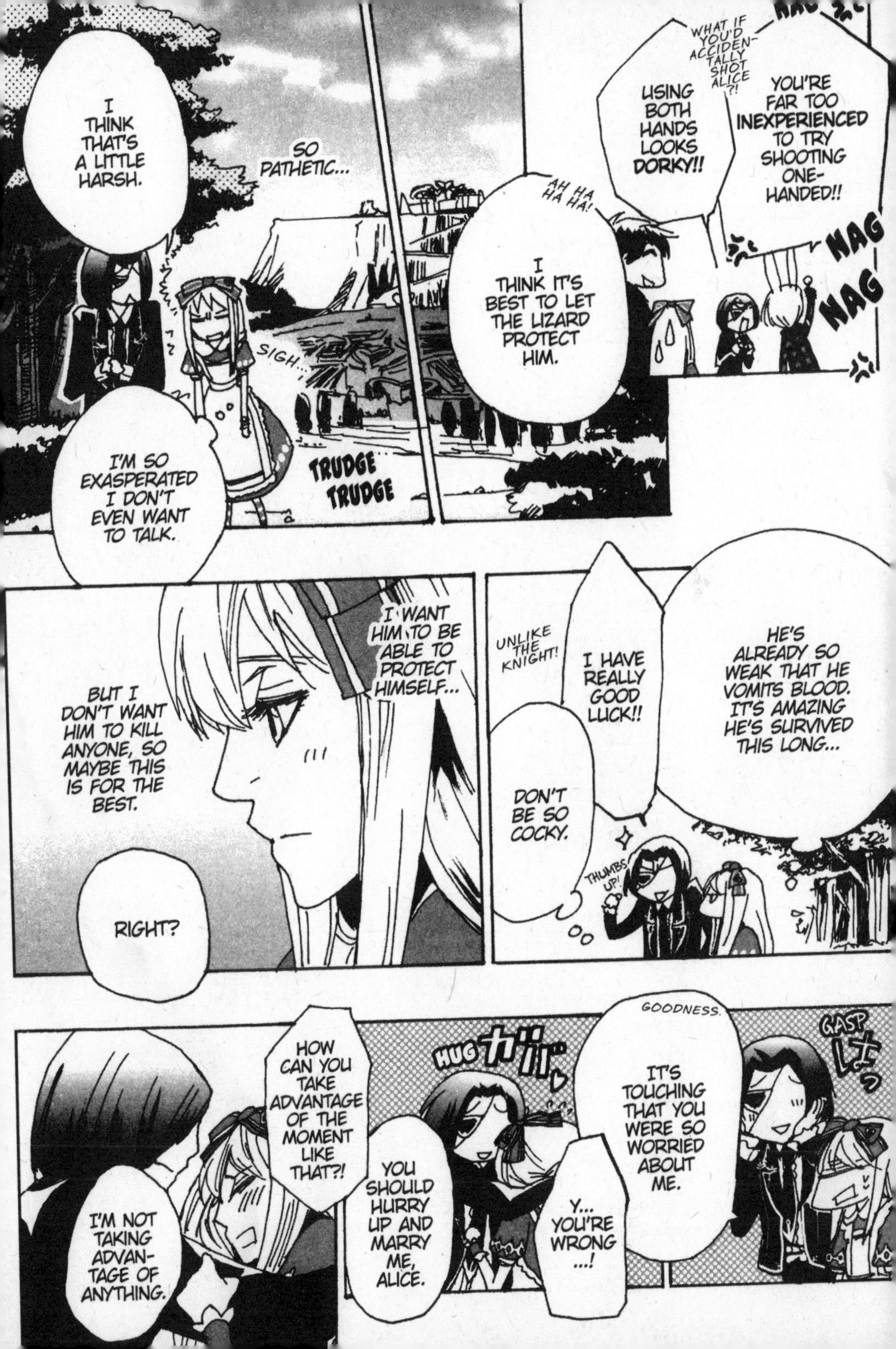
NAG
YOU'RE FAR TOO INEXPERIENCED TO TRY SHOOTING ONE-HANDED!!
WHAT IF YOU'D ACCIDENTALLY SHOT ALICE?!
USING BOTH HANDS LOOKS DORKY!!
NAG
NAG
AH HA HA HA!
I THINK IT'S BEST TO LET THE LIZARD PROTECT HIM.
SO PATHETIC...
I THINK THAT'S A LITTLE HARSH.
SIGH...
TRUDGE TRUDGE
I'M SO EXASPERATED I DON'T EVEN WANT TO TALK.
HE'S ALREADY SO WEAK THAT HE VOMITS BLOOD. IT'S AMAZING HE'S SURVIVED THIS LONG...
I HAVE REALLY GOOD LUCK!!
UNLIKE THE KNIGHT!
DON'T BE SO COCKY.
THUMBS UP!
I WANT HIM TO BE ABLE TO PROTECT HIMSELF...
BUT I DON'T WANT HIM TO KILL ANYONE, SO MAYBE THIS IS FOR THE BEST.
RIGHT?
GASP
GOODNESS.
IT'S TOUCHING THAT YOU WERE SO WORRIED ABOUT ME.
Y... YOU'RE WRONG ...!
HUG
HOW CAN YOU TAKE ADVANTAGE OF THE MOMENT LIKE THAT?!
YOU SHOULD HURRY UP AND MARRY ME, ALICE.
I'M NOT TAKING ADVANTAGE OF ANYTHING.

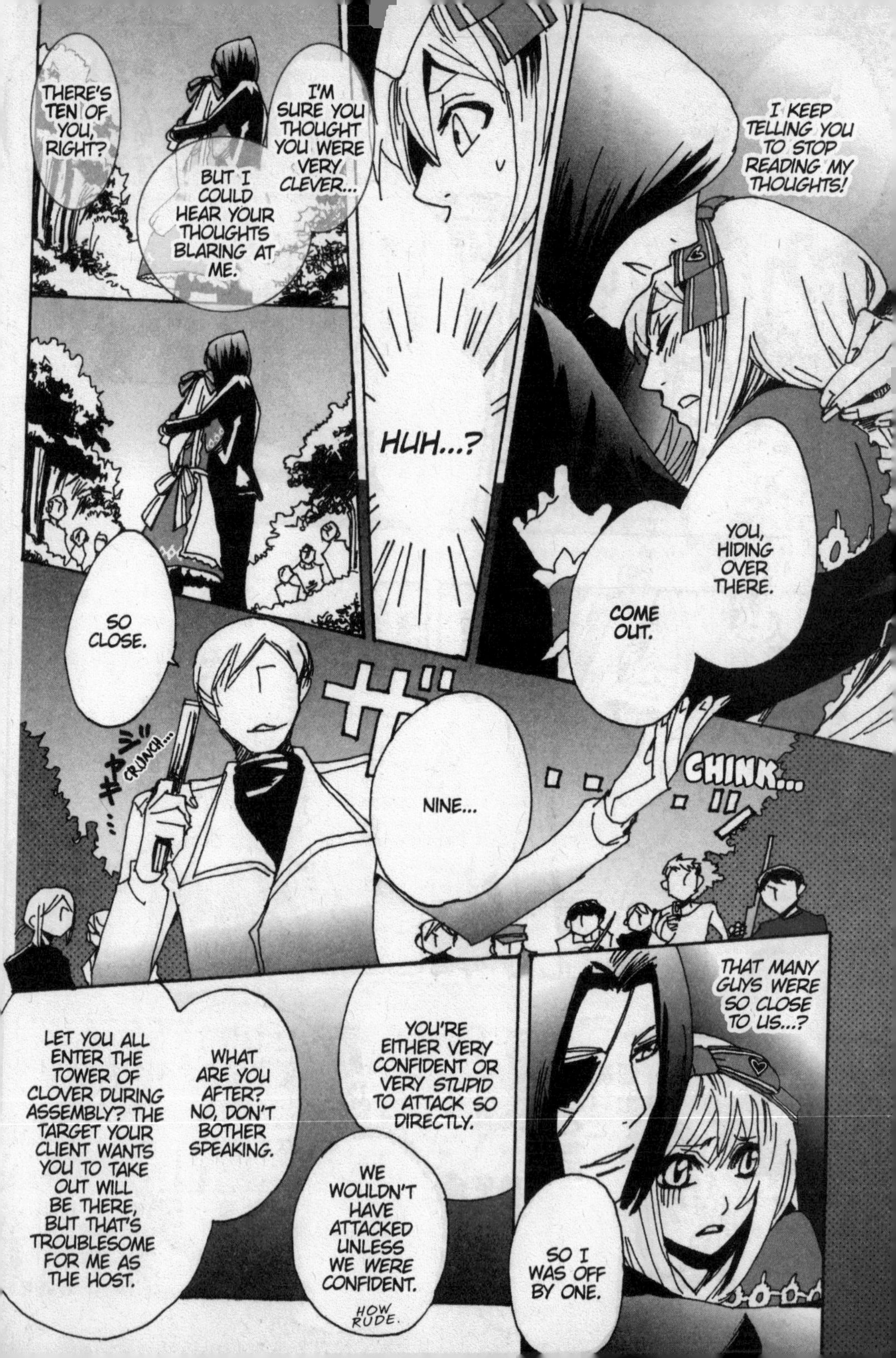
I KEEP TELLING YOU TO STOP READING MY THOUGHTS!
YOU, HIDING OVER THERE.
COME OUT.
HUH...?
I'M SURE YOU THOUGHT YOU WERE VERY CLEVER...
THERE'S TEN OF YOU, RIGHT?
BUT I COULD HEAR YOUR THOUGHTS BLARING AT ME.
CHINK...
NINE...
SO CLOSE.
CRUNCH...
THAT MANY GUYS WERE SO CLOSE TO US...?
SO I WAS OFF BY ONE.
YOU'RE EITHER VERY CONFIDENT OR VERY STUPID TO ATTACK SO DIRECTLY.
WE WOULDN'T HAVE ATTACKED UNLESS WE WERE CONFIDENT.
HOW RUDE.
WHAT ARE YOU AFTER? NO, DON'T BOTHER SPEAKING.
LET YOU ALL ENTER THE TOWER OF CLOVER DURING ASSEMBLY? THE TARGET YOUR CLIENT WANTS YOU TO TAKE OUT WILL BE THERE, BUT THAT'S TROUBLESOME FOR ME AS THE HOST.

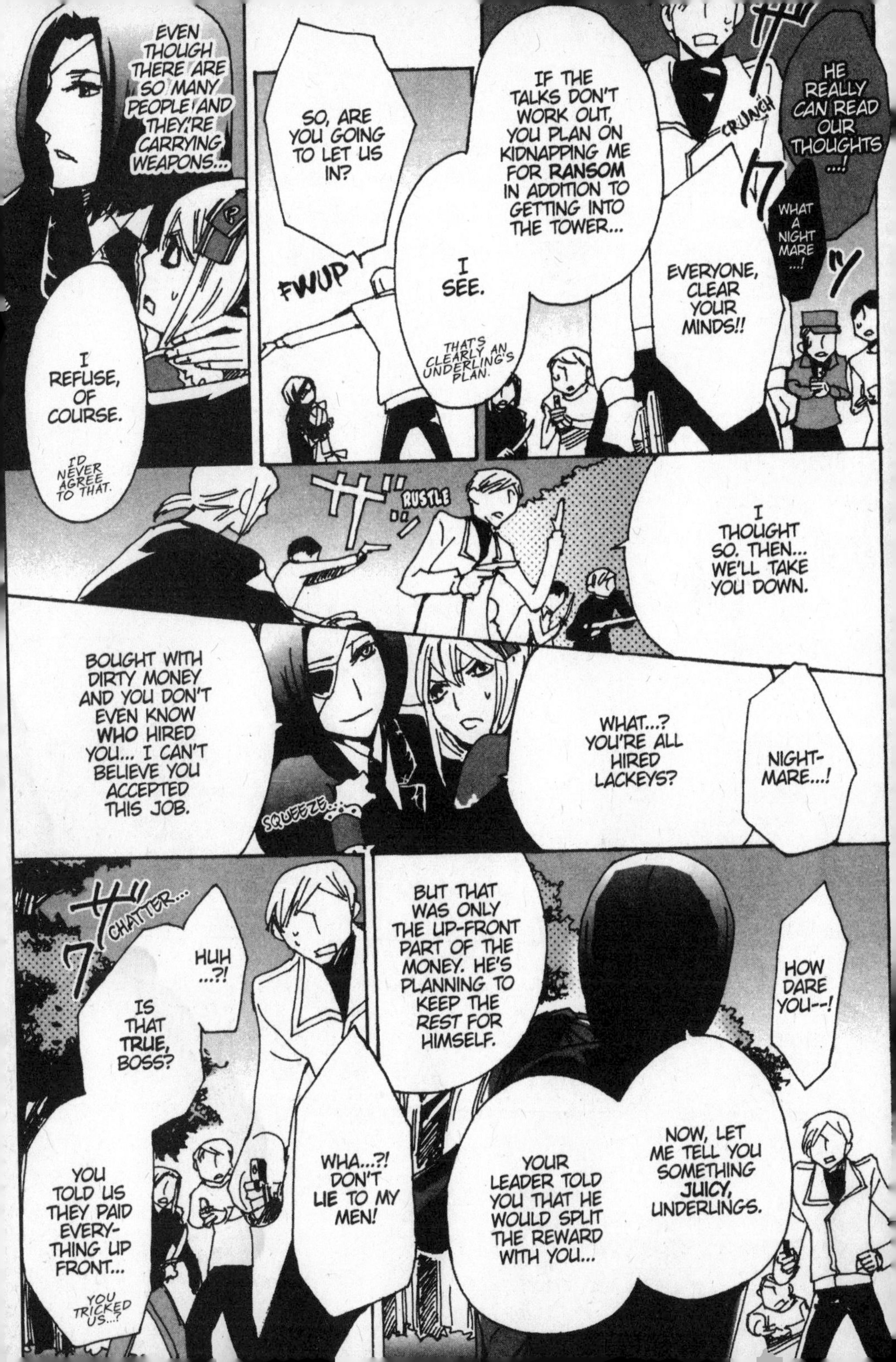
HE REALLY CAN READ OUR THOUGHTS...!
CRUNCH
IF THE TALKS DON'T WORK OUT, YOU PLAN ON KIDNAPPING ME FOR RANSOM IN ADDITION TO GETTING INTO THE TOWER...
WHAT A NIGHT MARE...!
EVERYONE, CLEAR YOUR MINDS!!
SO, ARE YOU GOING TO LET US IN?
FWUP
I SEE.
THAT'S CLEARLY AN UNDERLING'S PLAN.
EVEN THOUGH THERE ARE SO MANY PEOPLE AND THEY'RE CARRYING WEAPONS...
I REFUSE, OF COURSE.
ID NEVER AGREE TO THAT.
I THOUGHT SO. THEN... WE'LL TAKE YOU DOWN.
RUSTLE
NIGHT-MARE...!
WHAT...? YOU'RE ALL HIRED LACKEYS?
BOUGHT WITH DIRTY MONEY AND YOU DON'T EVEN KNOW WHO HIRED YOU... I CAN'T BELIEVE YOU ACCEPTED THIS JOB.
SQUEEZE...
HOW DARE YOU--!
NOW, LET ME TELL YOU SOMETHING JUICY, UNDERLINGS.
YOUR LEADER TOLD YOU THAT HE WOULD SPLIT THE REWARD WITH YOU...
BUT THAT WAS ONLY THE UP-FRONT PART OF THE MONEY. HE'S PLANNING TO KEEP THE REST FOR HIMSELF.
WHA...?! DON'T LIE TO MY MEN!
CHATTER...
HUH...?!
IS THAT TRUE, BOSS?
YOU TOLD US THEY PAID EVERY-THING UP FRONT...
YOU TRICKED US...?

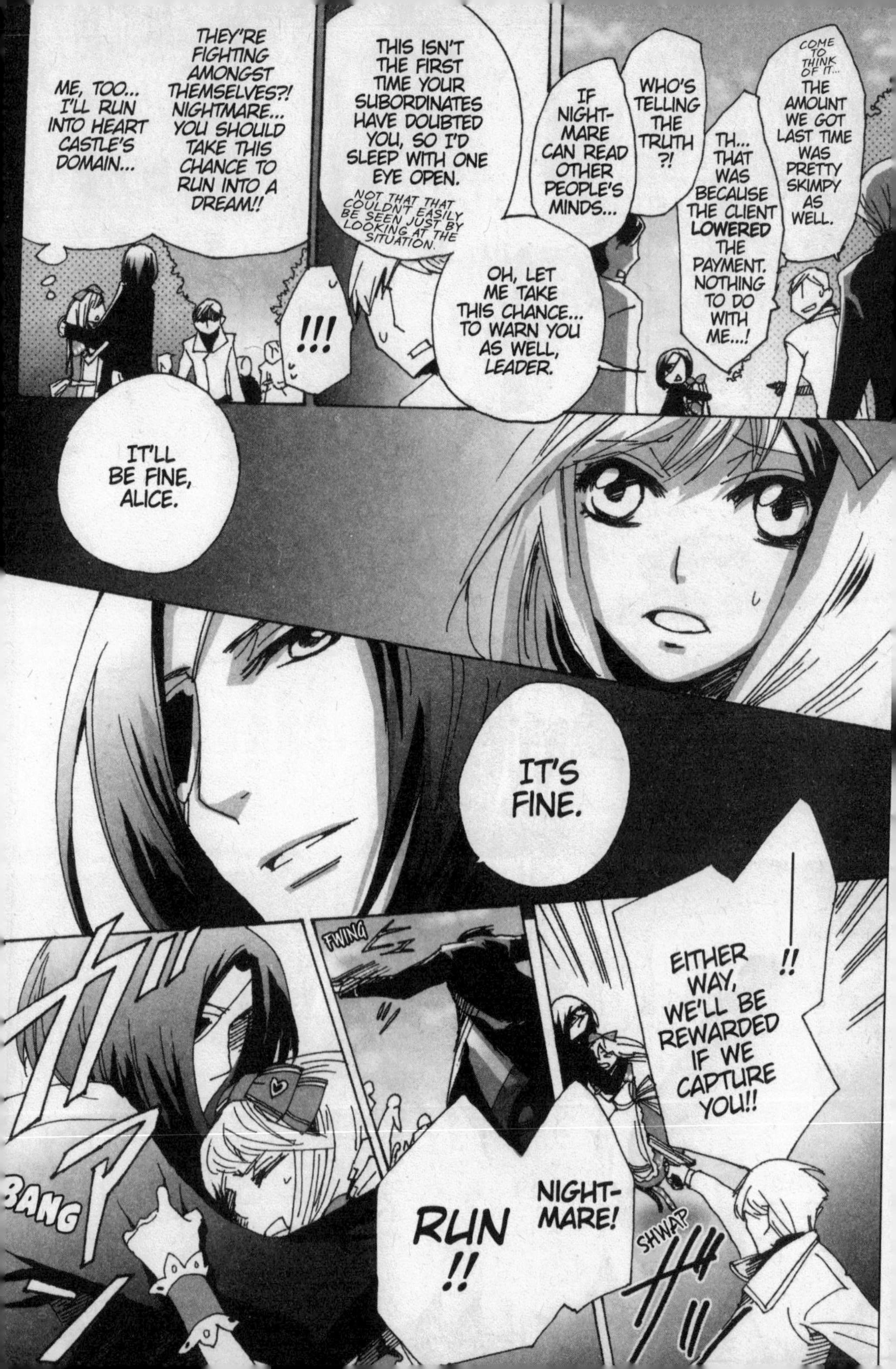
COME TO THINK OF IT... THE AMOUNT WE GOT LAST TIME WAS PRETTY SKIMPY AS WELL.
TH... THAT WAS BECAUSE THE CLIENT LOWERED THE PAYMENT. NOTHING TO DO WITH ME...!
WHO'S TELLING THE TRUTH?!
IF NIGHTMARE CAN READ OTHER PEOPLE'S MINDS...
THIS ISN'T THE FIRST TIME YOUR SUBORDINATES HAVE DOUBTED YOU, SO I'D SLEEP WITH ONE EYE OPEN.
NOT THAT THAT COULDN'T EASILY BE SEEN JUST BY LOOKING AT THE SITUATION.
OH, LET ME TAKE THIS CHANCE... TO WARN YOU AS WELL, LEADER.
!!!
THEY'RE FIGHTING AMONGST THEMSELVES?! NIGHTMARE... YOU SHOULD TAKE THIS CHANCE TO RUN INTO A DREAM!!
ME, TOO... I'LL RUN INTO HEART CASTLE'S DOMAIN...
IT'LL BE FINE, ALICE.
IT'S FINE.
—!!
EITHER WAY, WE'LL BE REWARDED IF WE CAPTURE YOU!!
NIGHTMARE!
RUN!!
SHWAP
FWING
BANG

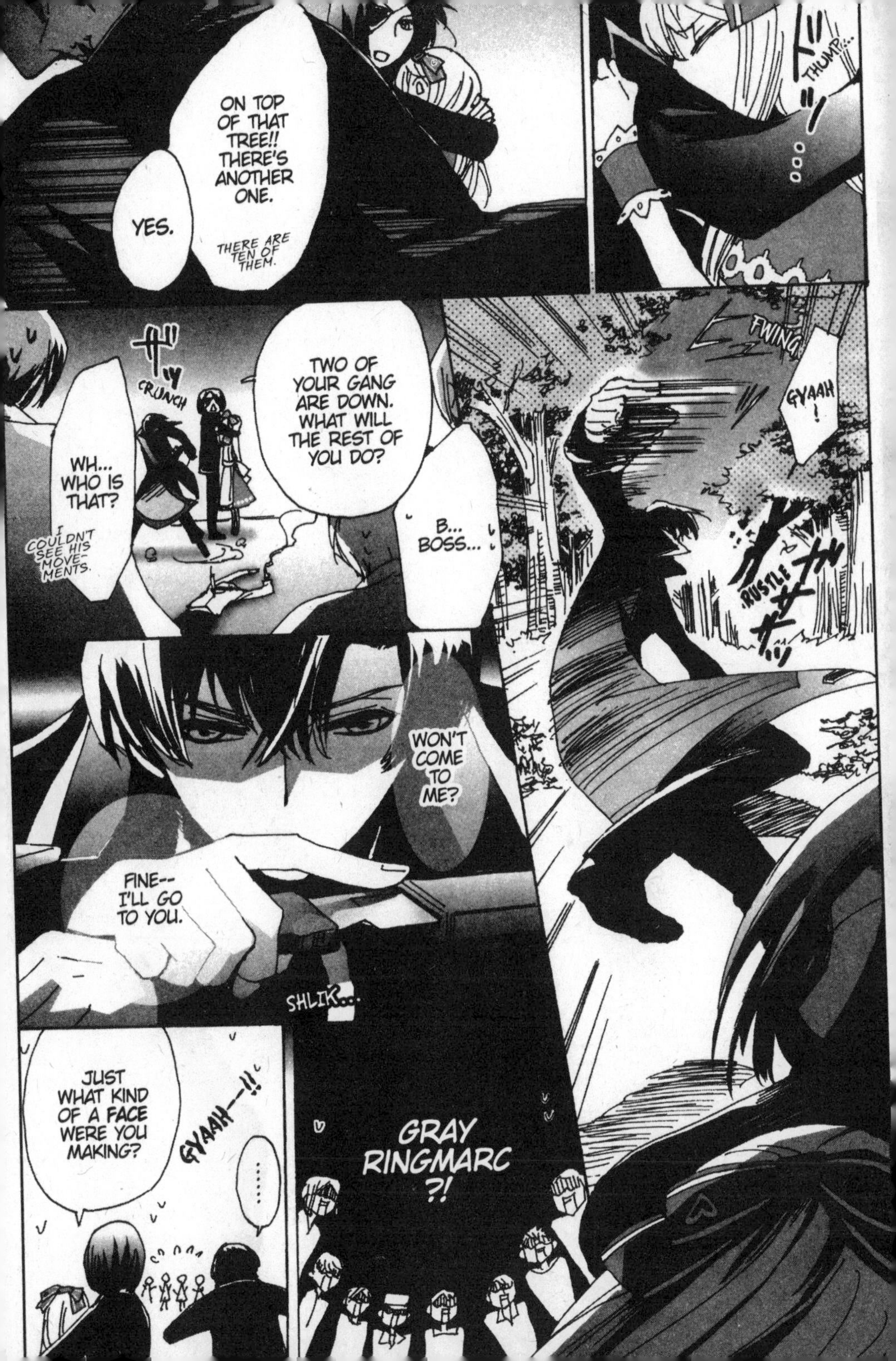
THUMP...
...
ON TOP OF THAT TREE!! THERE'S ANOTHER ONE.
YES.
THERE ARE TEN OF THEM.
FWING
GYAAH!
RUSTLE
TWO OF YOUR GANG ARE DOWN. WHAT WILL THE REST OF YOU DO?
B... BOSS...
CRUNCH
WH... WHO IS THAT?
I COULDN'T SEE HIS MOVEMENTS.
WON'T COME TO ME?
FINE-- I'LL GO TO YOU.
SHLIK...
GRAY RINGMARC ?!
JUST WHAT KIND OF A FACE WERE YOU MAKING?
GYAAH--!!
......

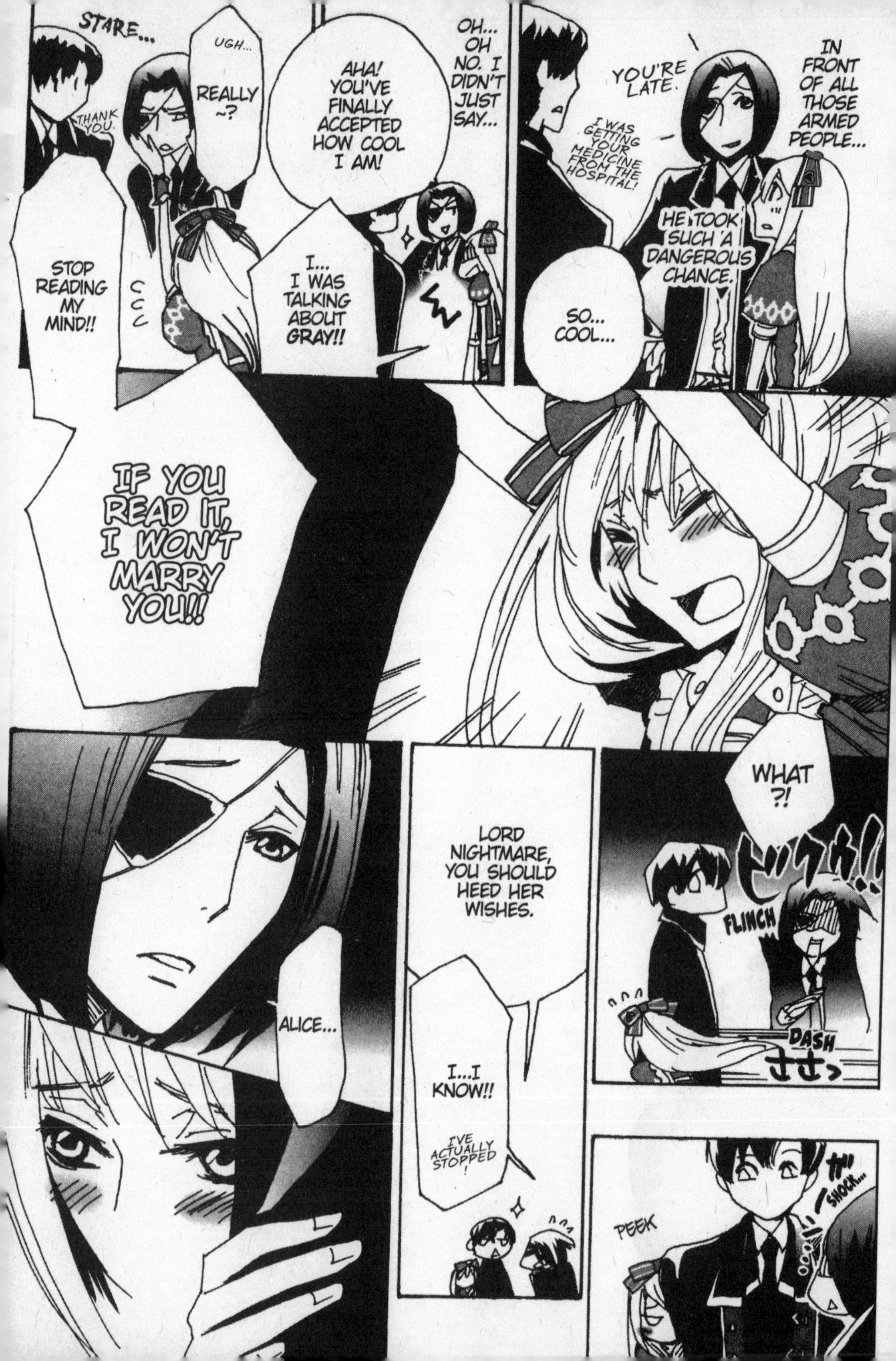
IN FRONT OF ALL THOSE ARMED PEOPLE...
YOU'RE LATE.
I WAS GETTING YOUR MEDICINE FROM THE HOSPITAL!
HE TOOK SUCH A DANGEROUS CHANCE.
SO... COOL...
OH... OH NO. I DIDN'T JUST SAY...
AHA! YOU'VE FINALLY ACCEPTED HOW COOL I AM!
I... I WAS TALKING ABOUT GRAY!!
UGH...
REALLY ~?
STARE...
THANK YOU.
STOP READING MY MIND!!
IF YOU READ IT, I WON'T MARRY YOU!!
WHAT ?!
FLINCH
DASH
ささっ
SHOCK...
PEEK
LORD NIGHTMARE, YOU SHOULD HEED HER WISHES.
I...I KNOW!!
I'VE ACTUALLY STOPPED!
ALICE...

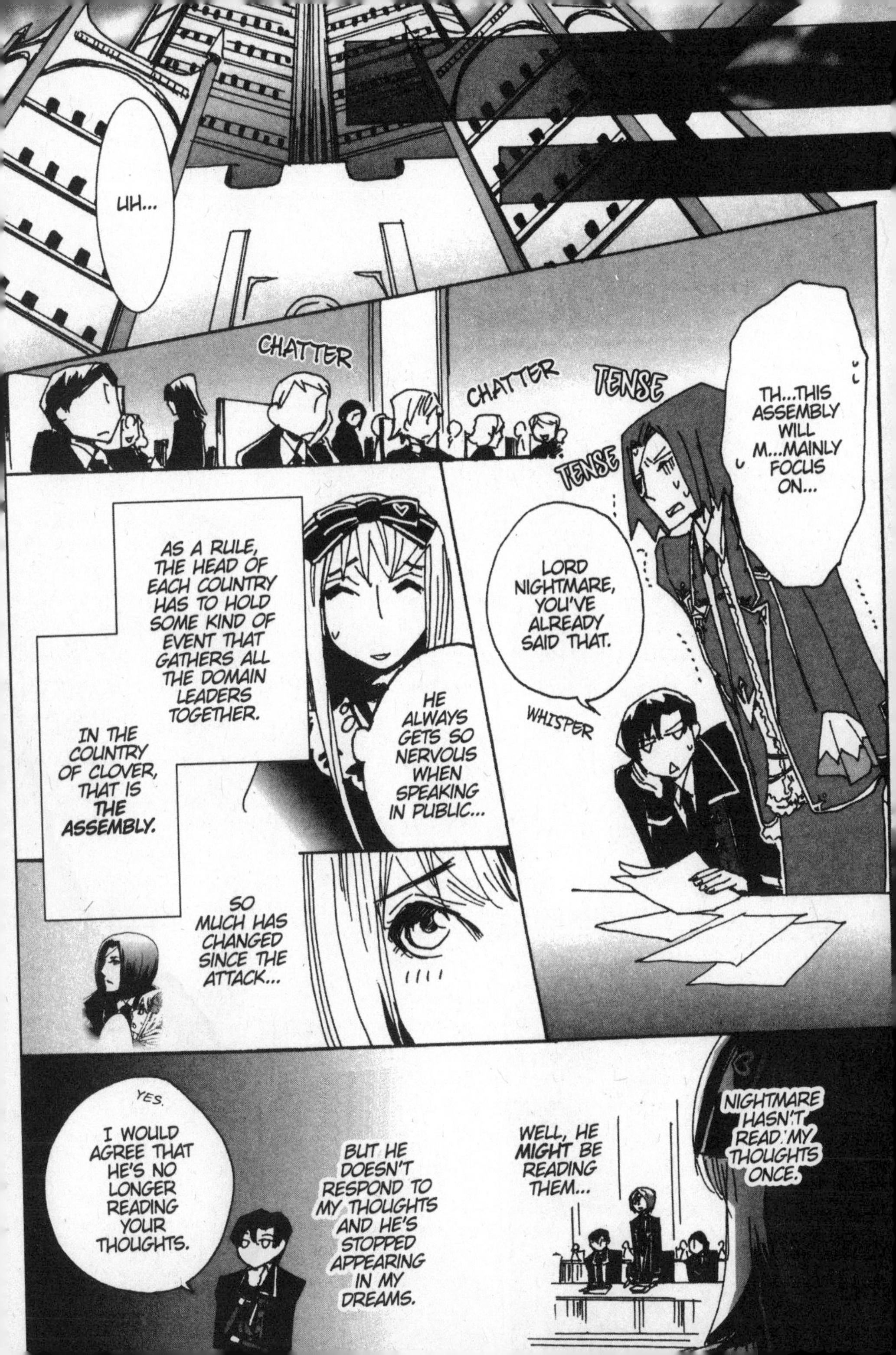
UH...
TH...THIS ASSEMBLY WILL M...MAINLY FOCUS ON...
TENSE
TENSE
CHATTER
CHATTER
LORD NIGHTMARE, YOU'VE ALREADY SAID THAT.
WHISPER
HE ALWAYS GETS SO NERVOUS WHEN SPEAKING IN PUBLIC...
AS A RULE, THE HEAD OF EACH COUNTRY HAS TO HOLD SOME KIND OF EVENT THAT GATHERS ALL THE DOMAIN LEADERS TOGETHER.
IN THE COUNTRY OF CLOVER, THAT IS THE ASSEMBLY.
SO MUCH HAS CHANGED SINCE THE ATTACK...
NIGHTMARE HASN'T READ MY THOUGHTS ONCE.
WELL, HE MIGHT BE READING THEM...
BUT HE DOESN'T RESPOND TO MY THOUGHTS AND HE'S STOPPED APPEARING IN MY DREAMS.
YES.
I WOULD AGREE THAT HE'S NO LONGER READING YOUR THOUGHTS.

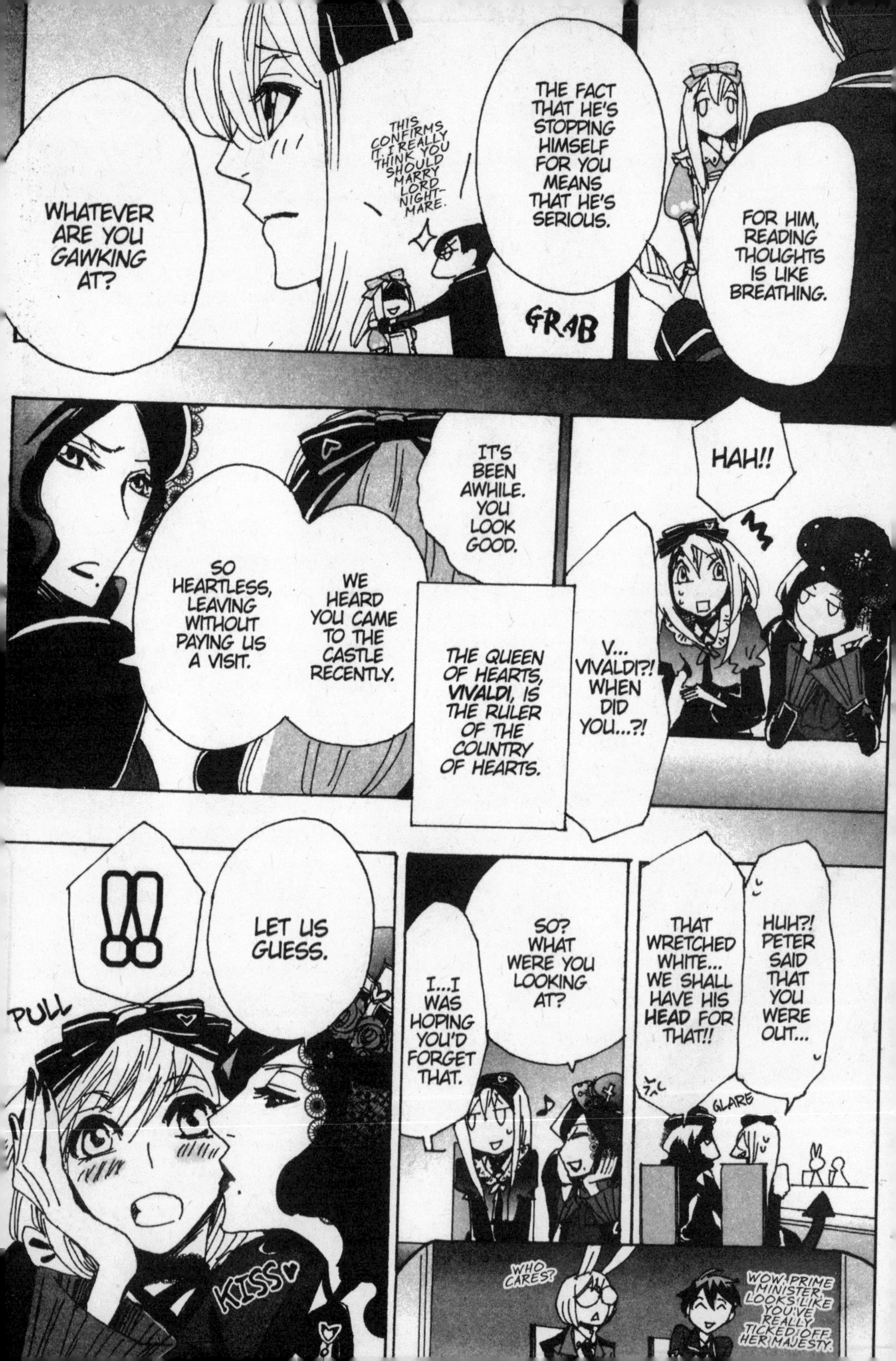
FOR HIM, READING THOUGHTS IS LIKE BREATHING.
THE FACT THAT HE'S STOPPING HIMSELF FOR YOU MEANS THAT HE'S SERIOUS.
GRAB
THIS CONFIRMS IT. I REALLY THINK YOU SHOULD MARRY LORD NIGHT-MARE.
WHATEVER ARE YOU GAWKING AT?
HAH!!
V... VIVALDI?! WHEN DID YOU...?!
THE QUEEN OF HEARTS, VIVALDI, IS THE RULER OF THE COUNTRY OF HEARTS.
IT'S BEEN AWHILE. YOU LOOK GOOD.
WE HEARD YOU CAME TO THE CASTLE RECENTLY.
SO HEARTLESS, LEAVING WITHOUT PAYING US A VISIT.
HUH?! PETER SAID THAT YOU WERE OUT...
THAT WRETCHED WHITE... WE SHALL HAVE HIS HEAD FOR THAT!!
GLARE
SO? WHAT WERE YOU LOOKING AT?
I...I WAS HOPING YOU'D FORGET THAT.
WOW, PRIME MINISTER, LOOKS LIKE YOU'VE REALLY TICKED OFF HER MAJESTY.
WHO CARES?
LET US GUESS.
!!
PULL
KISS♥

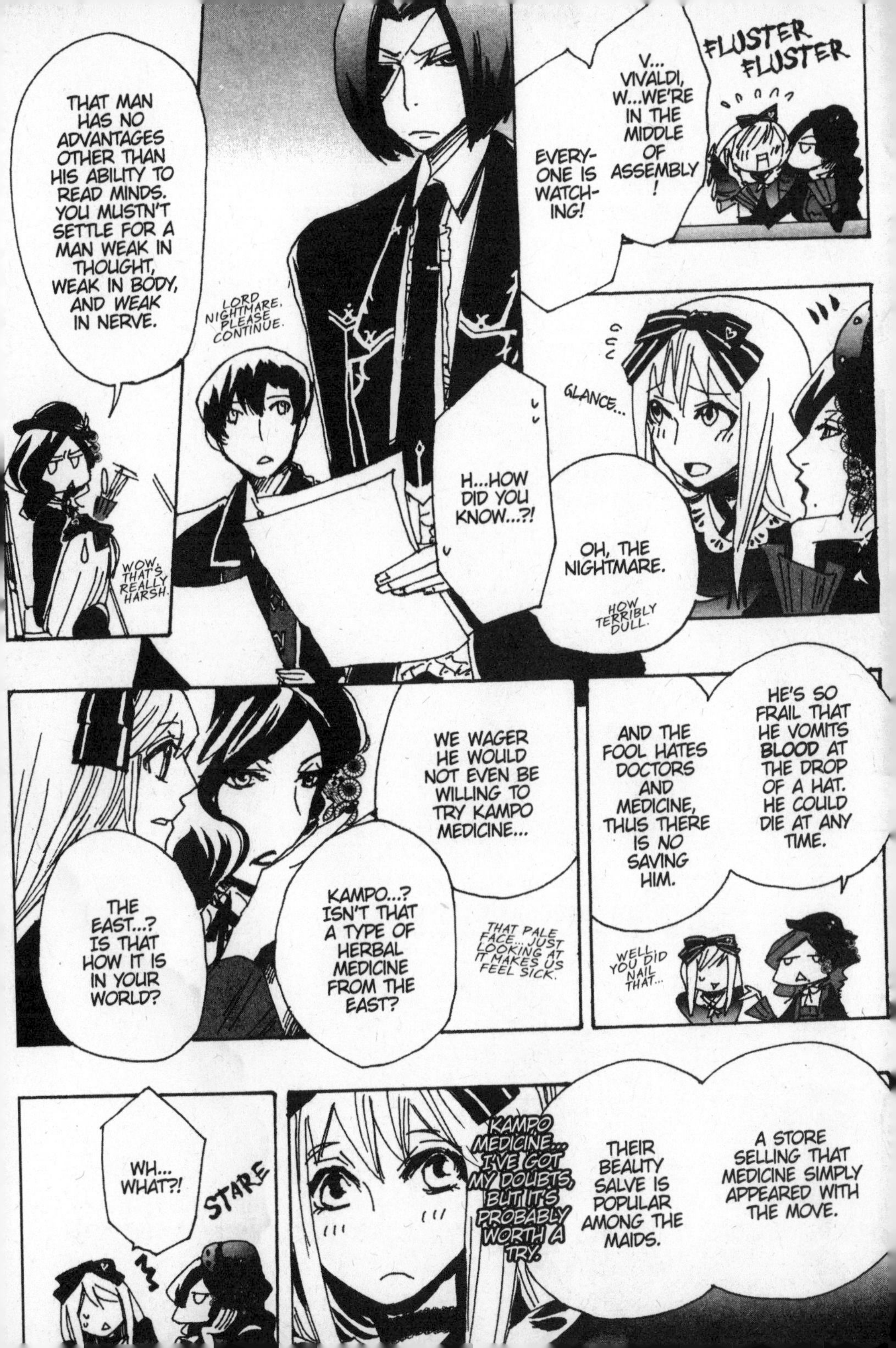

FLUSTER FLUSTER
V... VIVALDI, W...WE'RE IN THE MIDDLE OF ASSEMBLY!
EVERYONE IS WATCHING!
THAT MAN HAS NO ADVANTAGES OTHER THAN HIS ABILITY TO READ MINDS. YOU MUSTN'T SETTLE FOR A MAN WEAK IN THOUGHT, WEAK IN BODY, AND WEAK IN NERVE.
LORD NIGHTMARE, PLEASE CONTINUE.
WOW, THAT'S REALLY HARSH.
GUU
GLANCE...
OH, THE NIGHTMARE.
HOW TERRIBLY DULL.
H...HOW DID YOU KNOW...?!
HE'S SO FRAIL THAT HE VOMITS BLOOD AT THE DROP OF A HAT. HE COULD DIE AT ANY TIME.
AND THE FOOL HATES DOCTORS AND MEDICINE, THUS THERE IS NO SAVING HIM.
WELL YOU DID NAIL THAT...
WE WAGER HE WOULD NOT EVEN BE WILLING TO TRY KAMPO MEDICINE...
KAMPO...? ISN'T THAT A TYPE OF HERBAL MEDICINE FROM THE EAST?
THAT PALE FACE... JUST LOOKING AT IT MAKES US FEEL SICK.
THE EAST...? IS THAT HOW IT IS IN YOUR WORLD?
A STORE SELLING THAT MEDICINE SIMPLY APPEARED WITH THE MOVE.
THEIR BEAUTY SALVE IS POPULAR AMONG THE MAIDS.
KAMPO MEDICINE... I'VE GOT MY DOUBTS, BUT IT'S PROBABLY WORTH A TRY.
STARE
WH... WHAT?!

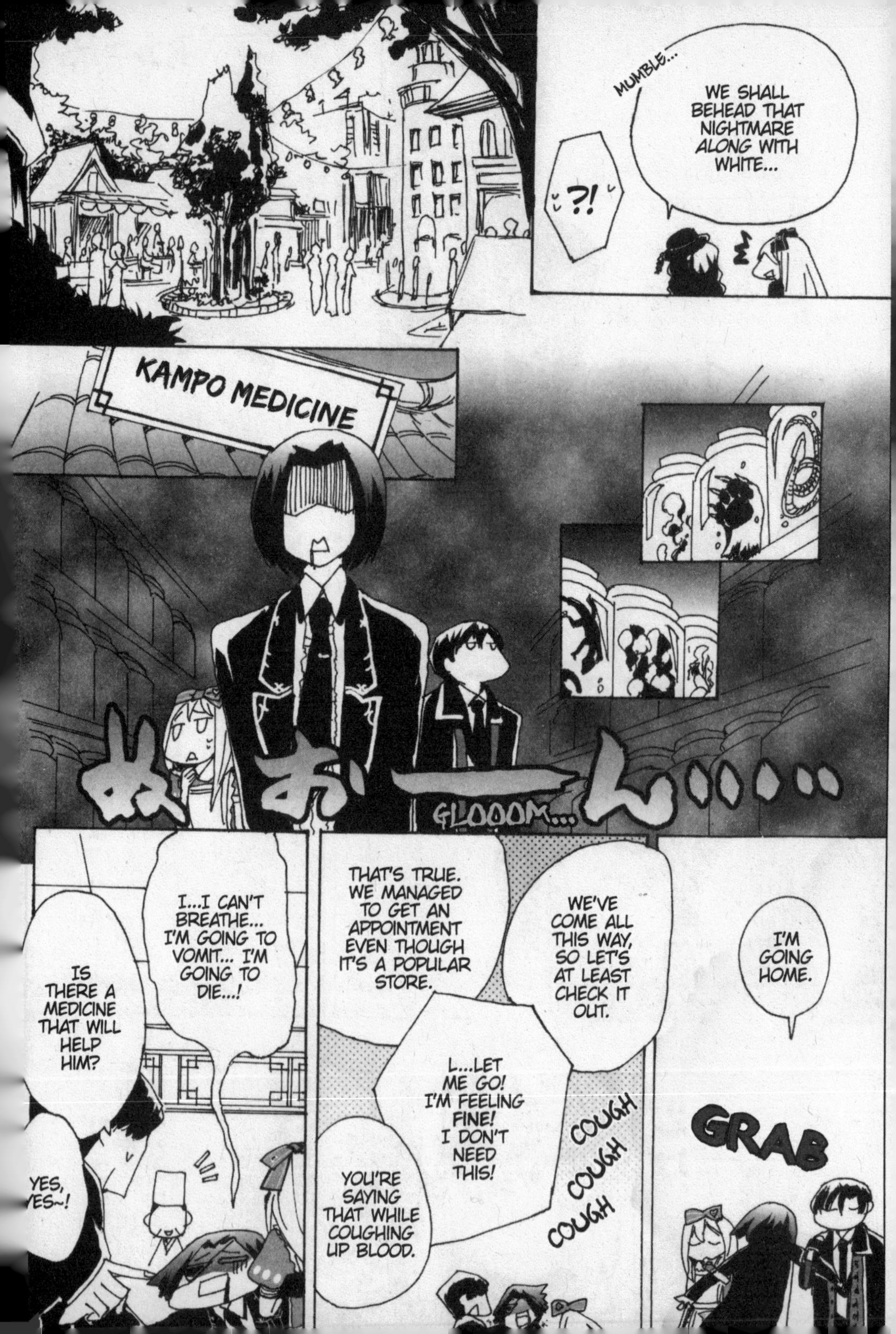
MUMBLE...
WE SHALL BEHEAD THAT NIGHTMARE ALONG WITH WHITE...
?!
KAMPO MEDICINE
GLOOOM...
I'M GOING HOME.
GRAB
WE'VE COME ALL THIS WAY, SO LET'S AT LEAST CHECK IT OUT.
THAT'S TRUE. WE MANAGED TO GET AN APPOINTMENT EVEN THOUGH IT'S A POPULAR STORE.
L...LET ME GO! I'M FEELING FINE! I DON'T NEED THIS!
COUGH COUGH COUGH
YOU'RE SAYING THAT WHILE COUGHING UP BLOOD.
I...I CAN'T BREATHE... I'M GOING TO VOMIT... I'M GOING TO DIE...!
IS THERE A MEDICINE THAT WILL HELP HIM?
YES, YES~!

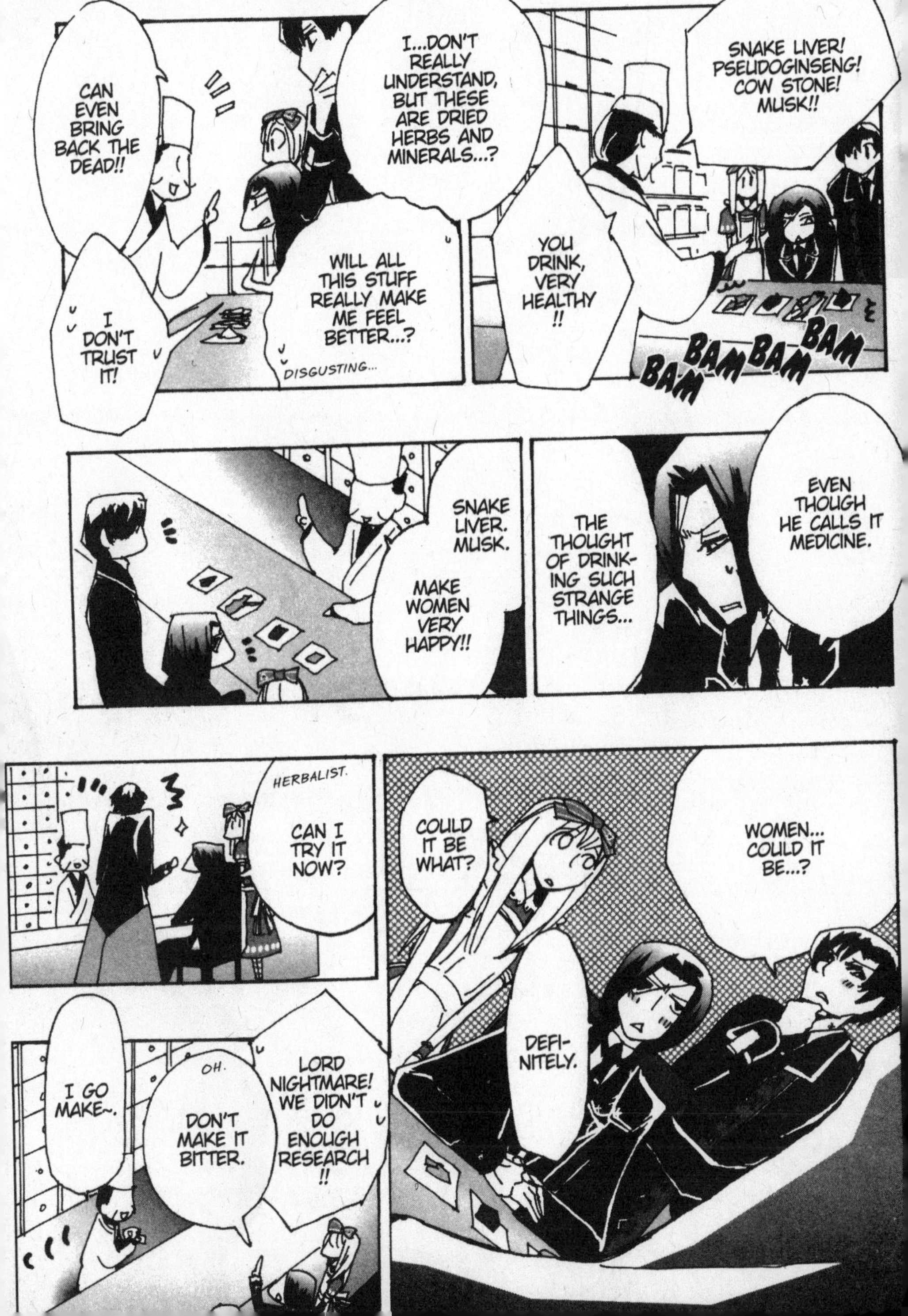
SNAKE LIVER! PSEUDOGINSENG! COW STONE! MUSK!!
YOU DRINK, VERY HEALTHY !!
BAM BAM BAM BAM
I...DON'T REALLY UNDERSTAND, BUT THESE ARE DRIED HERBS AND MINERALS...?
CAN EVEN BRING BACK THE DEAD!!
WILL ALL THIS STUFF REALLY MAKE ME FEEL BETTER...?
DISGUSTING...
I DON'T TRUST IT!
EVEN THOUGH HE CALLS IT MEDICINE.
THE THOUGHT OF DRINK-ING SUCH STRANGE THINGS...
SNAKE LIVER. MUSK.
MAKE WOMEN VERY HAPPY!!
WOMEN... COULD IT BE...?
COULD IT BE WHAT?
DEFI-NITELY.
HERBALIST.
CAN I TRY IT NOW?
LORD NIGHTMARE! WE DIDN'T DO ENOUGH RESEARCH !!
OH.
DON'T MAKE IT BITTER.
I GO MAKE~.

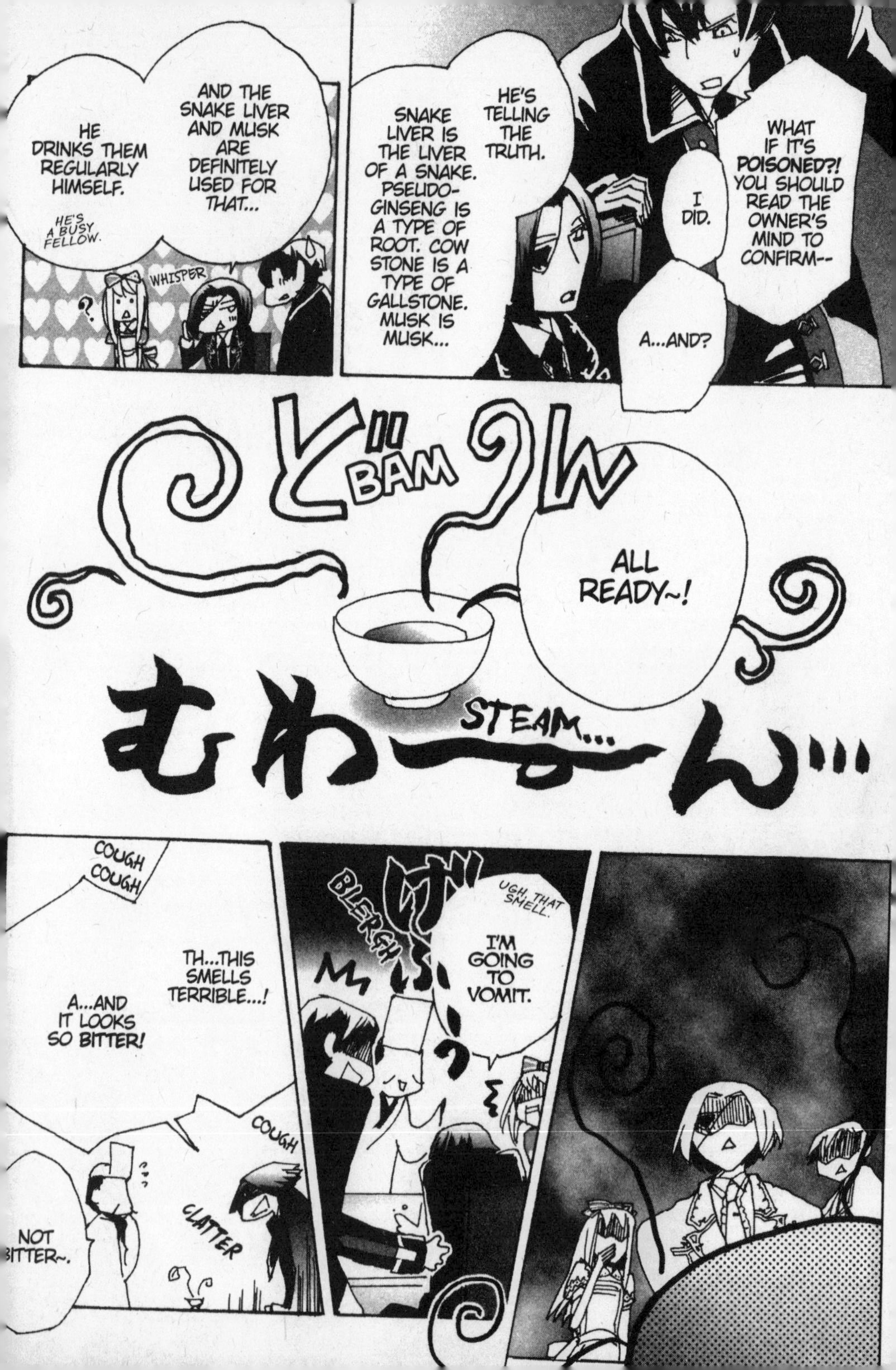
WHAT IF IT'S POISONED?! YOU SHOULD READ THE OWNER'S MIND TO CONFIRM--
I DID.
A...AND?
HE'S TELLING THE TRUTH.
SNAKE LIVER IS THE LIVER OF A SNAKE. PSEUDO-GINSENG IS A TYPE OF ROOT. COW STONE IS A TYPE OF GALLSTONE. MUSK IS MUSK...
AND THE SNAKE LIVER AND MUSK ARE DEFINITELY USED FOR THAT...
HE DRINKS THEM REGULARLY HIMSELF.
HE'S A BUSY FELLOW.
WHISPER
?
BAM
ALL READY~!
STEAM...
UGH, THAT SMELL.
I'M GOING TO VOMIT.
BLERGH
COUGH COUGH
TH...THIS SMELLS TERRIBLE...!
A...AND IT LOOKS SO BITTER!
COUGH
CLATTER
NOT BITTER~.

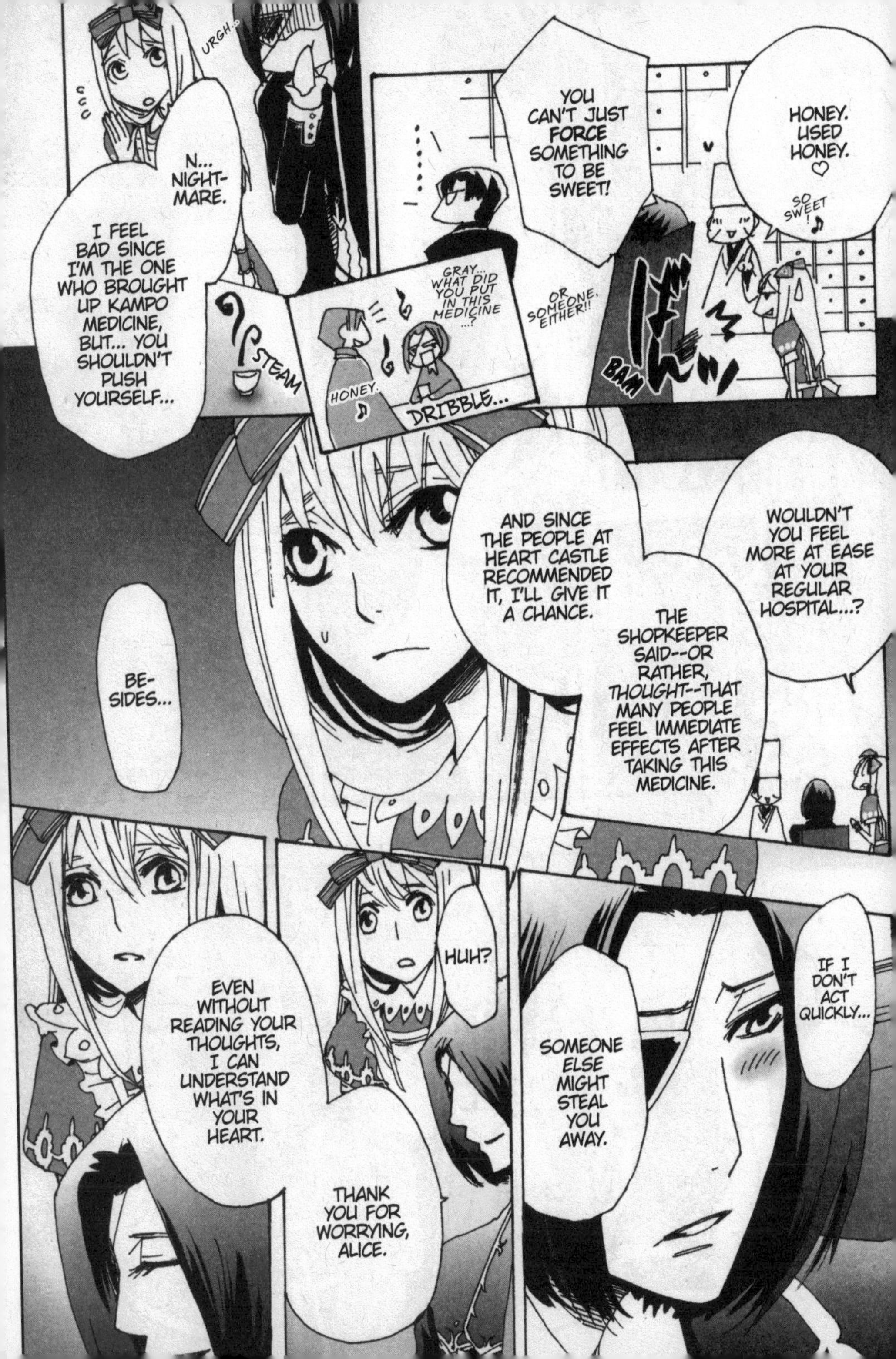
HONEY. USED HONEY. ♡
SO SWEET! ♪
BAM
YOU CAN'T JUST FORCE SOMETHING TO BE SWEET!
OR SOMEONE, EITHER!!
......
GRAY... WHAT DID YOU PUT IN THIS MEDICINE...?
HONEY. ♪
DRIBBLE...
STEAM
URGH...
N... NIGHT-MARE.
I FEEL BAD SINCE I'M THE ONE WHO BROUGHT UP KAMPO MEDICINE, BUT... YOU SHOULDN'T PUSH YOURSELF...
WOULDN'T YOU FEEL MORE AT EASE AT YOUR REGULAR HOSPITAL...?
AND SINCE THE PEOPLE AT HEART CASTLE RECOMMENDED IT, I'LL GIVE IT A CHANCE.
THE SHOPKEEPER SAID--OR RATHER, THOUGHT--THAT MANY PEOPLE FEEL IMMEDIATE EFFECTS AFTER TAKING THIS MEDICINE.
BE-SIDES...
IF I DON'T ACT QUICKLY...
SOMEONE ELSE MIGHT STEAL YOU AWAY.
HUH?
EVEN WITHOUT READING YOUR THOUGHTS, I CAN UNDERSTAND WHAT'S IN YOUR HEART.
THANK YOU FOR WORRYING, ALICE.

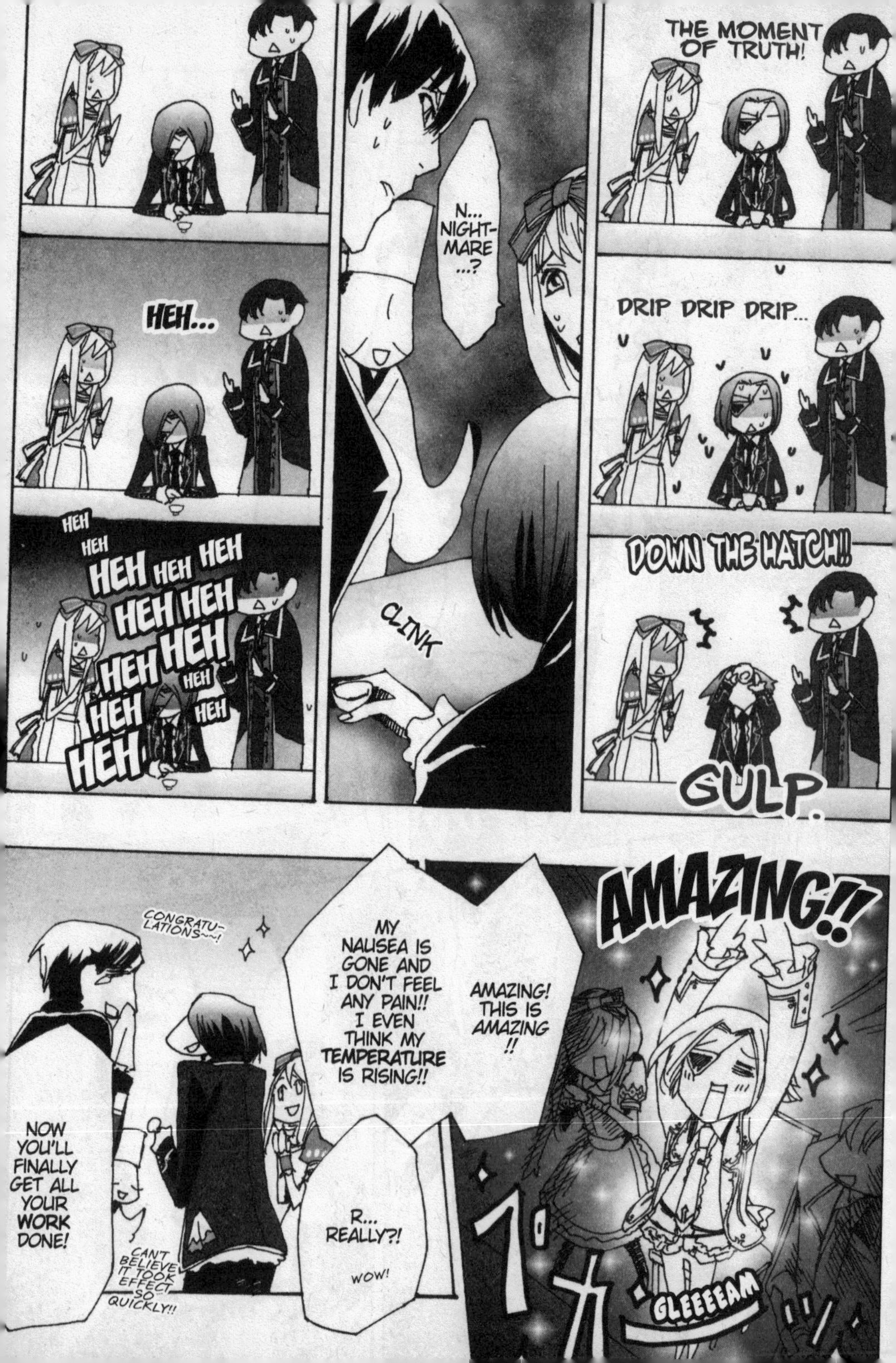

THE MOMENT OF TRUTH!
DRIP DRIP DRIP...
DOWN THE HATCH!!
GULP.
N... NIGHT-MARE ...?
CLINK
HEH...
HEH HEH HEH heh HEH HEH HEH HEH HEH HEH HEH HEH HEH
AMAZING!!
AMAZING! THIS IS AMAZING !!
MY NAUSEA IS GONE AND I DON'T FEEL ANY PAIN!! I EVEN THINK MY TEMPERATURE IS RISING!!
GLEEEEAM
R... REALLY?!
WOW!
CONGRATU-LATIONS~~!
CAN'T BELIEVE IT TOOK EFFECT SO QUICKLY!!
NOW YOU'LL FINALLY GET ALL YOUR WORK DONE!

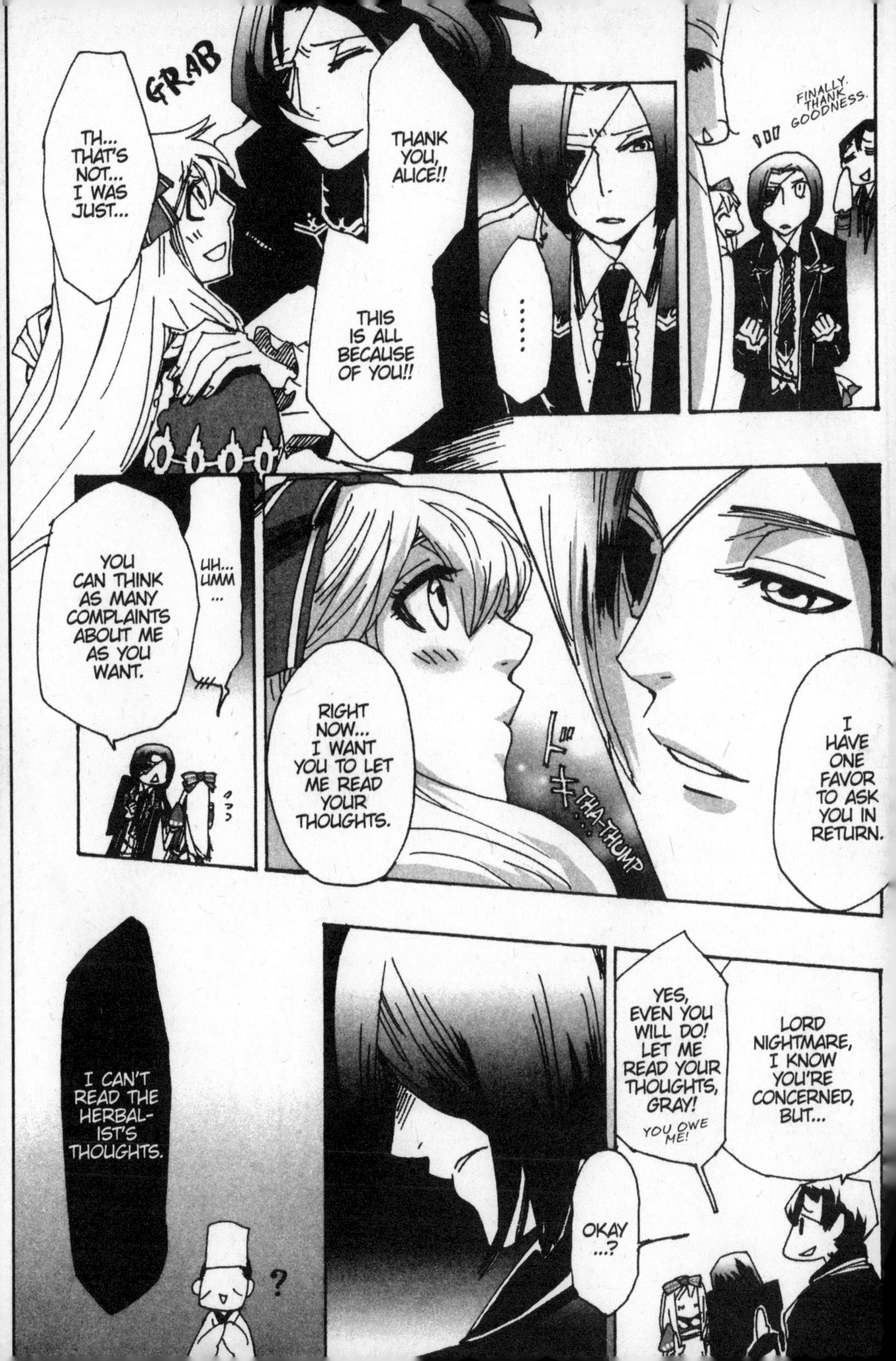
FINALLY. THANK GOODNESS.
!!!
......
THANK YOU, ALICE!!
GRAB
THIS IS ALL BECAUSE OF YOU!!
TH... THAT'S NOT... I WAS JUST...
I HAVE ONE FAVOR TO ASK YOU IN RETURN.
RIGHT NOW... I WANT YOU TO LET ME READ YOUR THOUGHTS.
THA-THUMP
UH... UMM...
YOU CAN THINK AS MANY COMPLAINTS ABOUT ME AS YOU WANT.
LORD NIGHTMARE, I KNOW YOU'RE CONCERNED, BUT...
YES, EVEN YOU WILL DO! LET ME READ YOUR THOUGHTS, GRAY!
YOU OWE ME!
OKAY ...?
I CAN'T READ THE HERBAL-IST'S THOUGHTS.
?

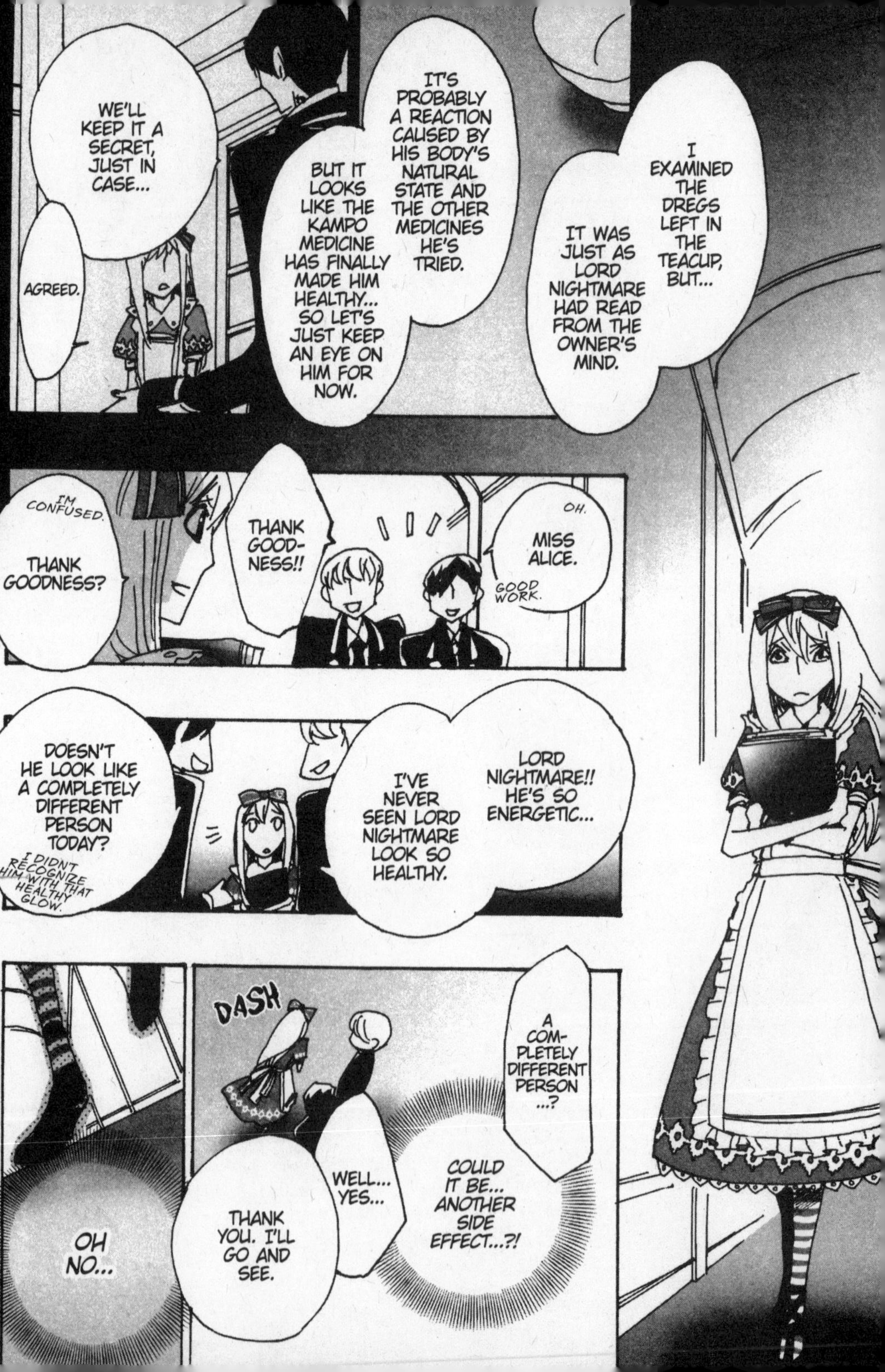
I EXAMINED THE DREGS LEFT IN THE TEACUP, BUT...
IT WAS JUST AS LORD NIGHTMARE HAD READ FROM THE OWNER'S MIND.
IT'S PROBABLY A REACTION CAUSED BY HIS BODY'S NATURAL STATE AND THE OTHER MEDICINES HE'S TRIED.
BUT IT LOOKS LIKE THE KAMPO MEDICINE HAS FINALLY MADE HIM HEALTHY... SO LET'S JUST KEEP AN EYE ON HIM FOR NOW.
WE'LL KEEP IT A SECRET, JUST IN CASE...
AGREED.
OH.
MISS ALICE.
GOOD WORK.
THANK GOOD-NESS!!
THANK GOODNESS?
I'M CONFUSED.
LORD NIGHTMARE!! HE'S SO ENERGETIC...
I'VE NEVER SEEN LORD NIGHTMARE LOOK SO HEALTHY.
DOESN'T HE LOOK LIKE A COMPLETELY DIFFERENT PERSON TODAY?
I DIDN'T RECOGNIZE HIM WITH THAT HEALTHY GLOW.
A COM-PLETELY DIFFERENT PERSON ...?
COULD IT BE... ANOTHER SIDE EFFECT...?!
WELL... YES...
THANK YOU. I'LL GO AND SEE.
DASH
OH NO...

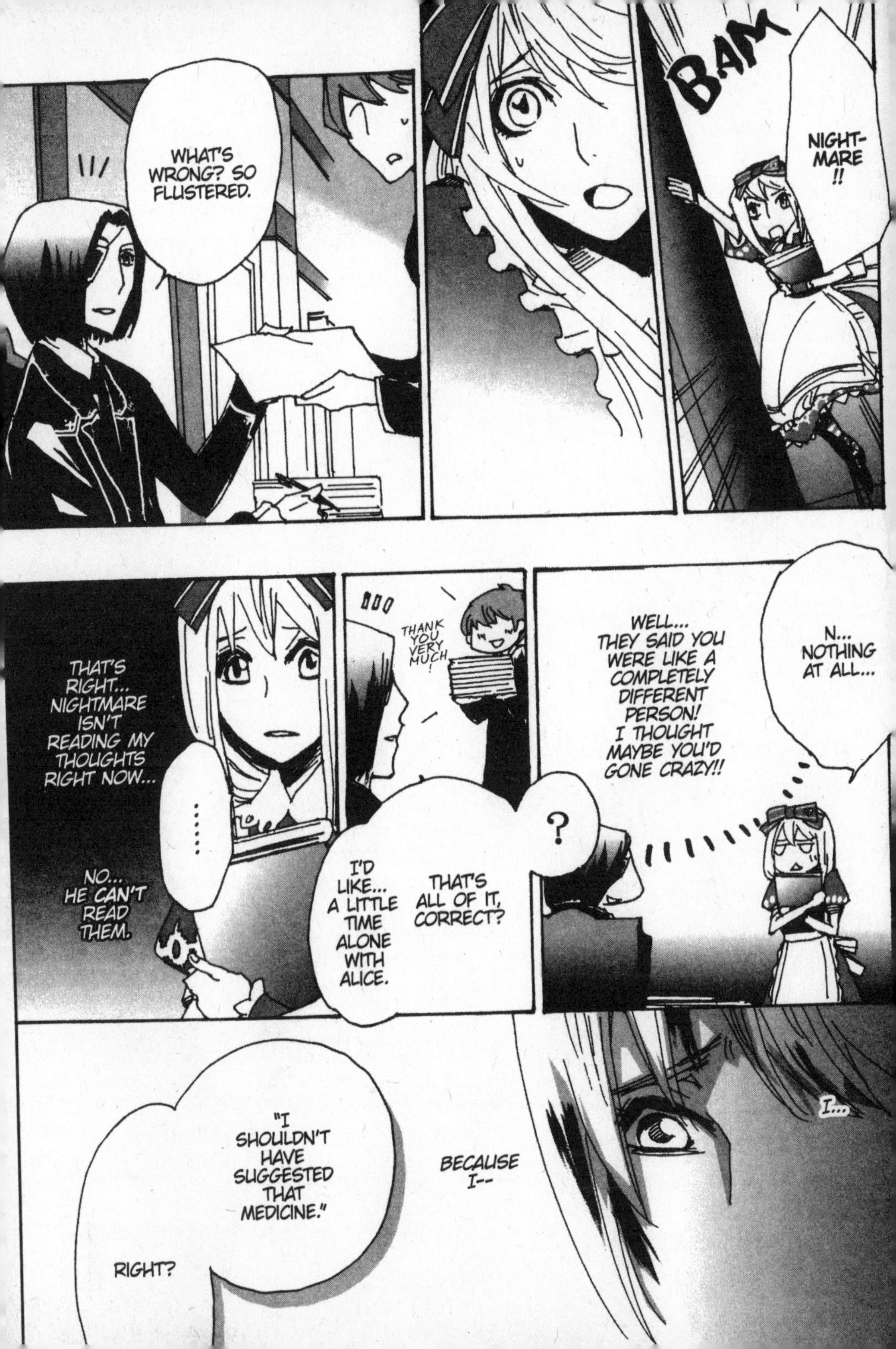
BAM
NIGHT-MARE !!
WHAT'S WRONG? SO FLUSTERED.
N... NOTHING AT ALL...
WELL... THEY SAID YOU WERE LIKE A COMPLETELY DIFFERENT PERSON! I THOUGHT MAYBE YOU'D GONE CRAZY!!
?
THANK YOU VERY MUCH!
THAT'S ALL OF IT, CORRECT?
I'D LIKE... A LITTLE TIME ALONE WITH ALICE.
THAT'S RIGHT... NIGHTMARE ISN'T READING MY THOUGHTS RIGHT NOW...
......
NO... HE CAN'T READ THEM.
I...
BECAUSE I--
"I SHOULDN'T HAVE SUGGESTED THAT MEDICINE."
RIGHT?

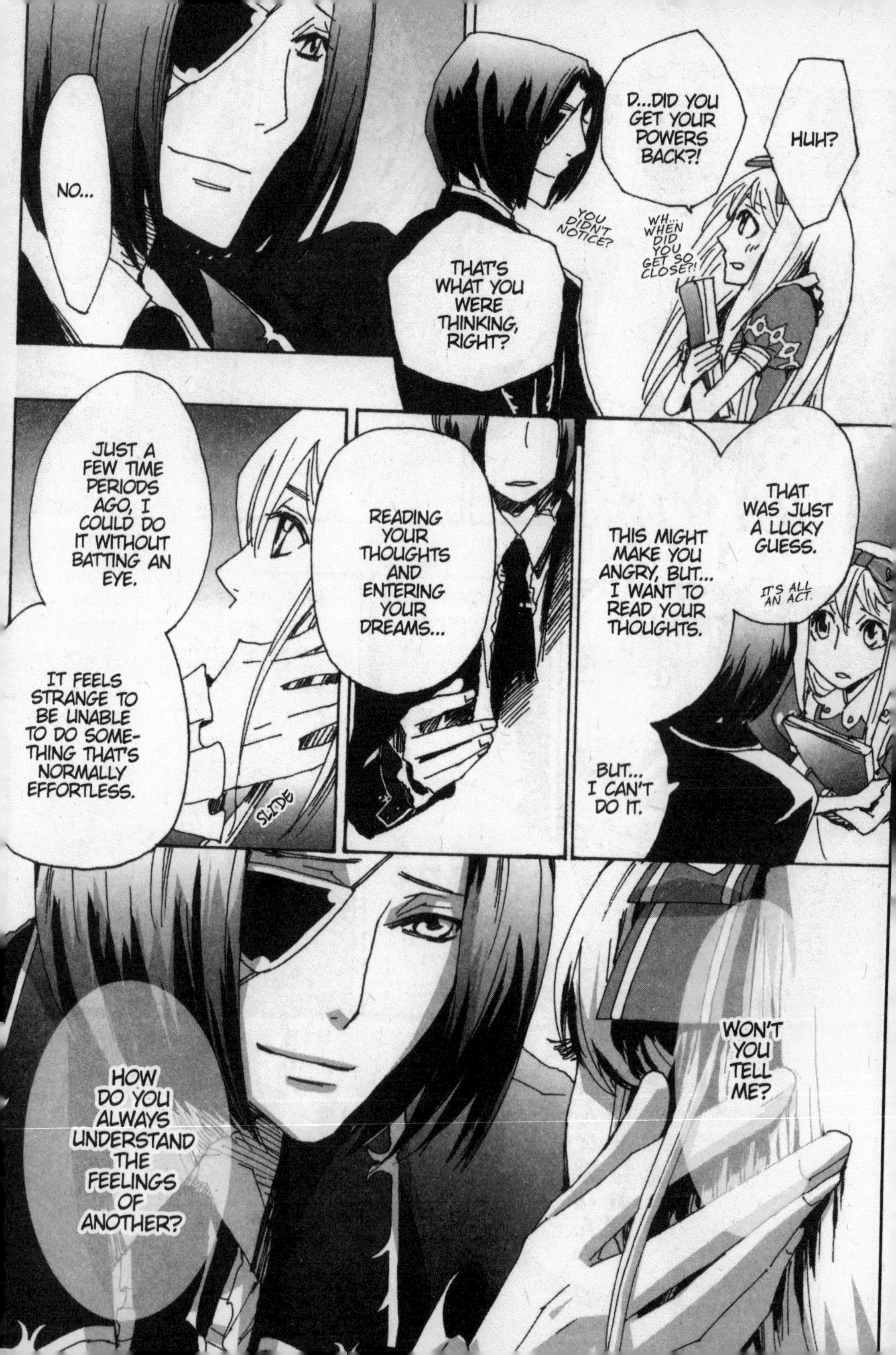
HUH?
D...DID YOU GET YOUR POWERS BACK?!
WH... WHEN DID YOU GET SO CLOSE?!
YOU DIDN'T NOTICE?
THAT'S WHAT YOU WERE THINKING, RIGHT?
NO...
THAT WAS JUST A LUCKY GUESS.
IT'S ALL AN ACT.
THIS MIGHT MAKE YOU ANGRY, BUT... I WANT TO READ YOUR THOUGHTS.
BUT... I CAN'T DO IT.
READING YOUR THOUGHTS AND ENTERING YOUR DREAMS...
JUST A FEW TIME PERIODS AGO, I COULD DO IT WITHOUT BATTING AN EYE.
IT FEELS STRANGE TO BE UNABLE TO DO SOMETHING THAT'S NORMALLY EFFORTLESS.
SLIDE
WON'T YOU TELL ME?
HOW DO YOU ALWAYS UNDERSTAND THE FEELINGS OF ANOTHER?

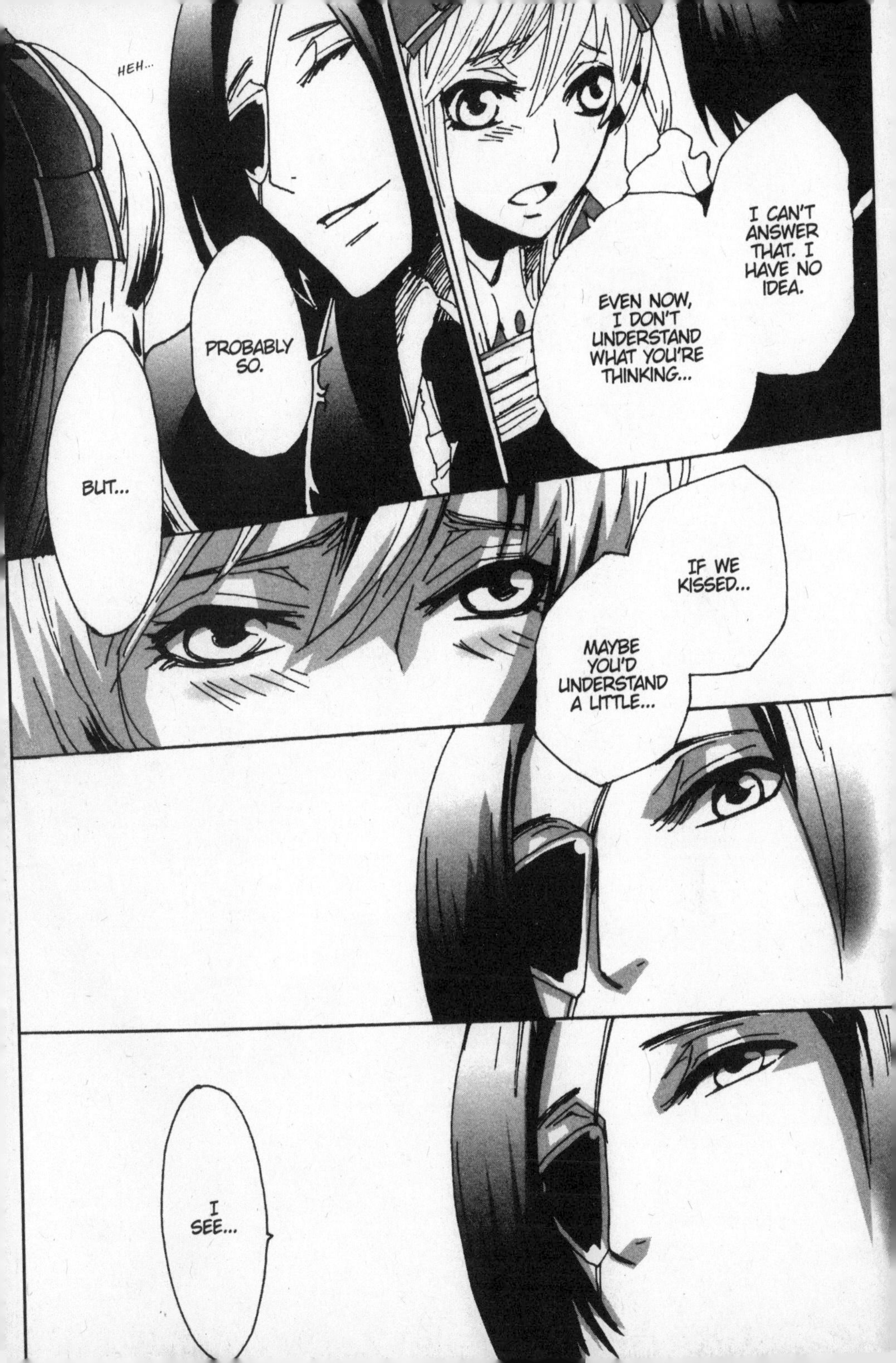
I CAN'T ANSWER THAT. I HAVE NO IDEA.
EVEN NOW, I DON'T UNDERSTAND WHAT YOU'RE THINKING...
HEH...
PROBABLY SO.
BUT...
IF WE KISSED...
MAYBE YOU'D UNDERSTAND A LITTLE...
I SEE...

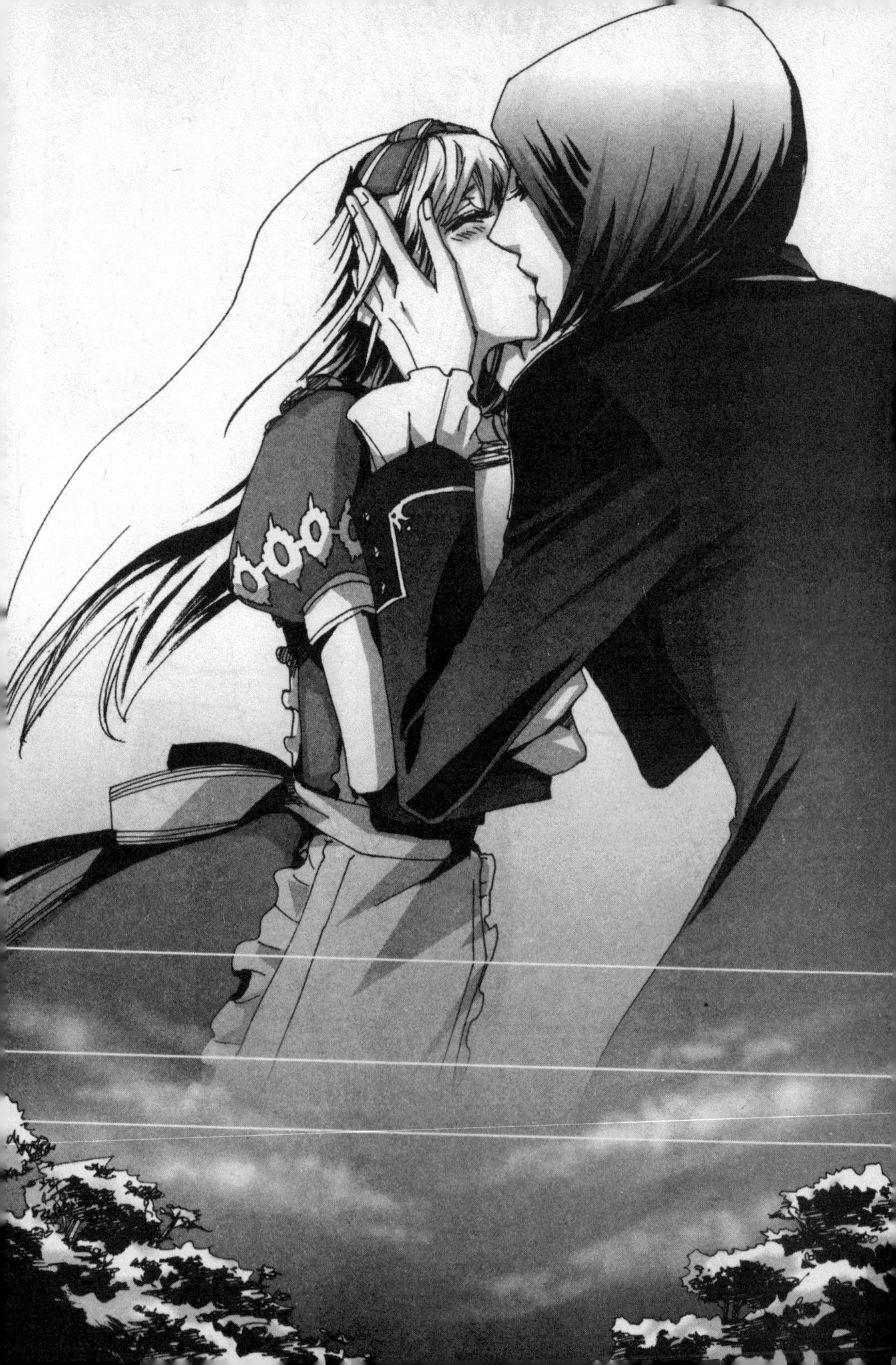

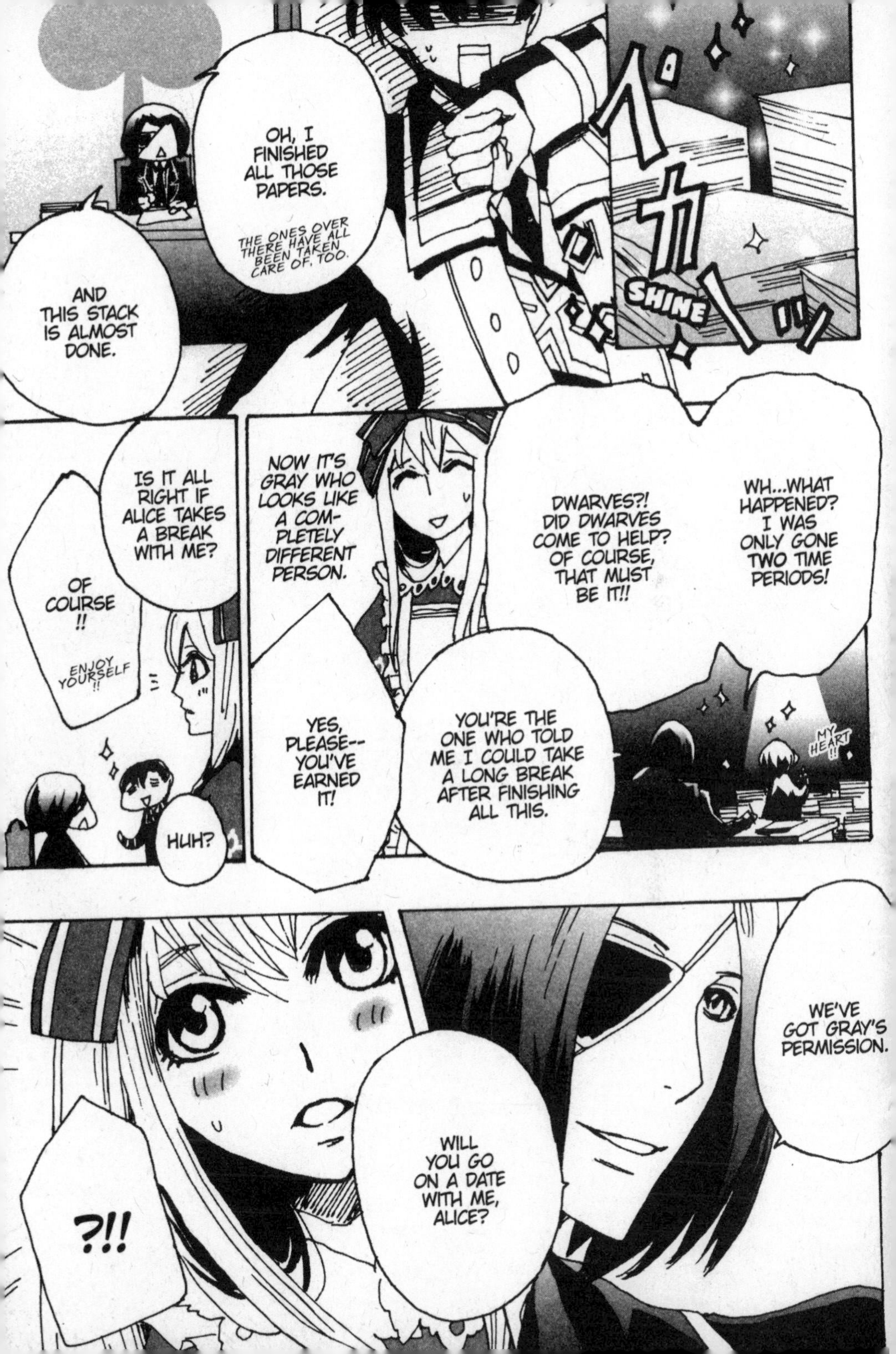

SHINE
OH, I FINISHED ALL THOSE PAPERS.
THE ONES OVER THERE HAVE ALL BEEN TAKEN CARE OF, TOO.
AND THIS STACK IS ALMOST DONE.
WH...WHAT HAPPENED? I WAS ONLY GONE TWO TIME PERIODS!
DWARVES?! DID DWARVES COME TO HELP? OF COURSE, THAT MUST BE IT!!
MY HEART!!
YOU'RE THE ONE WHO TOLD ME I COULD TAKE A LONG BREAK AFTER FINISHING ALL THIS.
NOW IT'S GRAY WHO LOOKS LIKE A COM-PLETELY DIFFERENT PERSON.
YES, PLEASE-- YOU'VE EARNED IT!
IS IT ALL RIGHT IF ALICE TAKES A BREAK WITH ME?
OF COURSE !!
ENJOY YOURSELF !!
HUH?
WE'VE GOT GRAY'S PERMISSION.
WILL YOU GO ON A DATE WITH ME, ALICE?
?!!

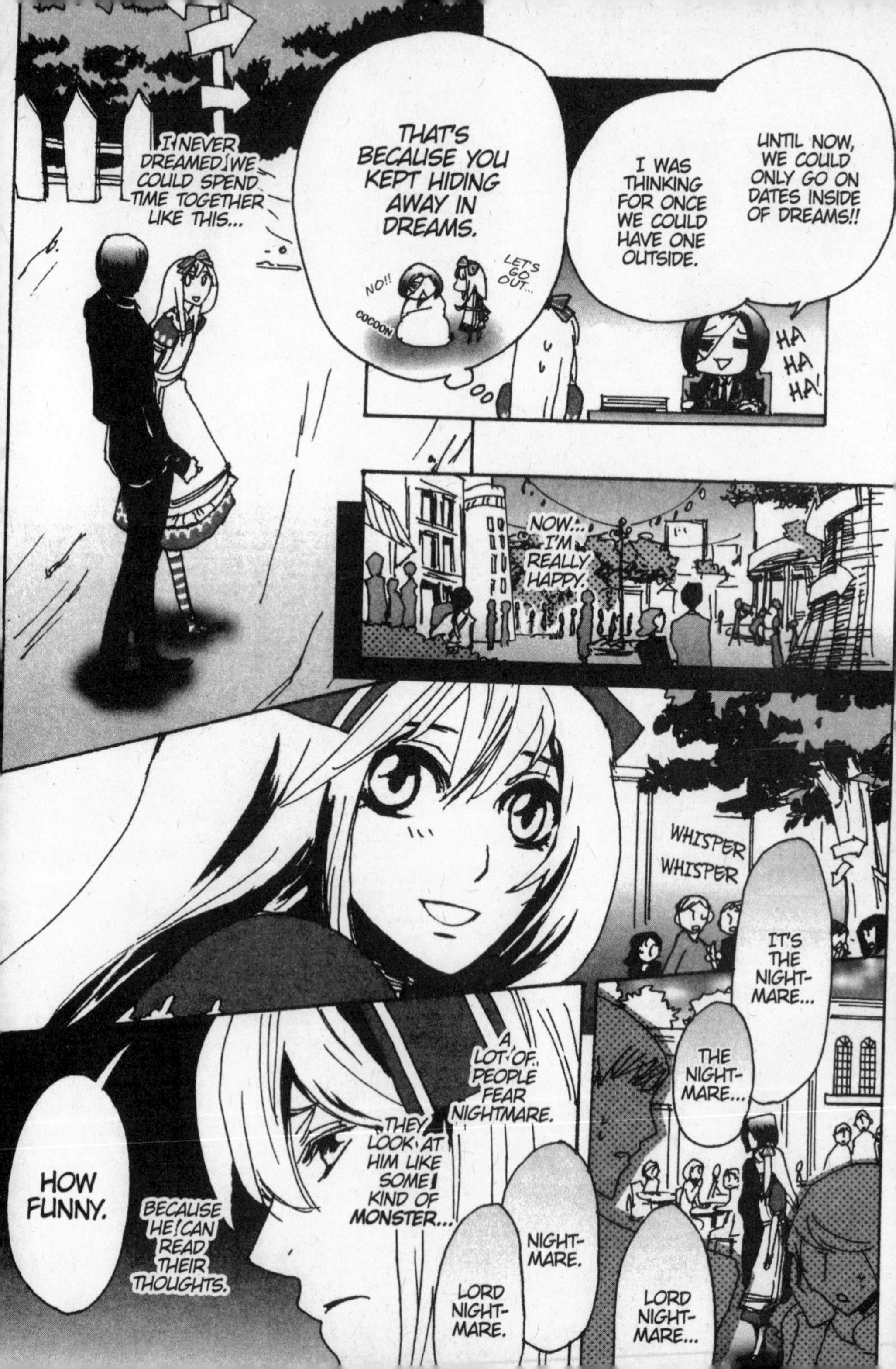
UNTIL NOW, WE COULD ONLY GO ON DATES INSIDE OF DREAMS!!
I WAS THINKING FOR ONCE WE COULD HAVE ONE OUTSIDE.
HA HA HA!
THAT'S BECAUSE YOU KEPT HIDING AWAY IN DREAMS.
LET'S GO OUT...
NO!!
COCOON
NOW... I'M REALLY HAPPY.
I NEVER DREAMED WE COULD SPEND TIME TOGETHER LIKE THIS...
WHISPER
WHISPER
IT'S THE NIGHT-MARE...
THE NIGHT-MARE...
LORD NIGHT-MARE...
NIGHT-MARE.
LORD NIGHT-MARE.
A LOT OF PEOPLE FEAR NIGHTMARE.
THEY LOOK AT HIM LIKE SOME KIND OF MONSTER...
BECAUSE HE CAN READ THEIR THOUGHTS.
HOW FUNNY.

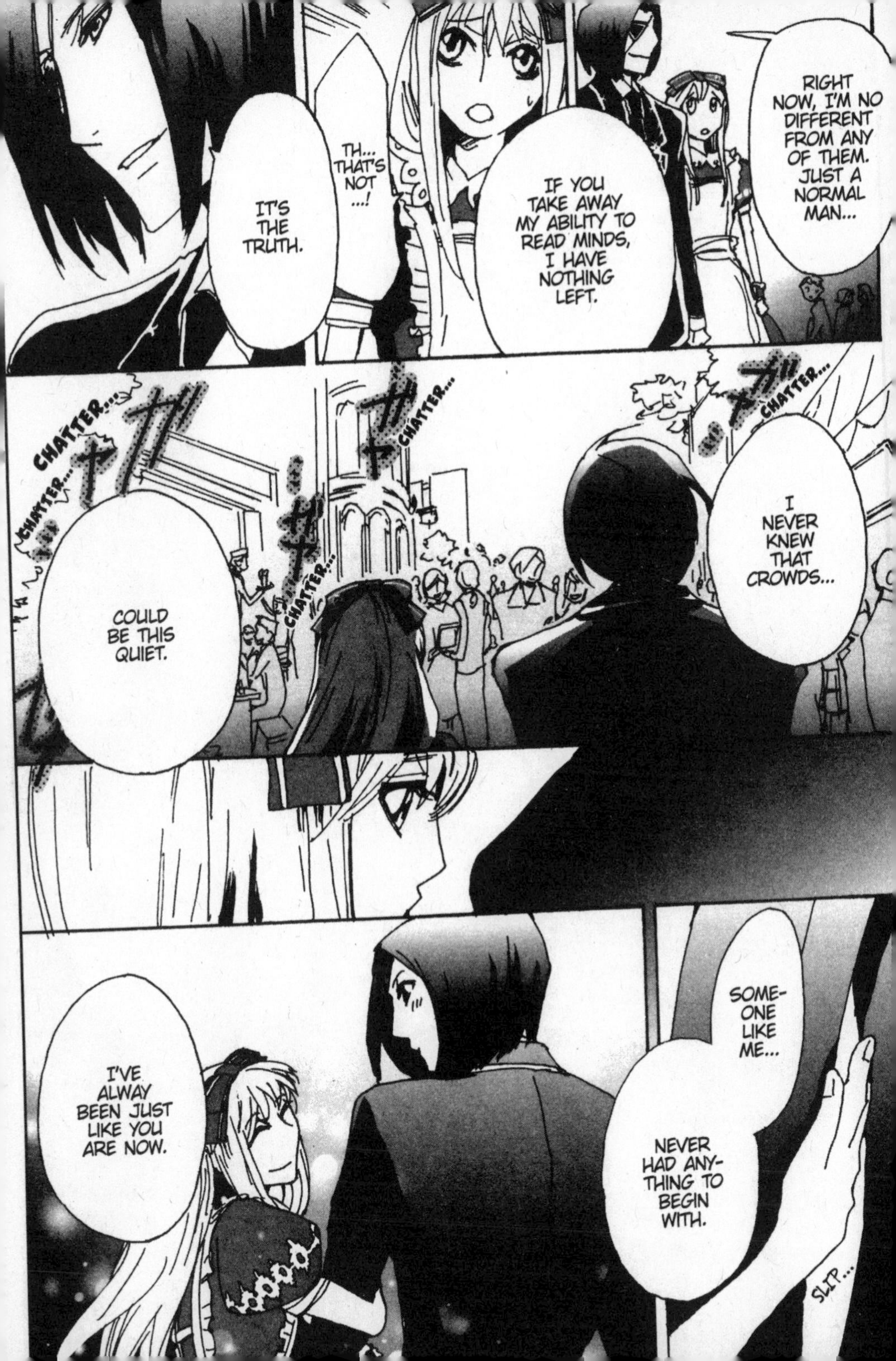
RIGHT NOW, I'M NO DIFFERENT FROM ANY OF THEM. JUST A NORMAL MAN...
IF YOU TAKE AWAY MY ABILITY TO READ MINDS, I HAVE NOTHING LEFT.
TH... THAT'S NOT ...!
IT'S THE TRUTH.
CHATTER...
CHATTER...
I NEVER KNEW THAT CROWDS...
CHATTER...
CHATTER...
CHATTER...
COULD BE THIS QUIET.
SOME-ONE LIKE ME...
NEVER HAD ANY-THING TO BEGIN WITH.
SLIP...
I'VE ALWAY BEEN JUST LIKE YOU ARE NOW.

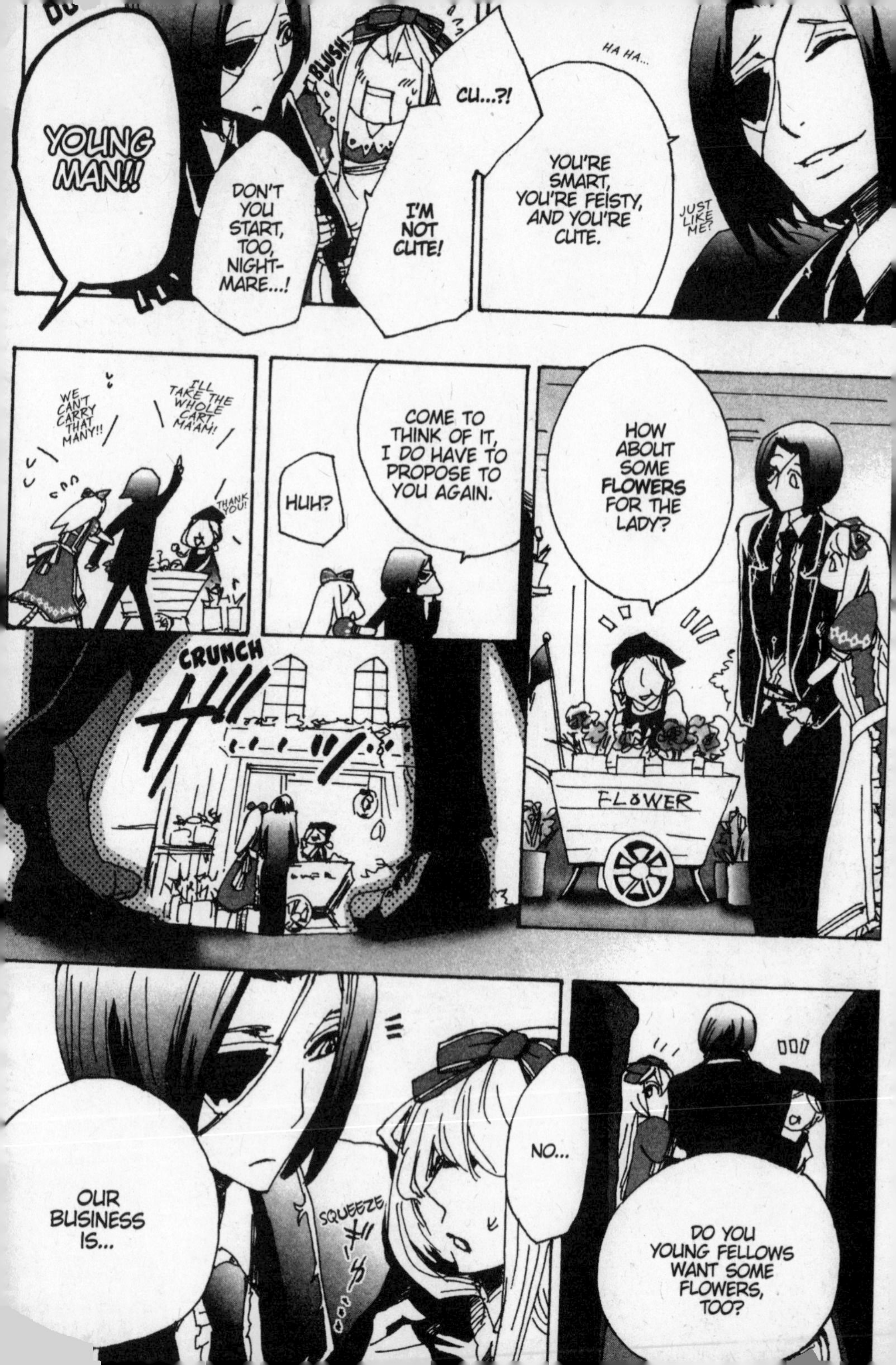
HA HA...
YOU'RE SMART, YOU'RE FEISTY, AND YOU'RE CUTE.
JUST LIKE ME?
CU...?!
I'M NOT CUTE!
BLUSH
DON'T YOU START, TOO, NIGHT-MARE...!
YOUNG MAN!!
HOW ABOUT SOME FLOWERS FOR THE LADY?
FLOWER
COME TO THINK OF IT, I DO HAVE TO PROPOSE TO YOU AGAIN.
HUH?
I'LL TAKE THE WHOLE CART, MA'AM!
THANK YOU!
WE CAN'T CARRY THAT MANY!!
CRUNCH
DO YOU YOUNG FELLOWS WANT SOME FLOWERS, TOO?
NO...
SQUEEZE
OUR BUSINESS IS...

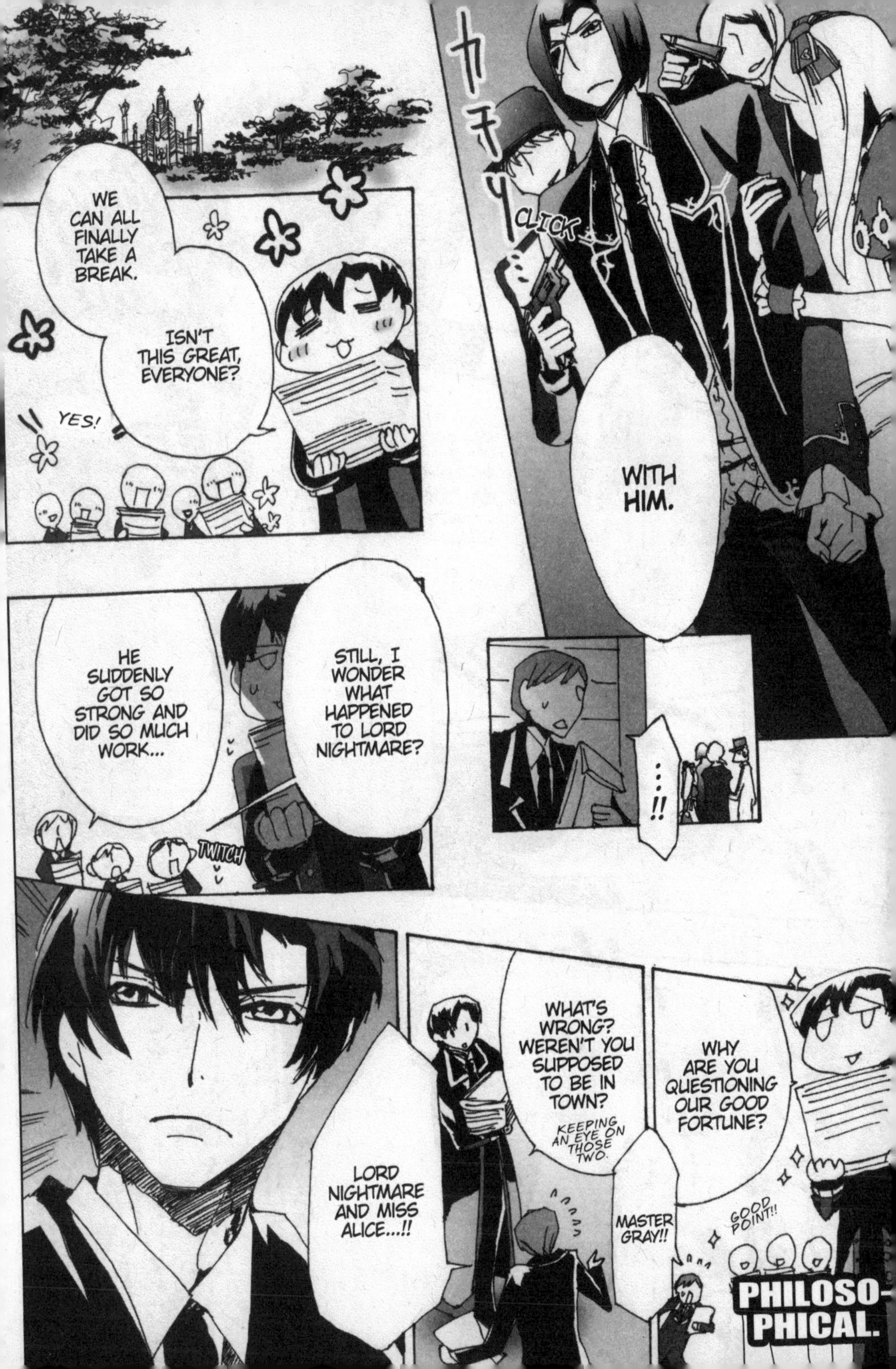

カチッ
CLICK
WITH HIM.
WE CAN ALL FINALLY TAKE A BREAK.
ISN'T THIS GREAT, EVERYONE?
YES!
STILL, I WONDER WHAT HAPPENED TO LORD NIGHTMARE?
HE SUDDENLY GOT SO STRONG AND DID SO MUCH WORK...
TWITCH
...!!
WHY ARE YOU QUESTIONING OUR GOOD FORTUNE?
GOOD POINT!!
PHILOSO-PHICAL.
WHAT'S WRONG? WEREN'T YOU SUPPOSED TO BE IN TOWN?
KEEPING AN EYE ON THOSE TWO.
MASTER GRAY!!
LORD NIGHTMARE AND MISS ALICE...!!

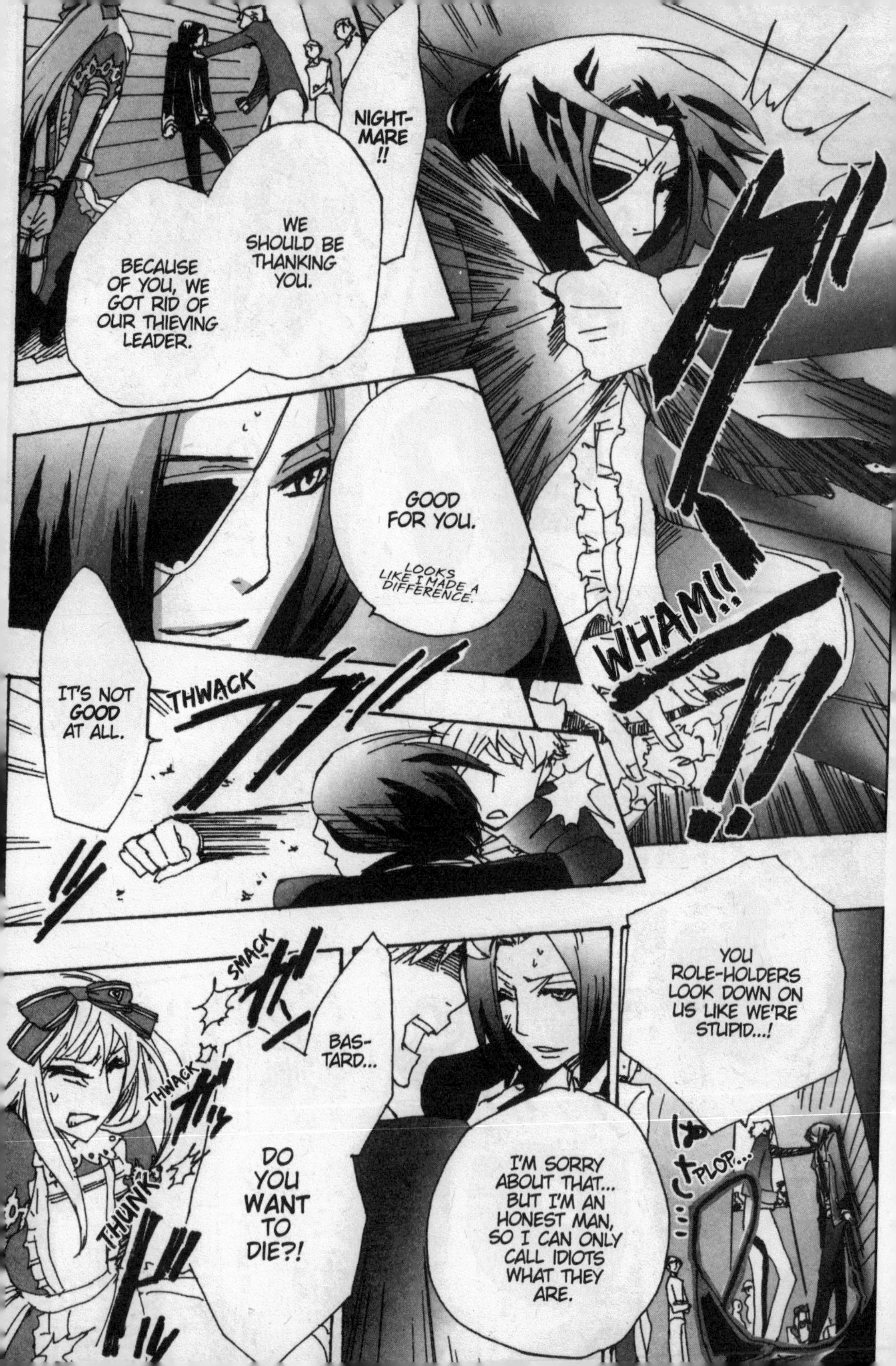
WHAM!!
NIGHT-MARE!!
WE SHOULD BE THANKING YOU.
BECAUSE OF YOU, WE GOT RID OF OUR THIEVING LEADER.
GOOD FOR YOU.
LOOKS LIKE I MADE A DIFFERENCE.
IT'S NOT GOOD AT ALL.
THWACK
YOU ROLE-HOLDERS LOOK DOWN ON US LIKE WE'RE STUPID...!
I'M SORRY ABOUT THAT... BUT I'M AN HONEST MAN, SO I CAN ONLY CALL IDIOTS WHAT THEY ARE.
PLOP...
BAS-TARD...
SMACK
THWACK
THUNK
DO YOU WANT TO DIE?!

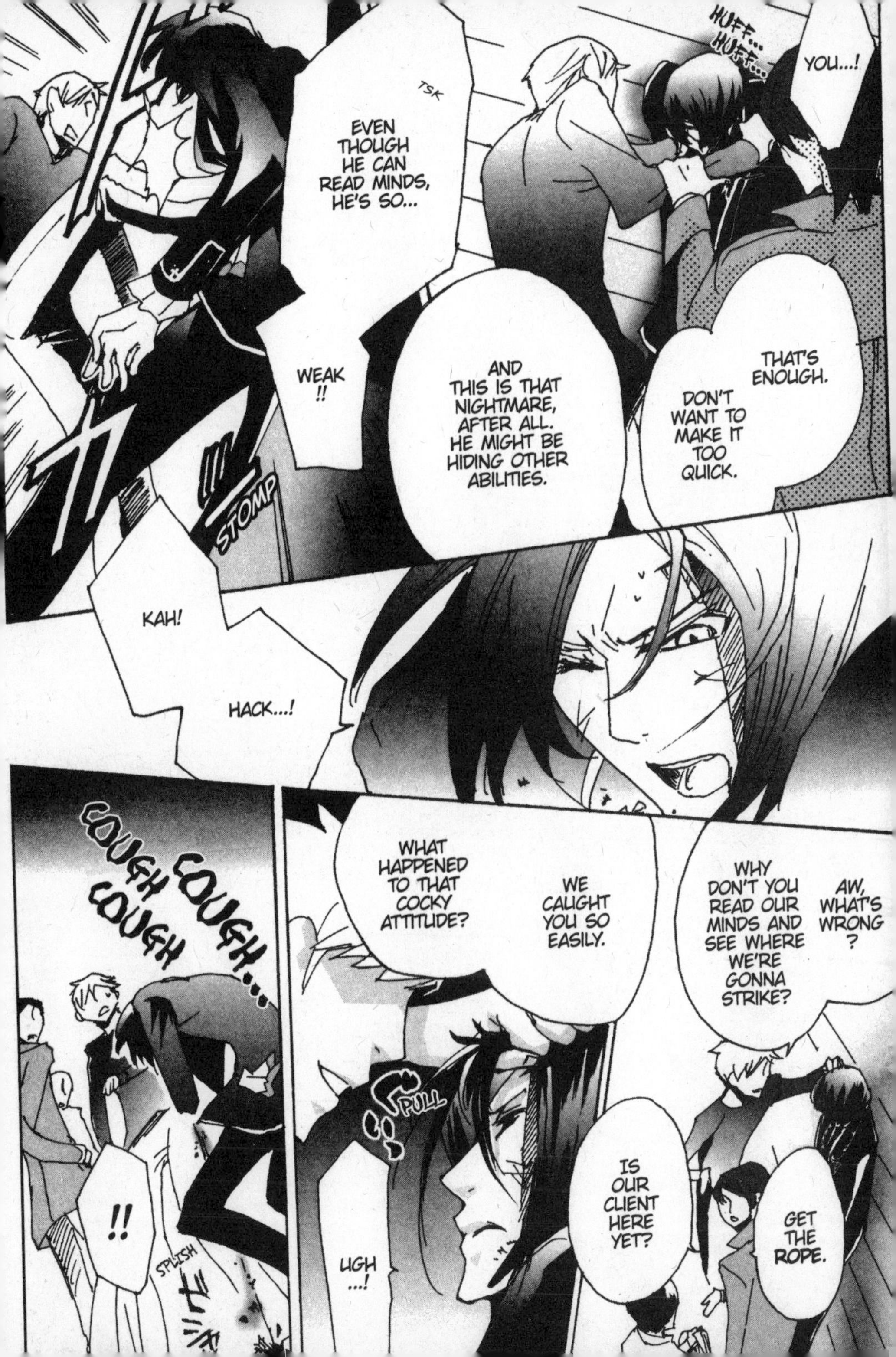
HUFF... HUFF...
YOU...!
THAT'S ENOUGH.
DON'T WANT TO MAKE IT TOO QUICK.
AND THIS IS THAT NIGHTMARE, AFTER ALL. HE MIGHT BE HIDING OTHER ABILITIES.
TSK
EVEN THOUGH HE CAN READ MINDS, HE'S SO...
WEAK!!
STOMP
KAH!
HACK...!
AW, WHAT'S WRONG?
WHY DON'T YOU READ OUR MINDS AND SEE WHERE WE'RE GONNA STRIKE?
WE CAUGHT YOU SO EASILY.
WHAT HAPPENED TO THAT COCKY ATTITUDE?
PULL
GET THE ROPE.
IS OUR CLIENT HERE YET?
UGH...!
COUGH... COUGH COUGH
!!
SPLISH

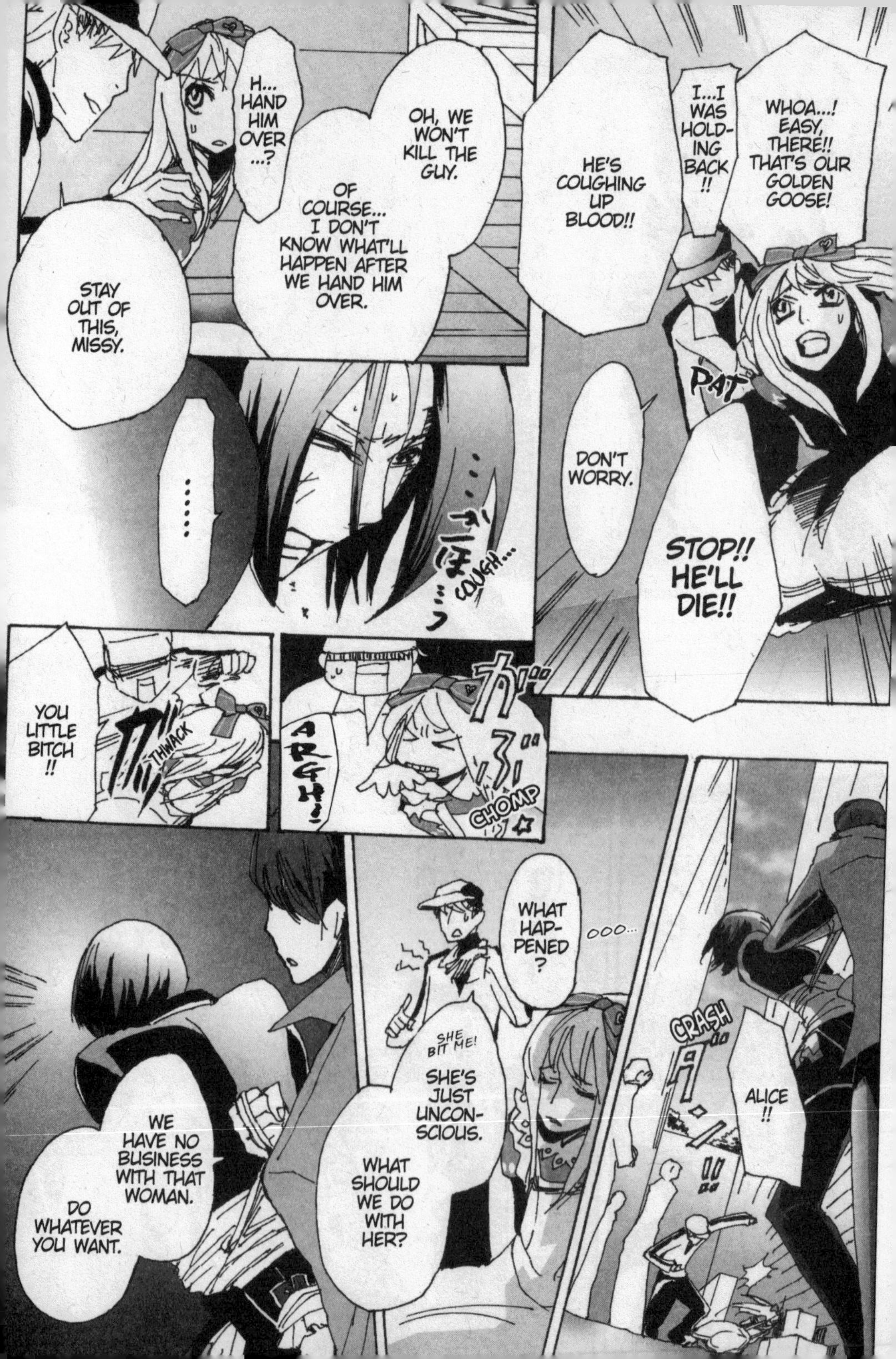

WHOA...! EASY, THERE!! THAT'S OUR GOLDEN GOOSE!
I...I WAS HOLDING-ING BACK!!
HE'S COUGHING UP BLOOD!!
PAT
DON'T WORRY.
STOP!! HE'LL DIE!!
OH, WE WON'T KILL THE GUY.
OF COURSE... I DON'T KNOW WHAT'LL HAPPEN AFTER WE HAND HIM OVER.
H... HAND HIM OVER ...?
STAY OUT OF THIS, MISSY.
......
COUGH...
ARGH!
CHOMP
YOU LITTLE BITCH!!
THWACK
ALICE!!
CRASH
WHAT HAP-PENED?
OOO...
SHE BIT ME!
SHE'S JUST UNCON-SCIOUS.
WHAT SHOULD WE DO WITH HER?
WE HAVE NO BUSINESS WITH THAT WOMAN.
DO WHATEVER YOU WANT.

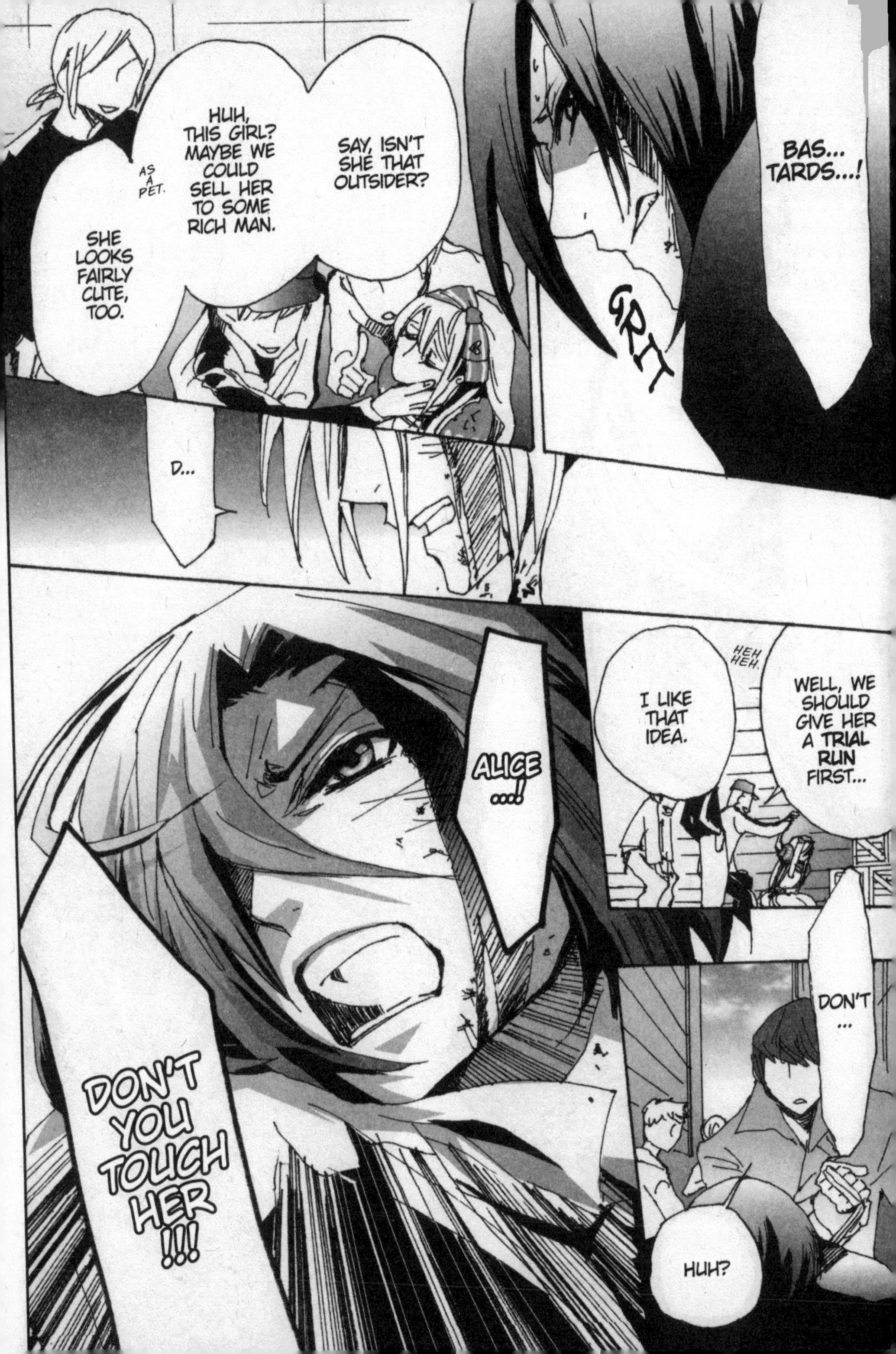

BAS... TARDS...!
GRIT
SAY, ISN'T SHE THAT OUTSIDER?
HUH, THIS GIRL? MAYBE WE COULD SELL HER TO SOME RICH MAN.
AS A PET.
SHE LOOKS FAIRLY CUTE, TOO.
D...
WELL, WE SHOULD GIVE HER A TRIAL RUN FIRST...
HEH HEH.
I LIKE THAT IDEA.
DON'T ...
HUH?
ALICE ...!
DON'T YOU TOUCH HER !!!

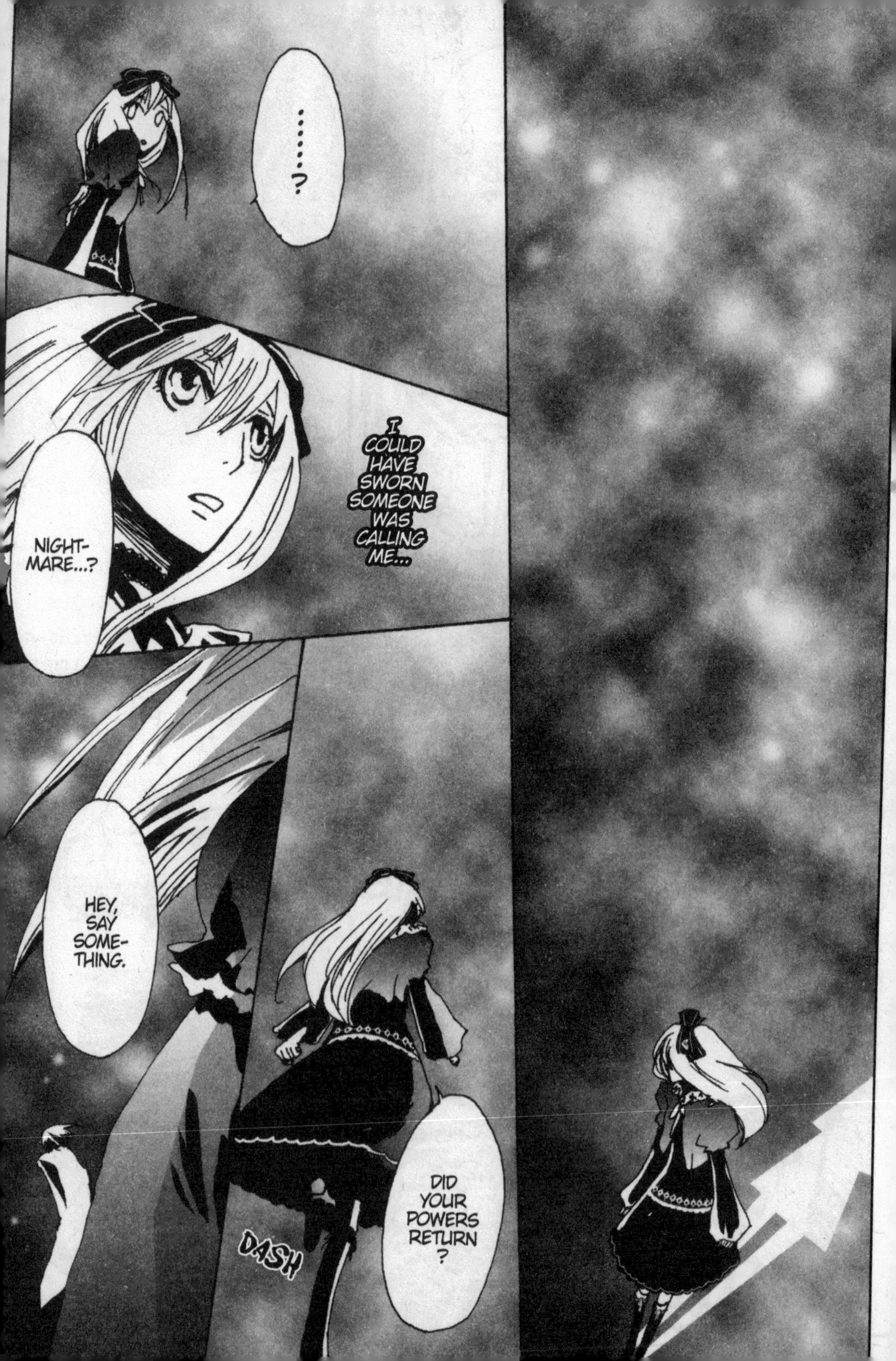
......?
I COULD HAVE SWORN SOMEONE WAS CALLING ME...
NIGHT-MARE...?
DID YOUR POWERS RETURN?
DASH
HEY, SAY SOME-THING.

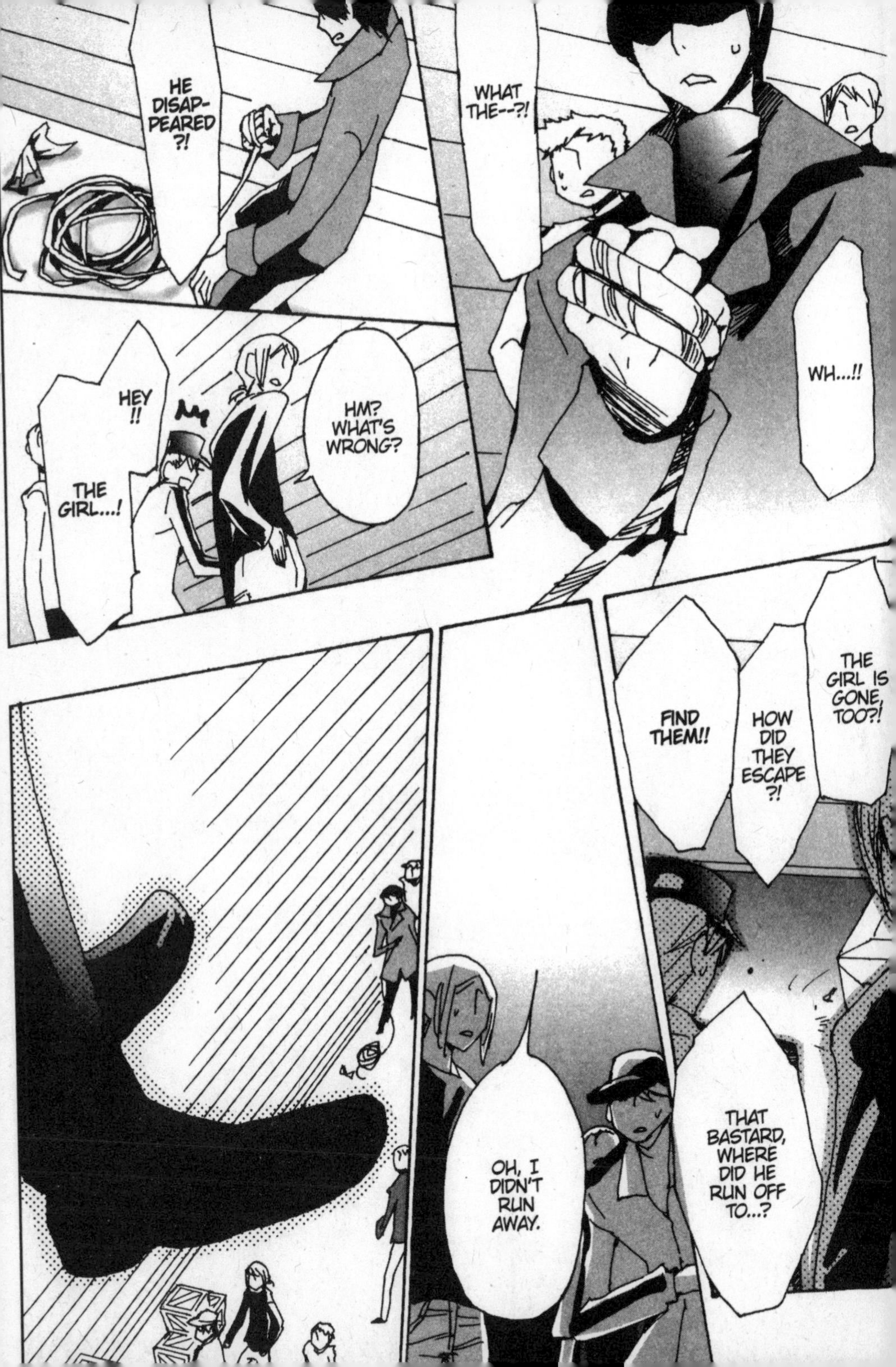
WHAT THE--?!
WH...!!
HE DISAP-PEARED ?!
HM? WHAT'S WRONG?
HEY !!
THE GIRL...!
THE GIRL IS GONE, TOO?!
HOW DID THEY ESCAPE ?!
FIND THEM!!
THAT BASTARD, WHERE DID HE RUN OFF TO...?
OH, I DIDN'T RUN AWAY.

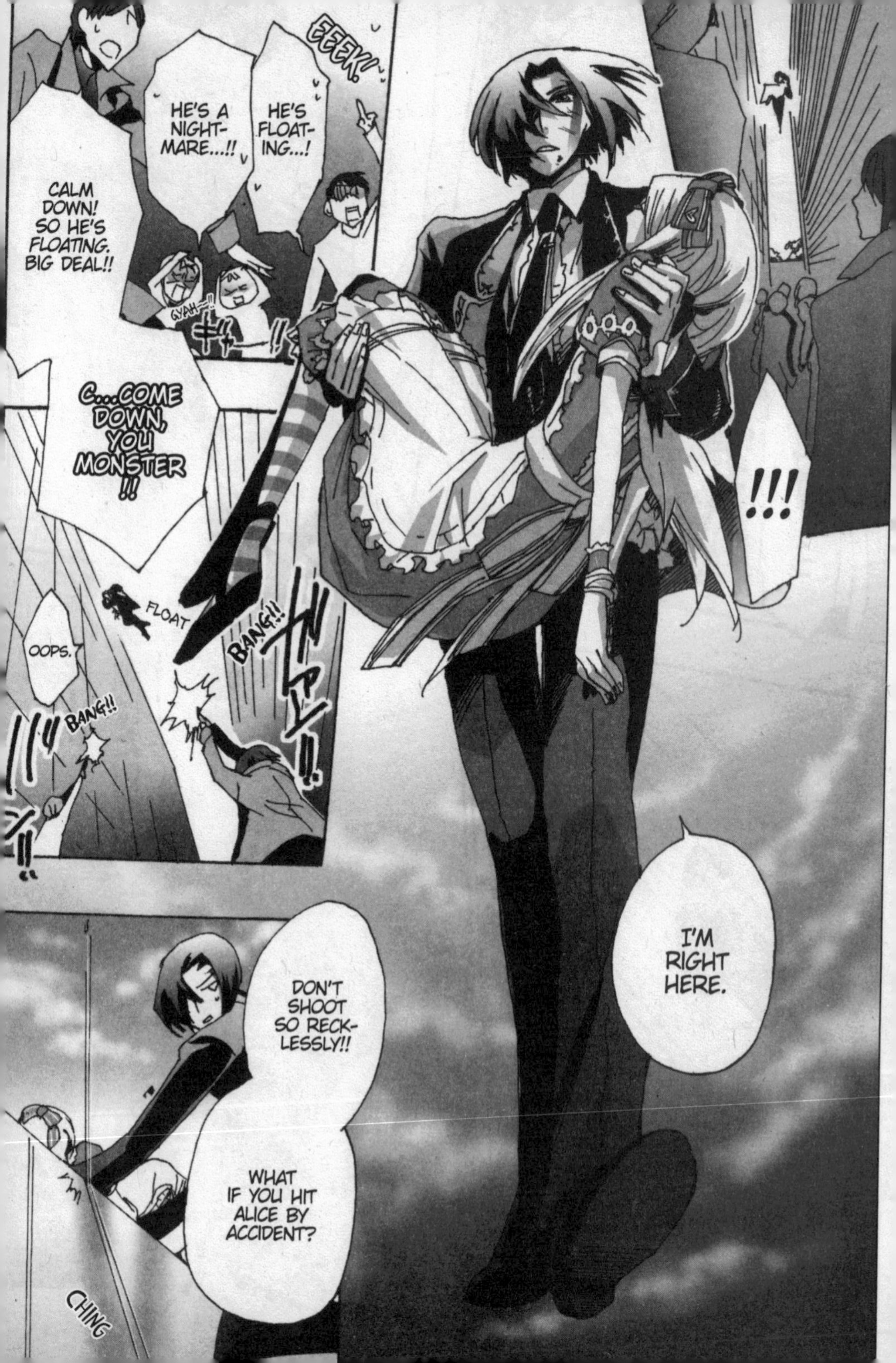
!!!
I'M RIGHT HERE.
EEEK!
HE'S FLOATING...!
HE'S A NIGHTMARE...!!
CALM DOWN! SO HE'S FLOATING. BIG DEAL!!
GYAH--!!
C...COME DOWN, YOU MONSTER!!
FLOAT
BANG!!
OOPS.
BANG!!
DON'T SHOOT SO RECKLESSLY!!
WHAT IF YOU HIT ALICE BY ACCIDENT?
CHING

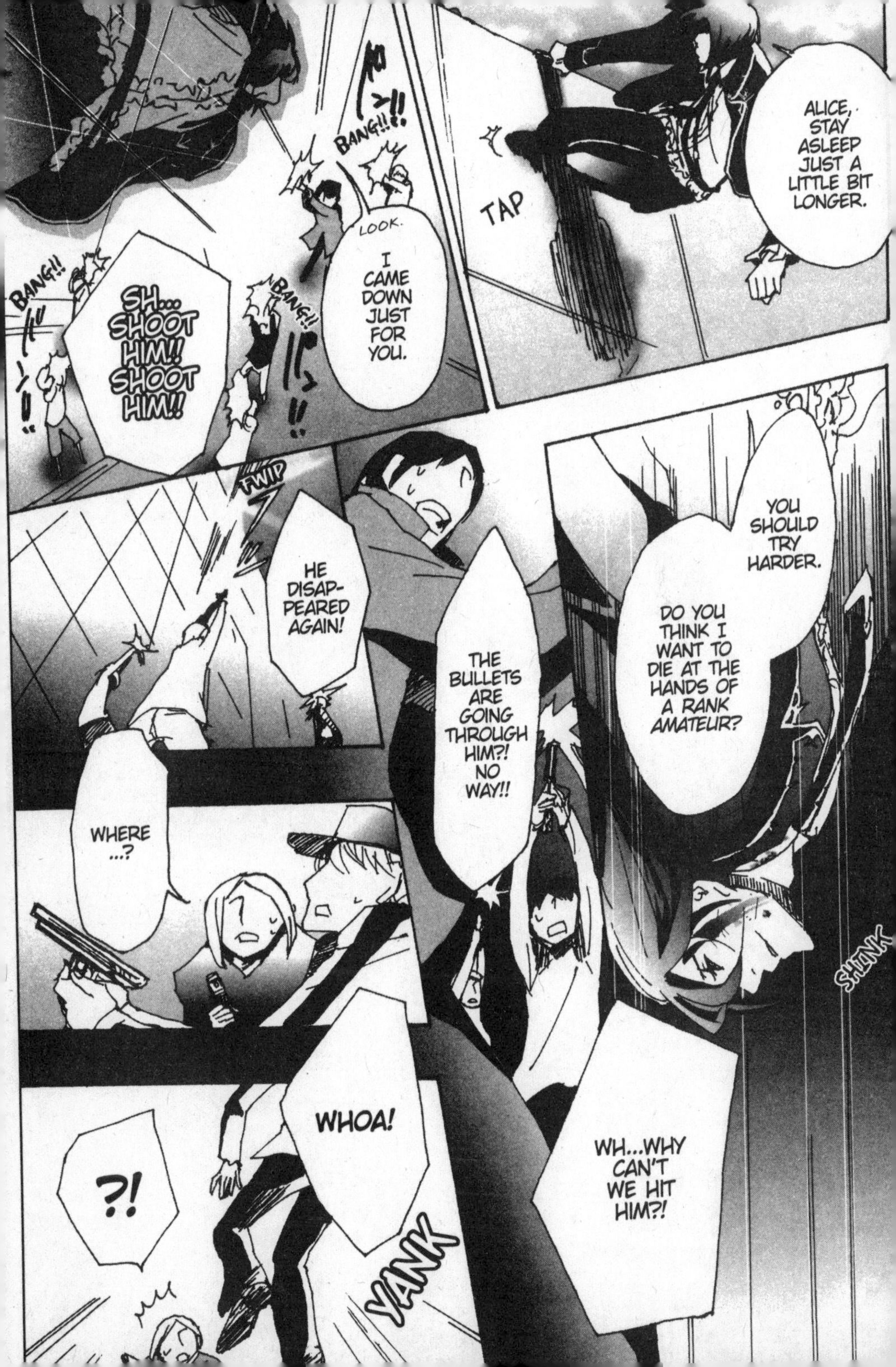
ALICE, STAY ASLEEP JUST A LITTLE BIT LONGER.
TAP
BANG!!!
LOOK.
I CAME DOWN JUST FOR YOU.
BANG!!
SH... SHOOT HIM!! SHOOT HIM!!
BANG!!
YOU SHOULD TRY HARDER.
DO YOU THINK I WANT TO DIE AT THE HANDS OF A RANK AMATEUR?
SHINK
FWIP
HE DISAP-PEARED AGAIN!
THE BULLETS ARE GOING THROUGH HIM?! NO WAY!!
WHERE ...?
WH...WHY CAN'T WE HIT HIM?!
WHOA!
YANK
?!

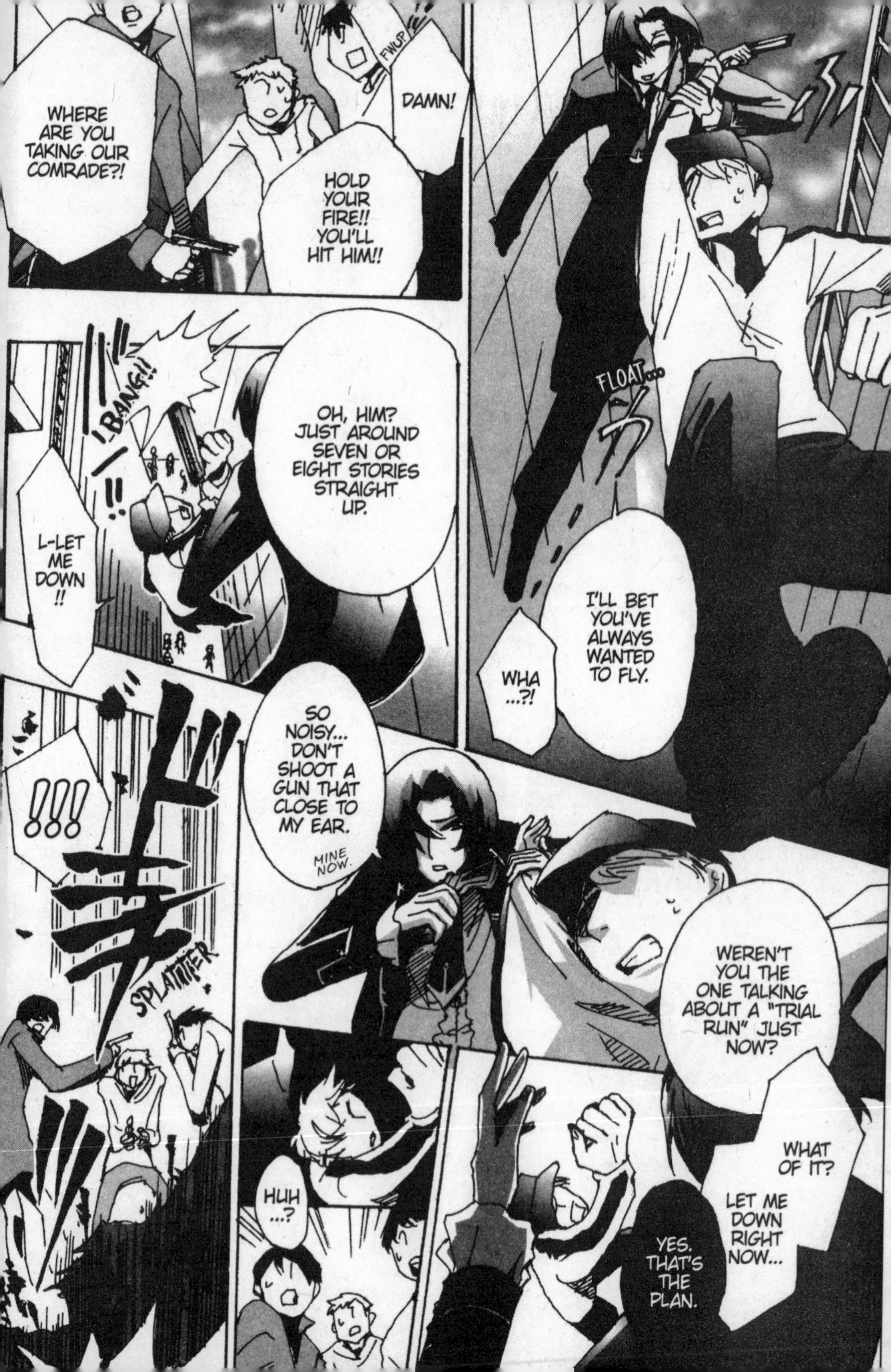

FLOAT...
I'LL BET YOU'VE ALWAYS WANTED TO FLY.
WHA ...?!
WHERE ARE YOU TAKING OUR COMRADE?!
FWUP
DAMN!
HOLD YOUR FIRE!! YOU'LL HIT HIM!!
OH, HIM? JUST AROUND SEVEN OR EIGHT STORIES STRAIGHT UP.
BANG!!
!!
L-LET ME DOWN !!
WEREN'T YOU THE ONE TALKING ABOUT A "TRIAL RUN" JUST NOW?
SO NOISY... DON'T SHOOT A GUN THAT CLOSE TO MY EAR.
MINE NOW.
WHAT OF IT?
LET ME DOWN RIGHT NOW...
YES. THAT'S THE PLAN.
HUH ...?
!!!
SPLATTER

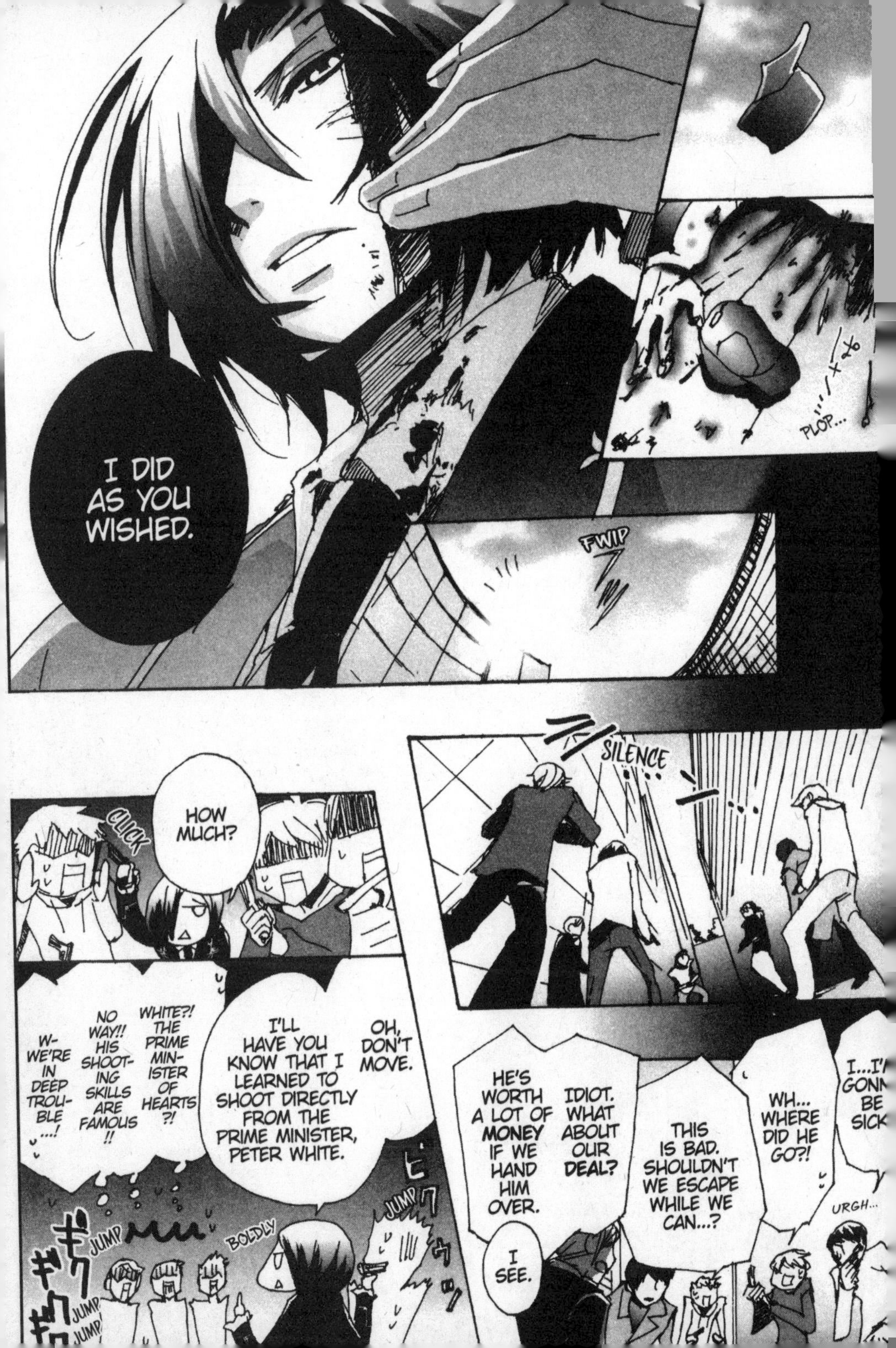
PLOP...
FWIP
I DID AS YOU WISHED.
SILENCE
...
HOW MUCH?
CLICK
I...I'M GONN BE SICK
WH... WHERE DID HE GO?!
THIS IS BAD. SHOULDN'T WE ESCAPE WHILE WE CAN...?
IDIOT. WHAT ABOUT OUR DEAL?
HE'S WORTH A LOT OF MONEY IF WE HAND HIM OVER.
I SEE.
URGH...
OH, DON'T MOVE.
I'LL HAVE YOU KNOW THAT I LEARNED TO SHOOT DIRECTLY FROM THE PRIME MINISTER, PETER WHITE.
WHITE?! THE PRIME MINISTER OF HEARTS?!
NO WAY!! HIS SHOOTING SKILLS ARE FAMOUS!!
W-WE'RE IN DEEP TROUBLE...!
JUMP
BOLDLY
JUMP
JUMP
JUMP

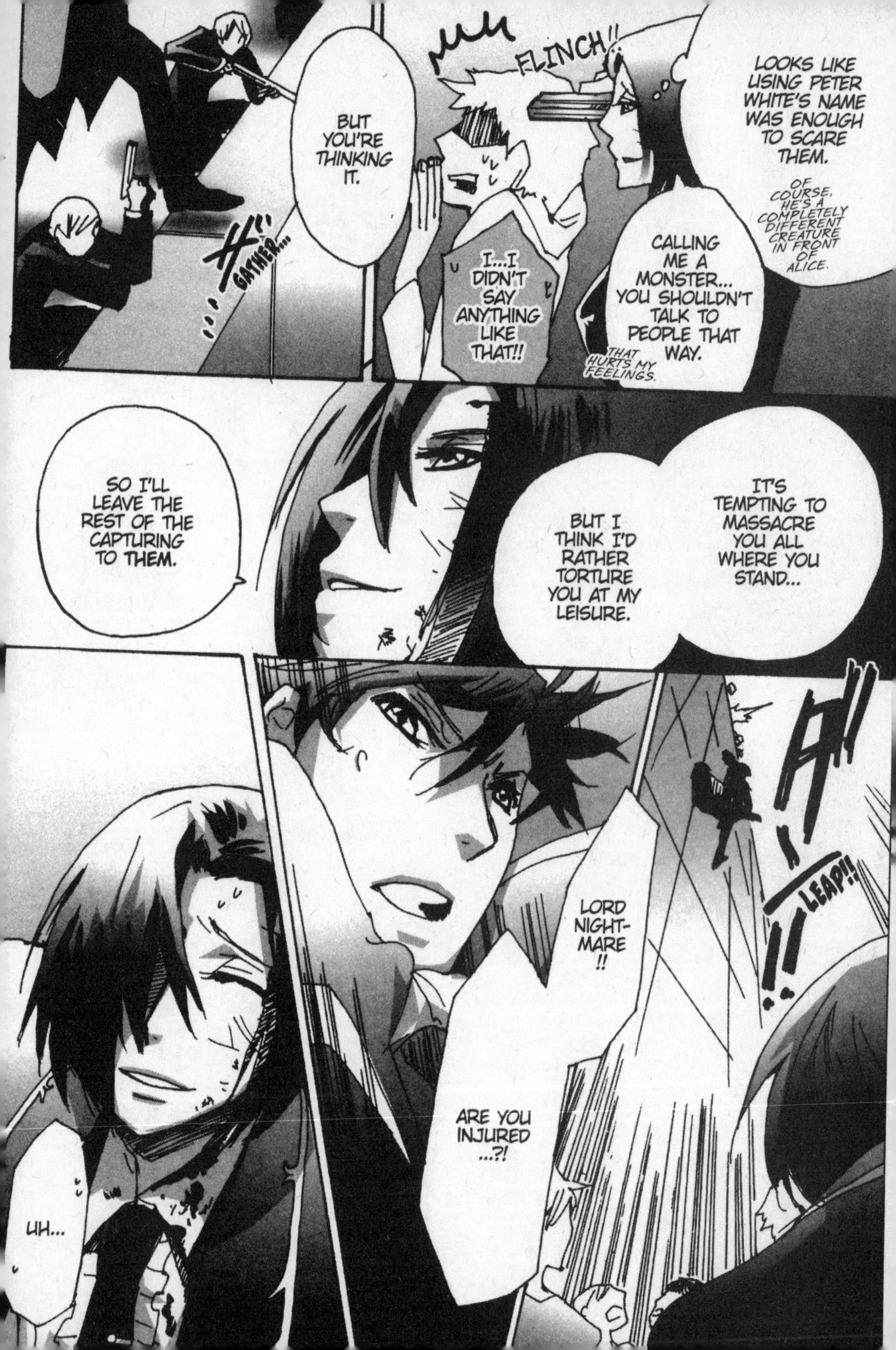
FLINCH!!
LOOKS LIKE USING PETER WHITE'S NAME WAS ENOUGH TO SCARE THEM.
OF COURSE, HE'S A COMPLETELY DIFFERENT CREATURE IN FRONT OF ALICE.
CALLING ME A MONSTER... YOU SHOULDN'T TALK TO PEOPLE THAT WAY.
THAT HURTS MY FEELINGS.
I...I DIDN'T SAY ANYTHING LIKE THAT!!
BUT YOU'RE THINKING IT.
GATHER...
IT'S TEMPTING TO MASSACRE YOU ALL WHERE YOU STAND...
BUT I THINK I'D RATHER TORTURE YOU AT MY LEISURE.
SO I'LL LEAVE THE REST OF THE CAPTURING TO THEM.
LEAP!!
LORD NIGHT-MARE!!
ARE YOU INJURED...?!
UH...

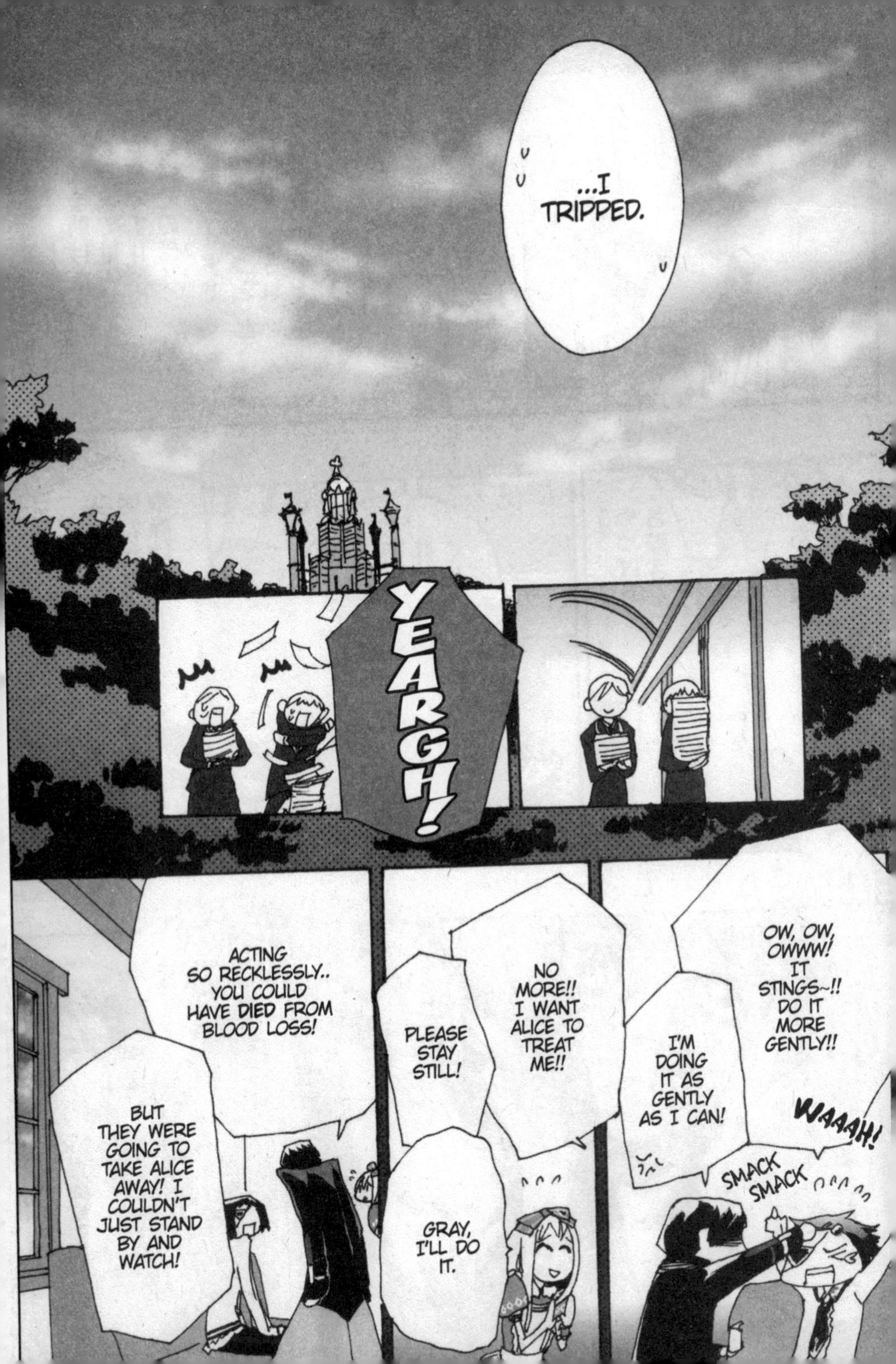
...I TRIPPED.
YEARGH!
OW, OW, OWWW! IT STINGS~!! DO IT MORE GENTLY!!
I'M DOING IT AS GENTLY AS I CAN!
WAAAH!
SMACK SMACK
NO MORE!! I WANT ALICE TO TREAT ME!!
PLEASE STAY STILL!
GRAY, I'LL DO IT.
ACTING SO RECKLESSLY.. YOU COULD HAVE DIED FROM BLOOD LOSS!
BUT THEY WERE GOING TO TAKE ALICE AWAY! I COULDN'T JUST STAND BY AND WATCH!

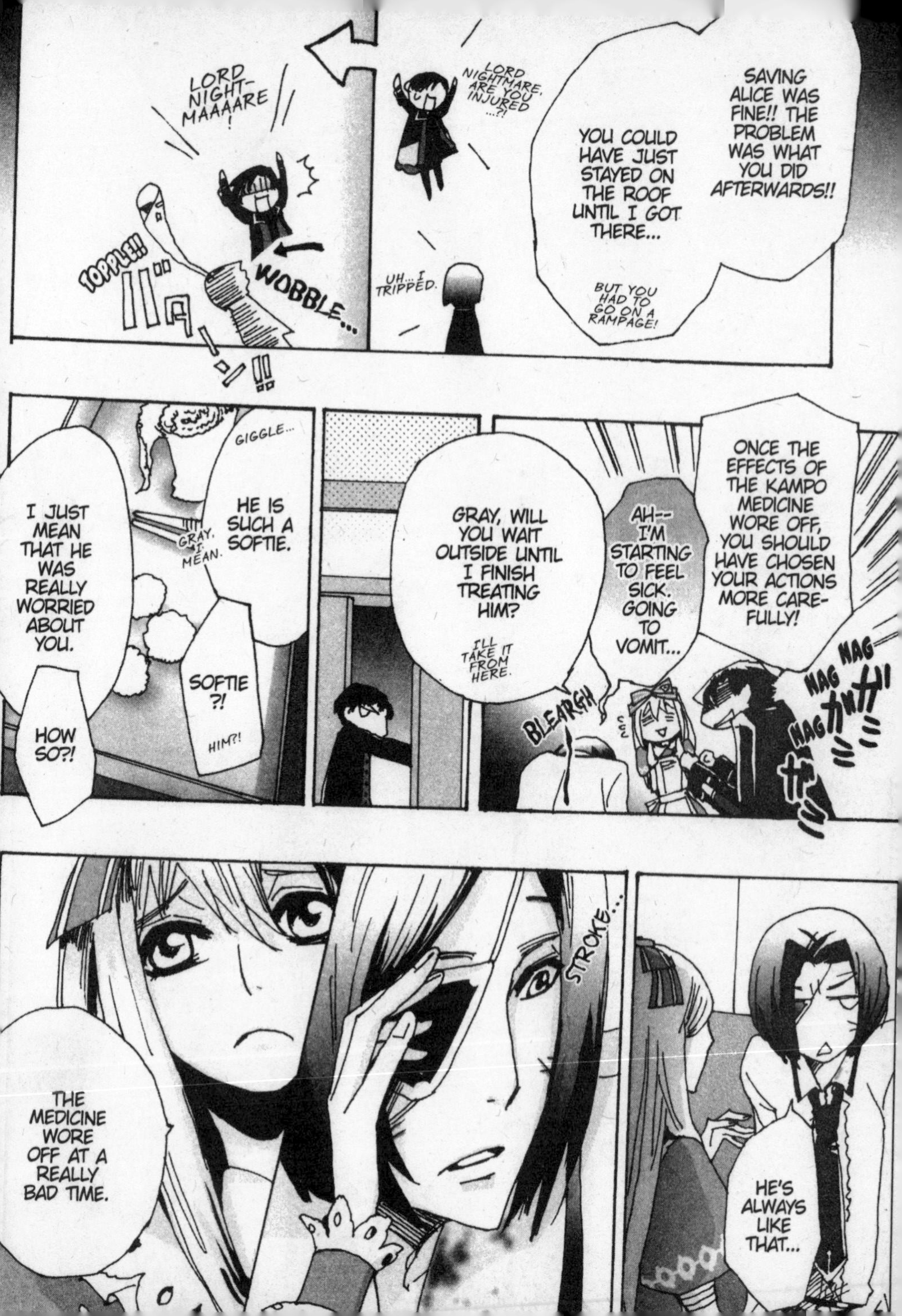
SAVING ALICE WAS FINE!! THE PROBLEM WAS WHAT YOU DID AFTERWARDS!!
YOU COULD HAVE JUST STAYED ON THE ROOF UNTIL I GOT THERE...
BUT YOU HAD TO GO ON A RAMPAGE!
LORD NIGHTMARE, ARE YOU INJURED ...?!
UH... I TRIPPED.
LORD NIGHT-MAAAARE!
WOBBLE...
TOPPLE!!
ONCE THE EFFECTS OF THE KAMPO MEDICINE WORE OFF, YOU SHOULD HAVE CHOSEN YOUR ACTIONS MORE CARE-FULLY!
NAG NAG NAG
AH-- I'M STARTING TO FEEL SICK. GOING TO VOMIT...
GRAY, WILL YOU WAIT OUTSIDE UNTIL I FINISH TREATING HIM?
I'LL TAKE IT FROM HERE.
BLEARGH
GIGGLE...
HE IS SUCH A SOFTIE.
GRAY, I MEAN.
SOFTIE?!
HIM?!
I JUST MEAN THAT HE WAS REALLY WORRIED ABOUT YOU.
HOW SO?!
HE'S ALWAYS LIKE THAT...
STROKE...
THE MEDICINE WORE OFF AT A REALLY BAD TIME.

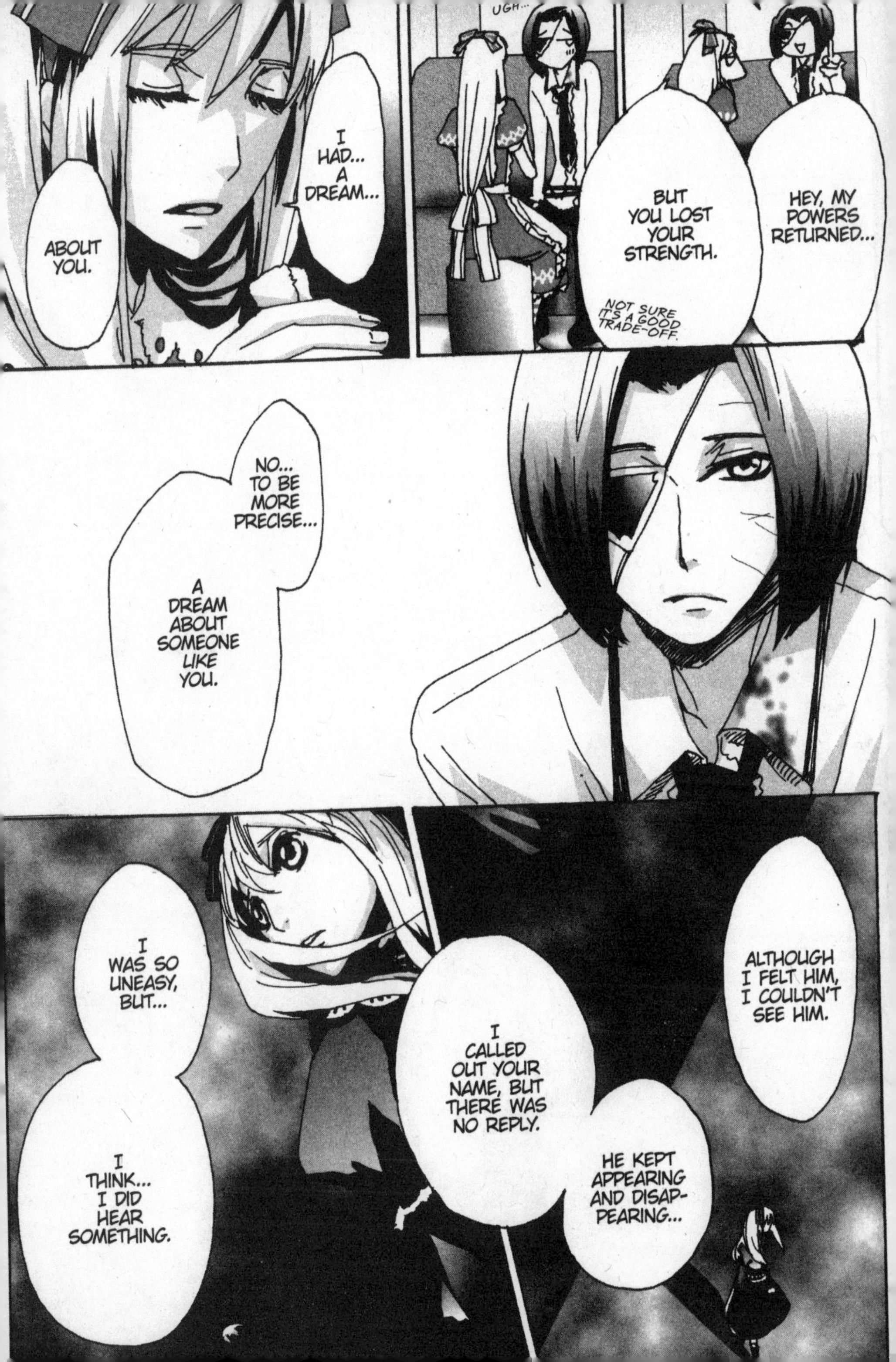
HEY, MY POWERS RETURNED...
BUT YOU LOST YOUR STRENGTH.
NOT SURE IT'S A GOOD TRADE-OFF.
UGH...
I HAD... A DREAM...
ABOUT YOU.
NO... TO BE MORE PRECISE...
A DREAM ABOUT SOMEONE LIKE YOU.
ALTHOUGH I FELT HIM, I COULDN'T SEE HIM.
HE KEPT APPEARING AND DISAP-PEARING...
I CALLED OUT YOUR NAME, BUT THERE WAS NO REPLY.
I WAS SO UNEASY, BUT...
I THINK... I DID HEAR SOMETHING.

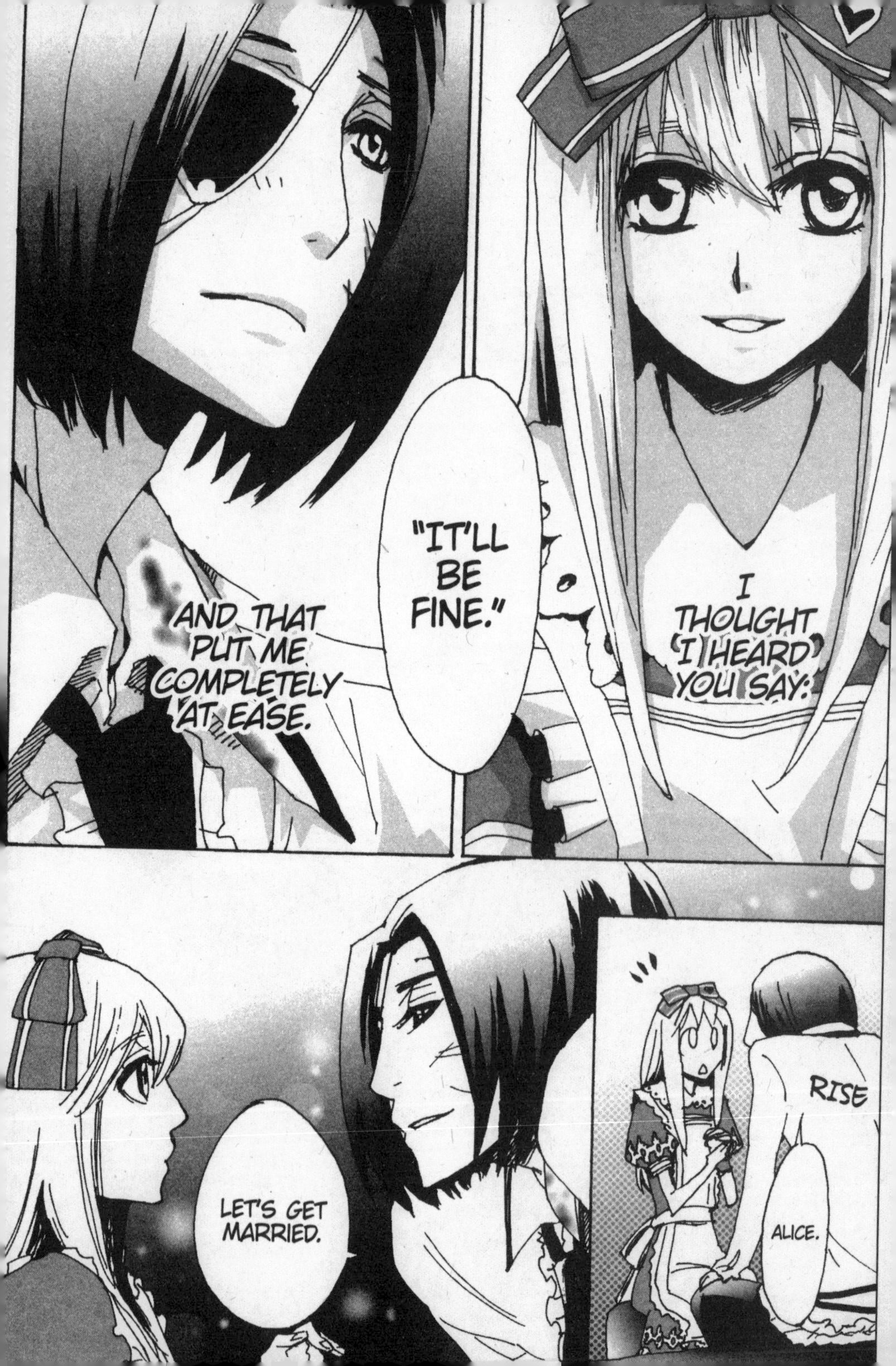
I THOUGHT I HEARD YOU SAY:
"IT'LL BE FINE."
AND THAT PUT ME COMPLETELY AT EASE.
RISE
ALICE.
LET'S GET MARRIED.

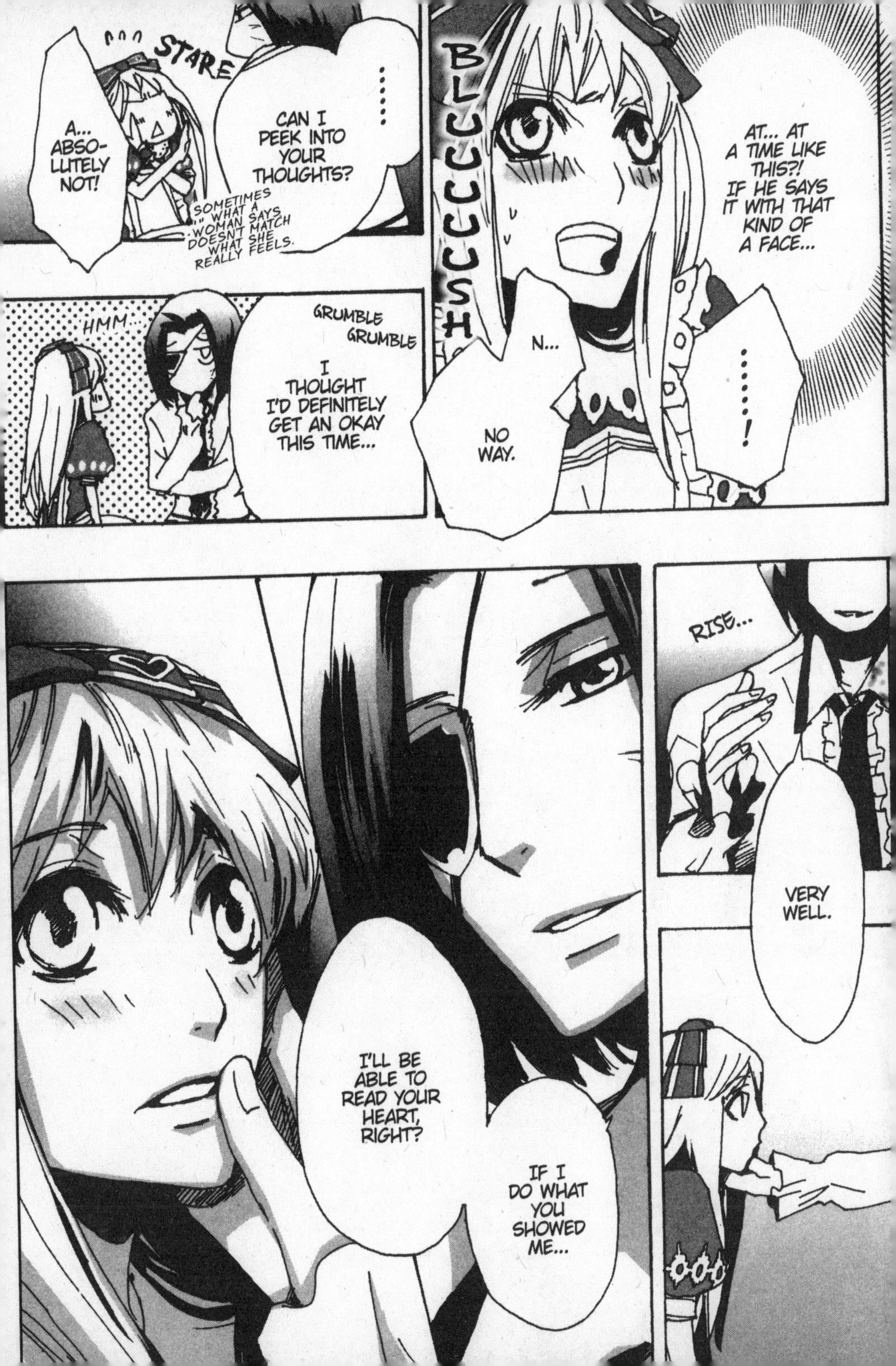
AT... AT A TIME LIKE THIS?! IF HE SAYS IT WITH THAT KIND OF A FACE...
......!
BLUUUUUUSH
N...
NO WAY.
......
CAN I PEEK INTO YOUR THOUGHTS?
STARE
A... ABSOLUTELY NOT!
SOMETIMES WHAT A WOMAN SAYS DOESN'T MATCH WHAT SHE REALLY FEELS.
GRUMBLE GRUMBLE
I THOUGHT I'D DEFINITELY GET AN OKAY THIS TIME...
HMM...
RISE...
VERY WELL.
IF I DO WHAT YOU SHOWED ME...
I'LL BE ABLE TO READ YOUR HEART, RIGHT?

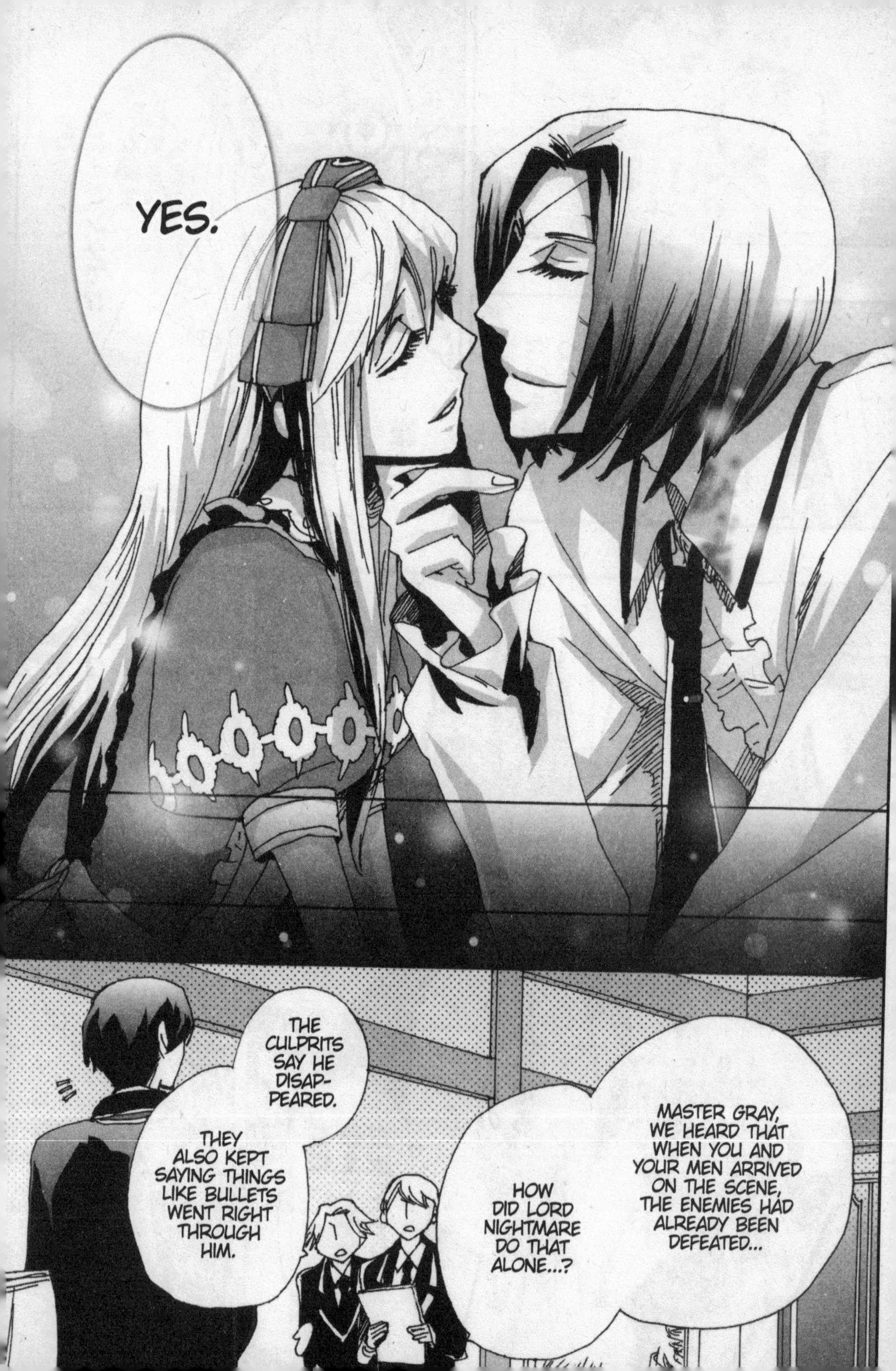
YES.
MASTER GRAY, WE HEARD THAT WHEN YOU AND YOUR MEN ARRIVED ON THE SCENE, THE ENEMIES HAD ALREADY BEEN DEFEATED...
HOW DID LORD NIGHTMARE DO THAT ALONE...?
THE CULPRITS SAY HE DISAPPEARED.
THEY ALSO KEPT SAYING THINGS LIKE BULLETS WENT RIGHT THROUGH HIM.

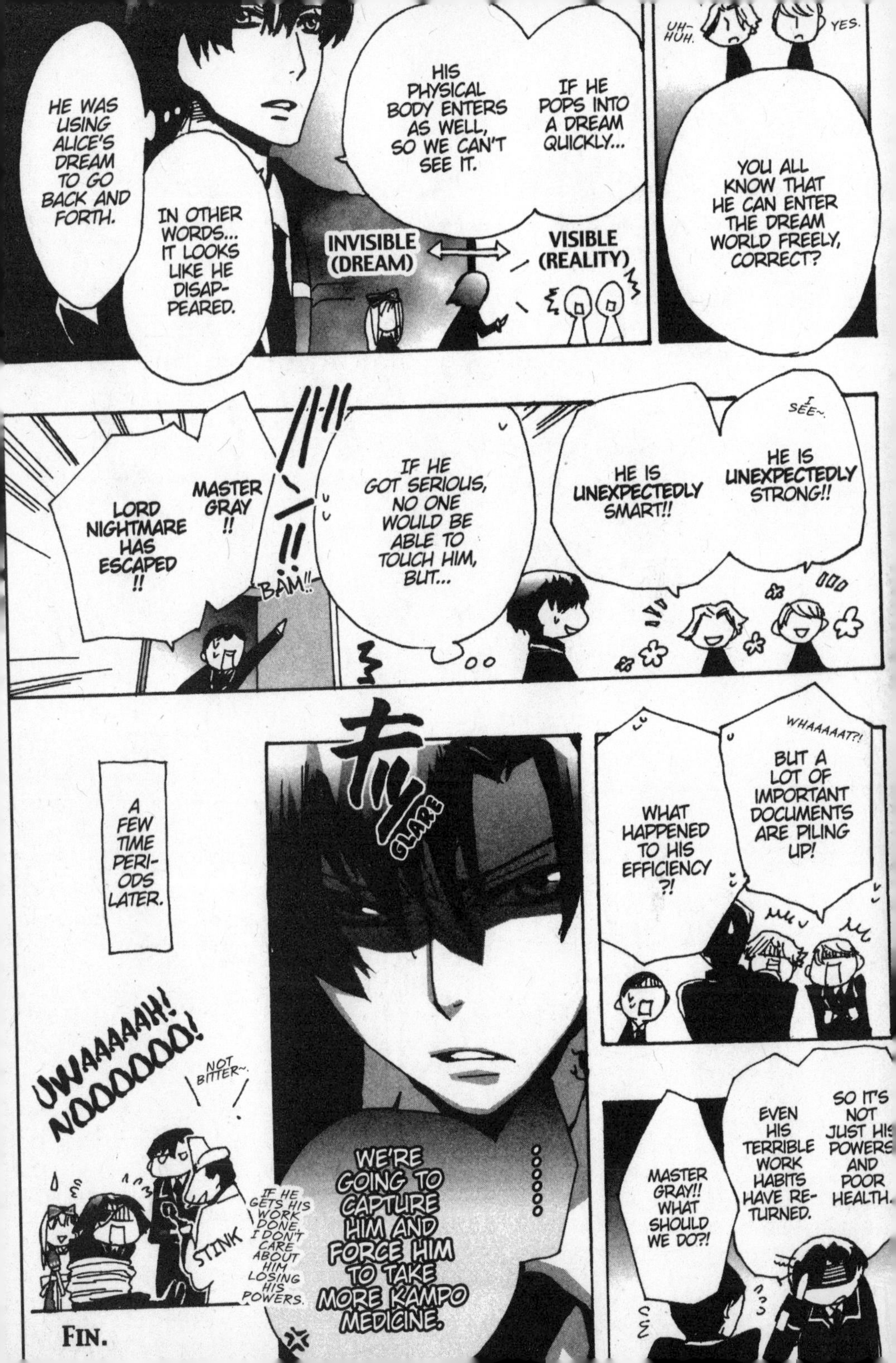
UH-HUH.
YES.
YOU ALL KNOW THAT HE CAN ENTER THE DREAM WORLD FREELY, CORRECT?
IF HE POPS INTO A DREAM QUICKLY...
HIS PHYSICAL BODY ENTERS AS WELL, SO WE CAN'T SEE IT.
VISIBLE (REALITY)
INVISIBLE (DREAM)
IN OTHER WORDS... IT LOOKS LIKE HE DISAPPEARED.
HE WAS USING ALICE'S DREAM TO GO BACK AND FORTH.
I SEE~.
HE IS UNEXPECTEDLY STRONG!!
HE IS UNEXPECTEDLY SMART!!
IF HE GOT SERIOUS, NO ONE WOULD BE ABLE TO TOUCH HIM, BUT...
MASTER GRAY!!
LORD NIGHTMARE HAS ESCAPED!!
BAM!!
WHAAAAAT?!
BUT A LOT OF IMPORTANT DOCUMENTS ARE PILING UP!
WHAT HAPPENED TO HIS EFFICIENCY?!
SO IT'S NOT JUST HIS POWERS AND POOR HEALTH.
EVEN HIS TERRIBLE WORK HABITS HAVE RETURNED.
MASTER GRAY!! WHAT SHOULD WE DO?!
GLARE
WE'RE GOING TO CAPTURE HIM AND FORCE HIM TO TAKE MORE KAMPO MEDICINE.
A FEW TIME PERIODS LATER.
UWAAAAAH! NOOOOOO!
NOT BITTER~.
IF HE GETS HIS WORK DONE, I DON'T CARE ABOUT HIM LOSING HIS POWERS.
STINK
FIN.

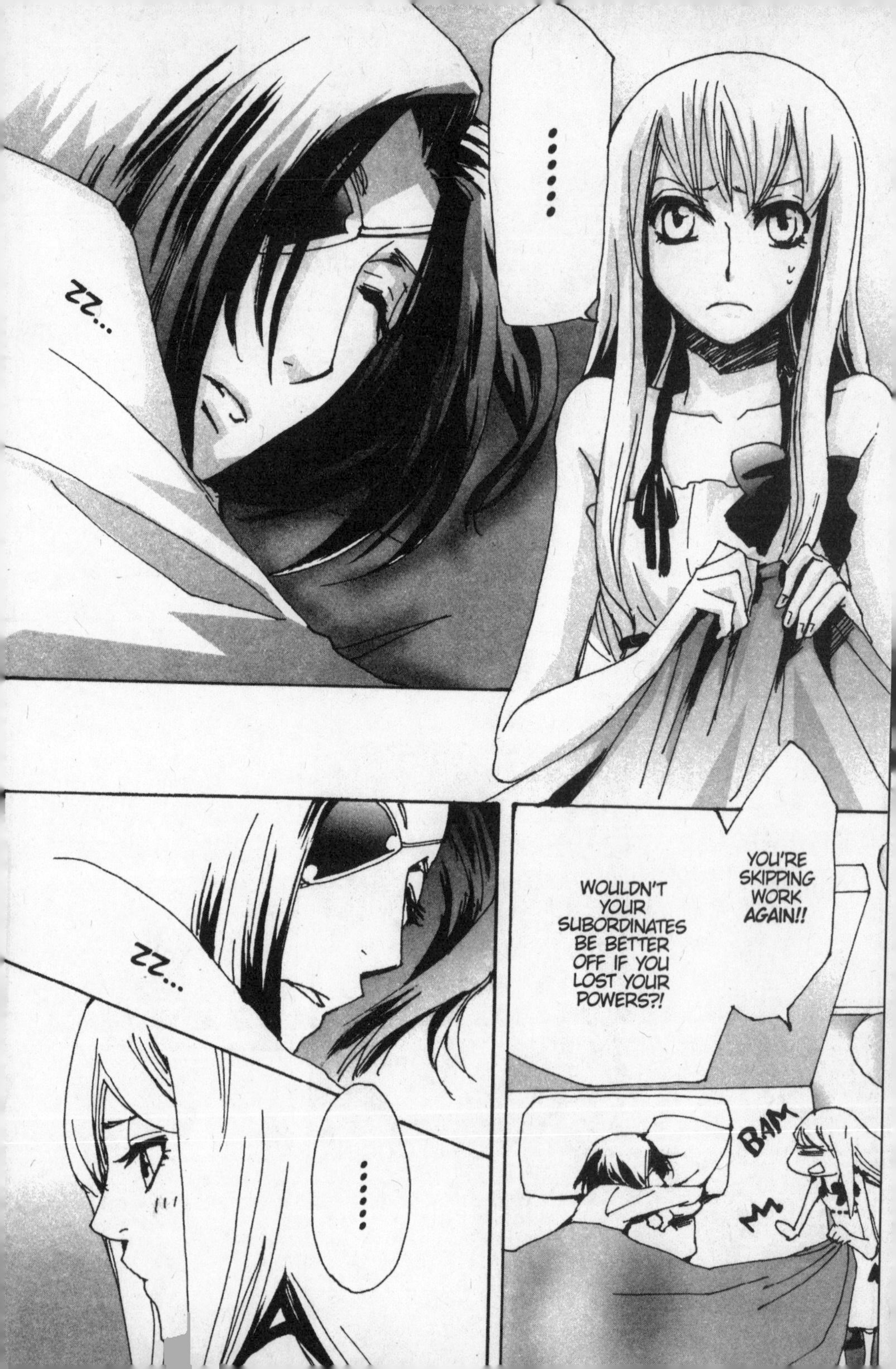
......
ZZ...
YOU'RE SKIPPING WORK AGAIN!!
WOULDN'T YOUR SUBORDINATES BE BETTER OFF IF YOU LOST YOUR POWERS?!
BAM
ZZ...
......

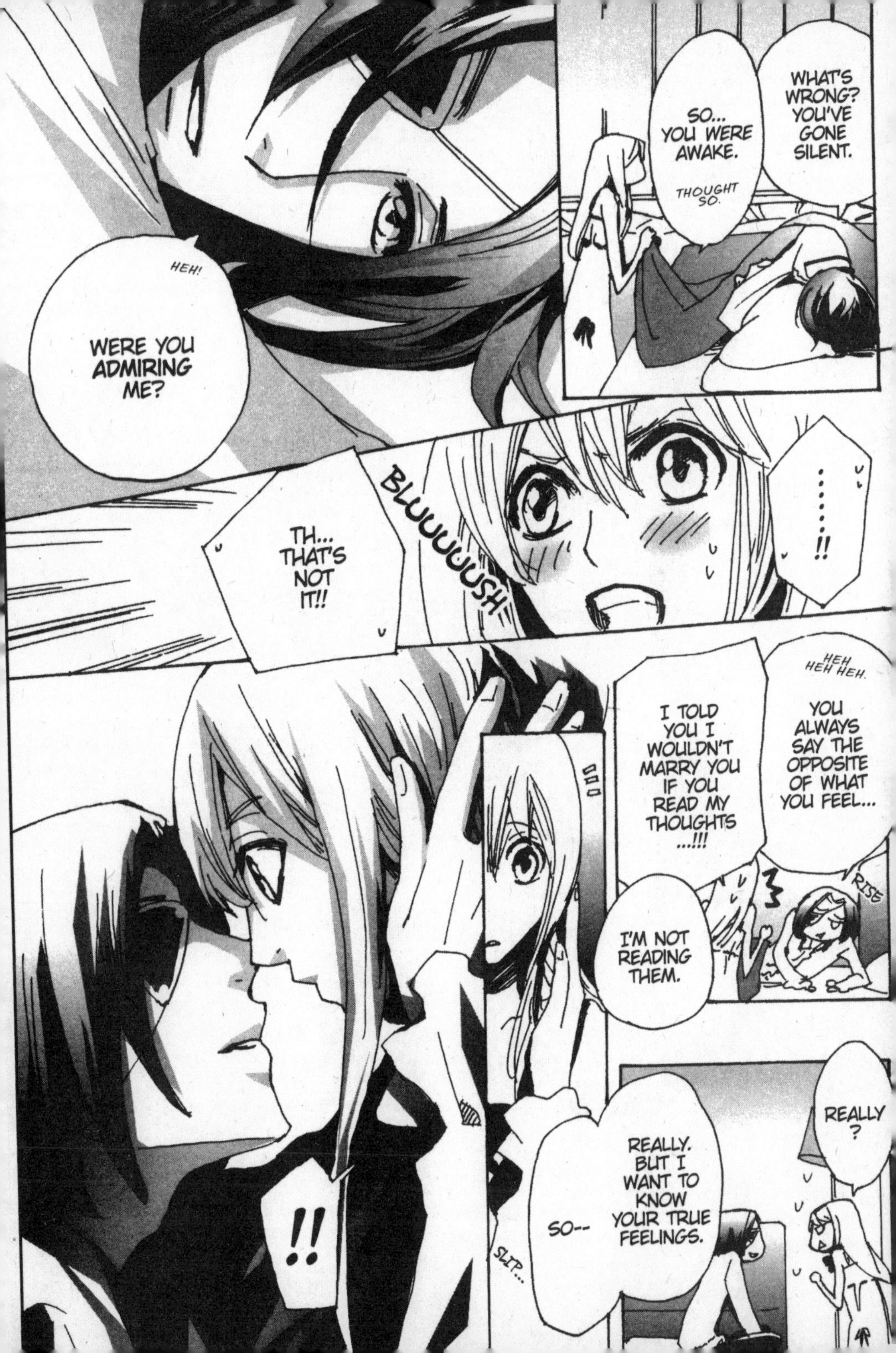
WHAT'S WRONG? YOU'VE GONE SILENT.
SO... YOU WERE AWAKE.
THOUGHT SO.
HEH!
WERE YOU ADMIRING ME?
......!!
BLUUUUUSH
TH... THAT'S NOT IT!!
HEH HEH HEH.
YOU ALWAYS SAY THE OPPOSITE OF WHAT YOU FEEL...
I TOLD YOU I WOULDN'T MARRY YOU IF YOU READ MY THOUGHTS ...!!!
RISE
I'M NOT READING THEM.
REALLY?
REALLY. BUT I WANT TO KNOW YOUR TRUE FEELINGS.
SO--
SLIP...
!!

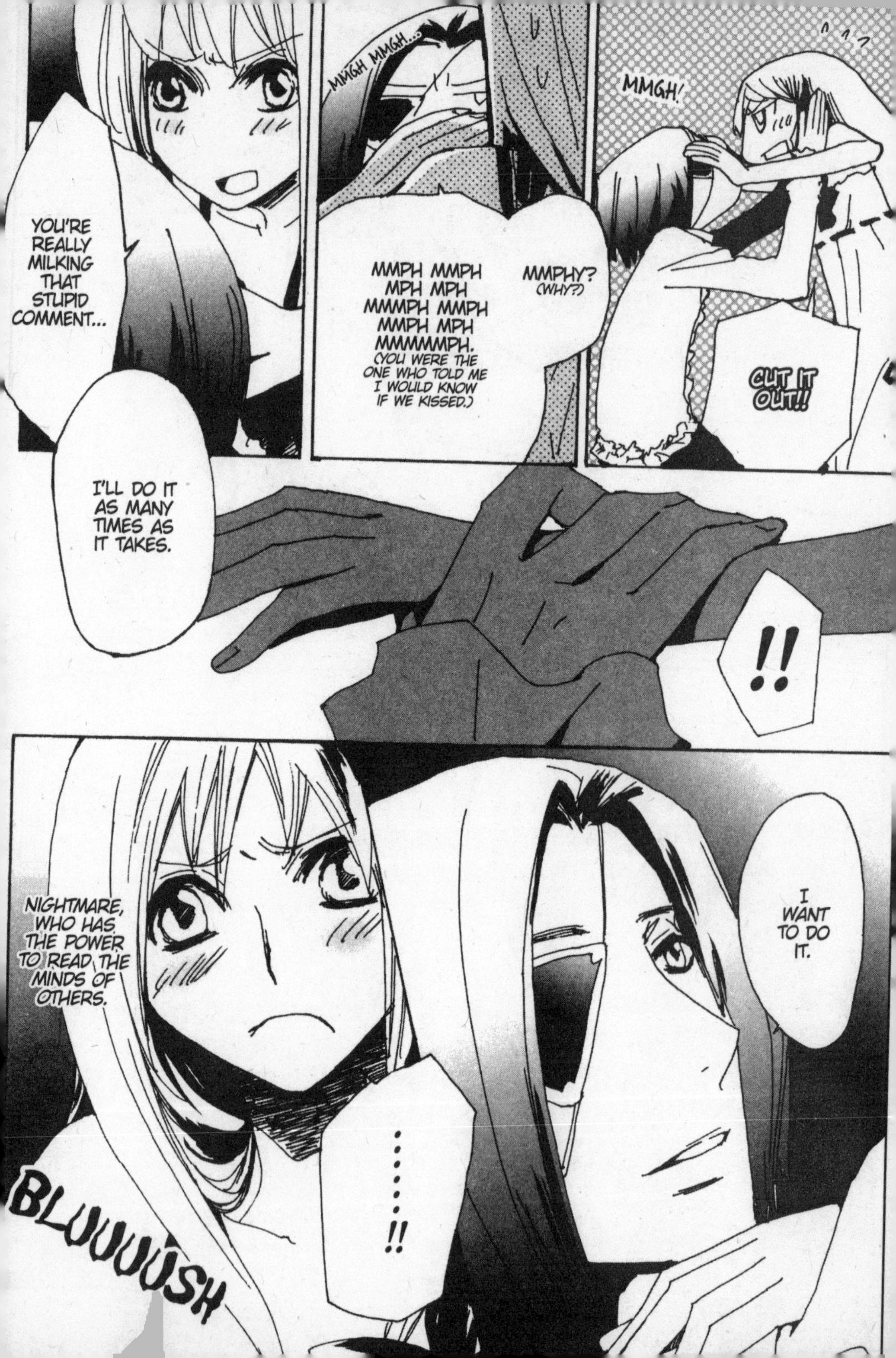
MMGH!
CUT IT OUT!!
MMGH MMGH...
MMPHY? (WHY?)
MMPH MMPH MPH MPH MMMPH MMPH MMPH MPH MMMMMPH. (YOU WERE THE ONE WHO TOLD ME I WOULD KNOW IF WE KISSED.)
YOU'RE REALLY MILKING THAT STUPID COMMENT...
!!
I'LL DO IT AS MANY TIMES AS IT TAKES.
I WANT TO DO IT.
NIGHTMARE, WHO HAS THE POWER TO READ THE MINDS OF OTHERS.
......!!
BLUUUUSH

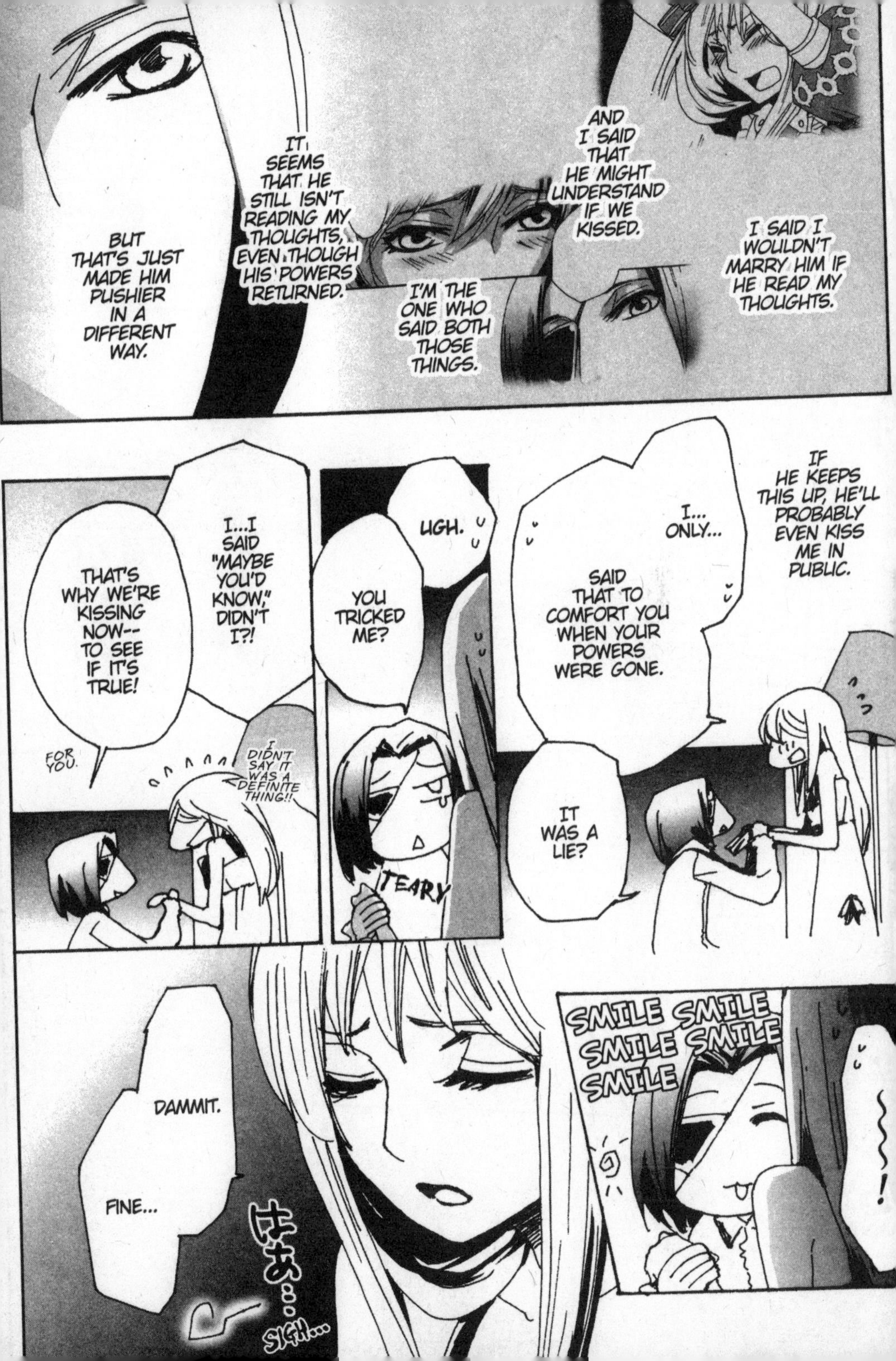
I SAID I WOULDN'T MARRY HIM IF HE READ MY THOUGHTS.
AND I SAID THAT HE MIGHT UNDERSTAND IF WE KISSED.
I'M THE ONE WHO SAID BOTH THOSE THINGS.
IT SEEMS THAT HE STILL ISN'T READING MY THOUGHTS, EVEN THOUGH HIS POWERS RETURNED.
BUT THAT'S JUST MADE HIM PUSHIER IN A DIFFERENT WAY.
IF HE KEEPS THIS UP, HE'LL PROBABLY EVEN KISS ME IN PUBLIC.
I... ONLY...
SAID THAT TO COMFORT YOU WHEN YOUR POWERS WERE GONE.
IT WAS A LIE?
UGH.
YOU TRICKED ME?
TEARY
I...I SAID "MAYBE YOU'D KNOW," DIDN'T I?!
THAT'S WHY WE'RE KISSING NOW-- TO SEE IF IT'S TRUE!
I DIDN'T SAY IT WAS A DEFINITE THING!!
FOR YOU.
SMILE SMILE SMILE SMILE SMILE
.....!
DAMMIT.
FINE...
はあ…
SIGH...

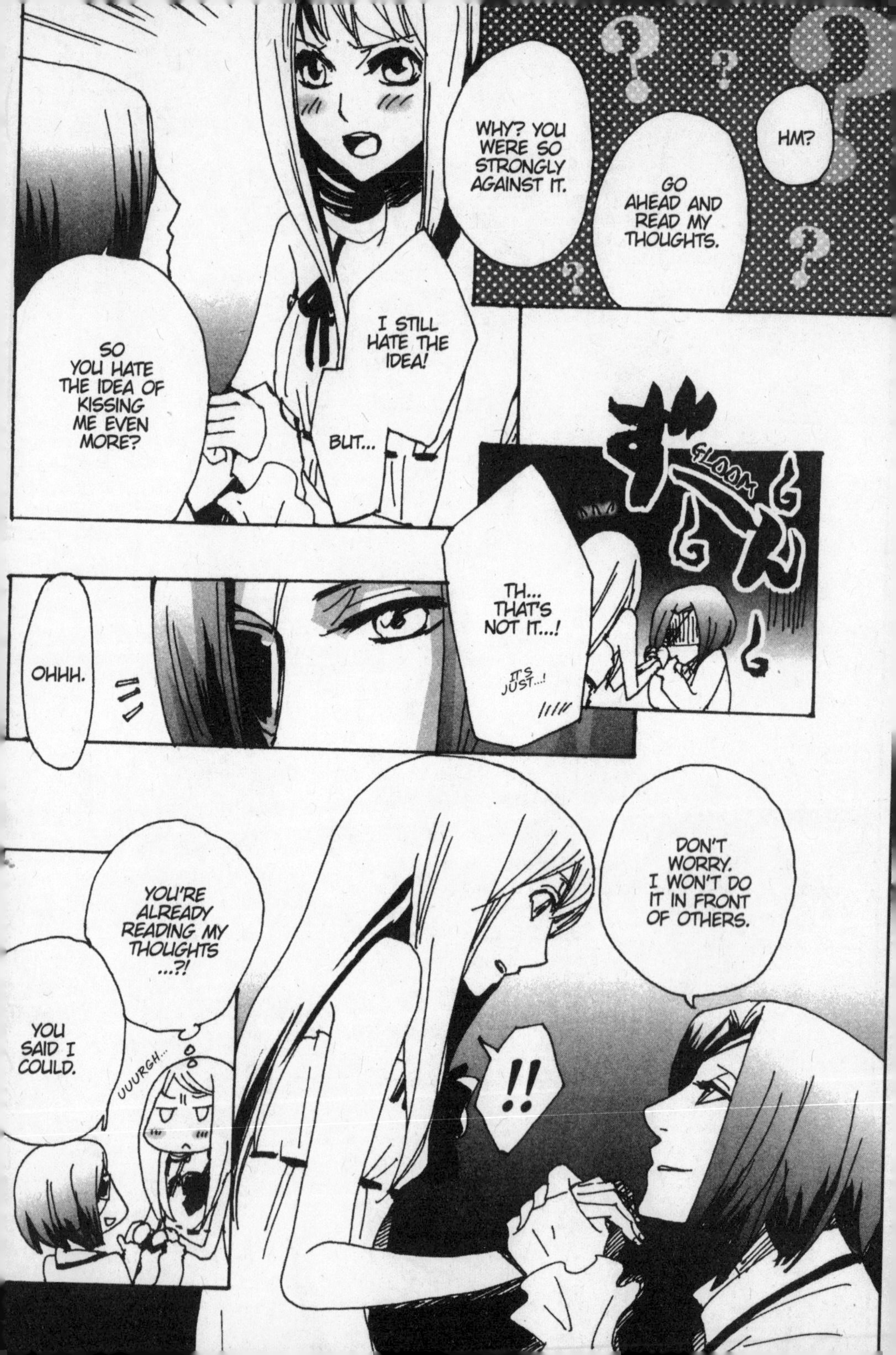
HM?
GO AHEAD AND READ MY THOUGHTS.
WHY? YOU WERE SO STRONGLY AGAINST IT.
I STILL HATE THE IDEA!
BUT...
SO YOU HATE THE IDEA OF KISSING ME EVEN MORE?
GLOOM
TH... THAT'S NOT IT...!
IT'S JUST...!
OHHH.
DON'T WORRY. I WON'T DO IT IN FRONT OF OTHERS.
!!
YOU'RE ALREADY READING MY THOUGHTS ...?!
UUURGH...
YOU SAID I COULD.

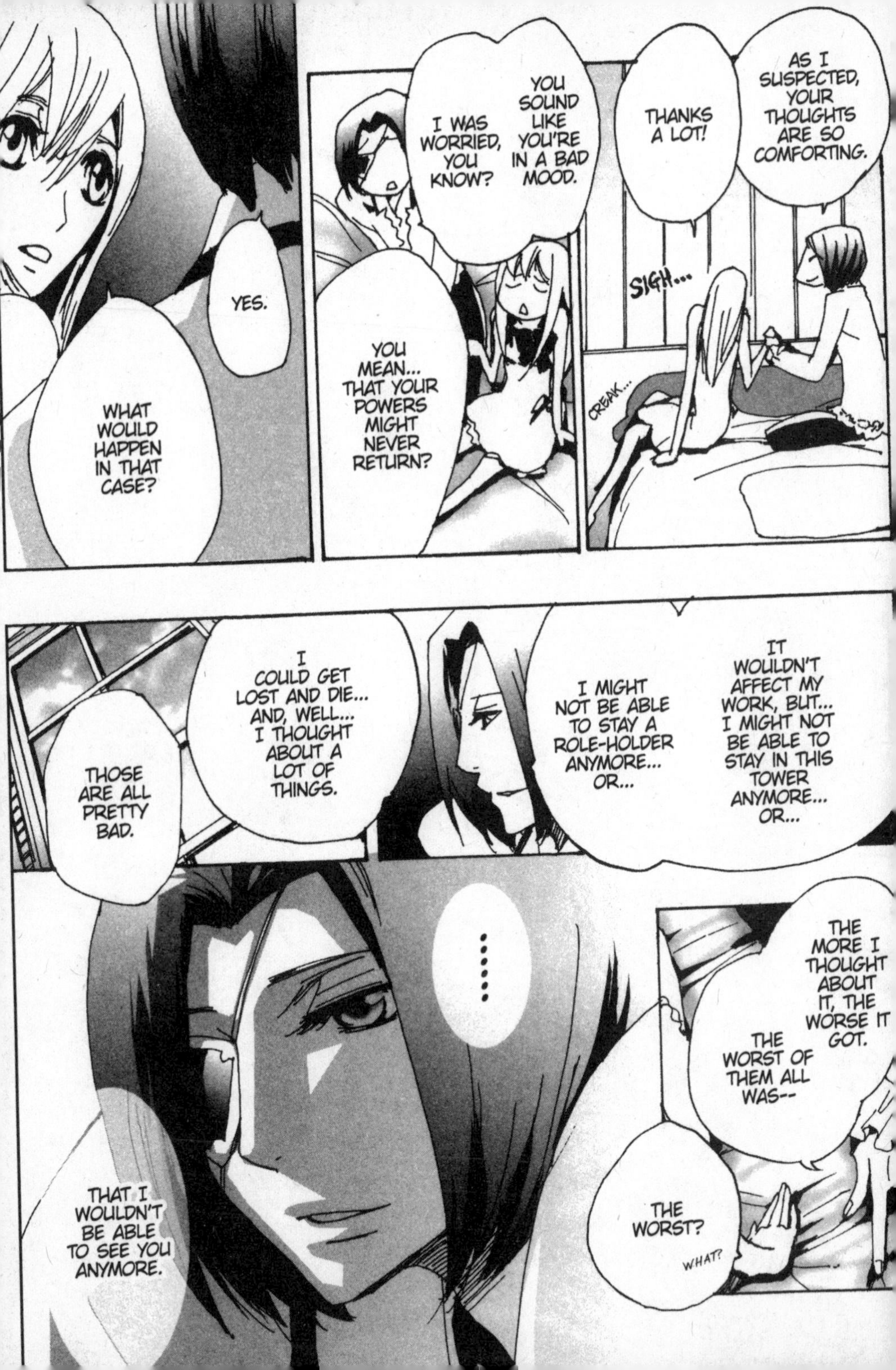
AS I SUSPECTED, YOUR THOUGHTS ARE SO COMFORTING.
THANKS A LOT!
SIGH...
CREAK...
YOU SOUND LIKE YOU'RE IN A BAD MOOD.
I WAS WORRIED, YOU KNOW?
YOU MEAN... THAT YOUR POWERS MIGHT NEVER RETURN?
YES.
WHAT WOULD HAPPEN IN THAT CASE?
IT WOULDN'T AFFECT MY WORK, BUT... I MIGHT NOT BE ABLE TO STAY IN THIS TOWER ANYMORE... OR...
I MIGHT NOT BE ABLE TO STAY A ROLE-HOLDER ANYMORE... OR...
I COULD GET LOST AND DIE... AND, WELL... I THOUGHT ABOUT A LOT OF THINGS.
THOSE ARE ALL PRETTY BAD.
THE MORE I THOUGHT ABOUT IT, THE WORSE IT GOT.
THE WORST OF THEM ALL WAS--
THE WORST?
WHAT?
......
THAT I WOULDN'T BE ABLE TO SEE YOU ANYMORE.

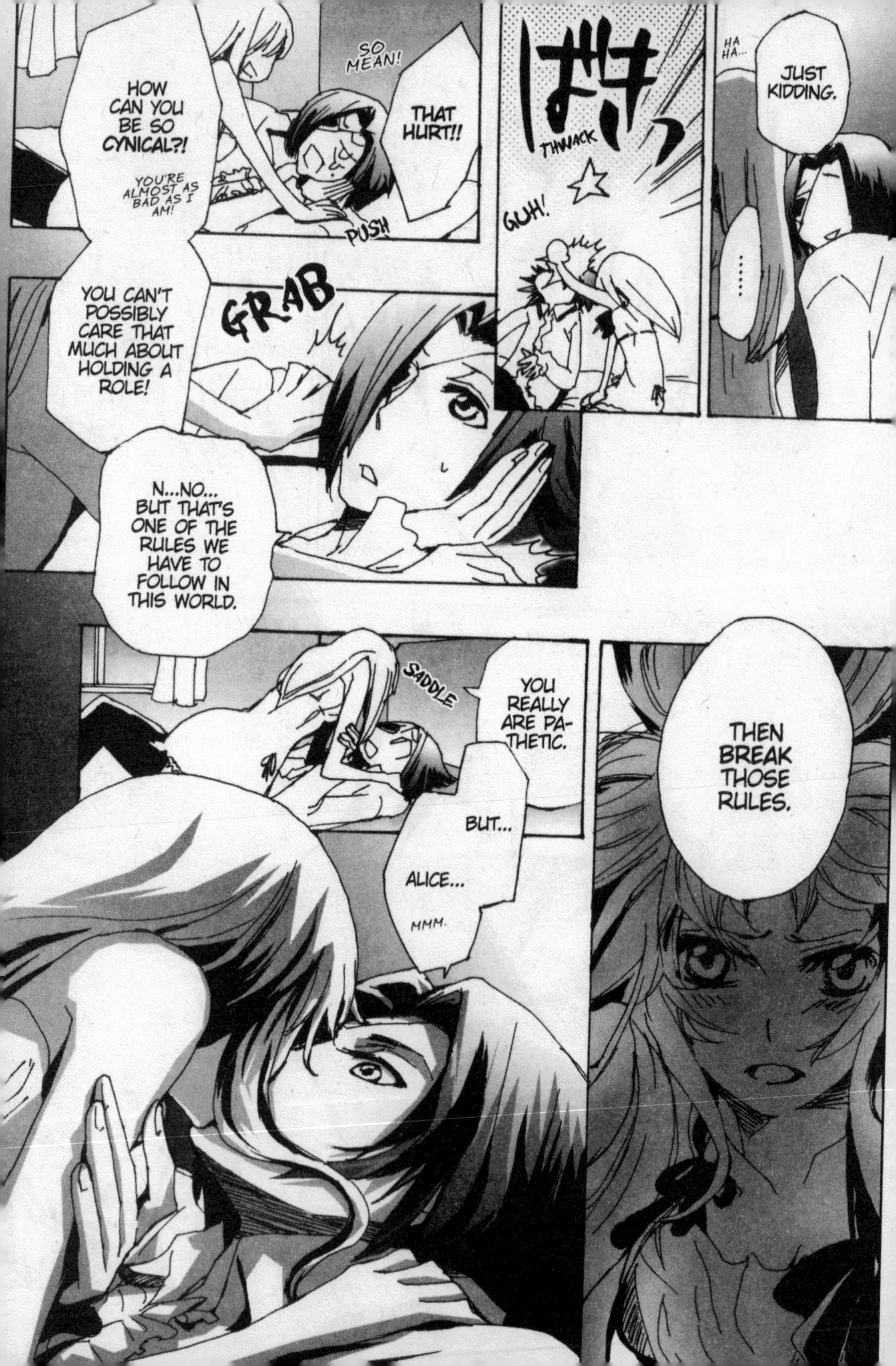

HA HA...
JUST KIDDING.
......
ばきっ
THWACK
GUH!
SO MEAN!
THAT HURT!!
HOW CAN YOU BE SO CYNICAL?!
YOU'RE ALMOST AS BAD AS I AM!
PUSH
GRAB
YOU CAN'T POSSIBLY CARE THAT MUCH ABOUT HOLDING A ROLE!
N...NO... BUT THAT'S ONE OF THE RULES WE HAVE TO FOLLOW IN THIS WORLD.
THEN BREAK THOSE RULES.
SADDLE
YOU REALLY ARE PA-THETIC.
BUT...
ALICE...
MMM.

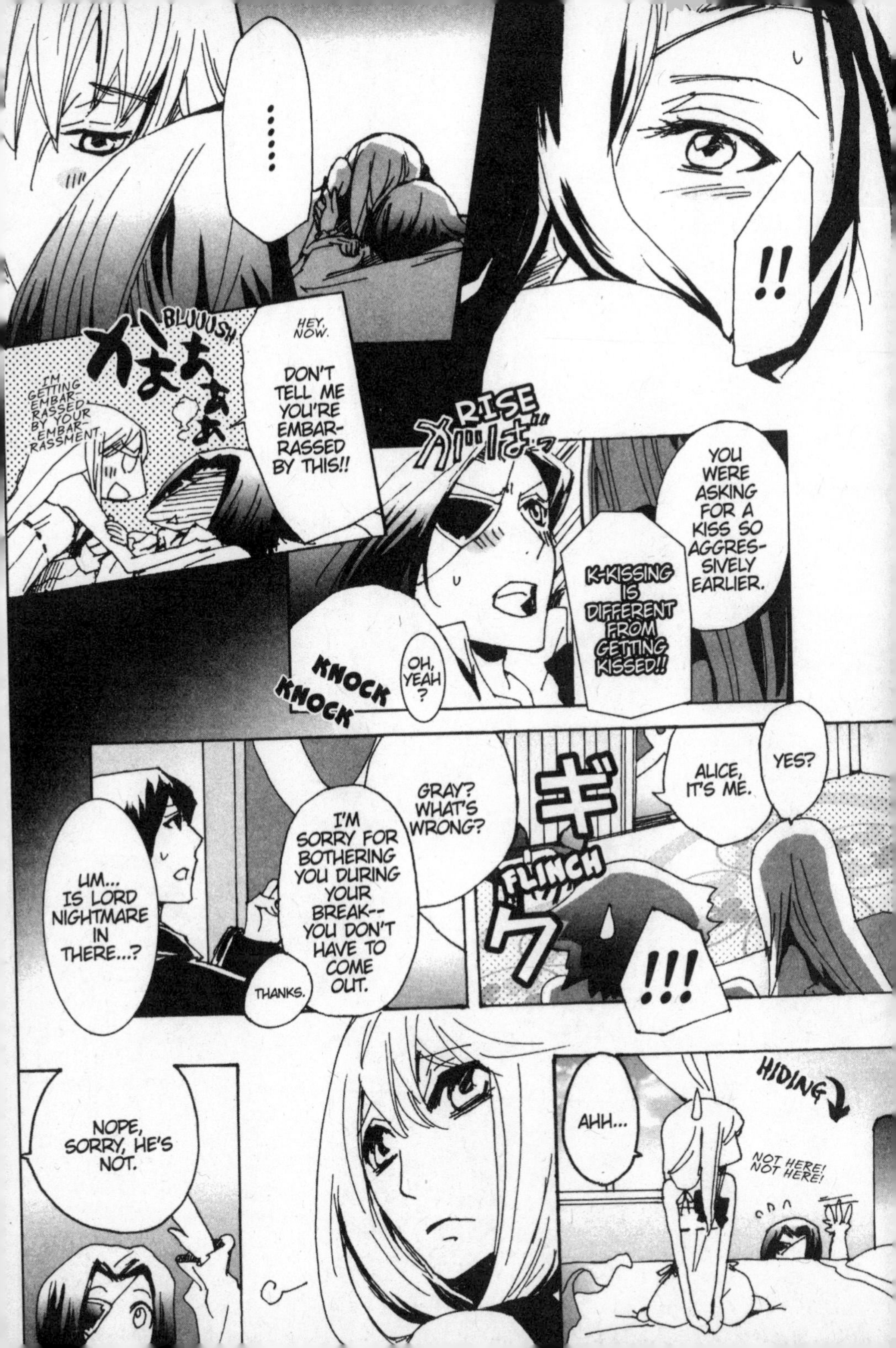
!!
......
BLUUUSH
かまぁぁぁ
I'M GETTING EMBARRASSED BY YOUR EMBARRASSMENT.
HEY, NOW.
DON'T TELL ME YOU'RE EMBARRASSED BY THIS!!
RISE
がばっ
YOU WERE ASKING FOR A KISS SO AGGRESSIVELY EARLIER.
K-KISSING IS DIFFERENT FROM GETTING KISSED!!
OH, YEAH?
KNOCK KNOCK
YES?
ALICE, IT'S ME.
FLINCH
ギクッ
!!!
GRAY? WHAT'S WRONG?
I'M SORRY FOR BOTHERING YOU DURING YOUR BREAK-- YOU DON'T HAVE TO COME OUT.
UM... IS LORD NIGHTMARE IN THERE...?
THANKS.
HIDING
AHH...
NOT HERE! NOT HERE!
NOPE, SORRY, HE'S NOT.

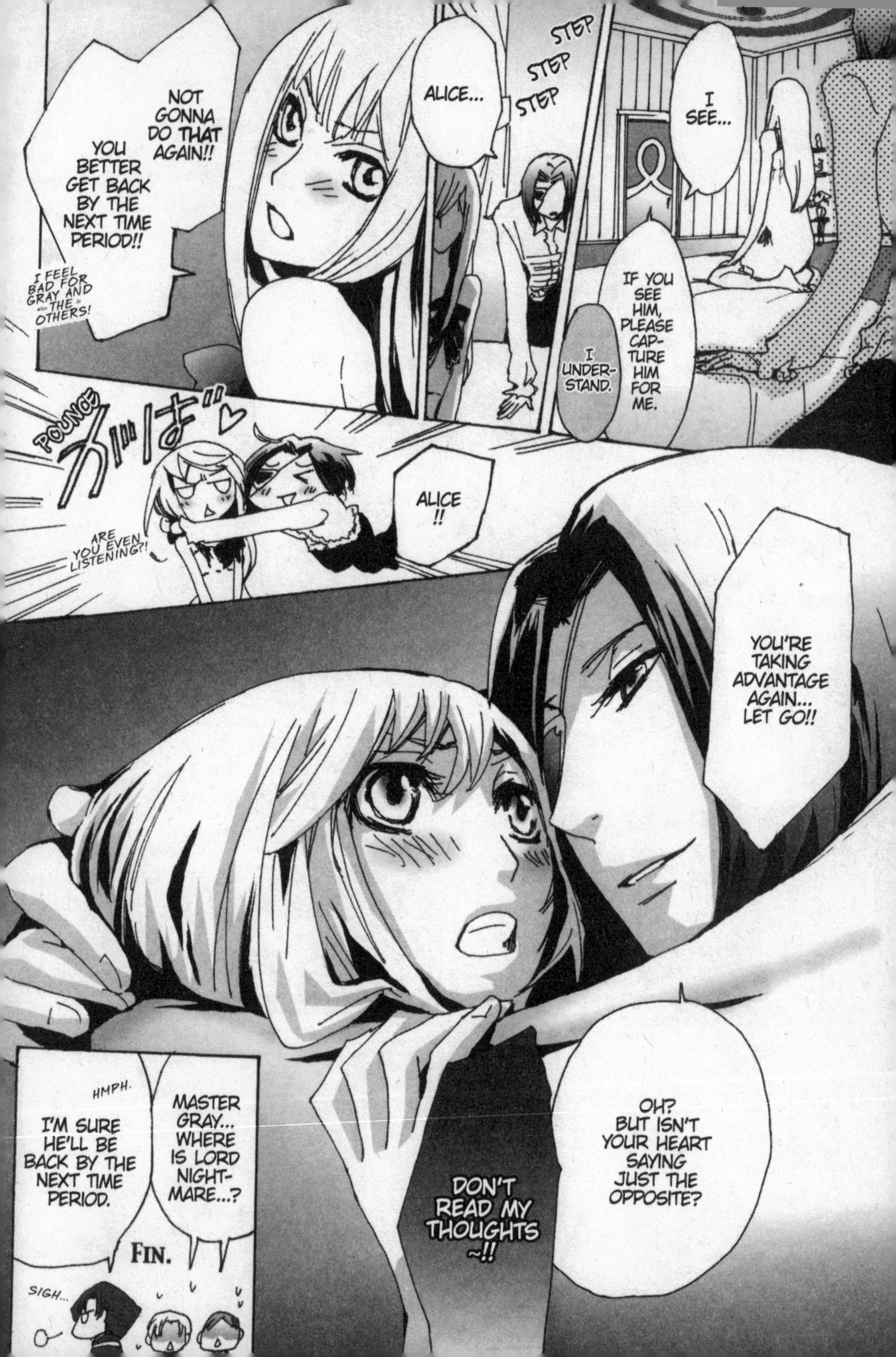
STEP
STEP
STEP
I SEE...
IF YOU SEE HIM, PLEASE CAPTURE HIM FOR ME.
I UNDER-STAND.
ALICE...
NOT GONNA DO THAT AGAIN!!
YOU BETTER GET BACK BY THE NEXT TIME PERIOD!!
I FEEL BAD FOR GRAY AND THE OTHERS!
ALICE!!
POUNCE
ARE YOU EVEN LISTENING?!
YOU'RE TAKING ADVANTAGE AGAIN... LET GO!!
OH? BUT ISN'T YOUR HEART SAYING JUST THE OPPOSITE?
DON'T READ MY THOUGHTS ~!!
MASTER GRAY... WHERE IS LORD NIGHT-MARE...?
HMPH.
I'M SURE HE'LL BE BACK BY THE NEXT TIME PERIOD.
FIN.
SIGH...

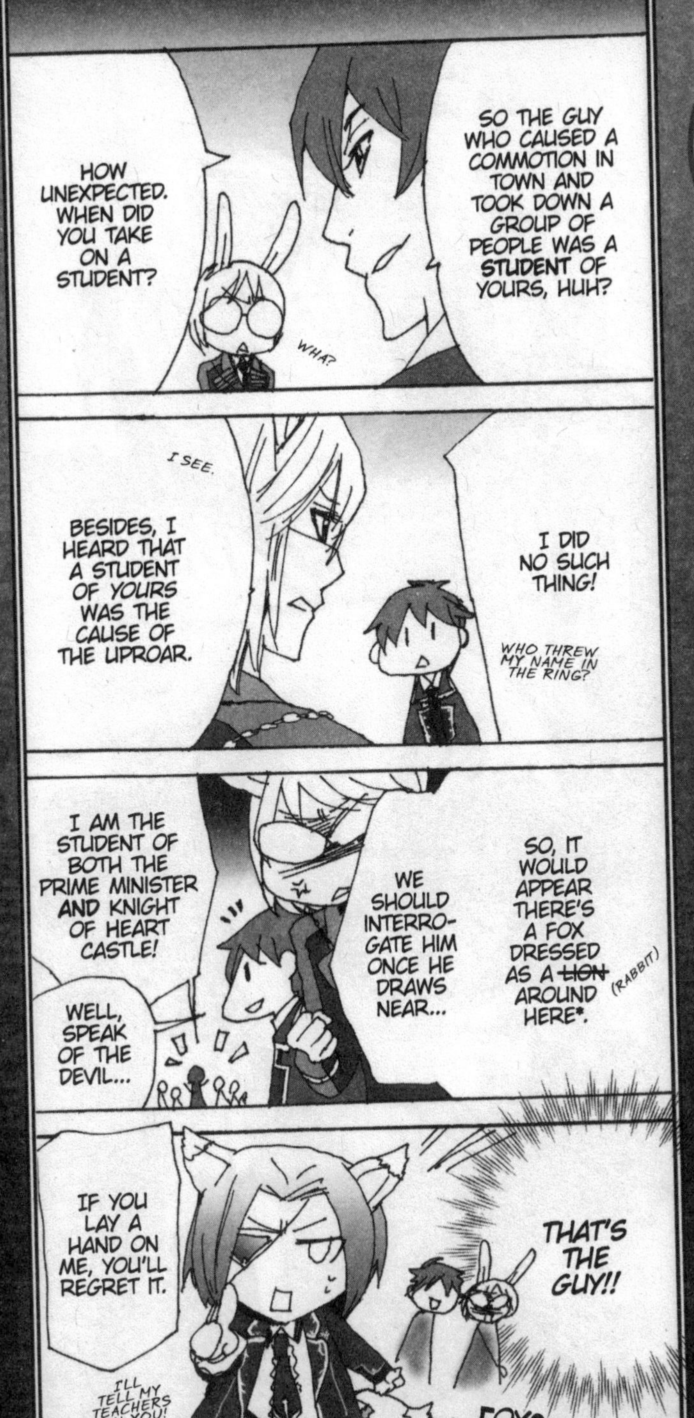
SO THE GUY WHO CAUSED A COMMOTION IN TOWN AND TOOK DOWN A GROUP OF PEOPLE WAS A STUDENT OF YOURS, HUH?
HOW UNEXPECTED. WHEN DID YOU TAKE ON A STUDENT?
WHA?
I SEE.
BESIDES, I HEARD THAT A STUDENT OF YOURS WAS THE CAUSE OF THE UPROAR.
I DID NO SUCH THING!
WHO THREW MY NAME IN THE RING?
SO, IT WOULD APPEAR THERE'S A FOX DRESSED AS A ~~LION~~ (RABBIT) AROUND HERE*.
WE SHOULD INTERROGATE HIM ONCE HE DRAWS NEAR...
I AM THE STUDENT OF BOTH THE PRIME MINISTER AND KNIGHT OF HEART CASTLE!
WELL, SPEAK OF THE DEVIL...
THAT'S THE GUY!!
IF YOU LAY A HAND ON ME, YOU'LL REGRET IT.
I'LL TELL MY TEACHERS ON YOU!
← FOX?

*The expression, "a fox is dressed as a lion" means someone is pretending to be something they're not, usually to impress or intimidate others.

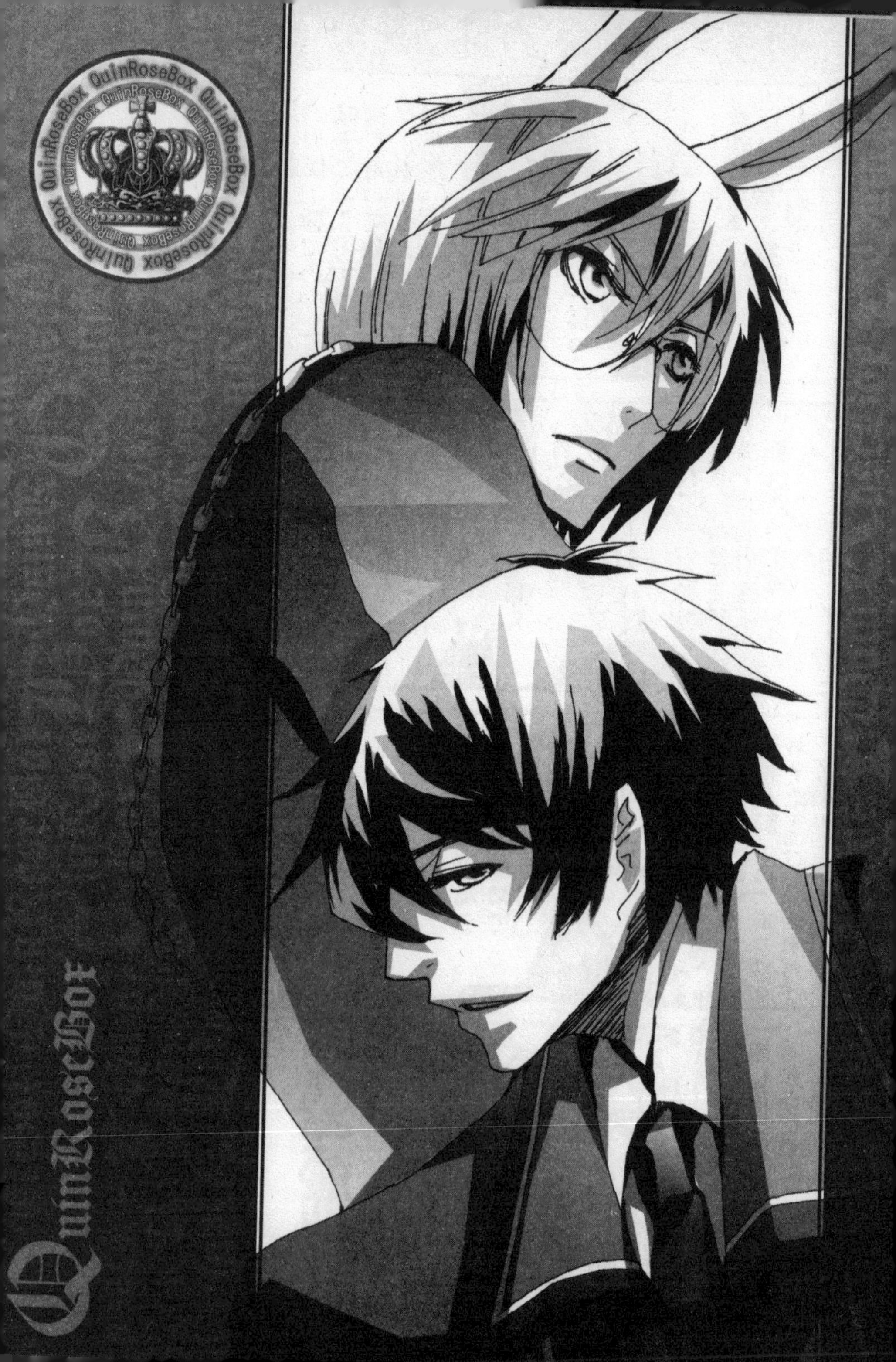
QuinRoseBox
QuinRoseBox

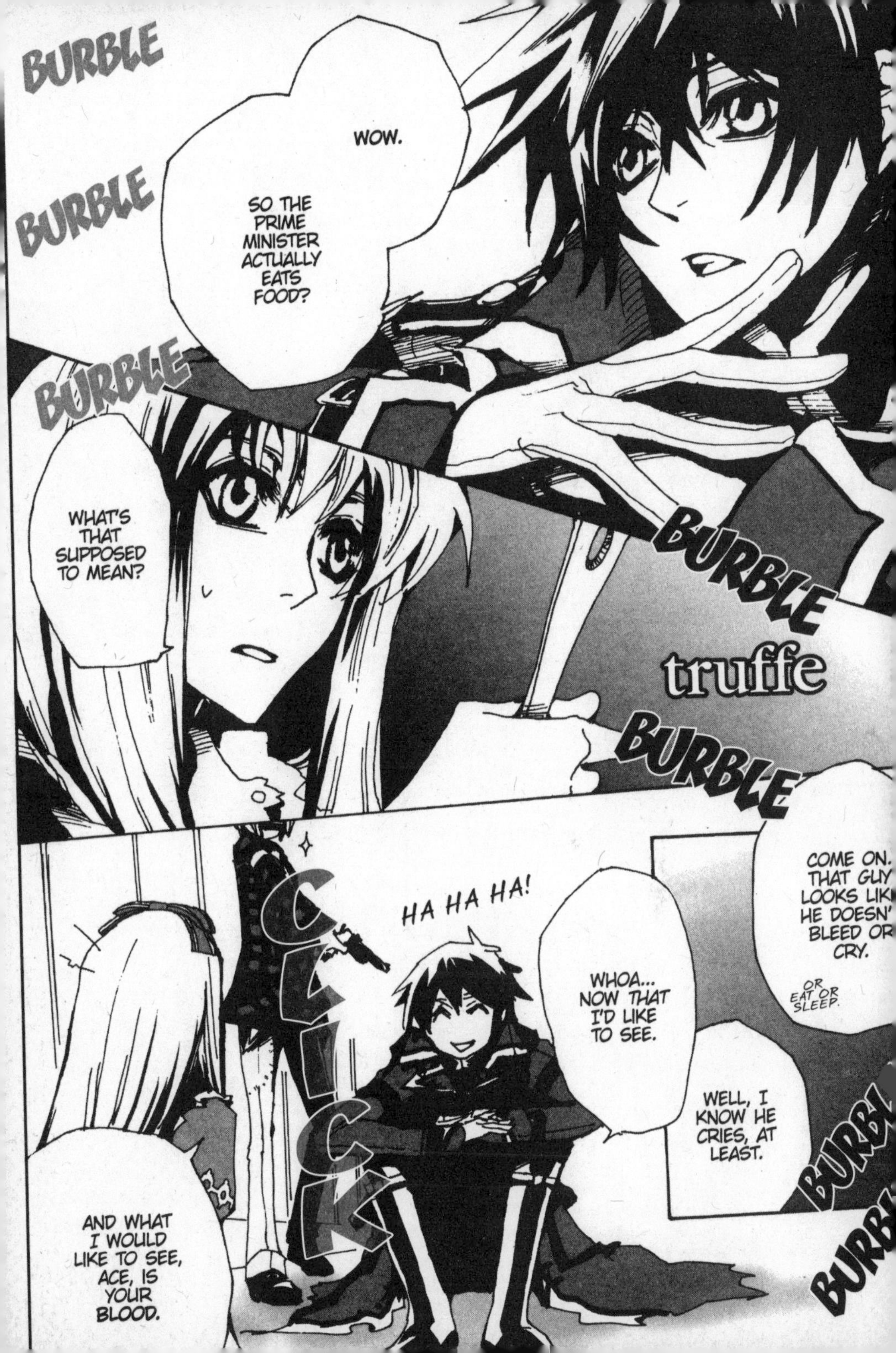
WOW.
SO THE PRIME MINISTER ACTUALLY EATS FOOD?
BURBLE
BURBLE
BURBLE
BURBLE
WHAT'S THAT SUPPOSED TO MEAN?
truffe
BURBLE
COME ON. THAT GUY LOOKS LIKE HE DOESN' BLEED OR CRY.
OR EAT OR SLEEP.
WHOA... NOW THAT I'D LIKE TO SEE.
HA HA HA!
WELL, I KNOW HE CRIES, AT LEAST.
CLICK
AND WHAT I WOULD LIKE TO SEE, ACE, IS YOUR BLOOD.

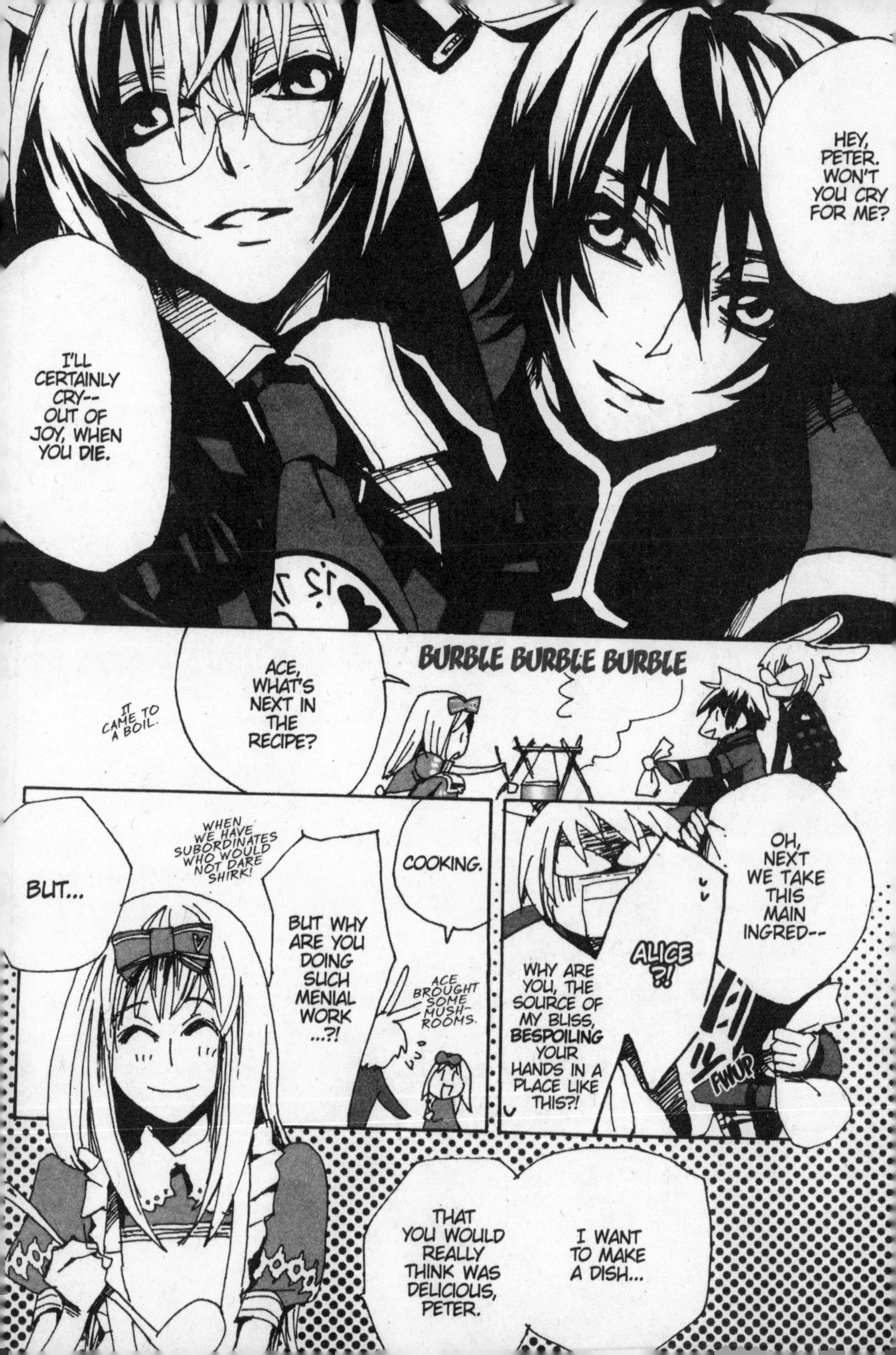

HEY, PETER. WON'T YOU CRY FOR ME?
I'LL CERTAINLY CRY-- OUT OF JOY, WHEN YOU DIE.
BURBLE BURBLE BURBLE
ACE, WHAT'S NEXT IN THE RECIPE?
IT CAME TO A BOIL.
OH, NEXT WE TAKE THIS MAIN INGRED--
ALICE ?!
WHY ARE YOU, THE SOURCE OF MY BLISS, BESPOILING YOUR HANDS IN A PLACE LIKE THIS?!
FWUP
COOKING.
BUT WHY ARE YOU DOING SUCH MENIAL WORK ...?!
WHEN WE HAVE SUBORDINATES WHO WOULD NOT DARE SHIRK!
ACE BROUGHT SOME MUSH-ROOMS.
BUT...
I WANT TO MAKE A DISH...
THAT YOU WOULD REALLY THINK WAS DELICIOUS, PETER.

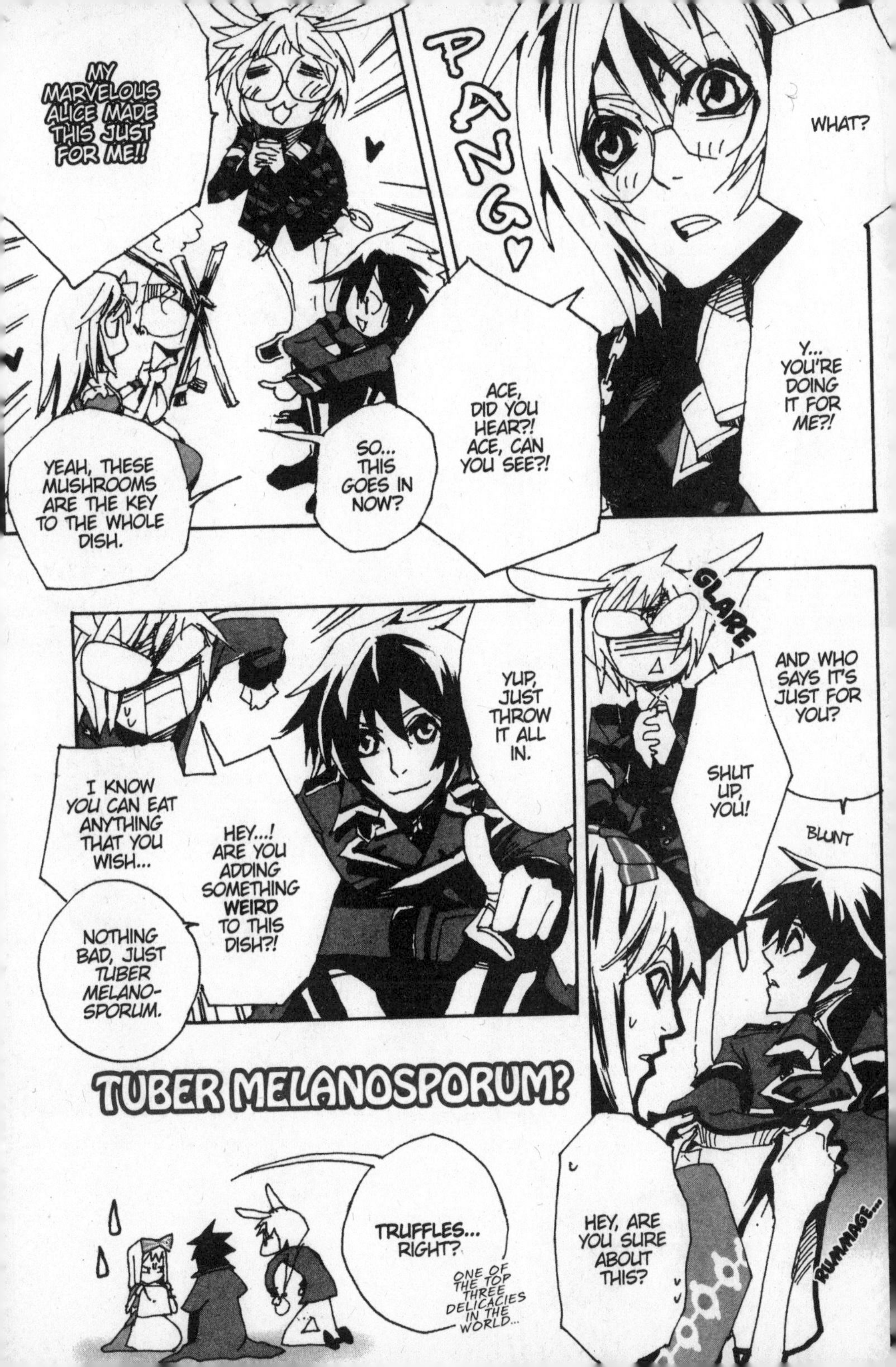
WHAT?
PANG
Y... YOU'RE DOING IT FOR ME?!
MY MARVELOUS ALICE MADE THIS JUST FOR ME!!
ACE, DID YOU HEAR?! ACE, CAN YOU SEE?!
SO... THIS GOES IN NOW?
YEAH, THESE MUSHROOMS ARE THE KEY TO THE WHOLE DISH.
GLARE
AND WHO SAYS IT'S JUST FOR YOU?
SHUT UP, YOU!
BLUNT
RUMMAGE...
HEY, ARE YOU SURE ABOUT THIS?
YUP, JUST THROW IT ALL IN.
HEY...! ARE YOU ADDING SOMETHING WEIRD TO THIS DISH?!
I KNOW YOU CAN EAT ANYTHING THAT YOU WISH...
NOTHING BAD, JUST TUBER MELANOSPORUM.
TUBER MELANOSPORUM?
TRUFFLES... RIGHT?
ONE OF THE TOP THREE DELICACIES IN THE WORLD...

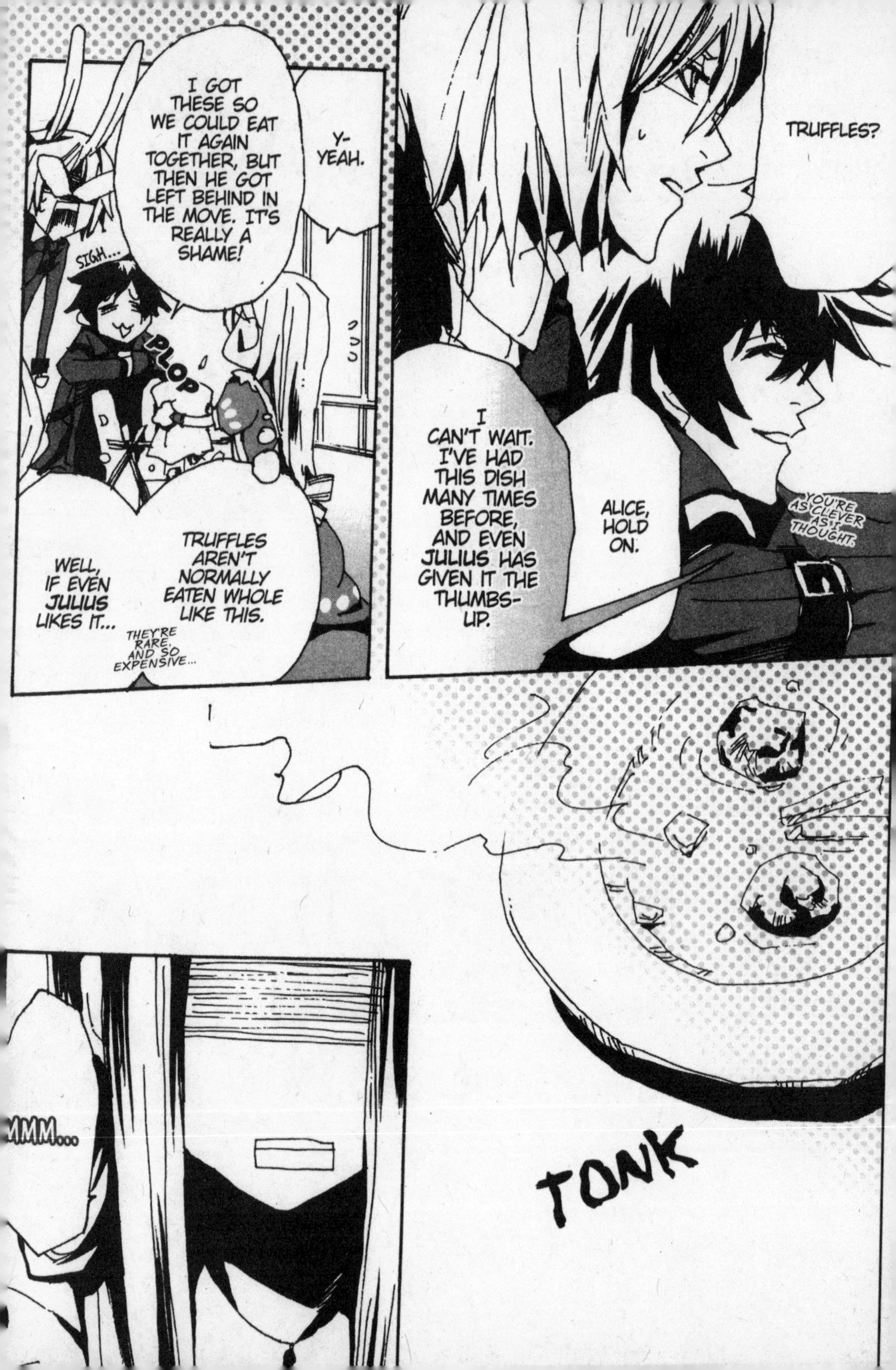
TRUFFLES?
I CAN'T WAIT. I'VE HAD THIS DISH MANY TIMES BEFORE, AND EVEN JULIUS HAS GIVEN IT THE THUMBS-UP.
ALICE, HOLD ON.
YOU'RE AS CLEVER AS I THOUGHT.
I GOT THESE SO WE COULD EAT IT AGAIN TOGETHER, BUT THEN HE GOT LEFT BEHIND IN THE MOVE. IT'S REALLY A SHAME!
Y-YEAH.
SIGH...
PLOP
TRUFFLES AREN'T NORMALLY EATEN WHOLE LIKE THIS.
WELL, IF EVEN JULIUS LIKES IT...
THEY'RE RARE, AND SO EXPENSIVE...
TONK
MMM...

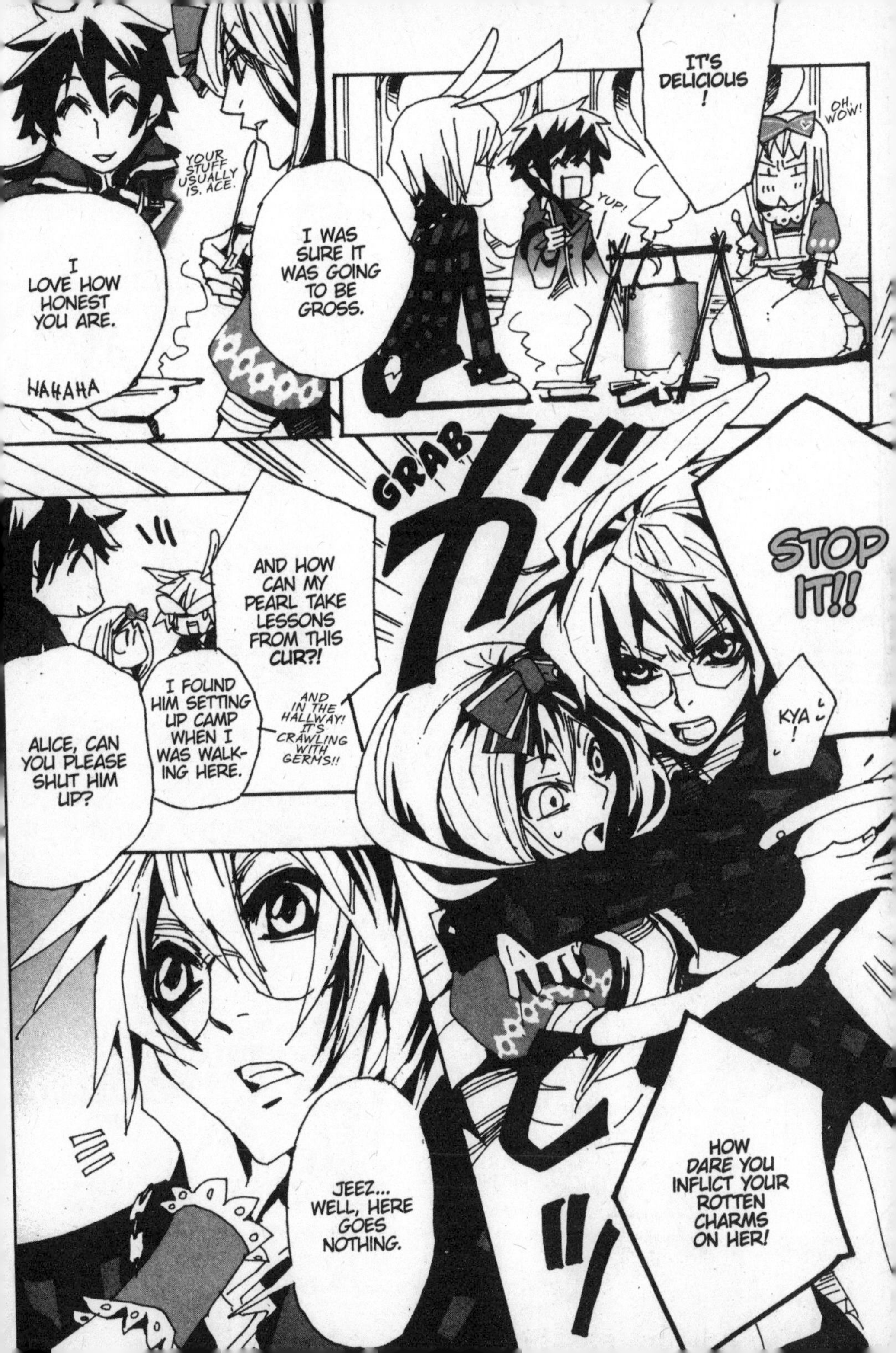
IT'S DELICIOUS!
OH, WOW!
YUP!
I WAS SURE IT WAS GOING TO BE GROSS.
YOUR STUFF USUALLY IS, ACE.
I LOVE HOW HONEST YOU ARE.
HAHAHA
GRAB
STOP IT!!
KYA!
HOW DARE YOU INFLICT YOUR ROTTEN CHARMS ON HER!
AND HOW CAN MY PEARL TAKE LESSONS FROM THIS CUR?!
I FOUND HIM SETTING UP CAMP WHEN I WAS WALKING HERE.
AND IN THE HALLWAY! IT'S CRAWLING WITH GERMS!!
ALICE, CAN YOU PLEASE SHUT HIM UP?
JEEZ... WELL, HERE GOES NOTHING.

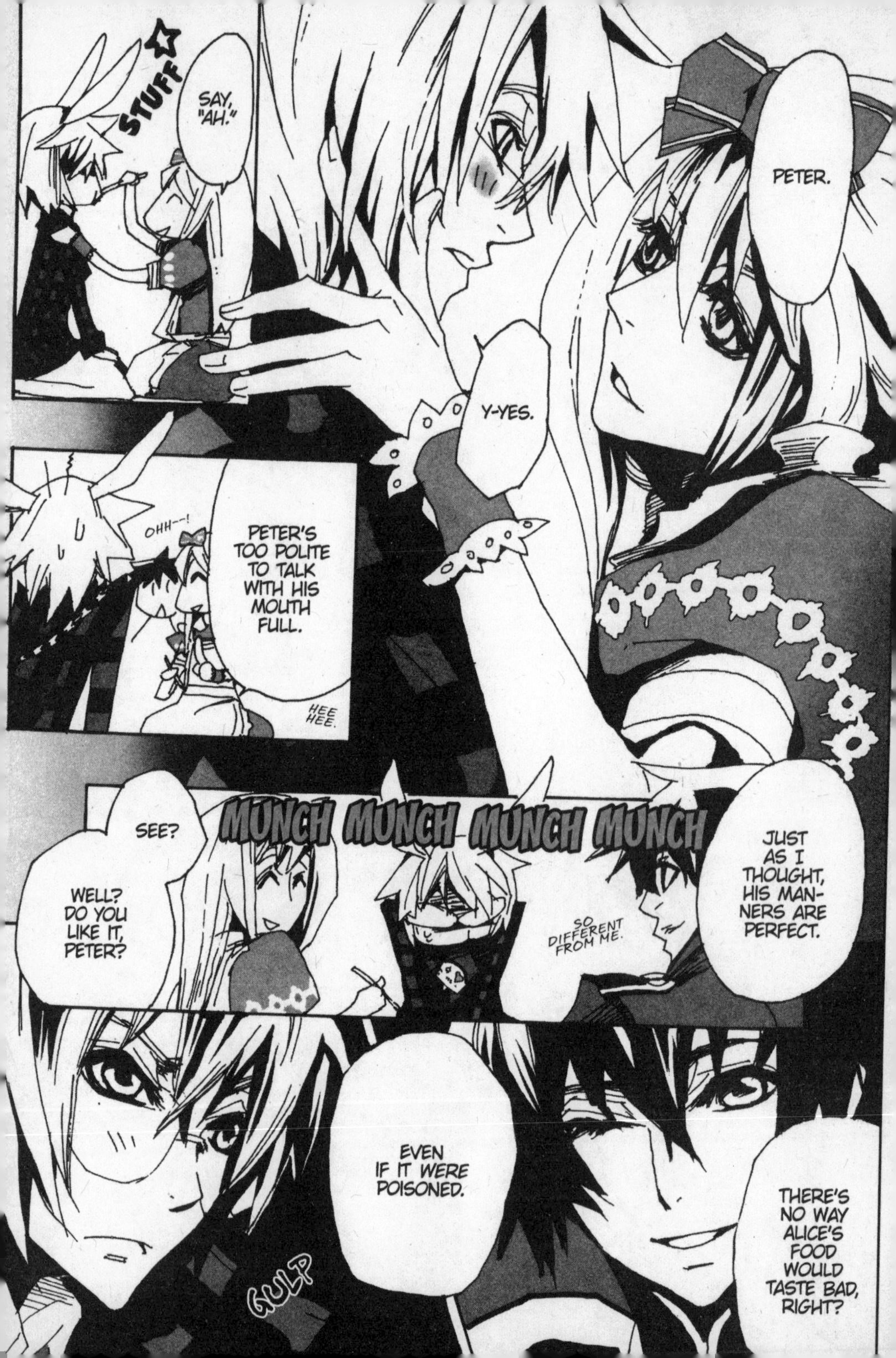
PETER.
Y-YES.
SAY, "AH."
STUFF
PETER'S TOO POLITE TO TALK WITH HIS MOUTH FULL.
OHH--!
HEE HEE.
JUST AS I THOUGHT, HIS MAN-NERS ARE PERFECT.
SO DIFFERENT FROM ME.
MUNCH MUNCH MUNCH MUNCH
SEE?
WELL? DO YOU LIKE IT, PETER?
THERE'S NO WAY ALICE'S FOOD WOULD TASTE BAD, RIGHT?
EVEN IF IT WERE POISONED.
GULP

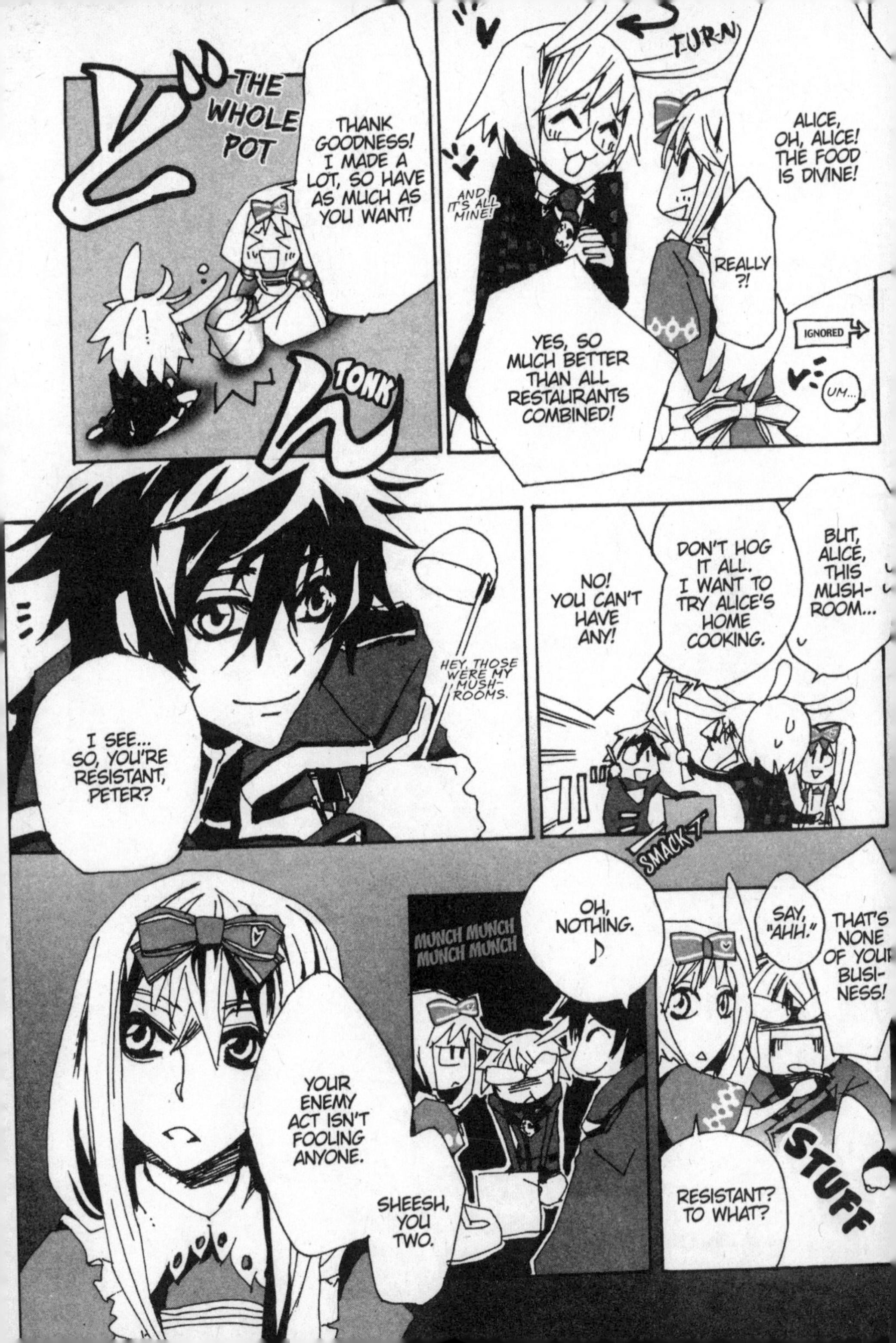
T-U-R-N
ALICE, OH, ALICE! THE FOOD IS DIVINE!
AND IT'S ALL MINE!
REALLY?!
IGNORED
YES, SO MUCH BETTER THAN ALL RESTAURANTS COMBINED!
UM...
THE WHOLE POT
THANK GOODNESS! I MADE A LOT, SO HAVE AS MUCH AS YOU WANT!
TONK
BUT, ALICE, THIS MUSH-ROOM...
DON'T HOG IT ALL. I WANT TO TRY ALICE'S HOME COOKING.
NO! YOU CAN'T HAVE ANY!
SMACK
HEY, THOSE WERE MY MUSH-ROOMS.
I SEE... SO, YOU'RE RESISTANT, PETER?
THAT'S NONE OF YOUR BUSI-NESS!
SAY, "AHH."
STUFF
RESISTANT? TO WHAT?
OH, NOTHING. ♪
MUNCH MUNCH MUNCH MUNCH
YOUR ENEMY ACT ISN'T FOOLING ANYONE.
SHEESH, YOU TWO.

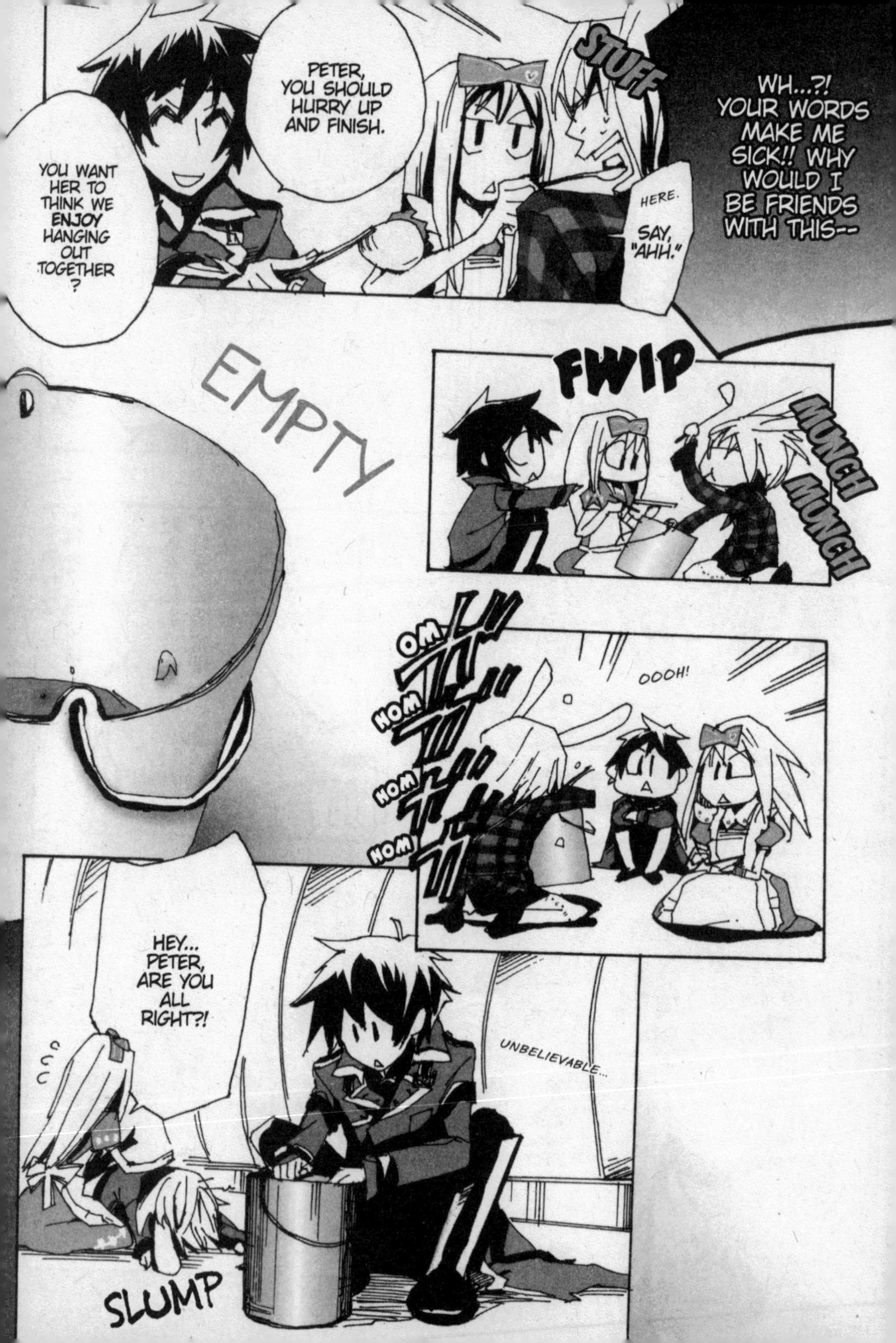

STUFF
WH...?! YOUR WORDS MAKE ME SICK!! WHY WOULD I BE FRIENDS WITH THIS--
HERE.
SAY, "AHH."
PETER, YOU SHOULD HURRY UP AND FINISH.
YOU WANT HER TO THINK WE ENJOY HANGING OUT TOGETHER?
FWIP
MUNCH MUNCH
EMPTY
OOOH!
OM NOM NOM NOM NOM
UNBELIEVABLE...
HEY... PETER, ARE YOU ALL RIGHT?!
SLUMP

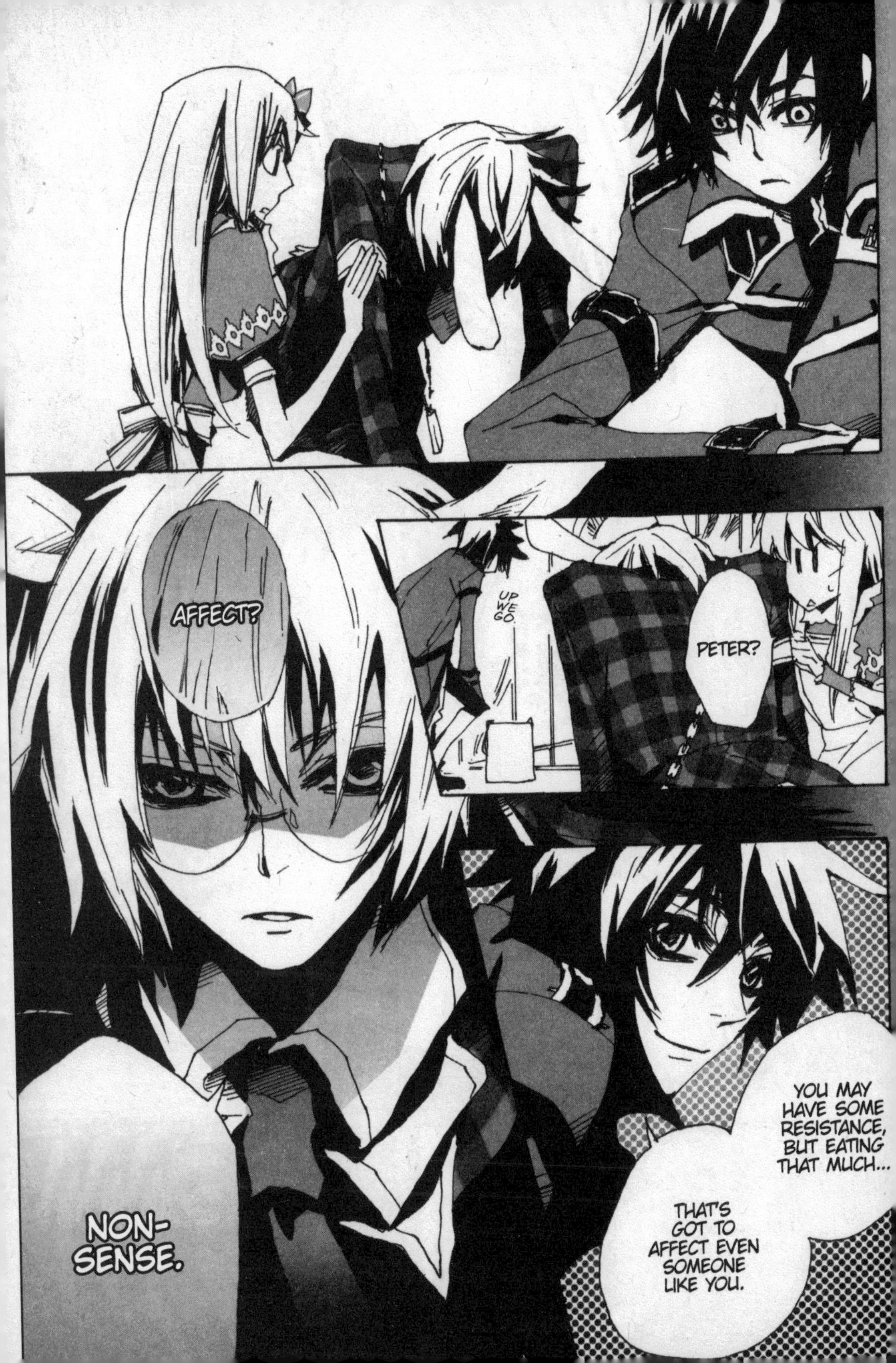
PETER?
UP WE GO.
YOU MAY HAVE SOME RESISTANCE, BUT EATING THAT MUCH...
THAT'S GOT TO AFFECT EVEN SOMEONE LIKE YOU.
AFFECT?
NON-SENSE.

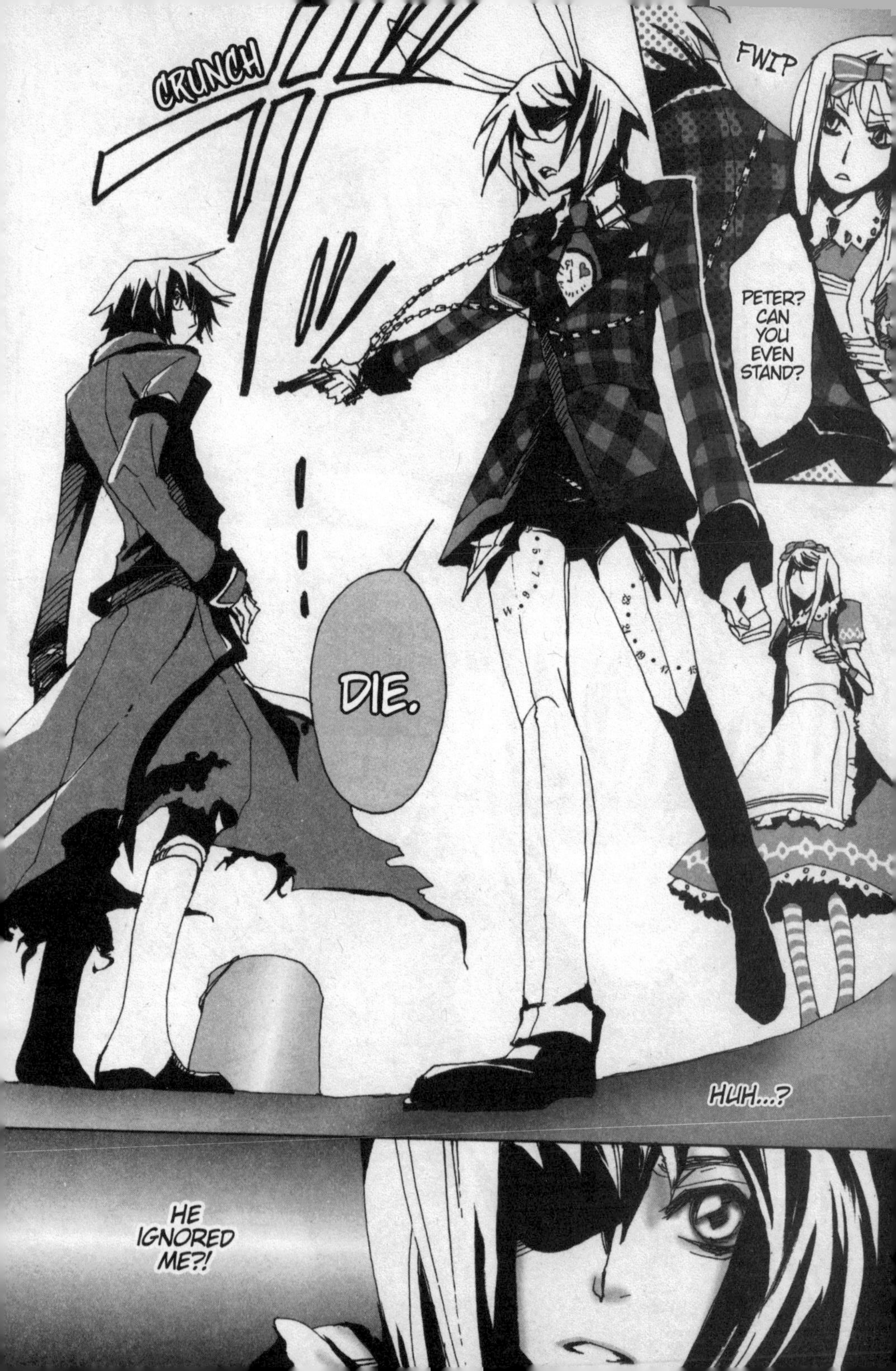
FWIP
PETER? CAN YOU EVEN STAND?
CRUNCH
DIE.
HUH...?
HE IGNORED ME?!

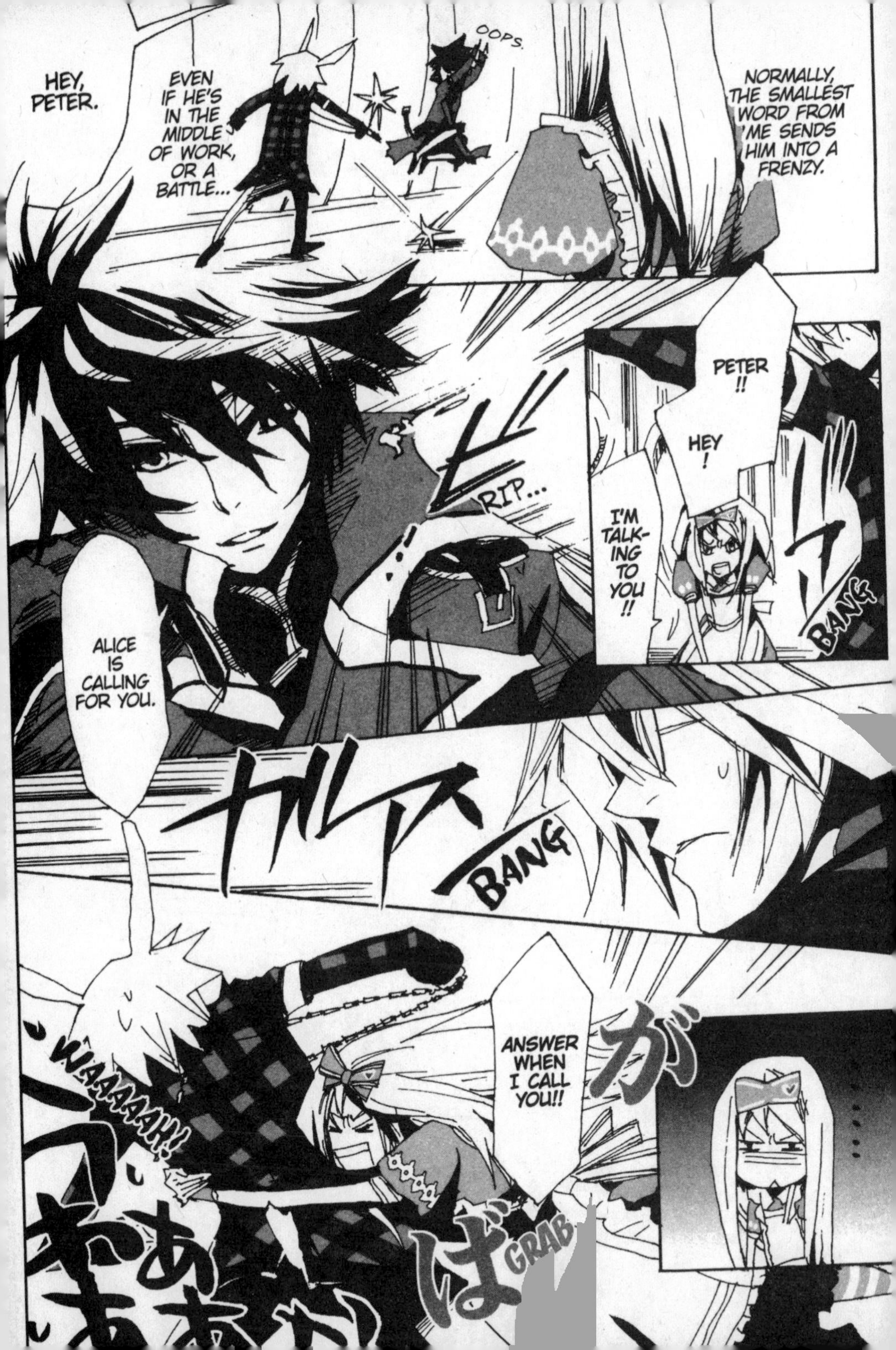

NORMALLY, THE SMALLEST WORD FROM ME SENDS HIM INTO A FRENZY.
OOPS.
EVEN IF HE'S IN THE MIDDLE OF WORK, OR A BATTLE...
HEY, PETER.
PETER!!
HEY!
I'M TALKING TO YOU!!
BANG
RIP...
ALICE IS CALLING FOR YOU.
BANG
...
ANSWER WHEN I CALL YOU!!
GRAB
WAAAAAAH!!

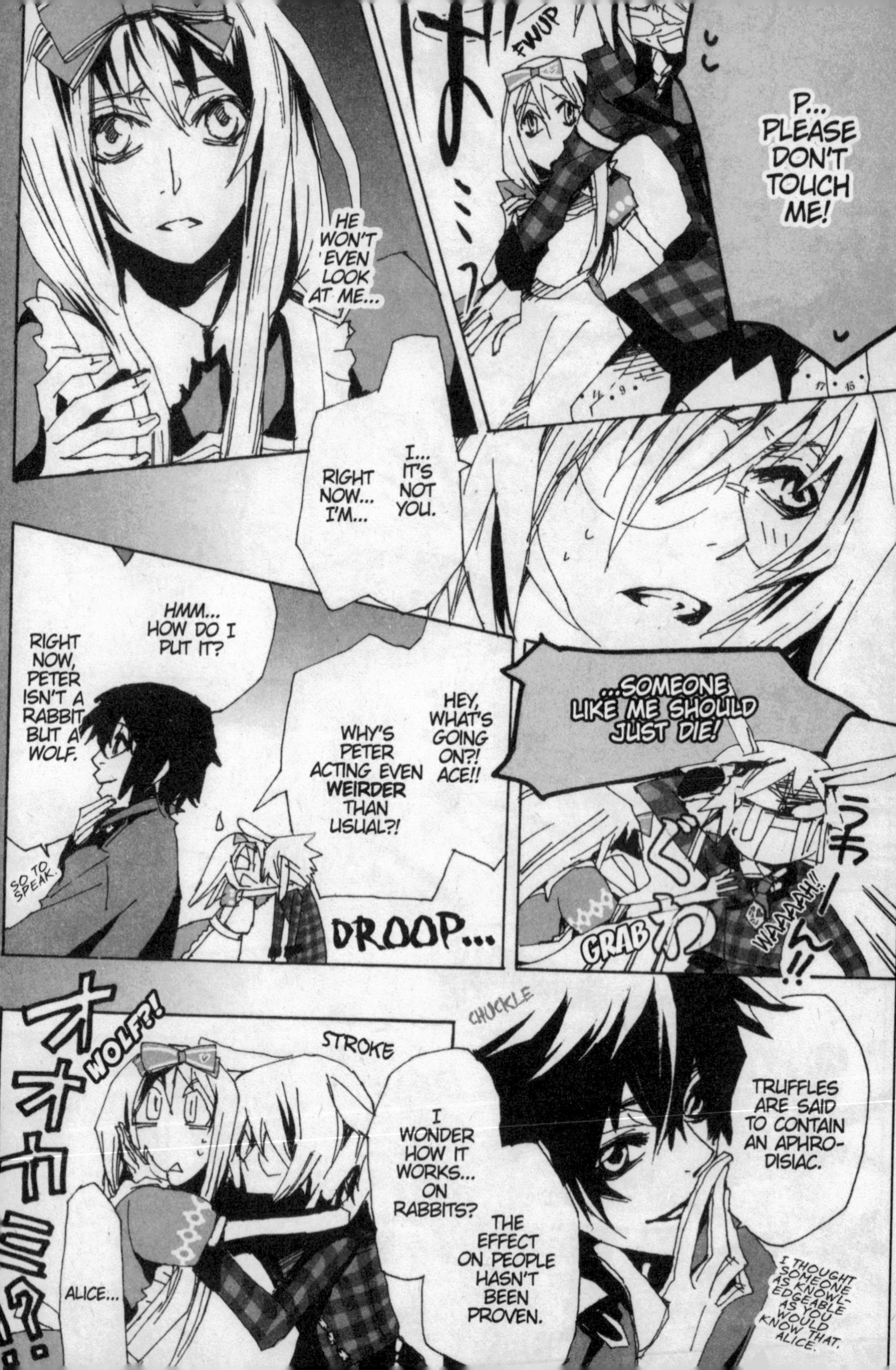
FWUP
P... PLEASE DON'T TOUCH ME!
HE WON'T EVEN LOOK AT ME...
I... IT'S NOT YOU.
RIGHT NOW... I'M...
...SOMEONE LIKE ME SHOULD JUST DIE!
GRAB
WAAAAH!!
HEY, WHAT'S GOING ON?! ACE!!
WHY'S PETER ACTING EVEN WEIRDER THAN USUAL?!
HMM... HOW DO I PUT IT?
RIGHT NOW, PETER ISN'T A RABBIT BUT A WOLF.
SO TO SPEAK.
DROOP...
CHUCKLE
TRUFFLES ARE SAID TO CONTAIN AN APHRODISIAC.
I THOUGHT SOMEONE AS KNOWLEDGEABLE AS YOU WOULD KNOW THAT, ALICE.
I WONDER HOW IT WORKS... ON RABBITS?
THE EFFECT ON PEOPLE HASN'T BEEN PROVEN.
WOLF?!
STROKE
ALICE...

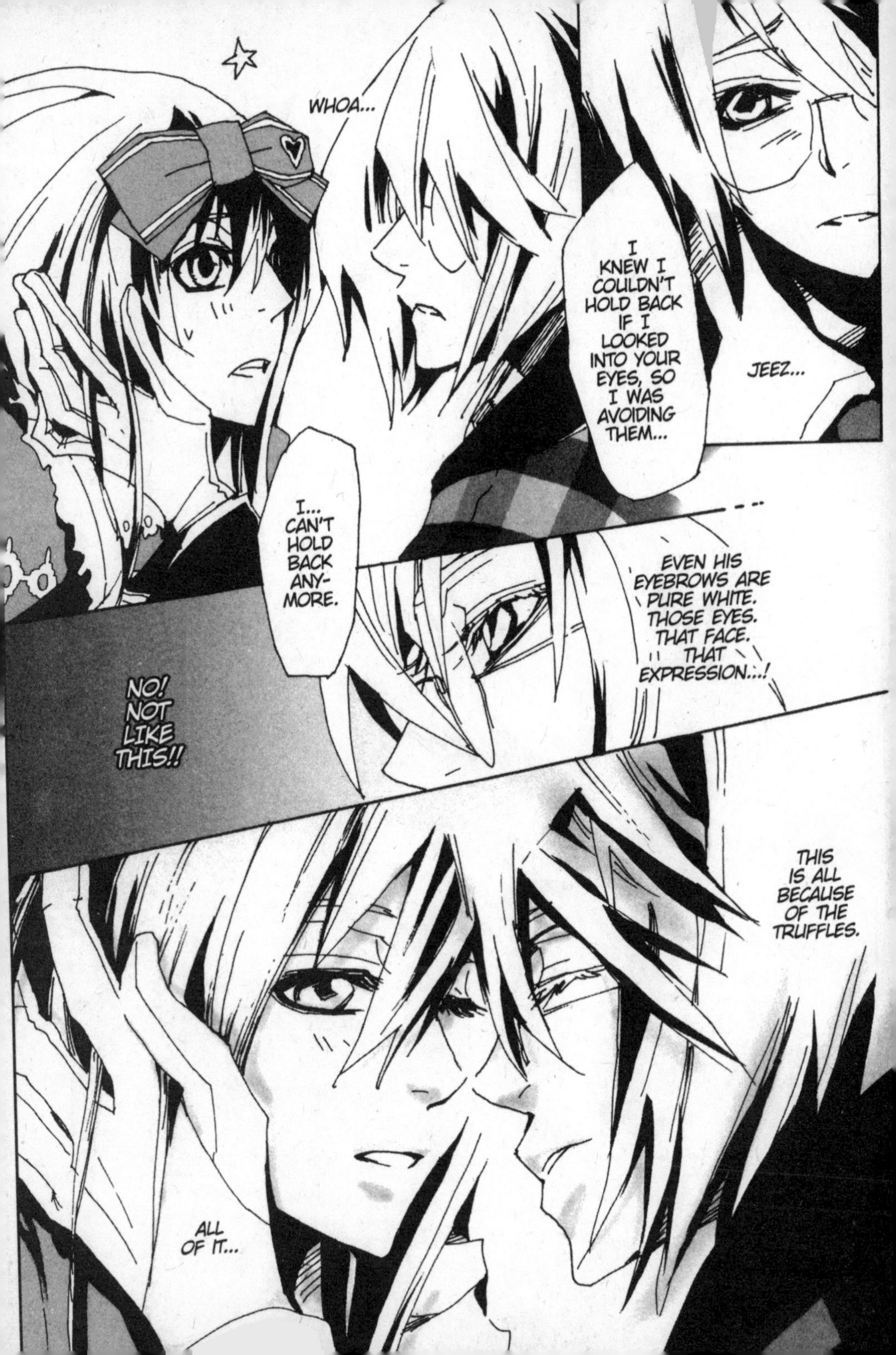
JEEZ...
WHOA...
I KNEW I COULDN'T HOLD BACK IF I LOOKED INTO YOUR EYES, SO I WAS AVOIDING THEM...
I... CAN'T HOLD BACK ANY-MORE.
EVEN HIS EYEBROWS ARE PURE WHITE. THOSE EYES. THAT FACE. THAT EXPRESSION...!
NO! NOT LIKE THIS!!
THIS IS ALL BECAUSE OF THE TRUFFLES.
ALL OF IT...

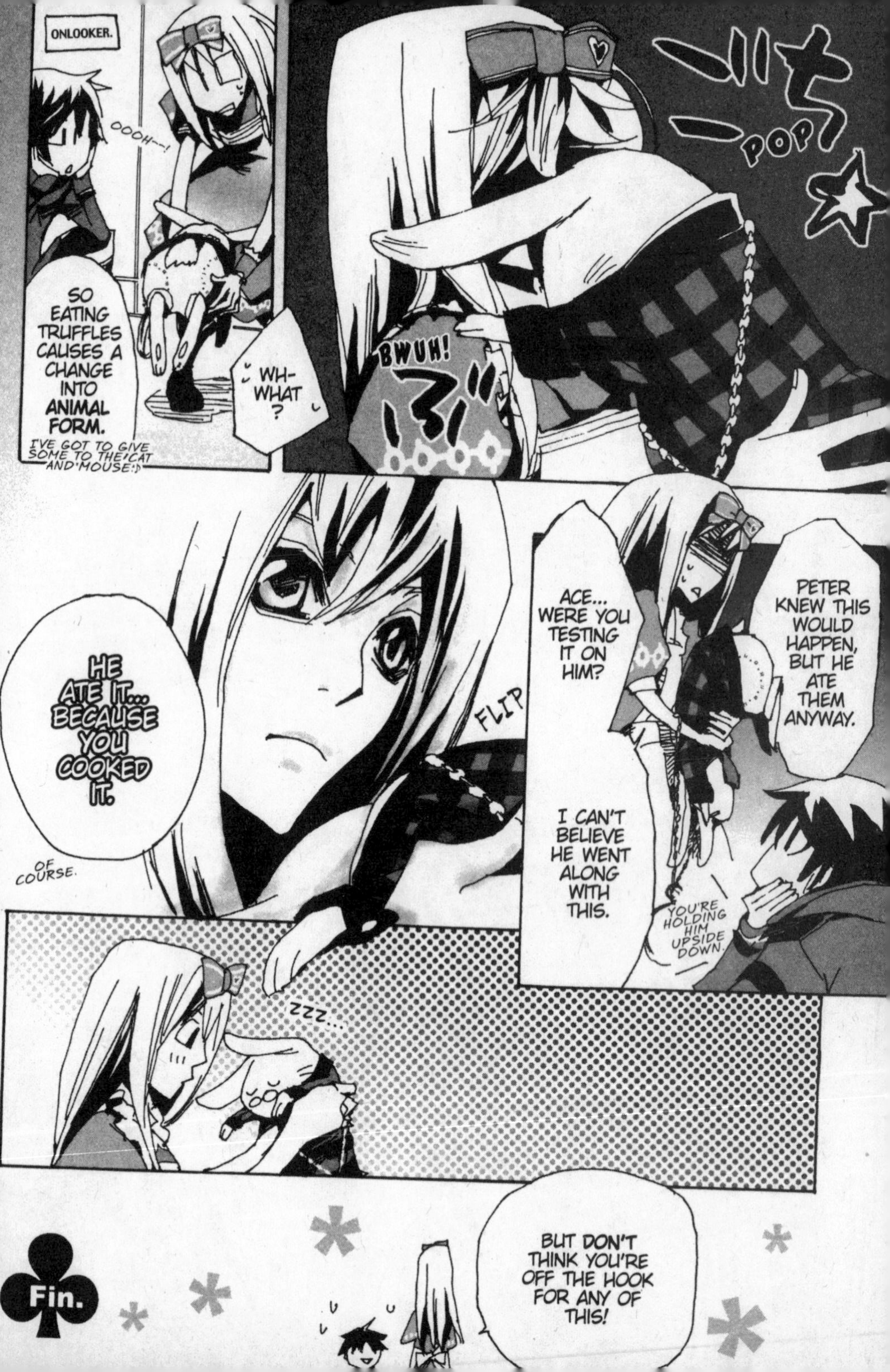

POP
BWUH!
WH-WHAT?
ONLOOKER.
OOOH~!
SO EATING TRUFFLES CAUSES A CHANGE INTO **ANIMAL FORM.**
I'VE GOT TO GIVE SOME TO THE CAT AND MOUSE! :)
PETER KNEW THIS WOULD HAPPEN, BUT HE ATE THEM ANYWAY.
ACE... WERE YOU TESTING IT ON HIM?
I CAN'T BELIEVE HE WENT ALONG WITH THIS.
YOU'RE HOLDING HIM UPSIDE DOWN.
FLIP
HE ATE IT... BECAUSE YOU COOKED IT.
OF COURSE.
ZZZ...
BUT DON'T THINK YOU'RE OFF THE HOOK FOR ANY OF THIS!
Fin.

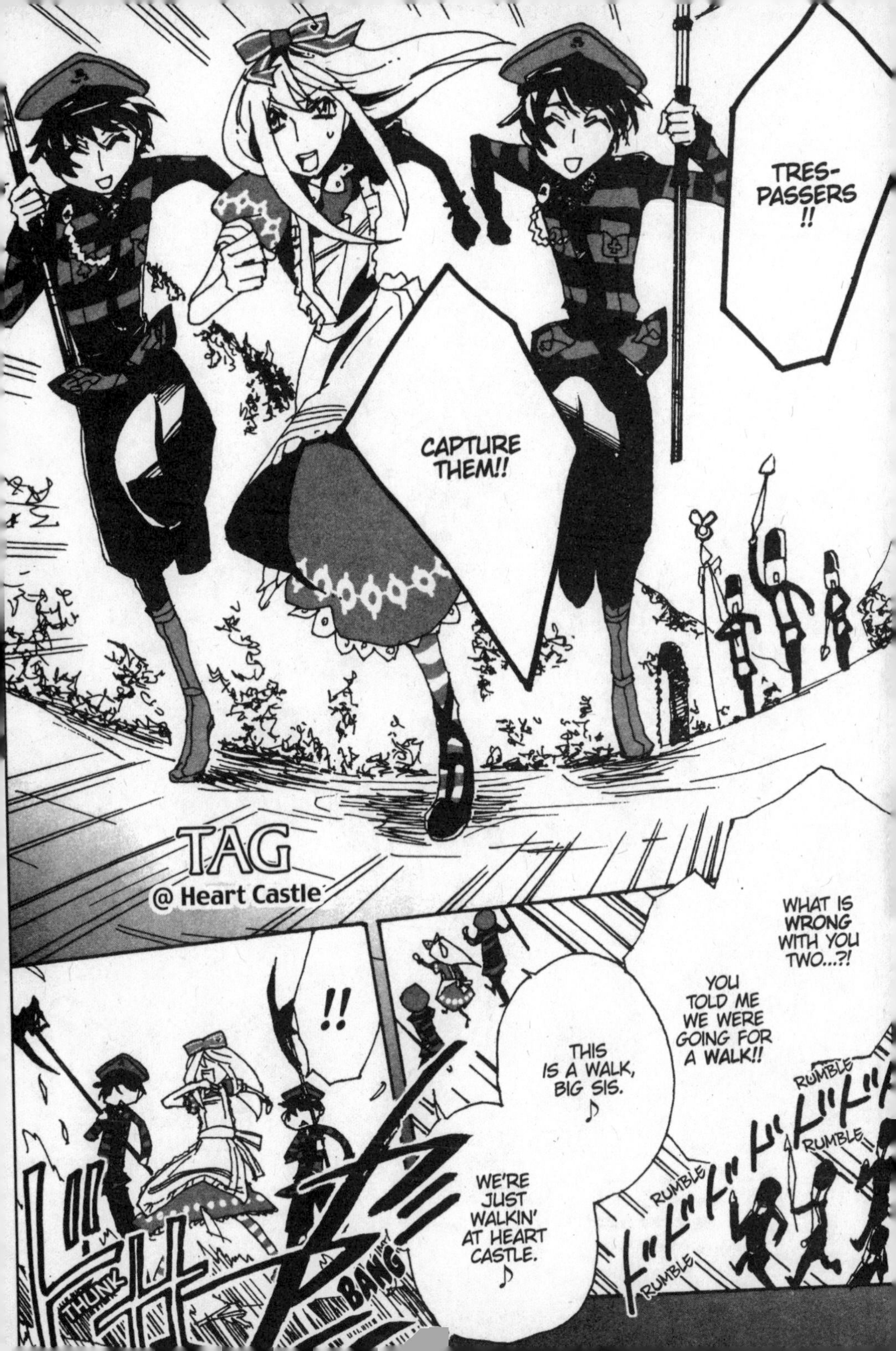
TRES-PASSERS!!
CAPTURE THEM!!
TAG
@ Heart Castle
WHAT IS WRONG WITH YOU TWO...?!
YOU TOLD ME WE WERE GOING FOR A WALK!!
RUMBLE
RUMBLE
RUMBLE
RUMBLE
THIS IS A WALK, BIG SIS. ♪
WE'RE JUST WALKIN' AT HEART CASTLE. ♪
!!
BANG
THUNK

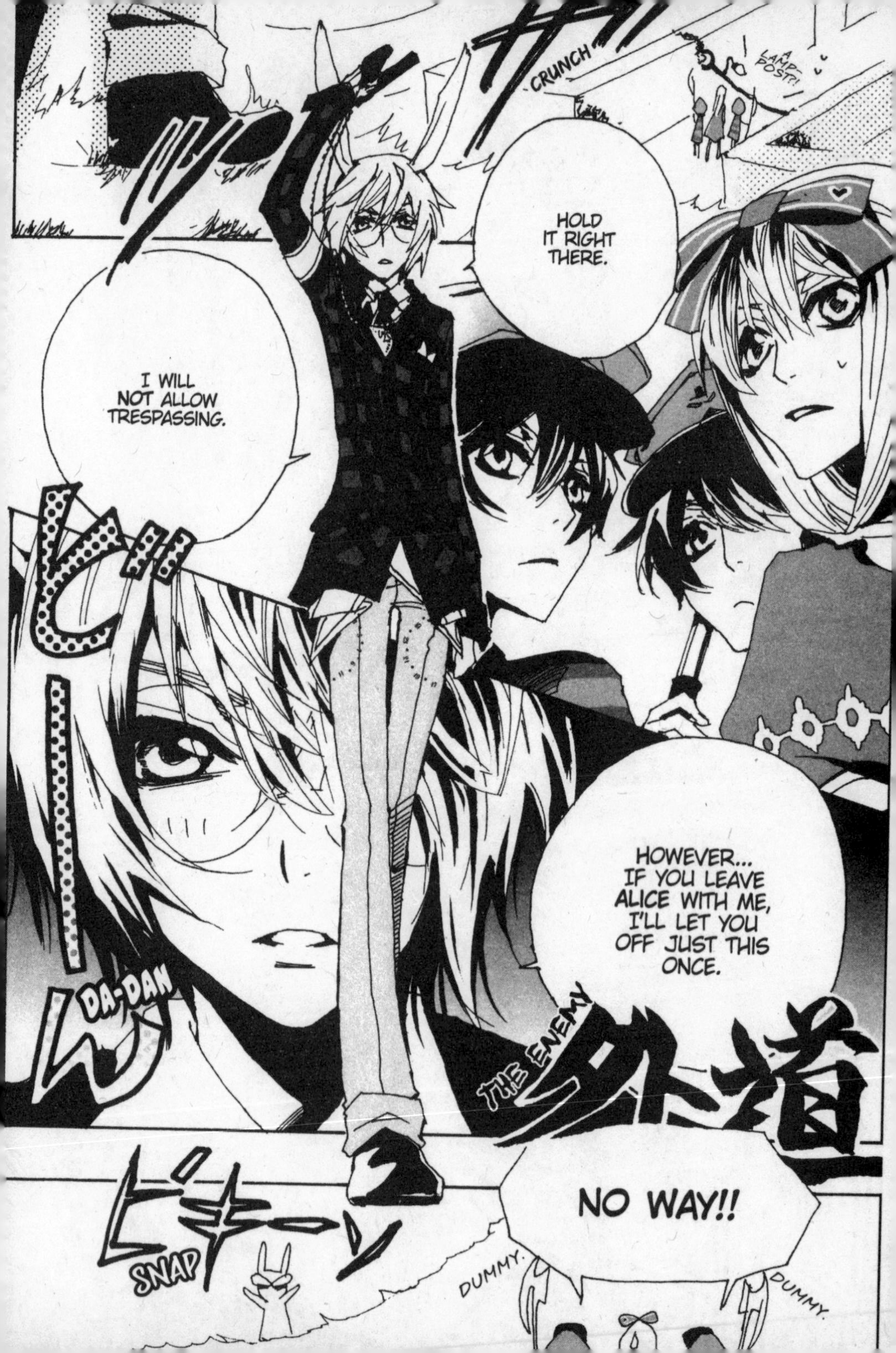
A LAMP-POST!?
CRUNCH
HOLD IT RIGHT THERE.
I WILL NOT ALLOW TRESPASSING.
HOWEVER... IF YOU LEAVE ALICE WITH ME, I'LL LET YOU OFF JUST THIS ONCE.
THE ENEMY
DA-DAN
DUMMY.
NO WAY!!
DUMMY.
SNAP

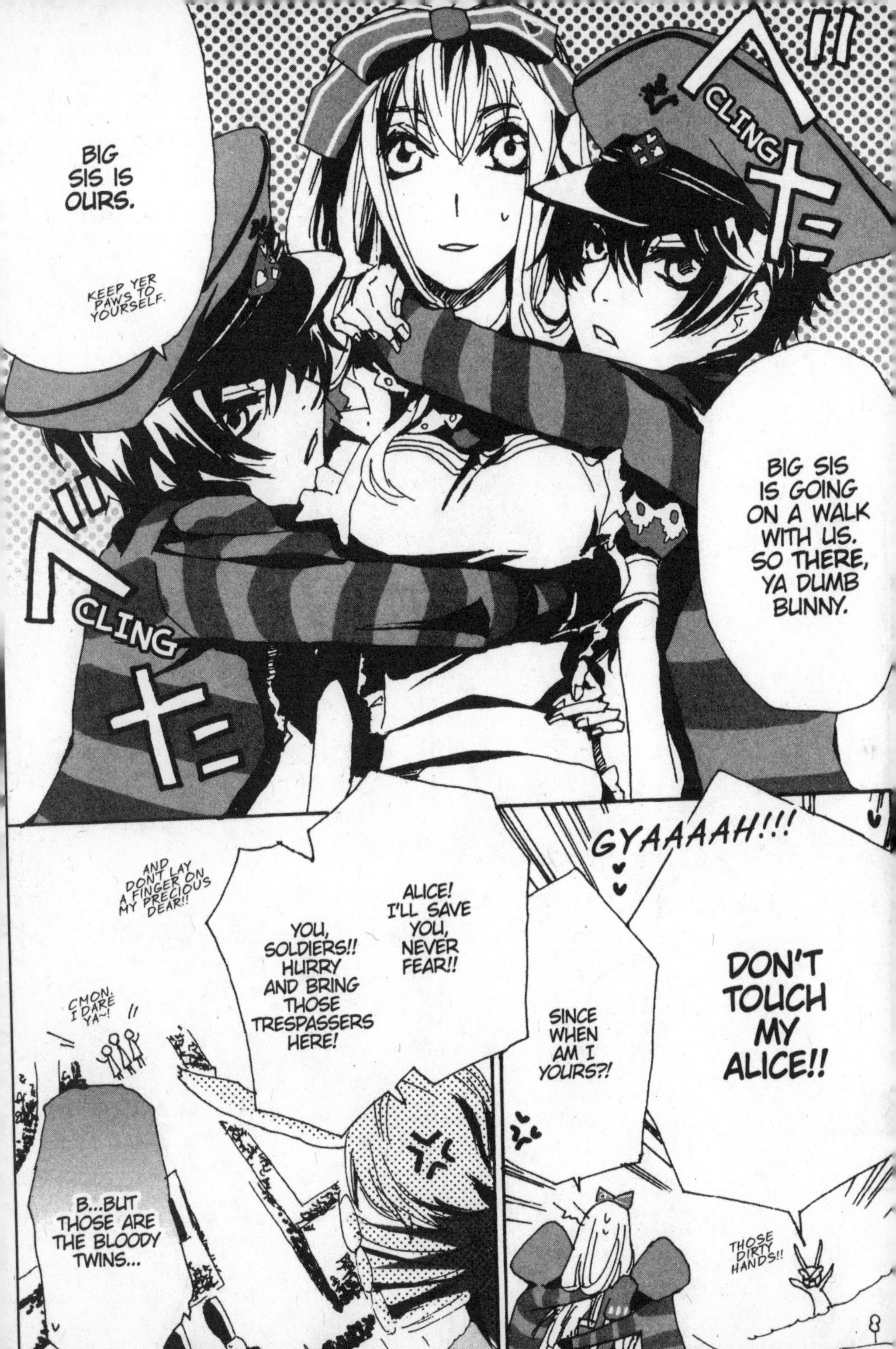
CLING
BIG SIS IS GOING ON A WALK WITH US. SO THERE, YA DUMB BUNNY.
BIG SIS IS OURS.
KEEP YER PAWS TO YOURSELF.
CLING
GYAAAAH!!!
DON'T TOUCH MY ALICE!!
THOSE DIRTY HANDS!!
SINCE WHEN AM I YOURS?!
ALICE! I'LL SAVE YOU, NEVER FEAR!!
YOU, SOLDIERS!! HURRY AND BRING THOSE TRESPASSERS HERE!
AND DON'T LAY A FINGER ON MY PRECIOUS DEAR!!
C'MON, I DARE YA~!
B...BUT THOSE ARE THE BLOODY TWINS...

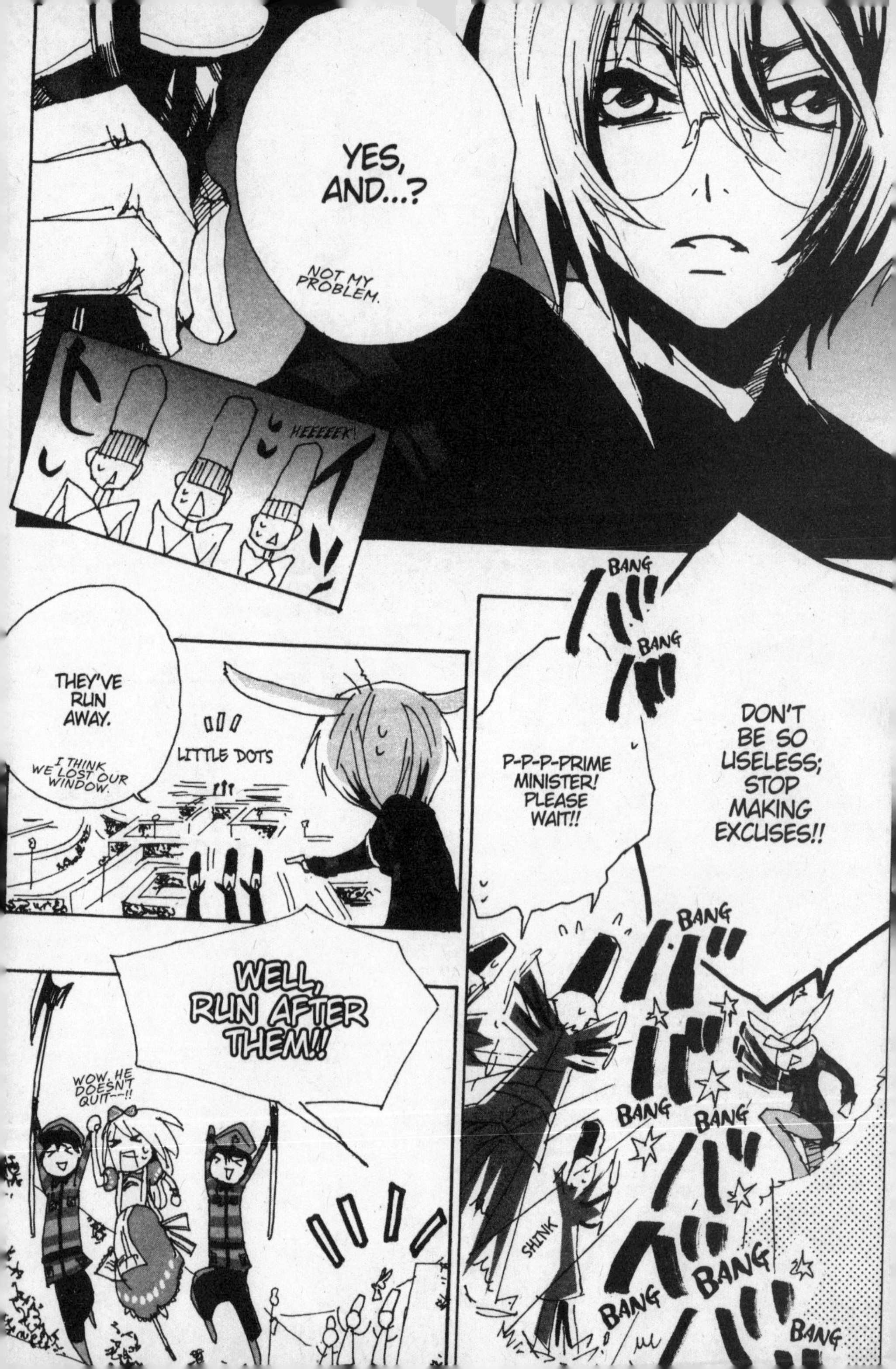
YES, AND...?
NOT MY PROBLEM.
HEEEEEK!
THEY'VE RUN AWAY.
I THINK WE LOST OUR WINDOW.
LITTLE DOTS
WELL, RUN AFTER THEM!!
WOW, HE DOESN'T QUIT--!!
BANG
BANG
DON'T BE SO USELESS; STOP MAKING EXCUSES!!
P-P-P-PRIME MINISTER! PLEASE WAIT!!
BANG
BANG
BANG
SHINK
BANG
BANG
BANG
BANG

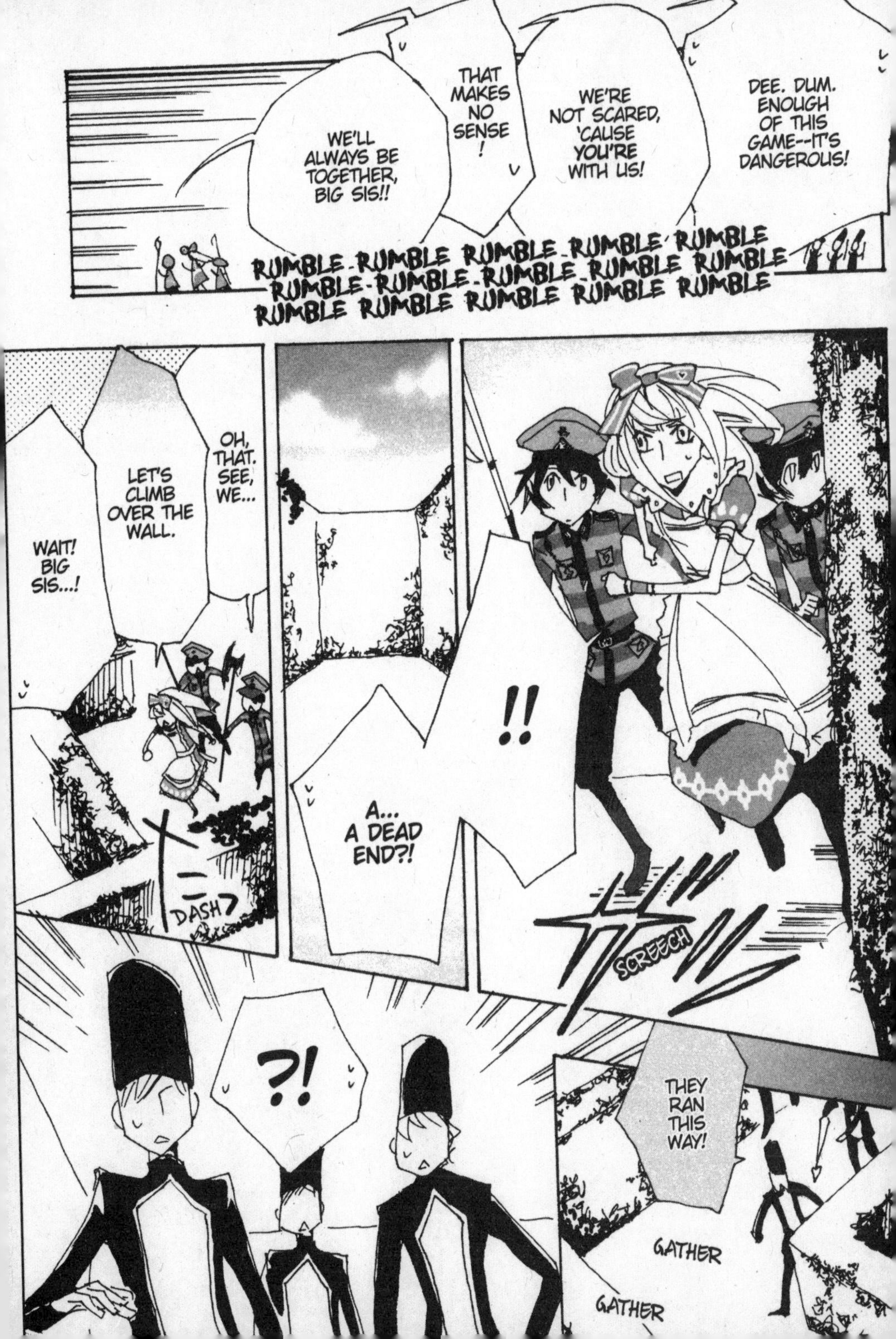
DEE. DUM. ENOUGH OF THIS GAME--IT'S DANGEROUS!
WE'RE NOT SCARED, 'CAUSE YOU'RE WITH US!
THAT MAKES NO SENSE!
WE'LL ALWAYS BE TOGETHER, BIG SIS!!
RUMBLE-RUMBLE RUMBLE-RUMBLE RUMBLE RUMBLE-RUMBLE-RUMBLE-RUMBLE RUMBLE RUMBLE RUMBLE RUMBLE RUMBLE RUMBLE RUMBLE
!!
A... A DEAD END?!
SCREECH
OH, THAT. SEE, WE...
LET'S CLIMB OVER THE WALL.
WAIT! BIG SIS...!
DASH
THEY RAN THIS WAY!
GATHER
GATHER
?!

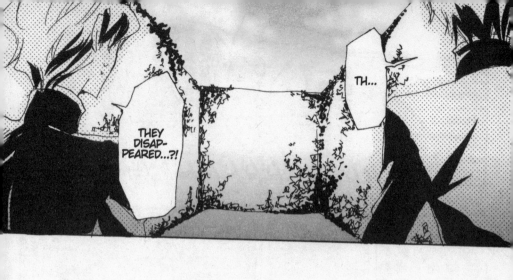

TH...

THEY DISAP- PEARED...?!

?!!

UNH...

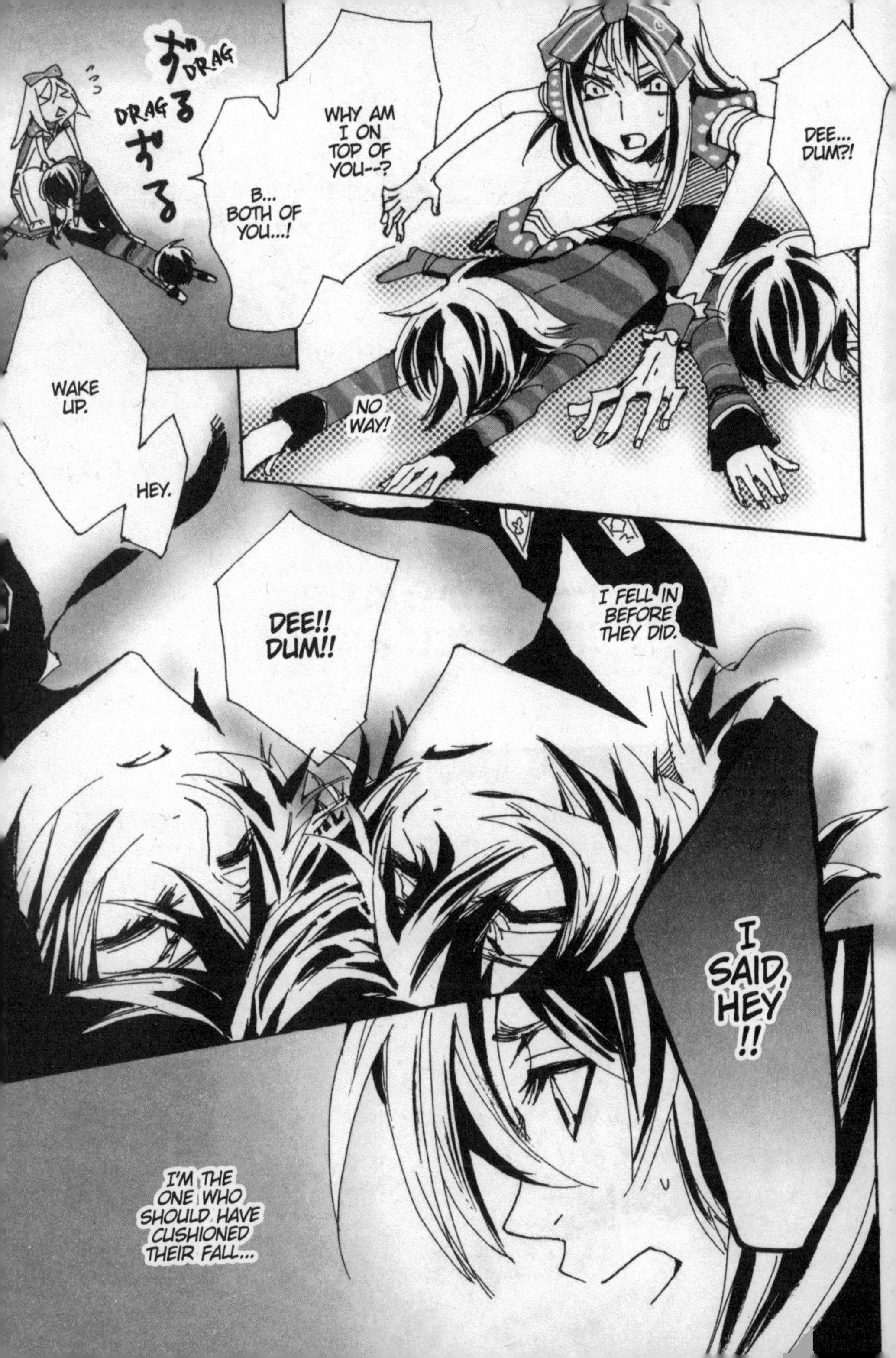
DEE... DUM?!
WHY AM I ON TOP OF YOU--?
B... BOTH OF YOU...!
NO WAY!
ずDRAG るDRAG ずる
I FELL IN BEFORE THEY DID.
DEE!! DUM!!
WAKE UP.
HEY.
I SAID, HEY!!
I'M THE ONE WHO SHOULD HAVE CUSHIONED THEIR FALL...

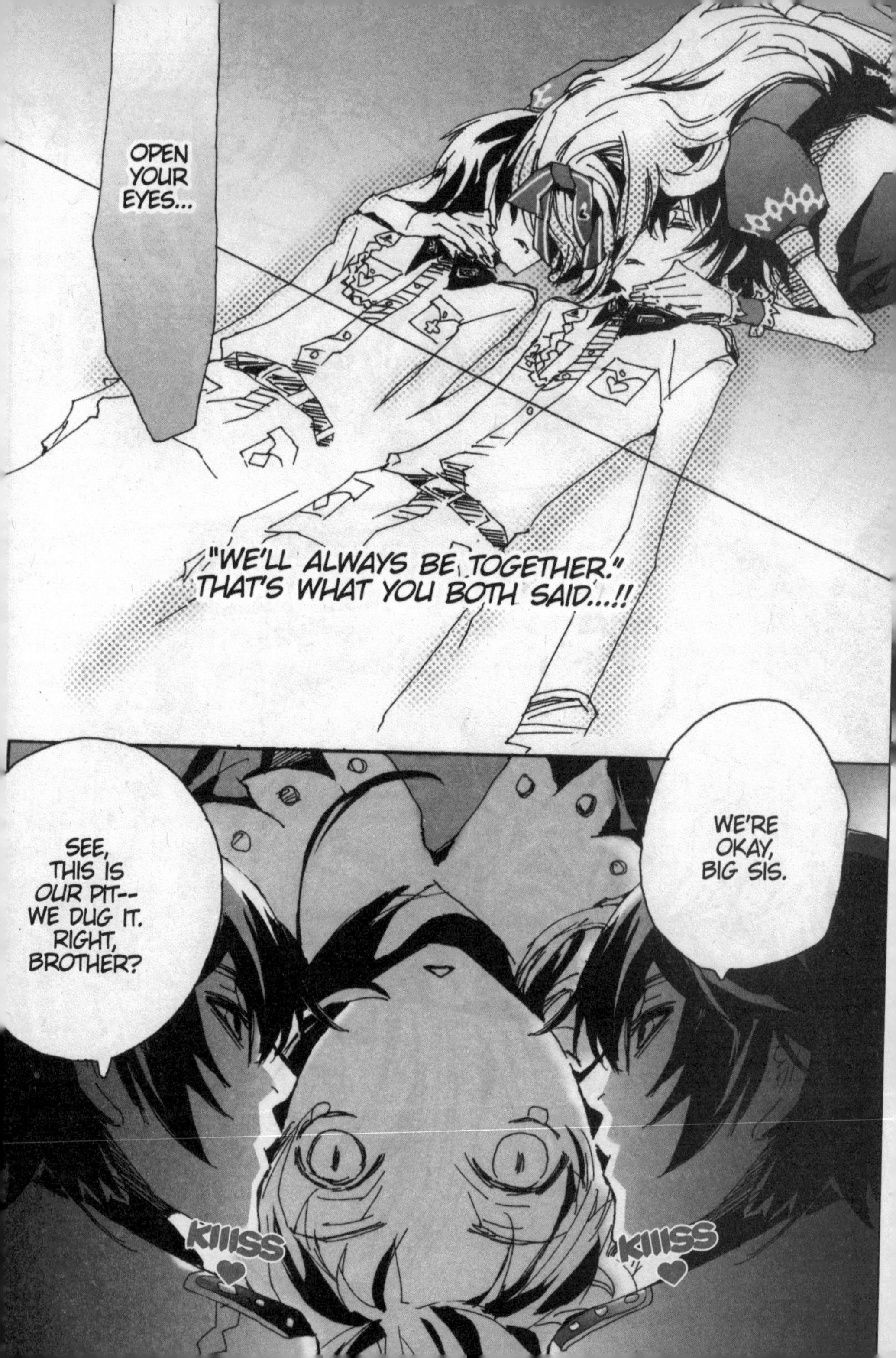
OPEN YOUR EYES...
"WE'LL ALWAYS BE TOGETHER." THAT'S WHAT YOU BOTH SAID...!!
WE'RE OKAY, BIG SIS.
SEE, THIS IS OUR PIT-- WE DUG IT. RIGHT, BROTHER?
KIIISS ♥
KIIISS ♥

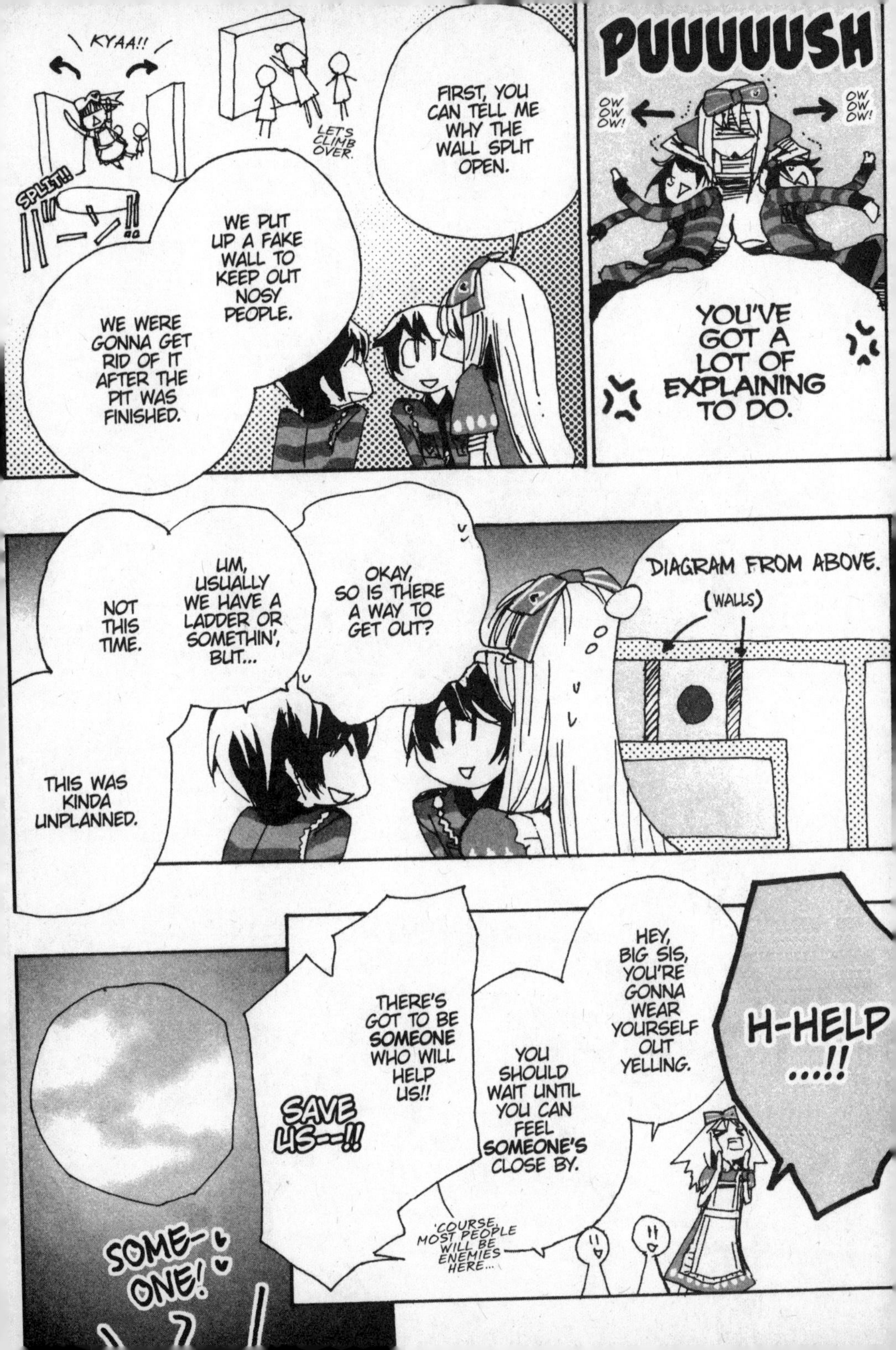
PUUUUUSH
OW OW OW!
OW OW OW!
YOU'VE GOT A LOT OF EXPLAINING TO DO.
FIRST, YOU CAN TELL ME WHY THE WALL SPLIT OPEN.
WE PUT UP A FAKE WALL TO KEEP OUT NOSY PEOPLE.
WE WERE GONNA GET RID OF IT AFTER THE PIT WAS FINISHED.
LET'S CLIMB OVER.
KYAA!!
SPLIT!!
DIAGRAM FROM ABOVE.
(WALLS)
OKAY, SO IS THERE A WAY TO GET OUT?
UM, USUALLY WE HAVE A LADDER OR SOMETHIN', BUT...
NOT THIS TIME.
THIS WAS KINDA UNPLANNED.
H-HELP ...!!
HEY, BIG SIS, YOU'RE GONNA WEAR YOURSELF OUT YELLING.
YOU SHOULD WAIT UNTIL YOU CAN FEEL SOMEONE'S CLOSE BY.
'COURSE, MOST PEOPLE WILL BE ENEMIES HERE...
THERE'S GOT TO BE SOMEONE WHO WILL HELP US!!
SAVE US--!!
SOME-ONE!

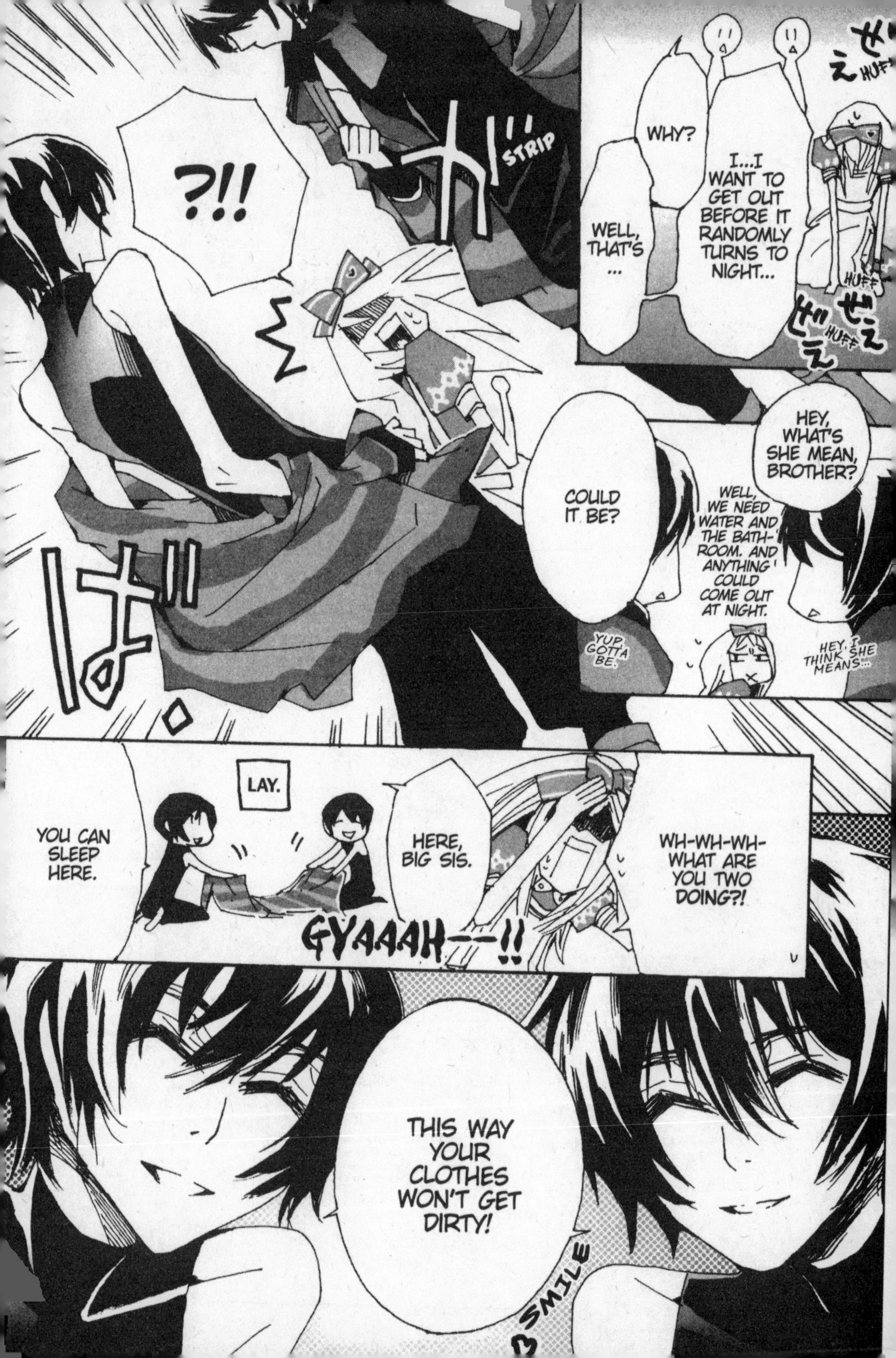
ぜえ
HUFF
WHY?
I...I WANT TO GET OUT BEFORE IT RANDOMLY TURNS TO NIGHT...
WELL, THAT'S ...
HUFF
ぜえ
HUFF
ぜえ
HEY, WHAT'S SHE MEAN, BROTHER?
WELL, WE NEED WATER AND THE BATH-ROOM. AND ANYTHING COULD COME OUT AT NIGHT.
COULD IT BE?
HEY, I THINK SHE MEANS...
YUP, GOTTA BE.
STRIP
?!!
WH-WH-WH-WHAT ARE YOU TWO DOING?!
HERE, BIG SIS.
LAY.
YOU CAN SLEEP HERE.
GYAAAH--!!
THIS WAY YOUR CLOTHES WON'T GET DIRTY!
SMILE

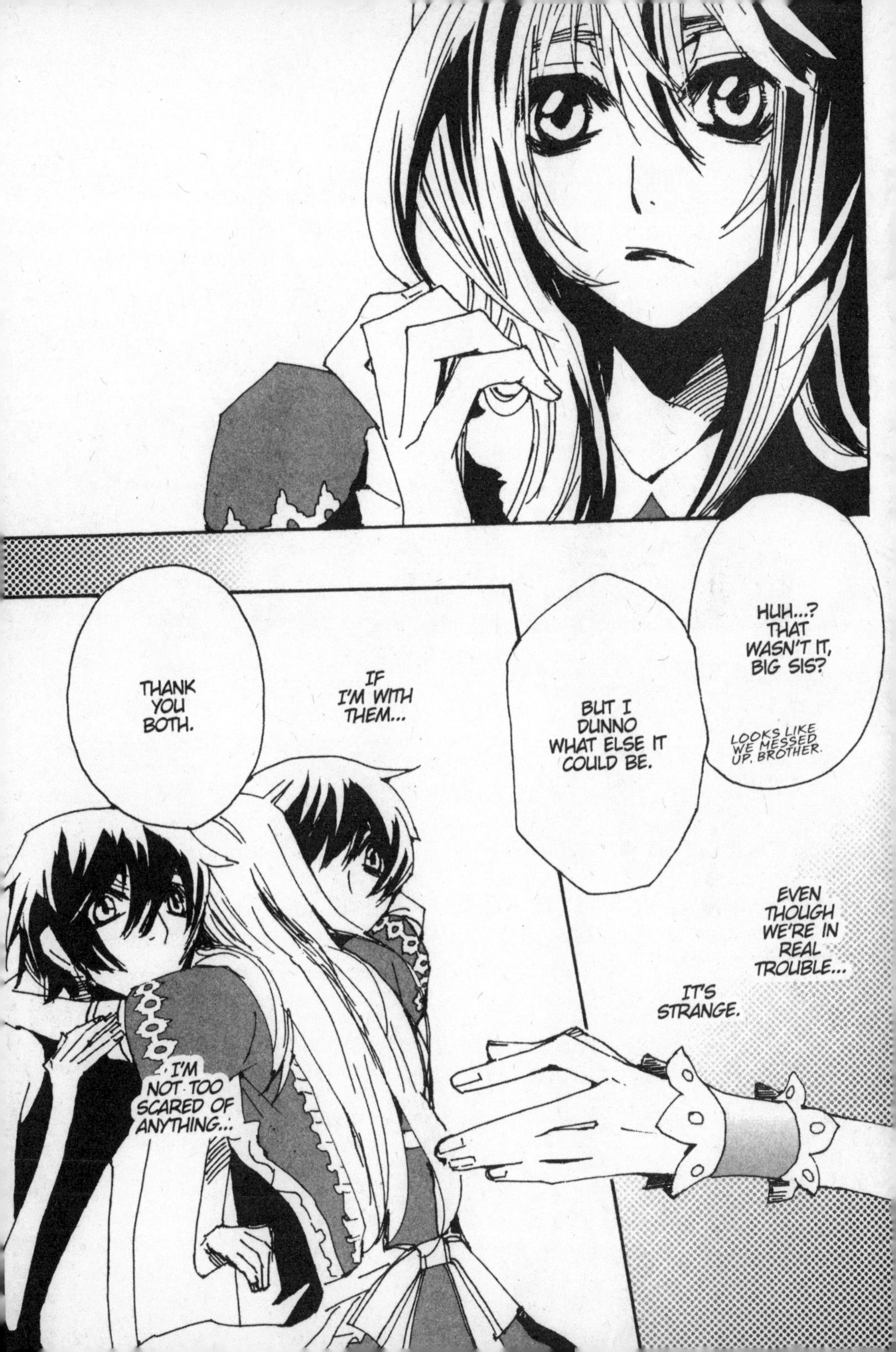
HUH...? THAT WASN'T IT, BIG SIS?
LOOKS LIKE WE MESSED UP, BROTHER.
BUT I DUNNO WHAT ELSE IT COULD BE.
EVEN THOUGH WE'RE IN REAL TROUBLE...
IT'S STRANGE.
IF I'M WITH THEM...
I'M NOT TOO SCARED OF ANYTHING...
THANK YOU BOTH.

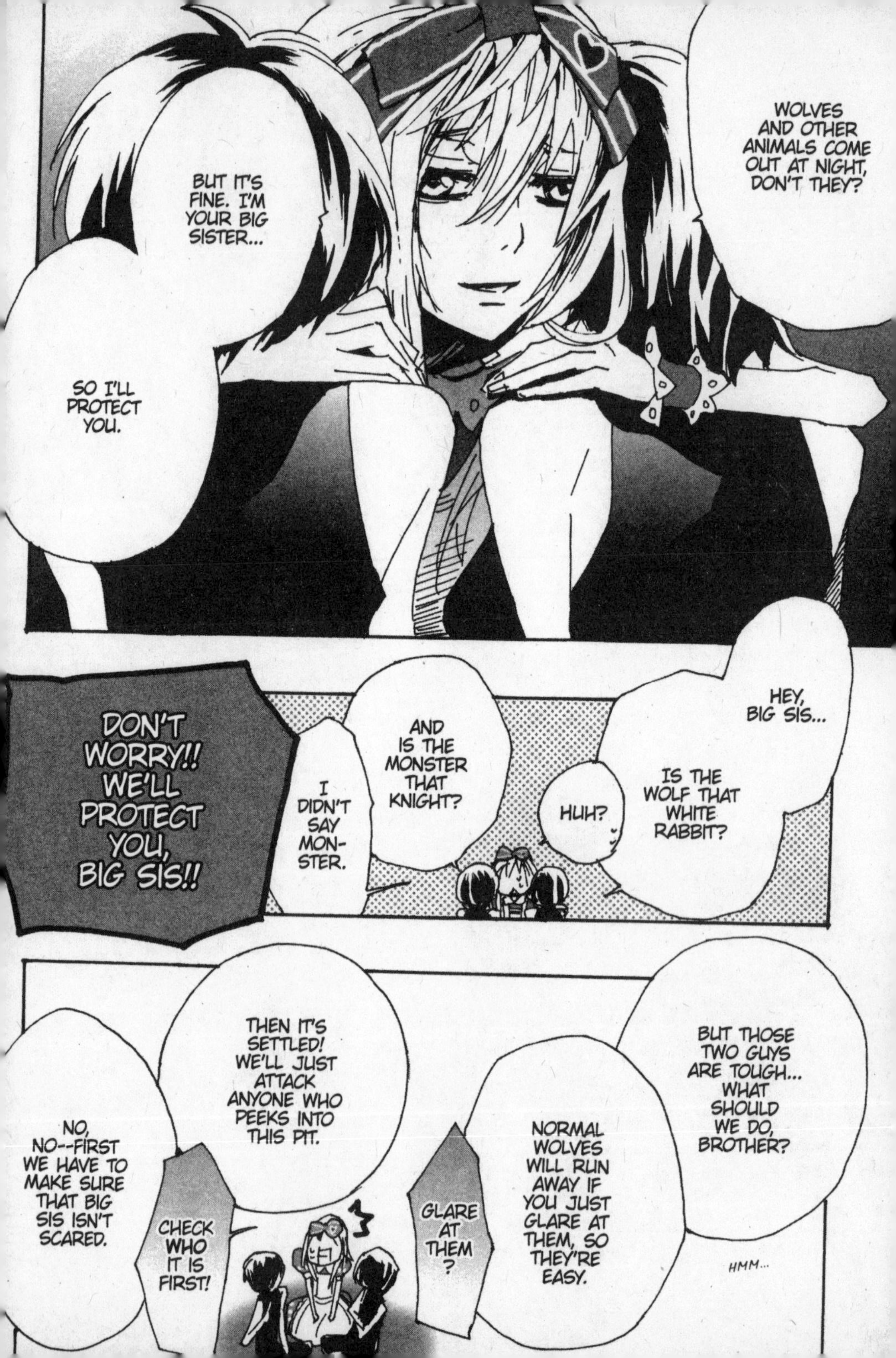

WOLVES AND OTHER ANIMALS COME OUT AT NIGHT, DON'T THEY?
BUT IT'S FINE. I'M YOUR BIG SISTER...
SO I'LL PROTECT YOU.
HEY, BIG SIS...
IS THE WOLF THAT WHITE RABBIT?
HUH?
AND IS THE MONSTER THAT KNIGHT?
I DIDN'T SAY MON-STER.
DON'T WORRY!! WE'LL PROTECT YOU, BIG SIS!!
BUT THOSE TWO GUYS ARE TOUGH... WHAT SHOULD WE DO, BROTHER?
HMM...
NORMAL WOLVES WILL RUN AWAY IF YOU JUST GLARE AT THEM, SO THEY'RE EASY.
GLARE AT THEM?
THEN IT'S SETTLED! WE'LL JUST ATTACK ANYONE WHO PEEKS INTO THIS PIT.
NO, NO--FIRST WE HAVE TO MAKE SURE THAT BIG SIS ISN'T SCARED.
CHECK WHO IT IS FIRST!

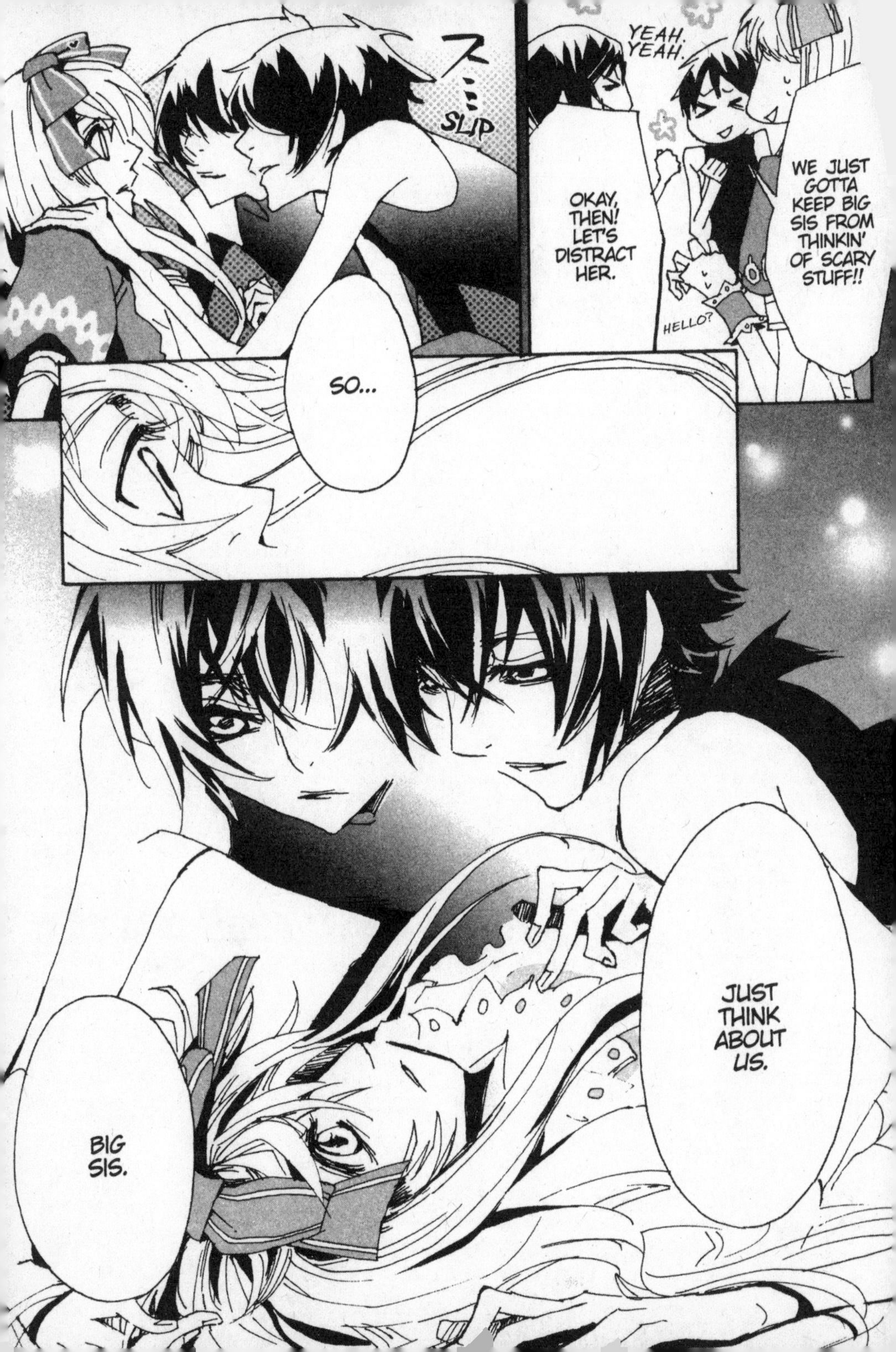
YEAH. YEAH.
WE JUST GOTTA KEEP BIG SIS FROM THINKIN' OF SCARY STUFF!!
OKAY, THEN! LET'S DISTRACT HER.
HELLO?
SLIP
SO...
JUST THINK ABOUT US.
BIG SIS.

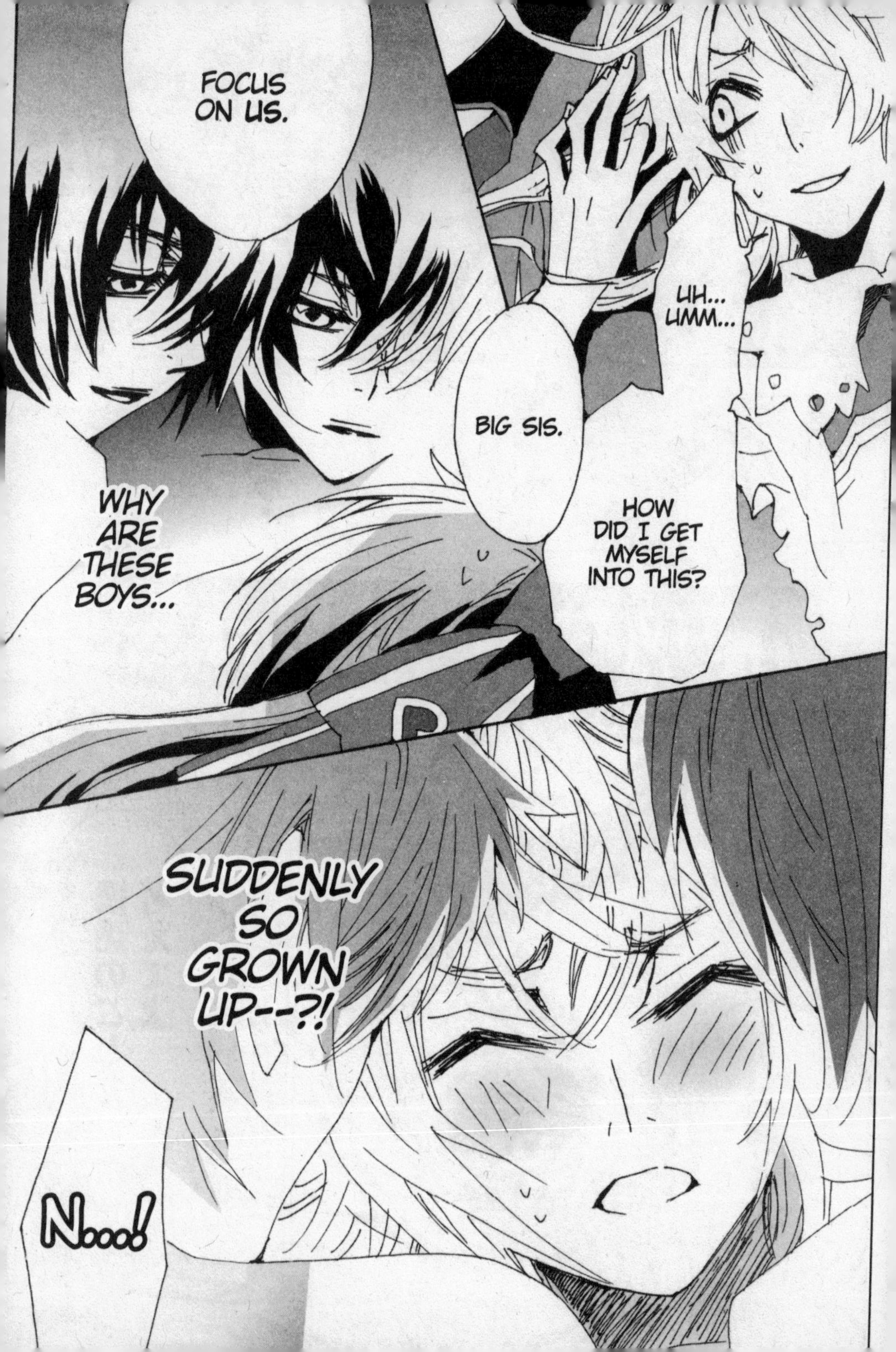
UH... UMM...
FOCUS ON US.
BIG SIS.
HOW DID I GET MYSELF INTO THIS?
WHY ARE THESE BOYS...
SUDDENLY SO GROWN UP--?!
Nooo!

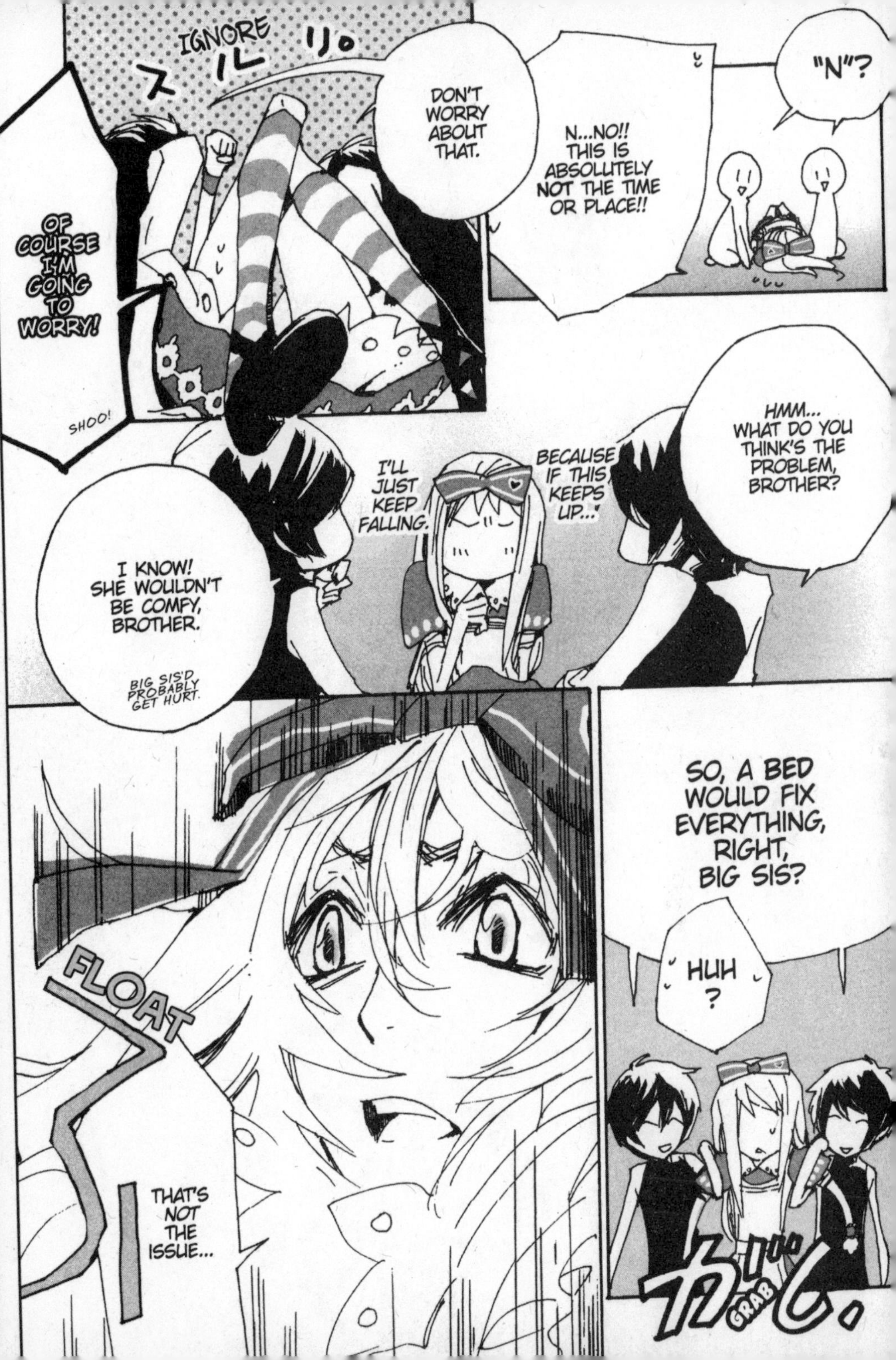
"N"?
N...NO!! THIS IS ABSOLUTELY NOT THE TIME OR PLACE!!
IGNORE
DON'T WORRY ABOUT THAT.
OF COURSE I'M GOING TO WORRY!
SHOO!
HMM... WHAT DO YOU THINK'S THE PROBLEM, BROTHER?
BECAUSE IF THIS KEEPS UP...
I'LL JUST KEEP FALLING.
I KNOW! SHE WOULDN'T BE COMFY, BROTHER.
BIG SIS'D PROBABLY GET HURT.
SO, A BED WOULD FIX EVERYTHING, RIGHT, BIG SIS?
HUH?
GRAB
FLOAT
THAT'S NOT THE ISSUE...

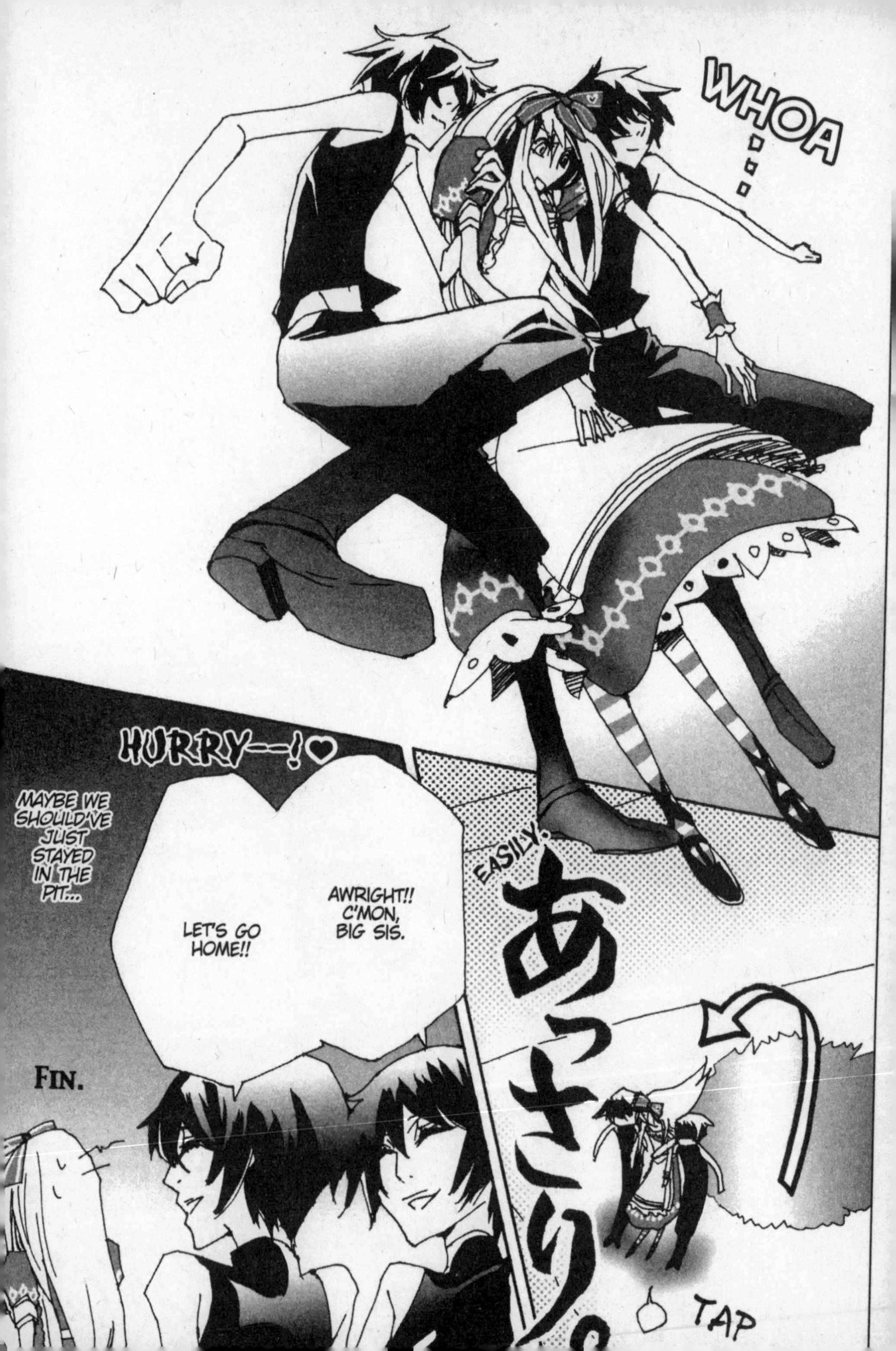
WHOA...
EASILY.
あっさり。
TAP
HURRY--!♥
AWRIGHT!! C'MON, BIG SIS.
LET'S GO HOME!!
MAYBE WE SHOULD'VE JUST STAYED IN THE PIT...
FIN.

CRIMSON ✦ EMPIRE

クリムゾン・エンパイア

~ *Circumstances to serve a noble* ~

**We devote our life proudly.
my life for you. For all you.**

Quin Rose 2008

- STORY -

The setting is a country of aristocrats: a tributary nation for Luxonne. *Crimson Empire* is a love adventure game about a maid, Sheila, who works in the luxurious royal castle. But behind the lavish façade, the castle is home to a savage—and bloody—political war.

Strong and skilled, Sheila uses her position as a maid to hide her true profession: bodyguard to Prince Edvard. Sheila carries a dark past of enslavement and murder. Now she survives day to day, with only a small wish in her heart.

While navigating the power struggle between Prince Edvard and his brother, the deceptive Prince Justin, Sheila must understand and use the dangerous people who surround her. But although a brilliant fighter and tactician, Sheila is unskilled when it comes to love and friendships. Such a gap between her power and her heart could lead to a dire ending indeed.

Crimson Empire Character Information

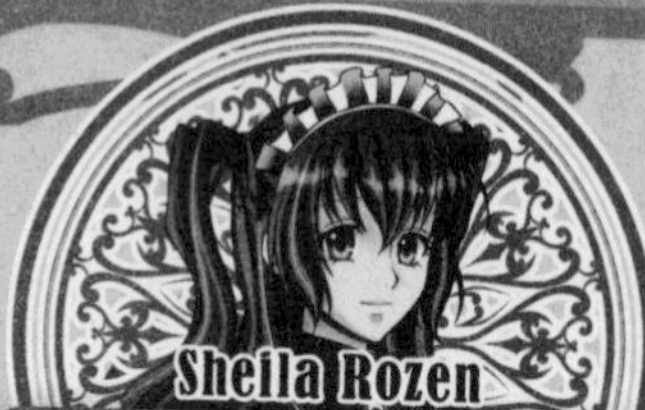

Sheila Rozen

The intensely loyal head maid to Prince Edvard—and his secret bodyguard. She's a skilled leader and shrewdly political, in addition to being fierce in combat. She doesn't hide her roots as a slave.

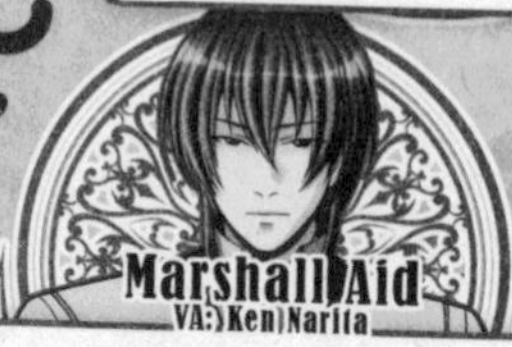

Marshall Aid
VA: Ken Narita

Prince Justin's head servant. He argues with Sheila in public but doesn't dislike her. In private, they're intimate enough to spar peacefully.

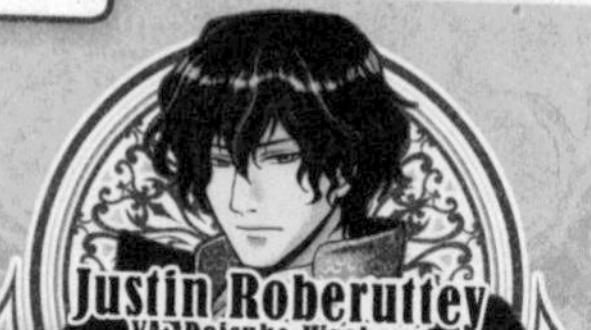

Justin Roberuttey
VA: Daisuke Hirakawa

The eldest prince, and Edvard's older half-brother. Since his mother is of lower status, Justin falls below his younger brother in line for the throne.

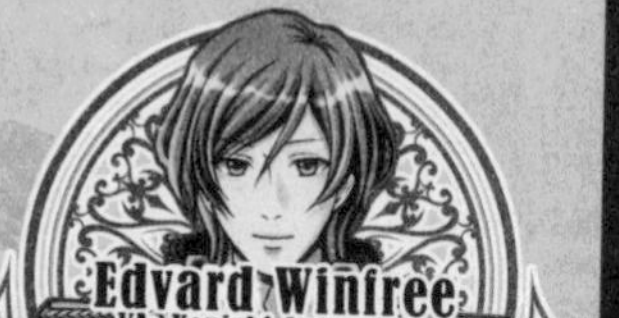

Edvard Winfree
VA: Kenichi Suzumura

Sheila's master. While friendly and regal on the surface, he's very condescending. He thinks of Sheila as more than a subordinate and loves her more than his own family... or so he *claims*.

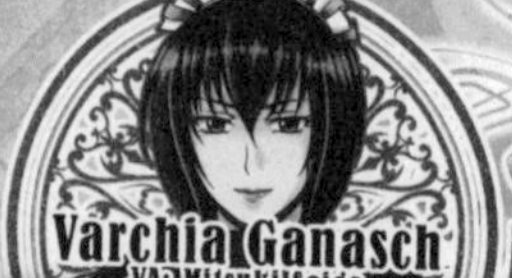

Varchia Ganasch
VA: Mitsuki Saiga

Varchia, the vice-maid, is a close friend of Sheila's, and is a former slave. Her actions and words are always painfully neutral. She's trustworthy and helps Sheila in both public and private.

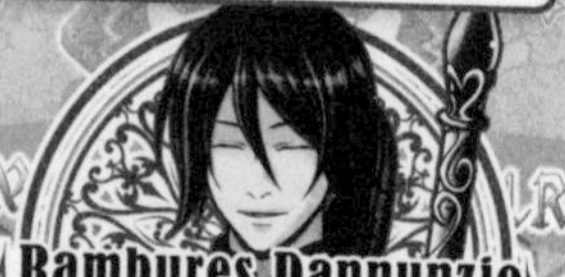

Rambures Dannunzio
VA: Taniyama Kisho

A commoner who was knighted after saving the king. He loves to lurk in his room and brew concoctions—which often stink and explode—instead of interacting with the nobility.

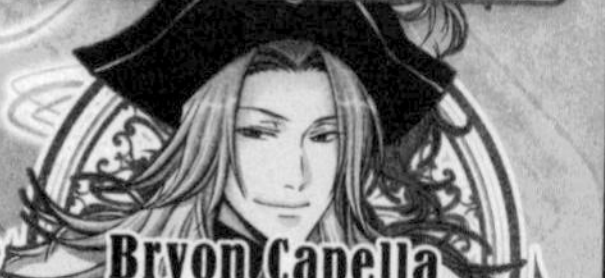

Bryon Capella
VA: Tatsuhisa Suzuki

Son of the marquis who one day will inherit the position and become an important pillar of the country. He seems cheerful and carefree, but rather guarded. Like his sister, he adores Sheila.

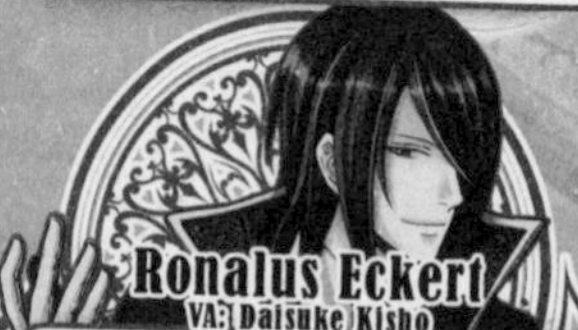

Ronalus Eckert
VA: Daisuke Kisho

Another guest in the royal castle, Ronalus is the servant to the Queen of Luxonne. Although he enjoys a higher status by serving the queen, he has a good relationship with other servants. His role is to monitor Meissen.

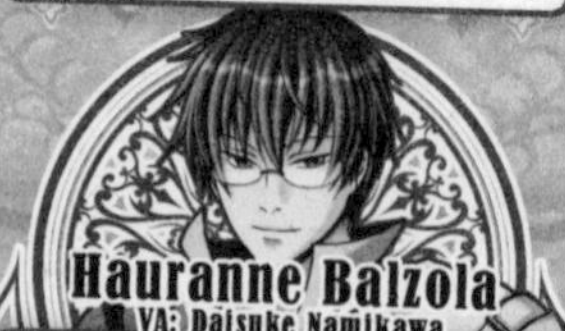

Hauranne Balzola
VA: Daisuke Namikawa

A wizard staying in the royal castle who is treated as a guest, but he's been in the castle longer than anyone. He's lived a *long* life...and his real age doesn't match his looks.

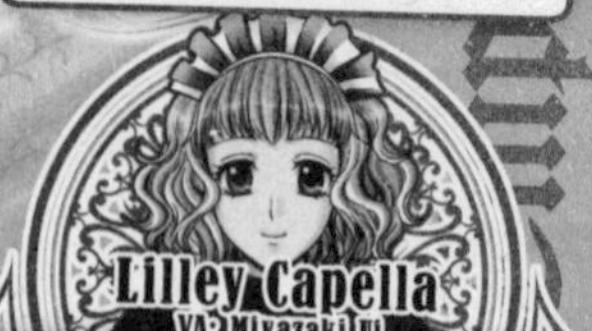

Lilley Capella
VA: Miyazaki Ui

Another battle maid, but of noble birth, Lilley is fiercely loyal to Sheila. She has innate skill, and her strength is second only to Sheila's. She and her brother Bryon are very close.

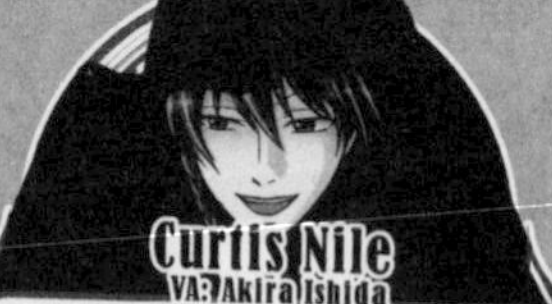

Curtis Nile
VA: Akira Ishida

A deadly assassin who specializes in poisons. He raised Sheila, and nearly killed her with his vicious training. Ever since, their relationship has been strained, to say the least.

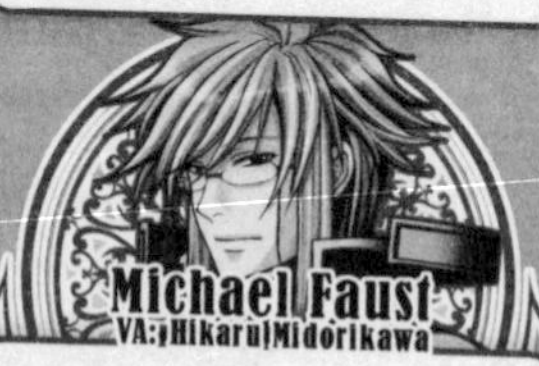

Michael Faust
VA: Hikaru Midorikawa

A demon who made a contract with Meissen. He's dangerously strong, monologues frequently, and is oddly nervous. His mental instability feeds his pessimism.

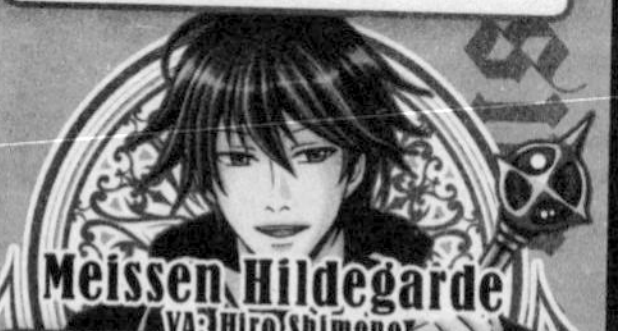

Meissen Hildegarde
VA: Hiro Shimono

Meissen has a tendency to wander, and he's traveled all over the world. His ladykiller persona hides a powerful wizard. He's searching for the truth and is trying to become a sage...supposedly.

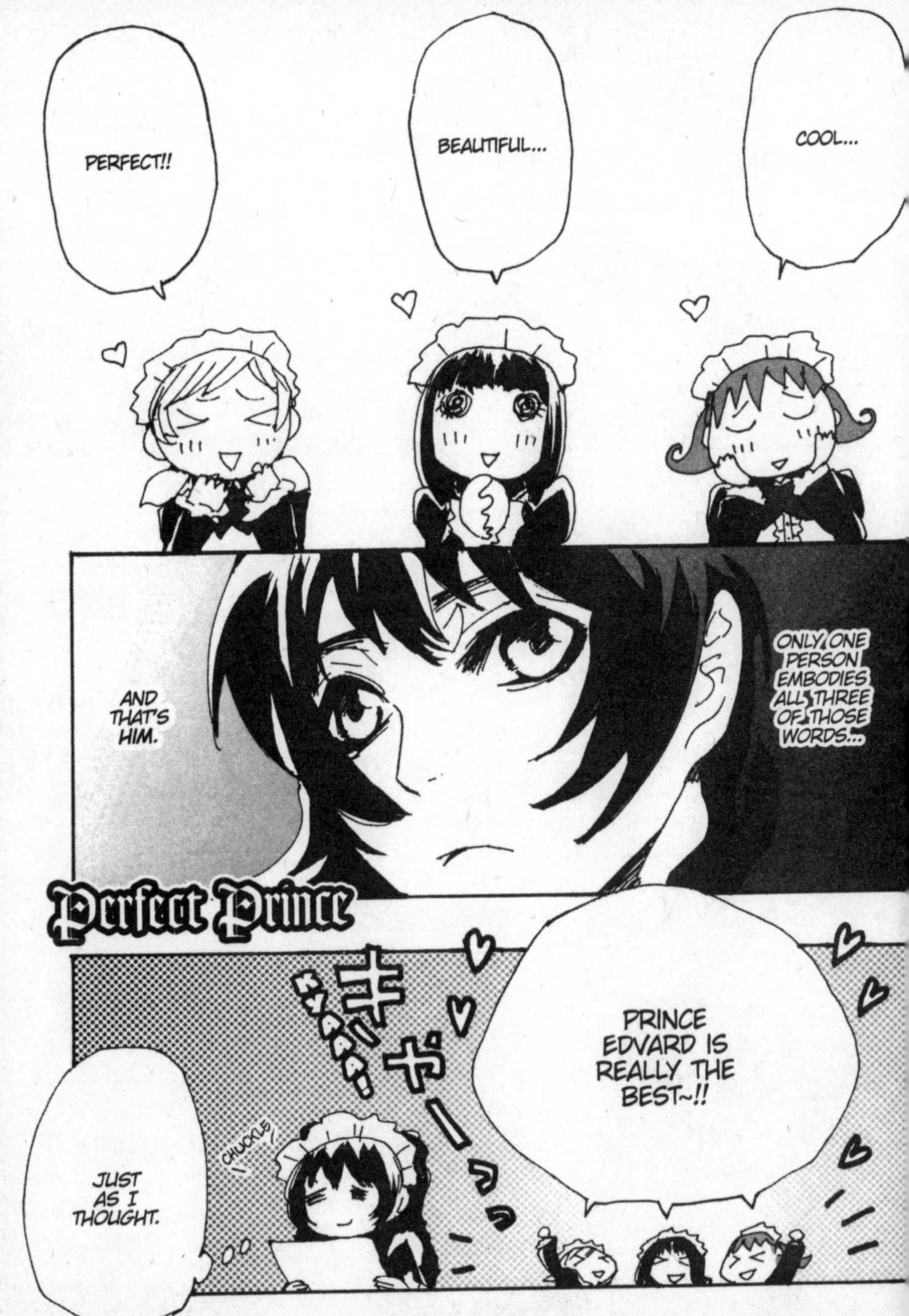
COOL...
BEAUTIFUL...
PERFECT!!
ONLY ONE PERSON EMBODIES ALL THREE OF THOSE WORDS...
AND THAT'S HIM.
Perfect Prince
PRINCE EDVARD IS REALLY THE BEST~!!
キャーッ
KYAAAA!
CHUCKLE
JUST AS I THOUGHT.

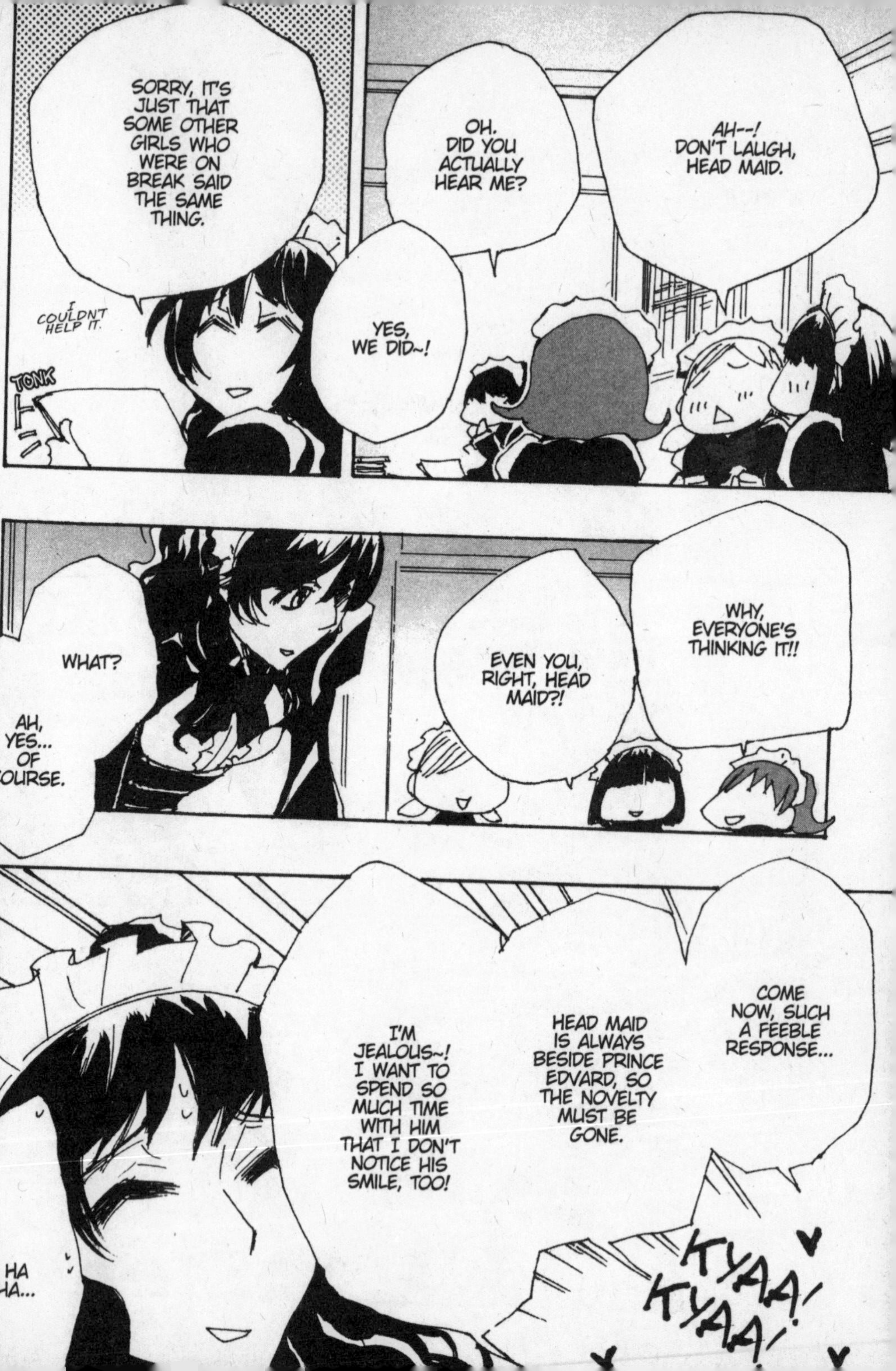
AH--! DON'T LAUGH, HEAD MAID.
OH. DID YOU ACTUALLY HEAR ME?
YES, WE DID~!
SORRY, IT'S JUST THAT SOME OTHER GIRLS WHO WERE ON BREAK SAID THE SAME THING.
I COULDN'T HELP IT.
TONK
WHY, EVERYONE'S THINKING IT!!
EVEN YOU, RIGHT, HEAD MAID?!
WHAT?
AH, YES... OF COURSE.
COME NOW, SUCH A FEEBLE RESPONSE...
HEAD MAID IS ALWAYS BESIDE PRINCE EDVARD, SO THE NOVELTY MUST BE GONE.
I'M JEALOUS~! I WANT TO SPEND SO MUCH TIME WITH HIM THAT I DON'T NOTICE HIS SMILE, TOO!
KYAA! KYAA!
HA HA...

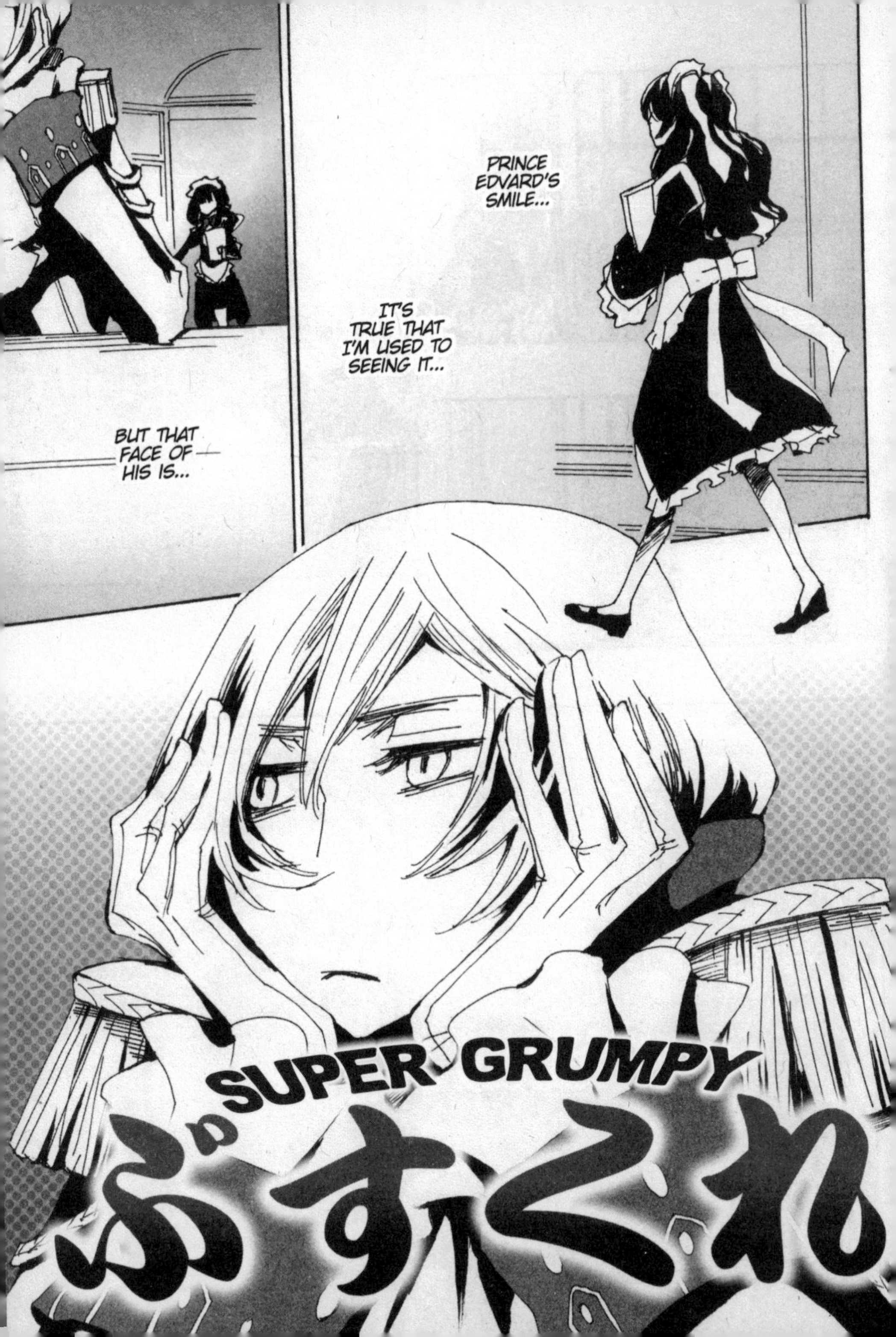
PRINCE EDVARD'S SMILE...
IT'S TRUE THAT I'M USED TO SEEING IT...
BUT THAT FACE OF HIS IS...
SUPER GRUMPY
ぶすくれ

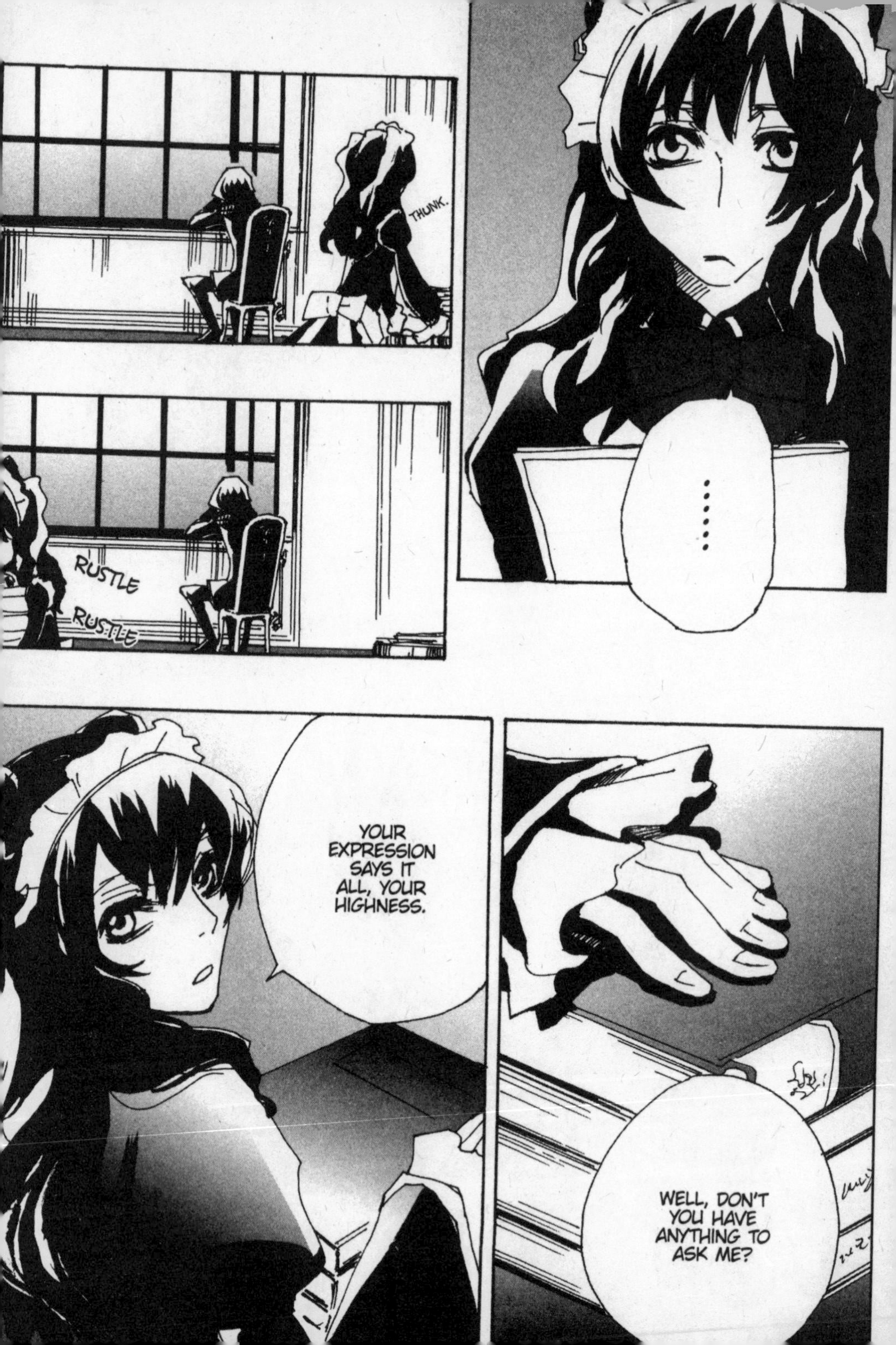
......
THUNK.
RUSTLE
RUSTLE
WELL, DON'T YOU HAVE ANYTHING TO ASK ME?
YOUR EXPRESSION SAYS IT ALL, YOUR HIGHNESS.

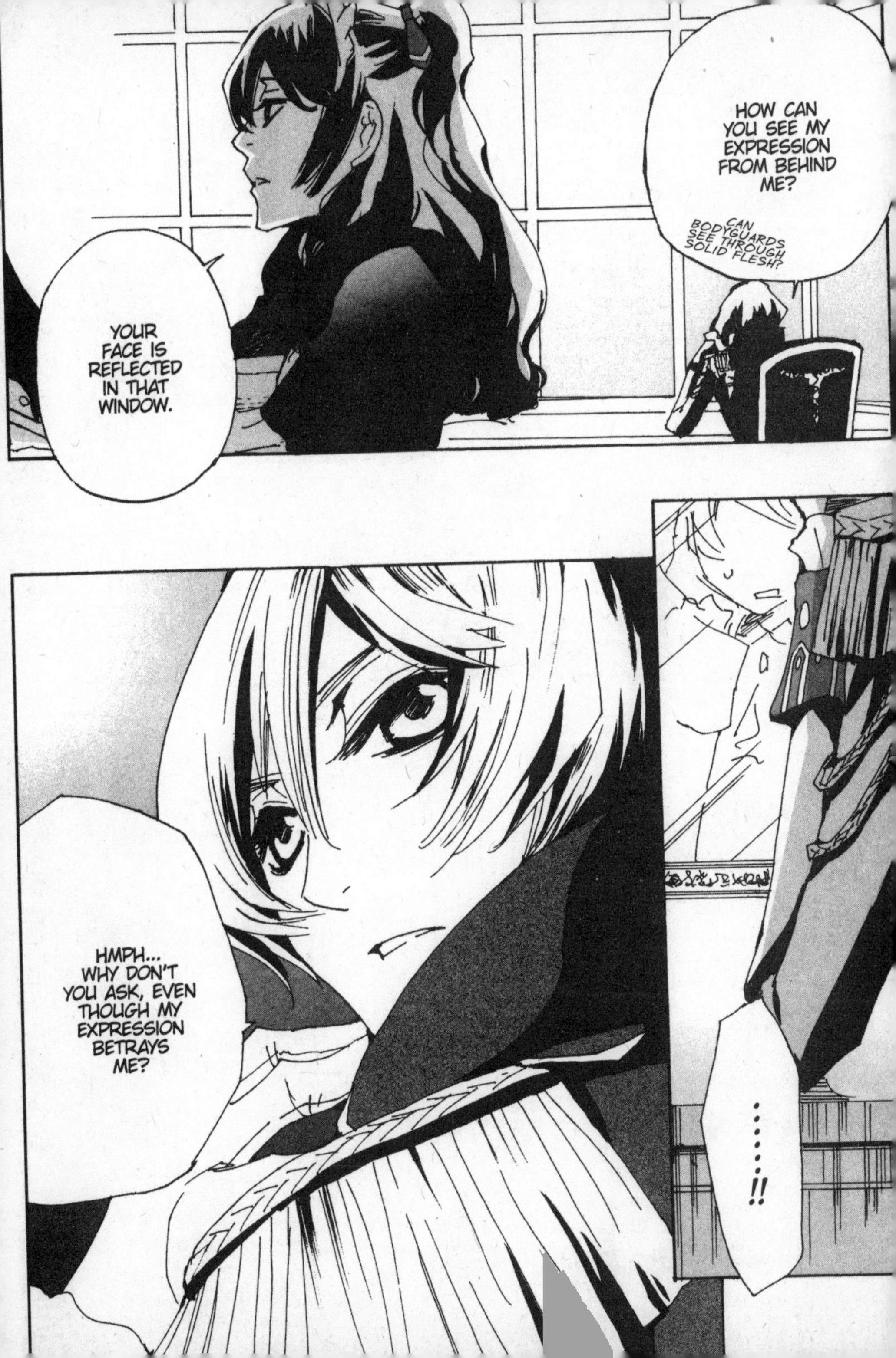
HOW CAN YOU SEE MY EXPRESSION FROM BEHIND ME?
CAN BODYGUARDS SEE THROUGH SOLID FLESH?
YOUR FACE IS REFLECTED IN THAT WINDOW.
......!!
HMPH... WHY DON'T YOU ASK, EVEN THOUGH MY EXPRESSION BETRAYS ME?

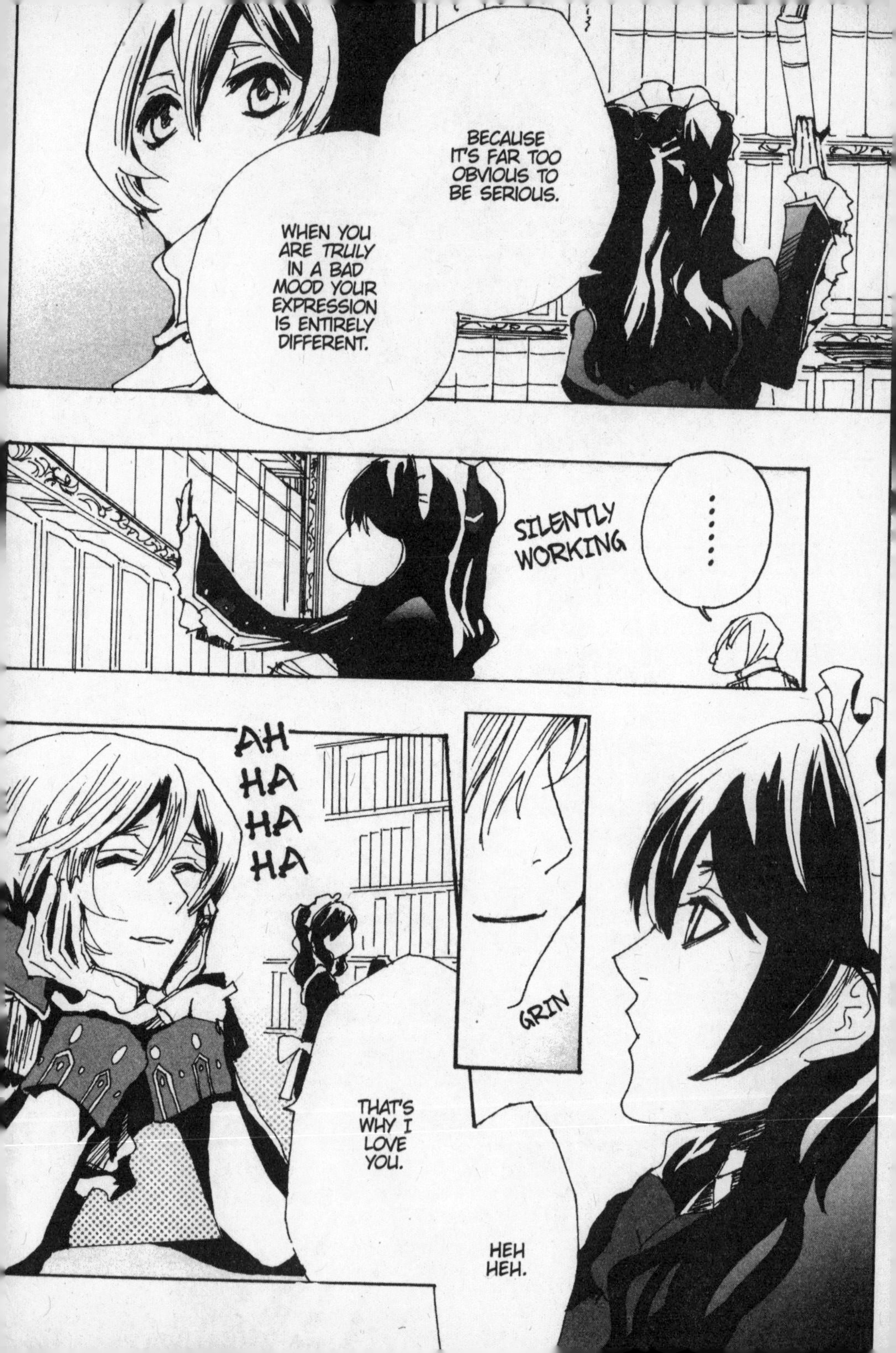
BECAUSE IT'S FAR TOO OBVIOUS TO BE SERIOUS.
WHEN YOU ARE TRULY IN A BAD MOOD YOUR EXPRESSION IS ENTIRELY DIFFERENT.
.....
SILENTLY WORKING
HEH HEH.
GRIN
AH HA HA HA
THAT'S WHY I LOVE YOU.

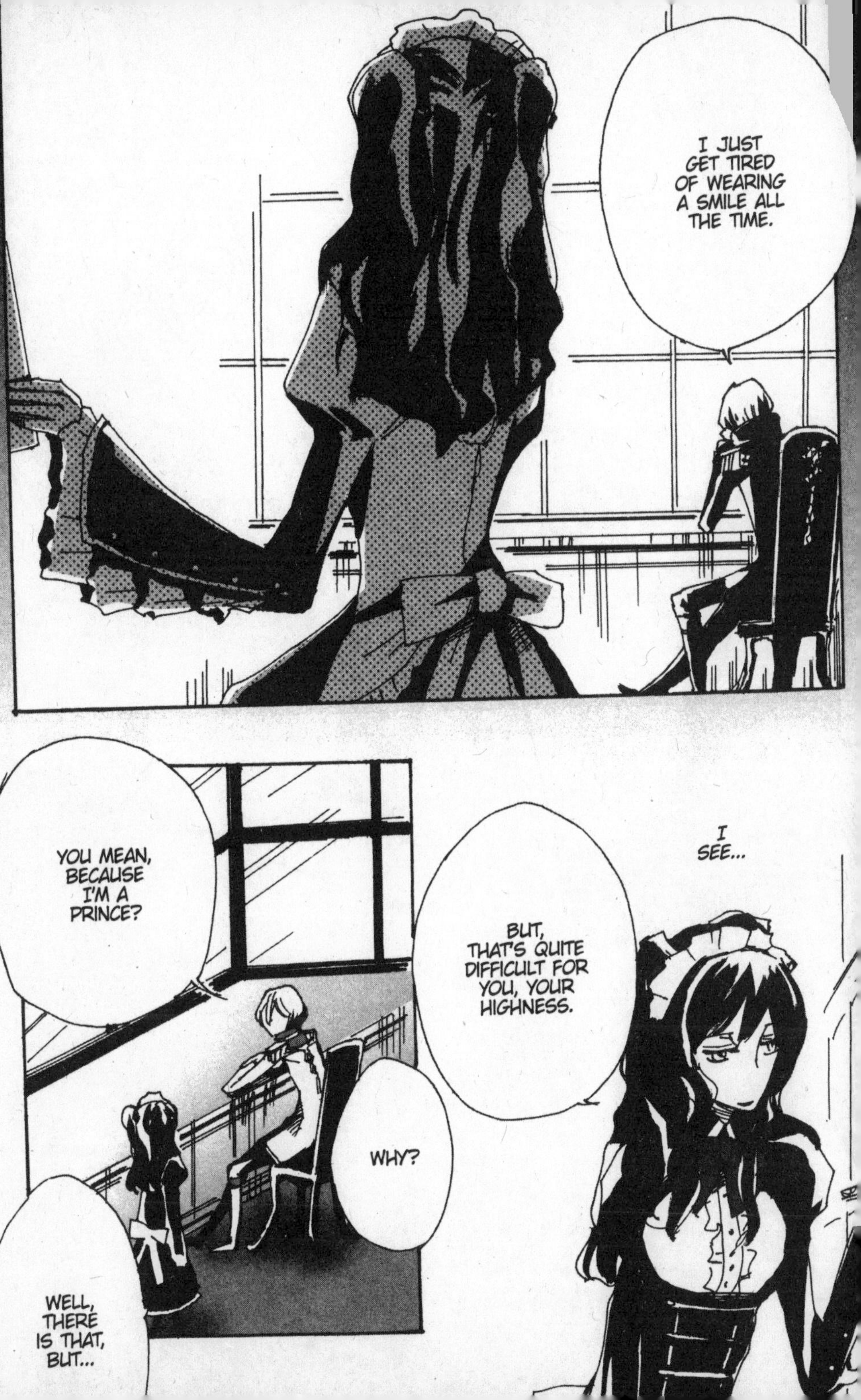
I JUST GET TIRED OF WEARING A SMILE ALL THE TIME.
I SEE...
BUT, THAT'S QUITE DIFFICULT FOR YOU, YOUR HIGHNESS.
WHY?
YOU MEAN, BECAUSE I'M A PRINCE?
WELL, THERE IS THAT, BUT...

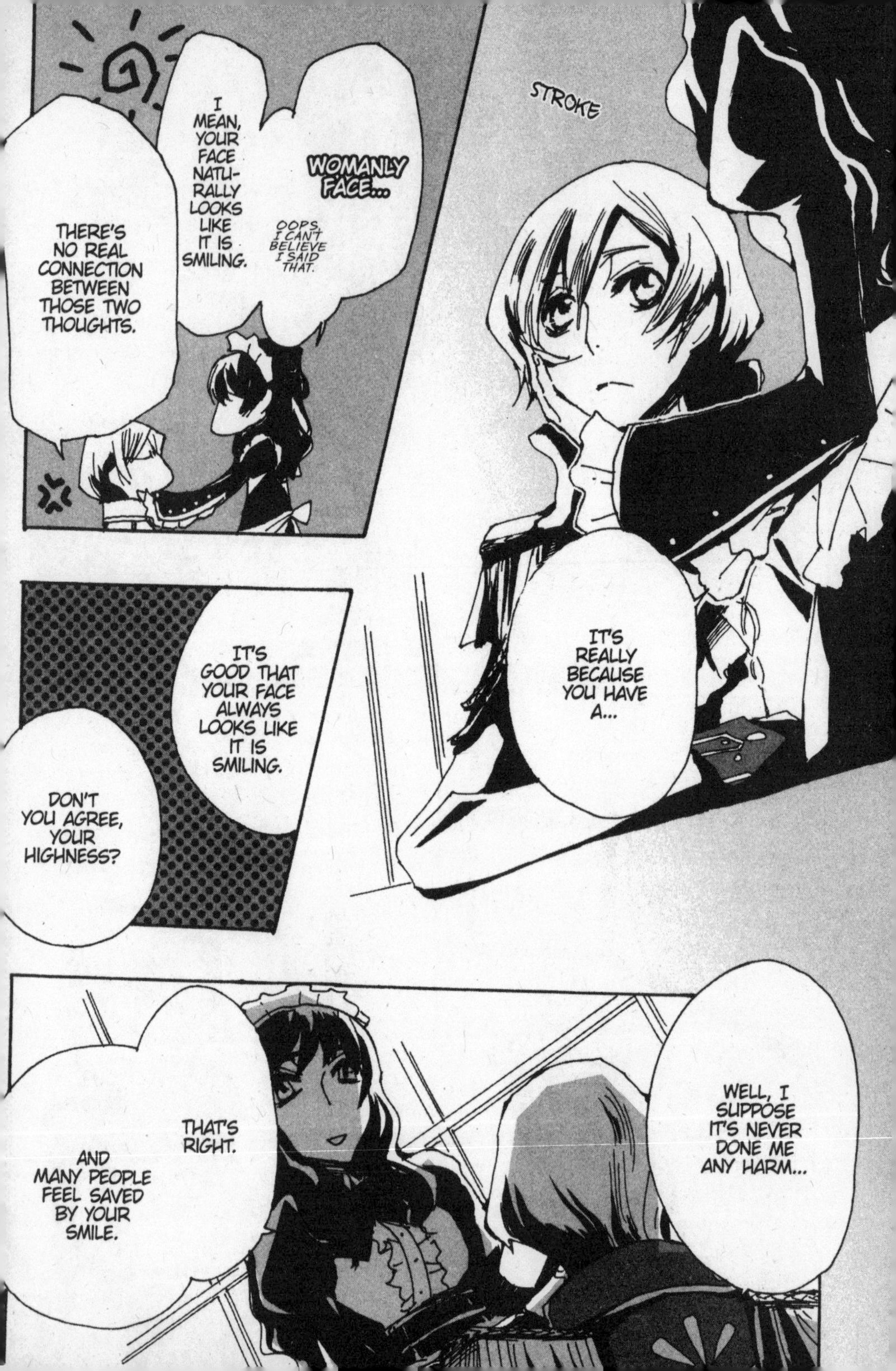
STROKE
IT'S REALLY BECAUSE YOU HAVE A...
WOMANLY FACE...
I MEAN, YOUR FACE NATU-RALLY LOOKS LIKE IT IS SMILING.
OOPS, I CAN'T BELIEVE I SAID THAT.
THERE'S NO REAL CONNECTION BETWEEN THOSE TWO THOUGHTS.
IT'S GOOD THAT YOUR FACE ALWAYS LOOKS LIKE IT IS SMILING.
DON'T YOU AGREE, YOUR HIGHNESS?
WELL, I SUPPOSE IT'S NEVER DONE ME ANY HARM...
THAT'S RIGHT.
AND MANY PEOPLE FEEL SAVED BY YOUR SMILE.

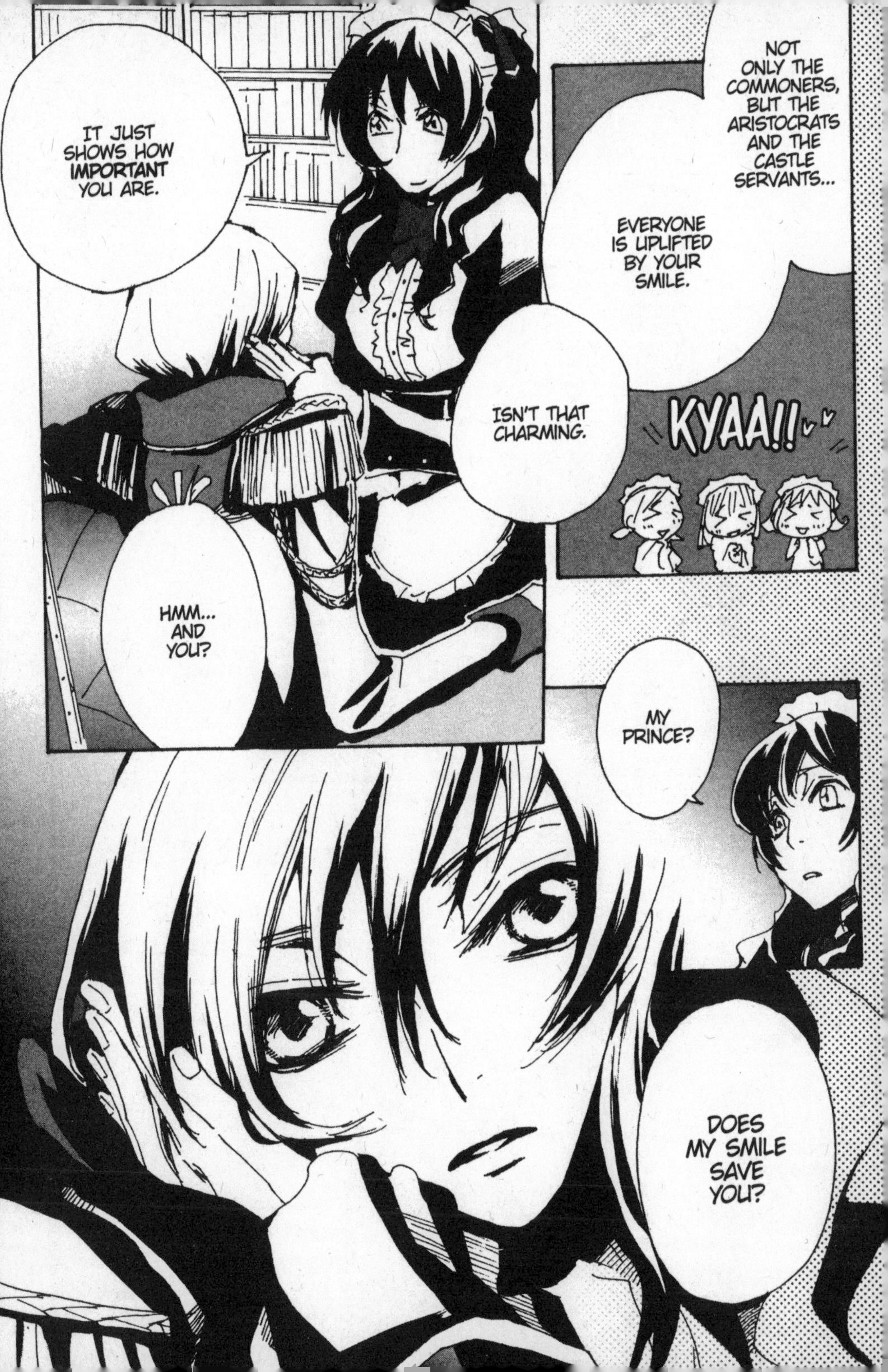
NOT ONLY THE COMMONERS, BUT THE ARISTOCRATS AND THE CASTLE SERVANTS...
EVERYONE IS UPLIFTED BY YOUR SMILE.
KYAA!!
IT JUST SHOWS HOW IMPORTANT YOU ARE.
ISN'T THAT CHARMING.
HMM... AND YOU?
MY PRINCE?
DOES MY SMILE SAVE YOU?

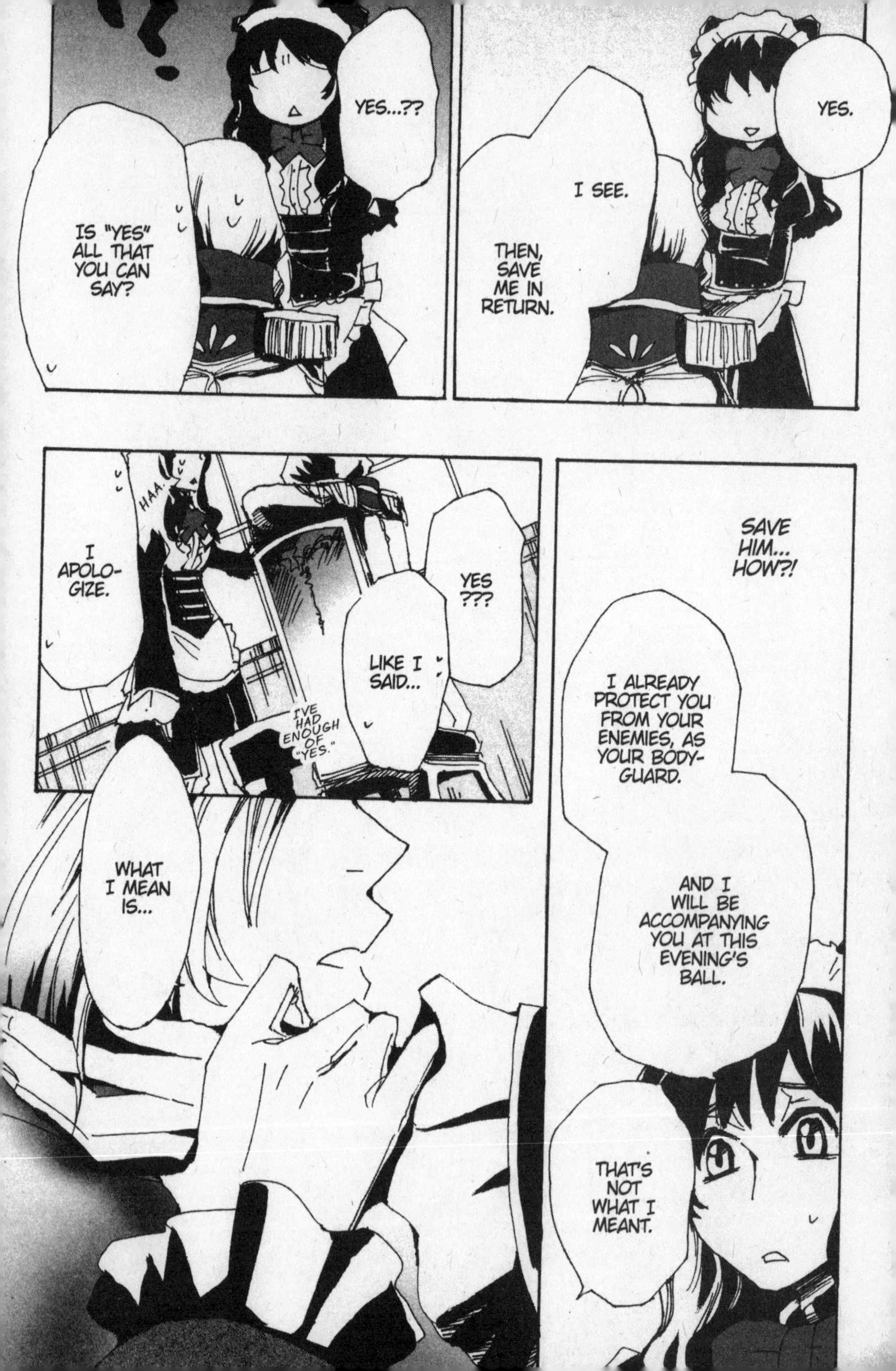
YES.
I SEE.
THEN, SAVE ME IN RETURN.
YES...??
IS "YES" ALL THAT YOU CAN SAY?
SAVE HIM... HOW?!
I ALREADY PROTECT YOU FROM YOUR ENEMIES, AS YOUR BODY-GUARD.
AND I WILL BE ACCOMPANYING YOU AT THIS EVENING'S BALL.
THAT'S NOT WHAT I MEANT.
YES ???
LIKE I SAID...
I'VE HAD ENOUGH OF "YES."
HAA.
I APOLOGIZE.
WHAT I MEAN IS...

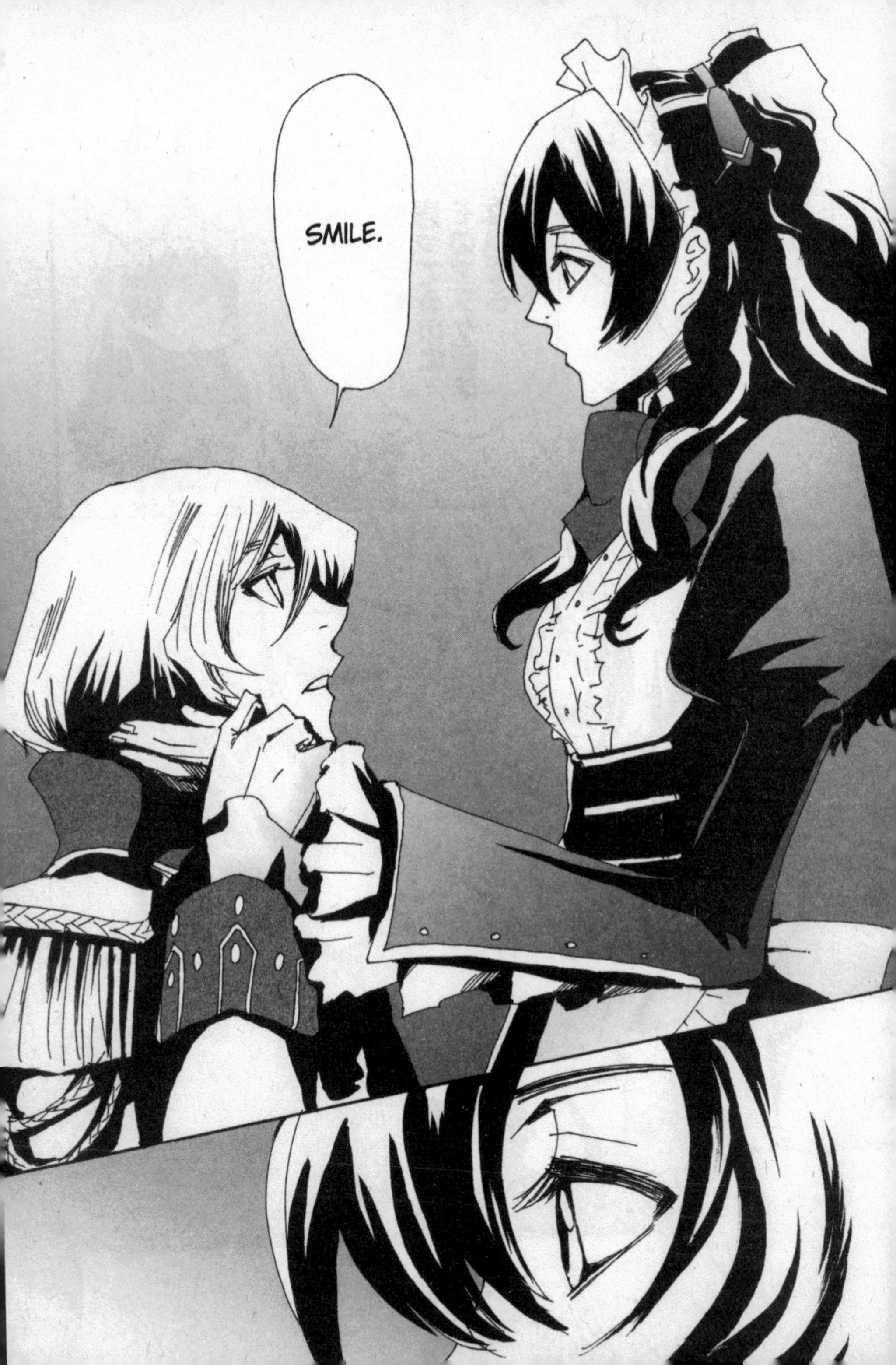
SMILE.

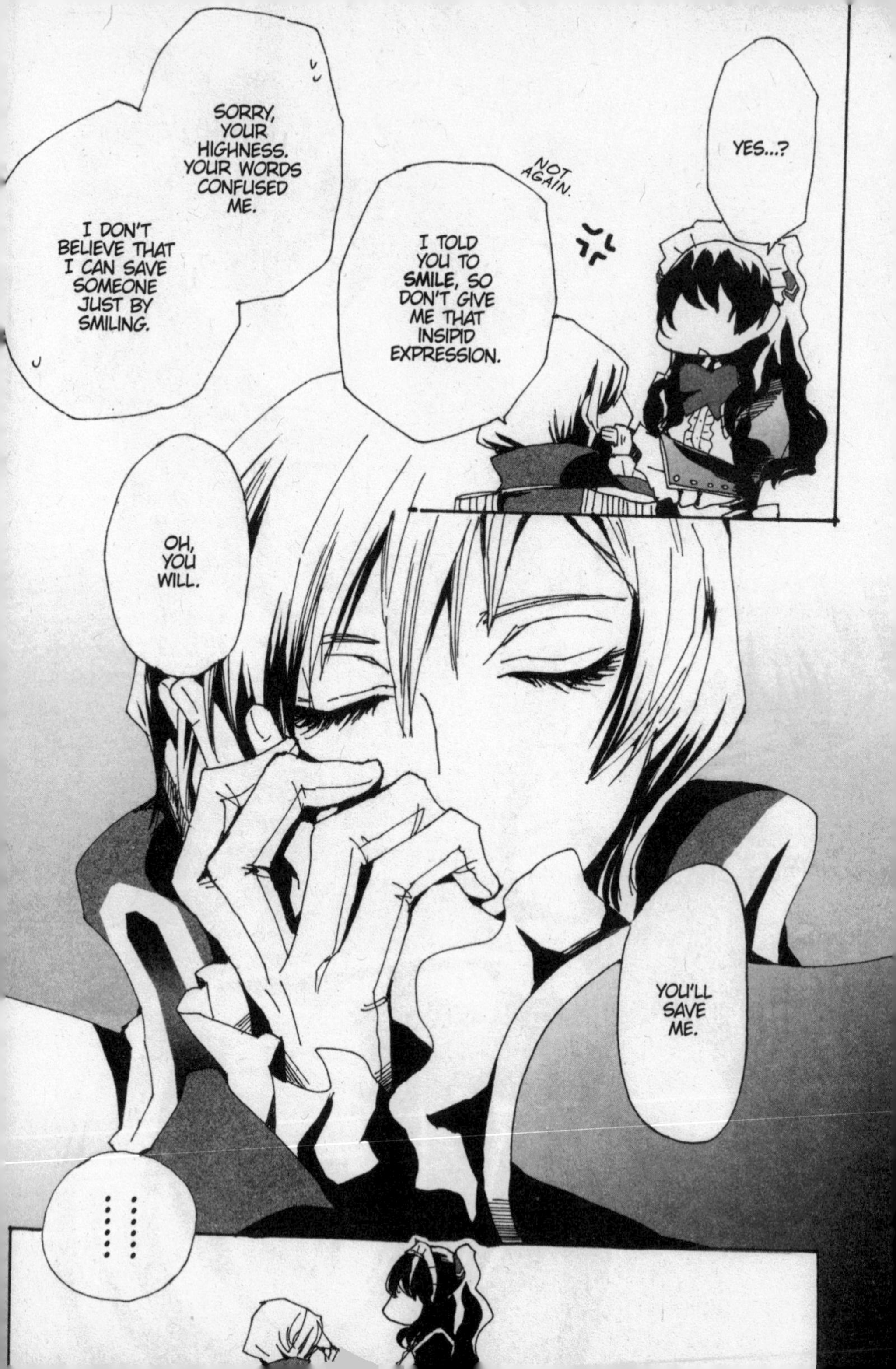
YES...?
NOT AGAIN.
I TOLD YOU TO SMILE, SO DON'T GIVE ME THAT INSIPID EXPRESSION.
SORRY, YOUR HIGHNESS. YOUR WORDS CONFUSED ME.
I DON'T BELIEVE THAT I CAN SAVE SOMEONE JUST BY SMILING.
OH, YOU WILL.
YOU'LL SAVE ME.
......

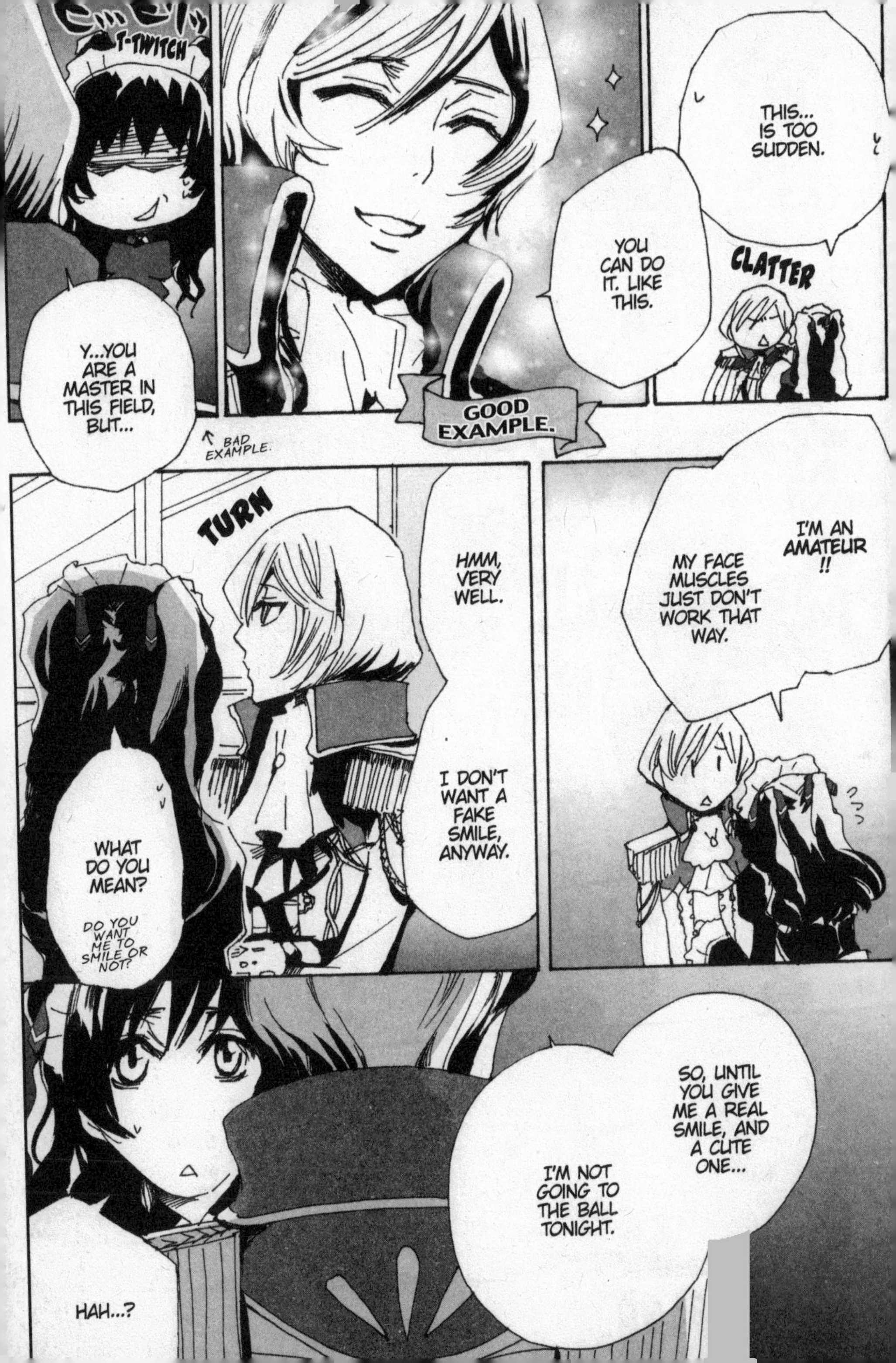
THIS... IS TOO SUDDEN.
YOU CAN DO IT. LIKE THIS.
CLATTER
GOOD EXAMPLE.
T-TWITCH
Y...YOU ARE A MASTER IN THIS FIELD, BUT...
BAD EXAMPLE.
I'M AN AMATEUR !!
MY FACE MUSCLES JUST DON'T WORK THAT WAY.
TURN
HMM, VERY WELL.
I DON'T WANT A FAKE SMILE, ANYWAY.
WHAT DO YOU MEAN?
DO YOU WANT ME TO SMILE OR NOT?
SO, UNTIL YOU GIVE ME A REAL SMILE, AND A CUTE ONE...
I'M NOT GOING TO THE BALL TONIGHT.
HAH...?

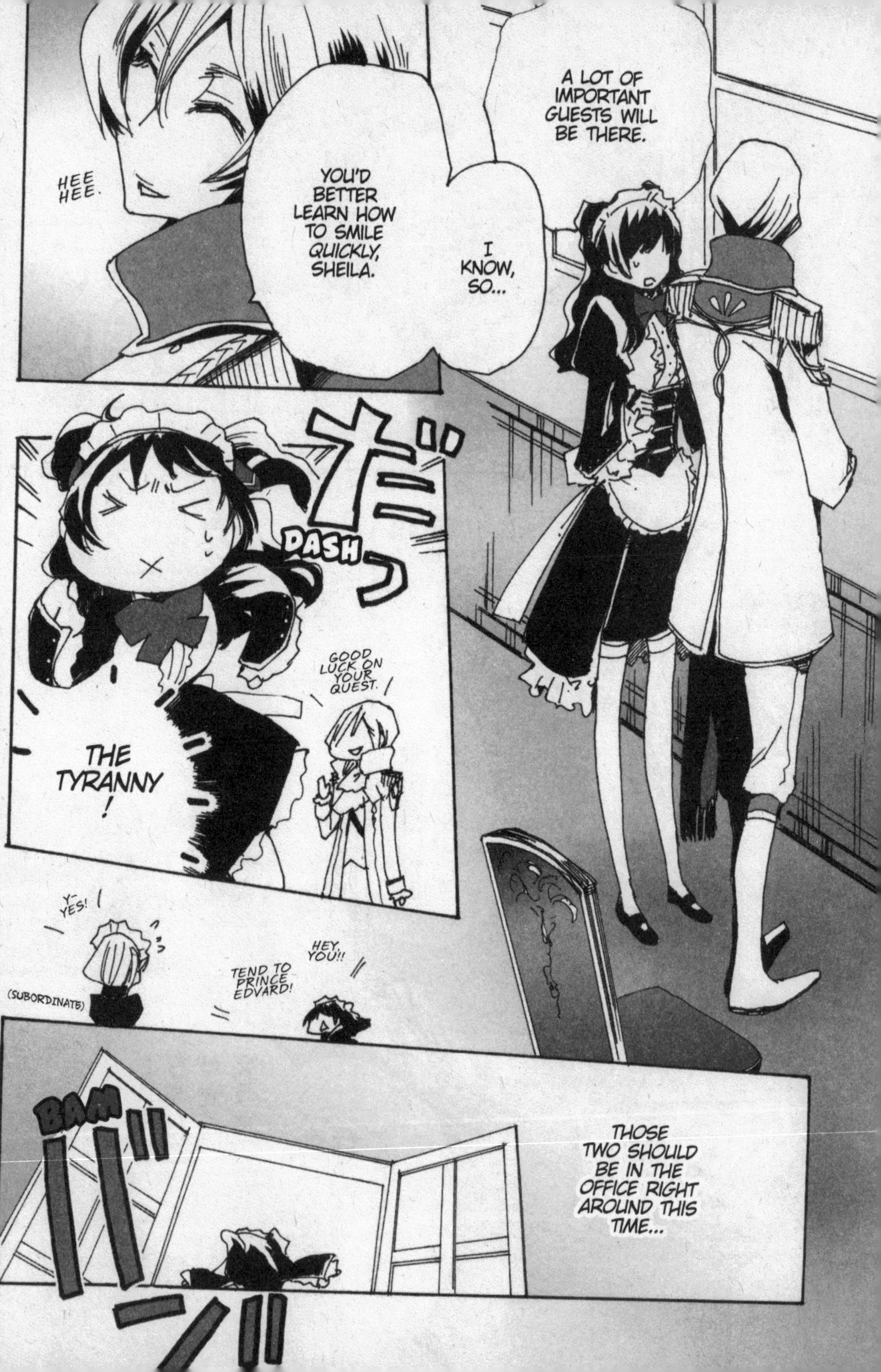

A LOT OF IMPORTANT GUESTS WILL BE THERE.
I KNOW, SO...
YOU'D BETTER LEARN HOW TO SMILE QUICKLY, SHEILA.
HEE HEE.
DASH
GOOD LUCK ON YOUR QUEST.
THE TYRANNY!
HEY, YOU!!
TEND TO PRINCE EDVARD!
Y-YES!
(SUBORDINATE)
THOSE TWO SHOULD BE IN THE OFFICE RIGHT AROUND THIS TIME...
BAM

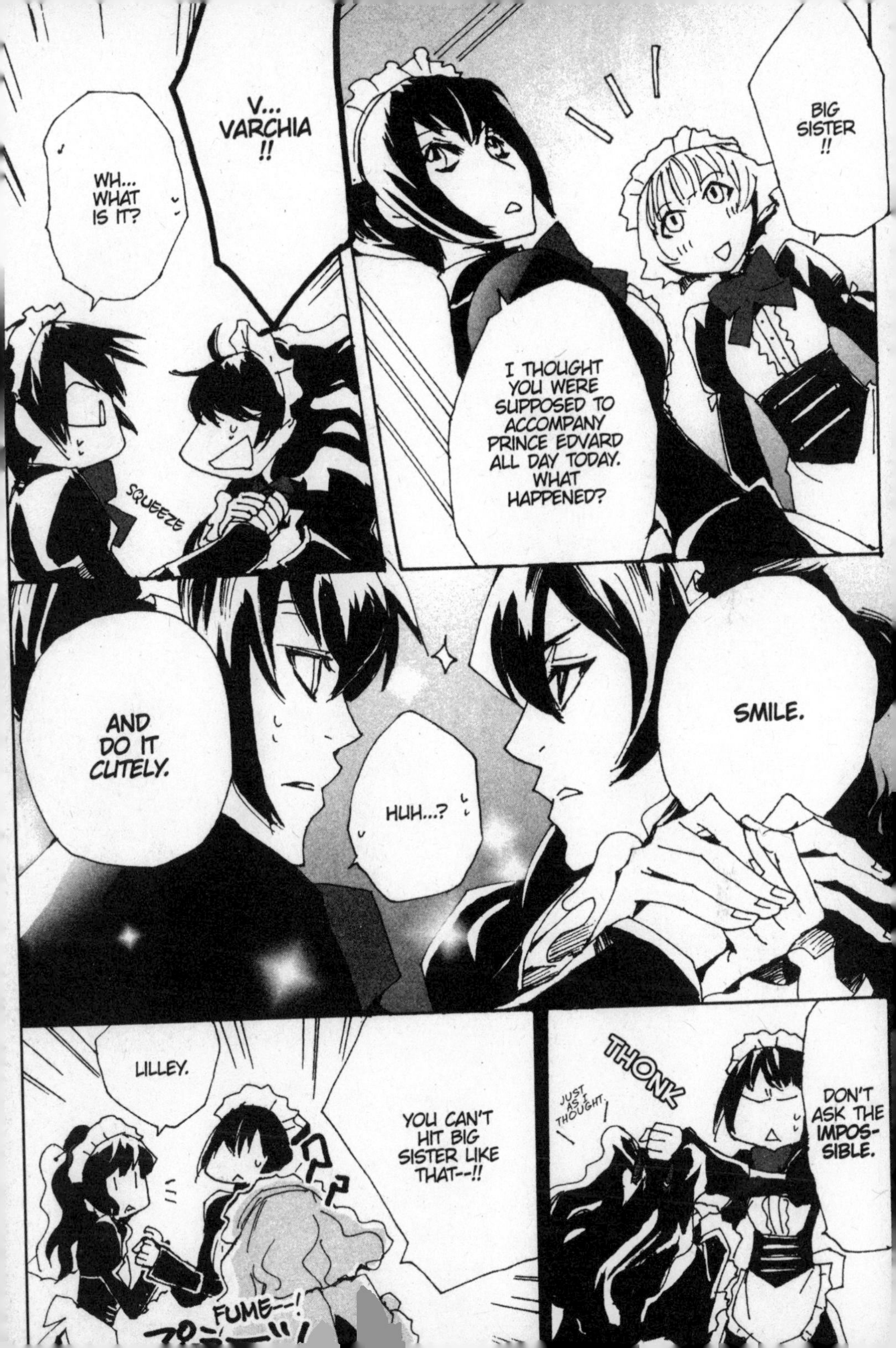
BIG SISTER!!
I THOUGHT YOU WERE SUPPOSED TO ACCOMPANY PRINCE EDVARD ALL DAY TODAY. WHAT HAPPENED?
V... VARCHIA!!
WH... WHAT IS IT?
SQUEEZE
SMILE.
HUH...?
AND DO IT CUTELY.
DON'T ASK THE IMPOS-SIBLE.
THONK
JUST AS I THOUGHT.
YOU CAN'T HIT BIG SISTER LIKE THAT--!!
LILLEY.
FUME--!

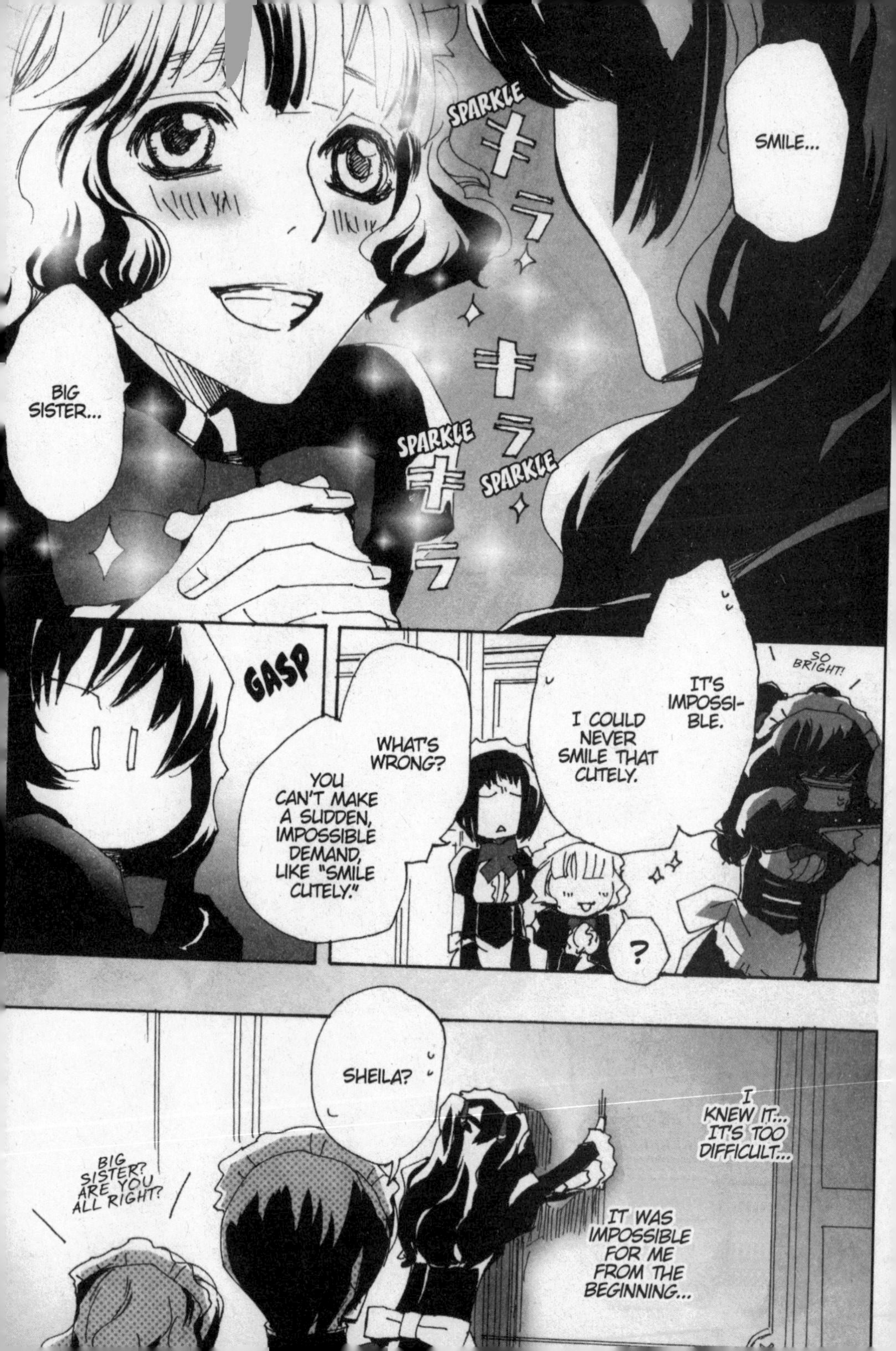
SMILE...
SPARKLE
キラ
キラ
SPARKLE
キラ
SPARKLE
BIG SISTER...
SO BRIGHT!
IT'S IMPOSSIBLE.
I COULD NEVER SMILE THAT CUTELY.
?
WHAT'S WRONG?
YOU CAN'T MAKE A SUDDEN, IMPOSSIBLE DEMAND, LIKE "SMILE CUTELY."
GASP
I KNEW IT... IT'S TOO DIFFICULT...
SHEILA?
IT WAS IMPOSSIBLE FOR ME FROM THE BEGINNING...
BIG SISTER? ARE YOU ALL RIGHT?

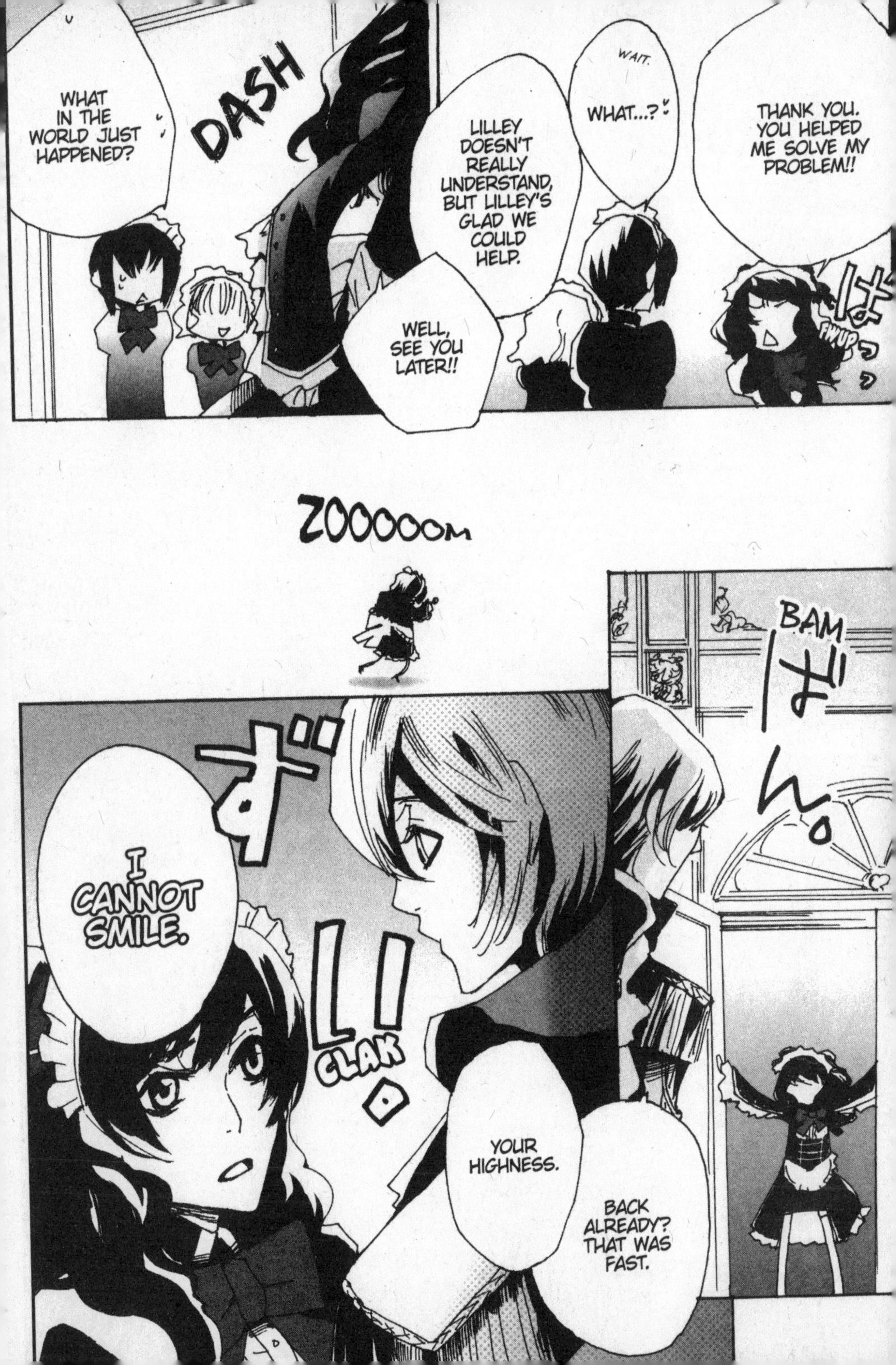
THANK YOU. YOU HELPED ME SOLVE MY PROBLEM!!
FWUP
WAIT.
WHAT...?
LILLEY DOESN'T REALLY UNDERSTAND, BUT LILLEY'S GLAD WE COULD HELP.
WELL, SEE YOU LATER!!
DASH
WHAT IN THE WORLD JUST HAPPENED?
ZOOOOOM
BAM
YOUR HIGHNESS.
BACK ALREADY? THAT WAS FAST.
CLAK
I CANNOT SMILE.

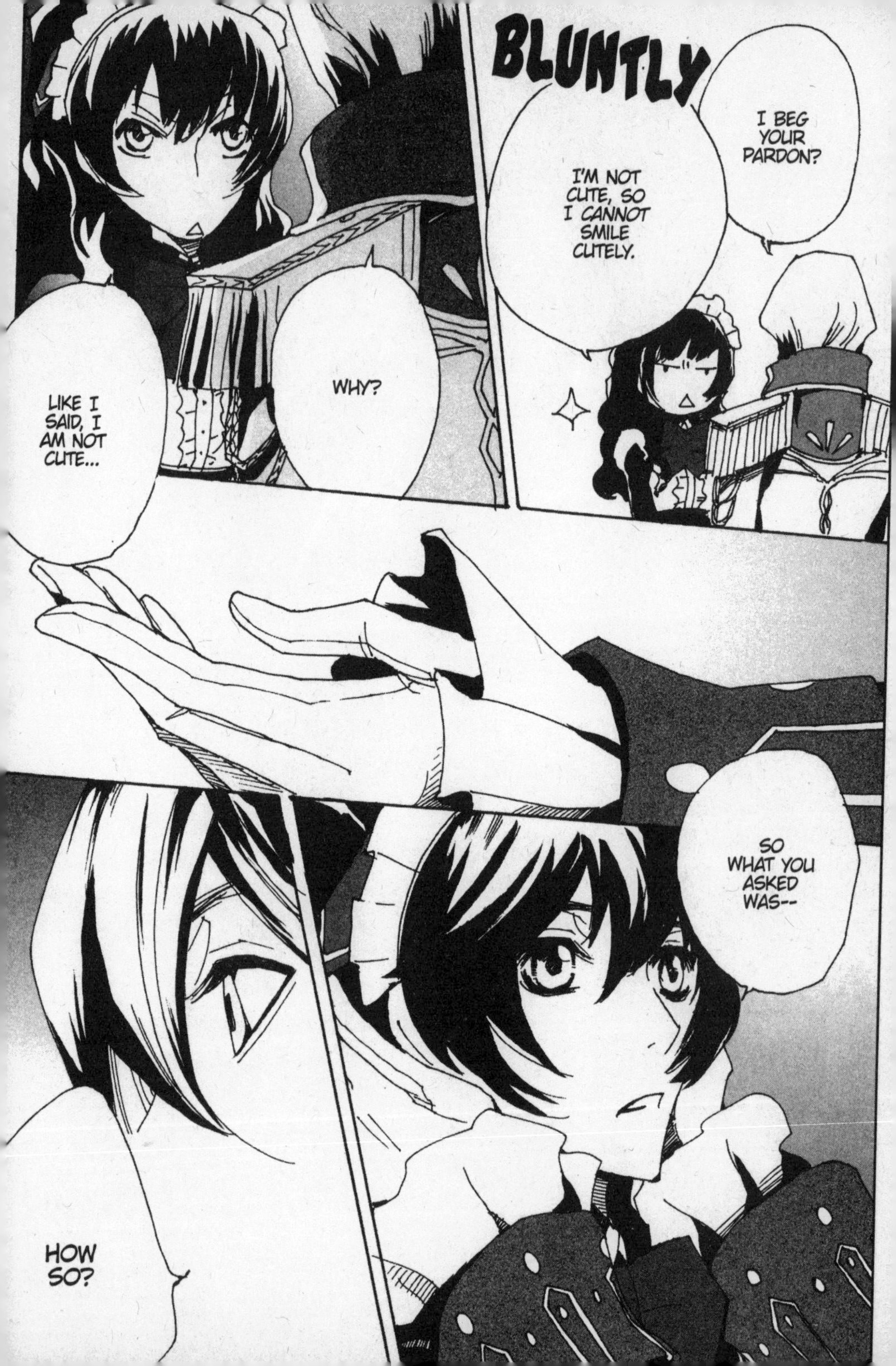
I BEG YOUR PARDON?
BLUNTLY
I'M NOT CUTE, SO I CANNOT SMILE CUTELY.
WHY?
LIKE I SAID, I AM NOT CUTE...
SO WHAT YOU ASKED WAS--
HOW SO?

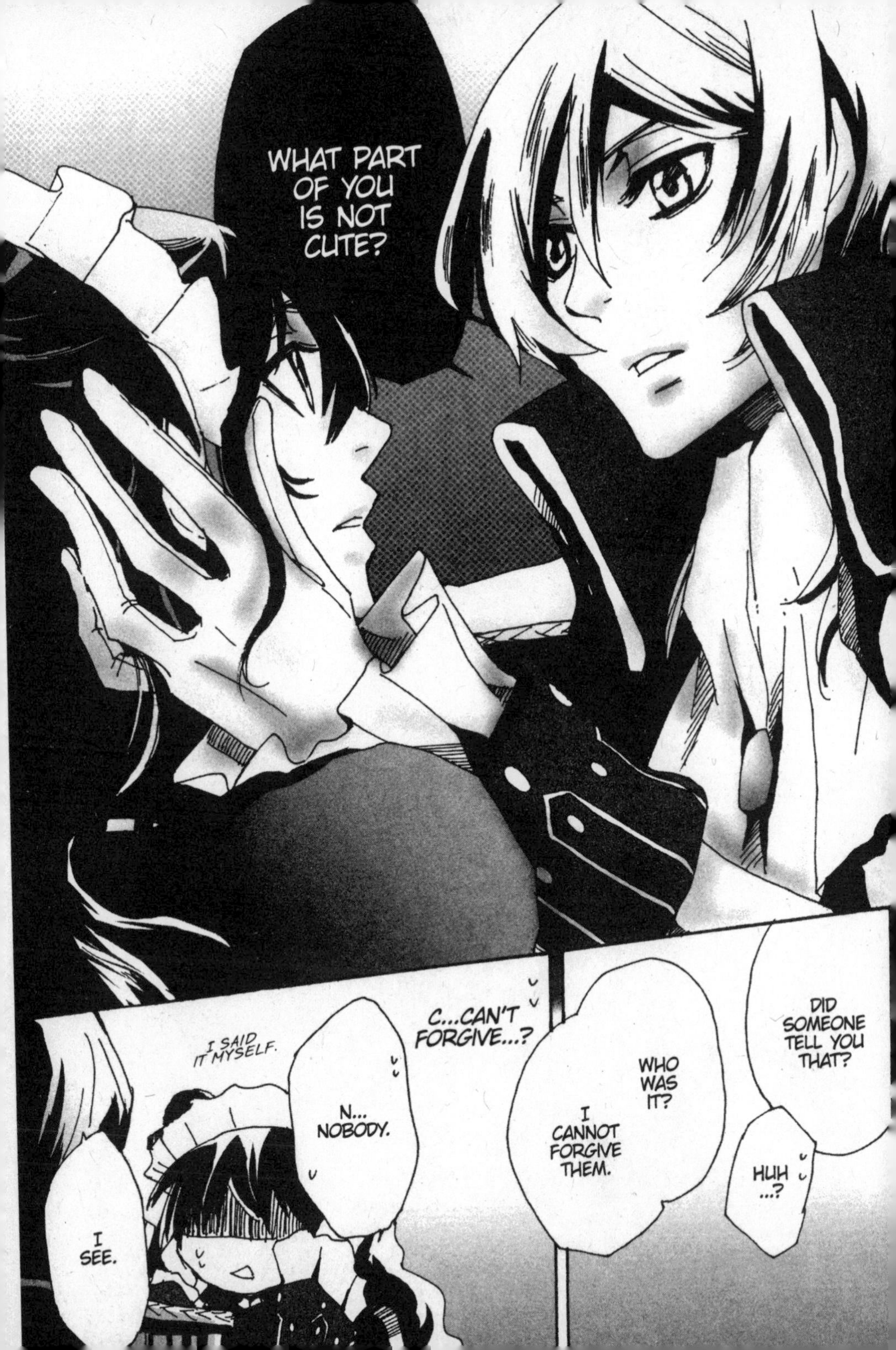
WHAT PART OF YOU IS NOT CUTE?
DID SOMEONE TELL YOU THAT?
HUH ...?
WHO WAS IT?
I CANNOT FORGIVE THEM.
C...CAN'T FORGIVE...?
N... NOBODY.
I SAID IT MYSELF.
I SEE.

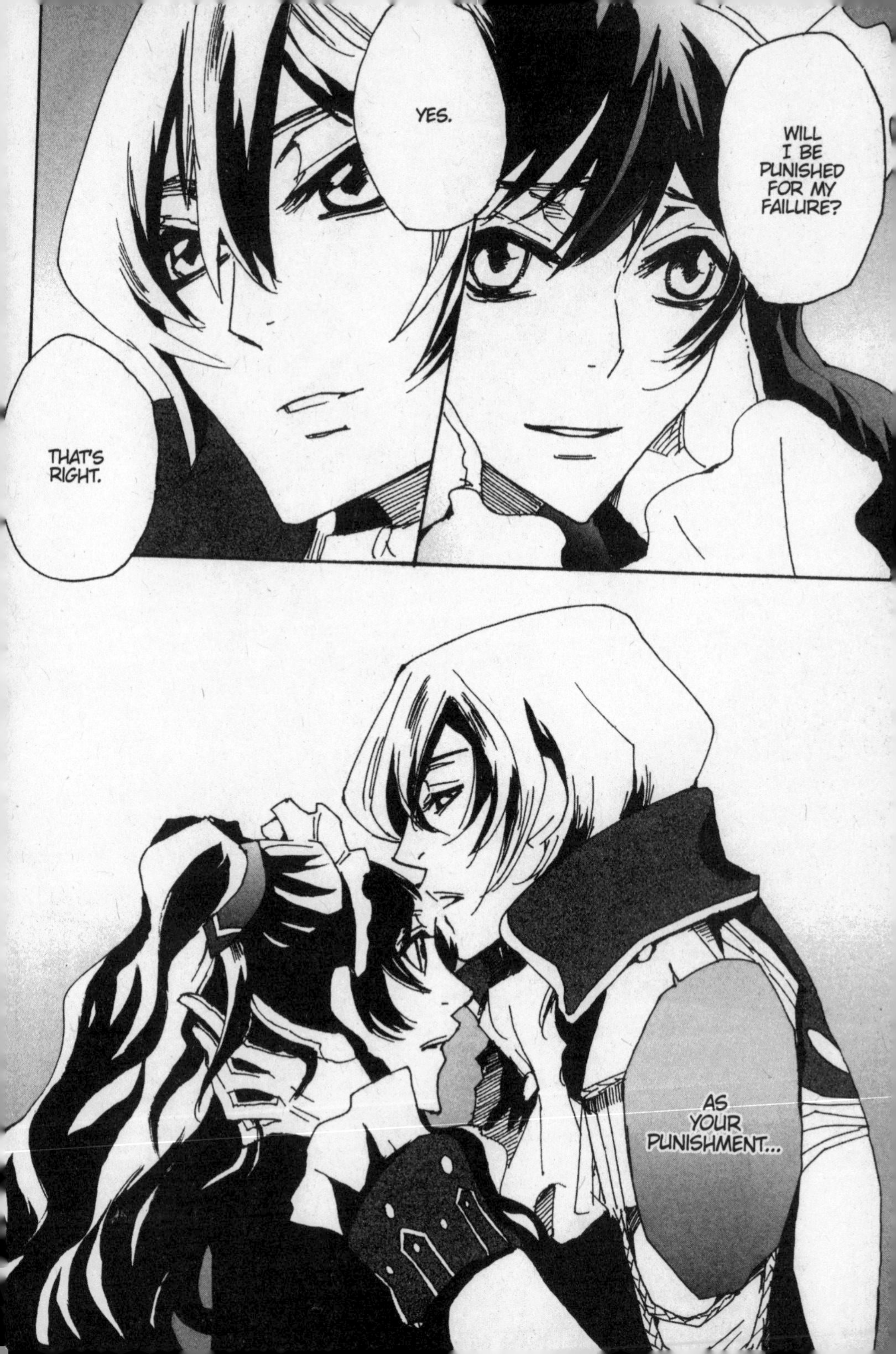
WILL I BE PUNISHED FOR MY FAILURE?
YES.
THAT'S RIGHT.
AS YOUR PUNISHMENT...

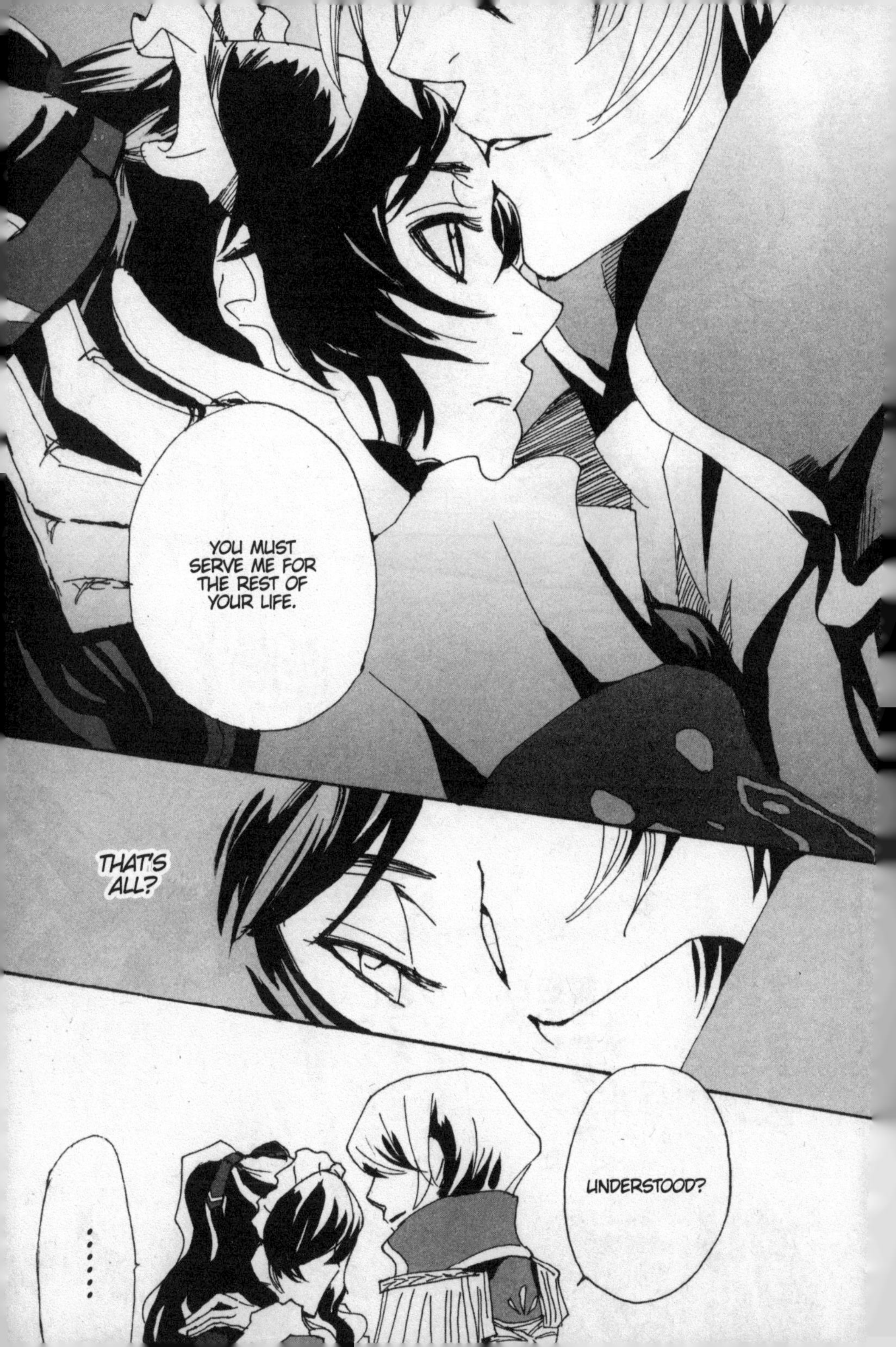
YOU MUST SERVE ME FOR THE REST OF YOUR LIFE.
THAT'S ALL?
UNDERSTOOD?
......

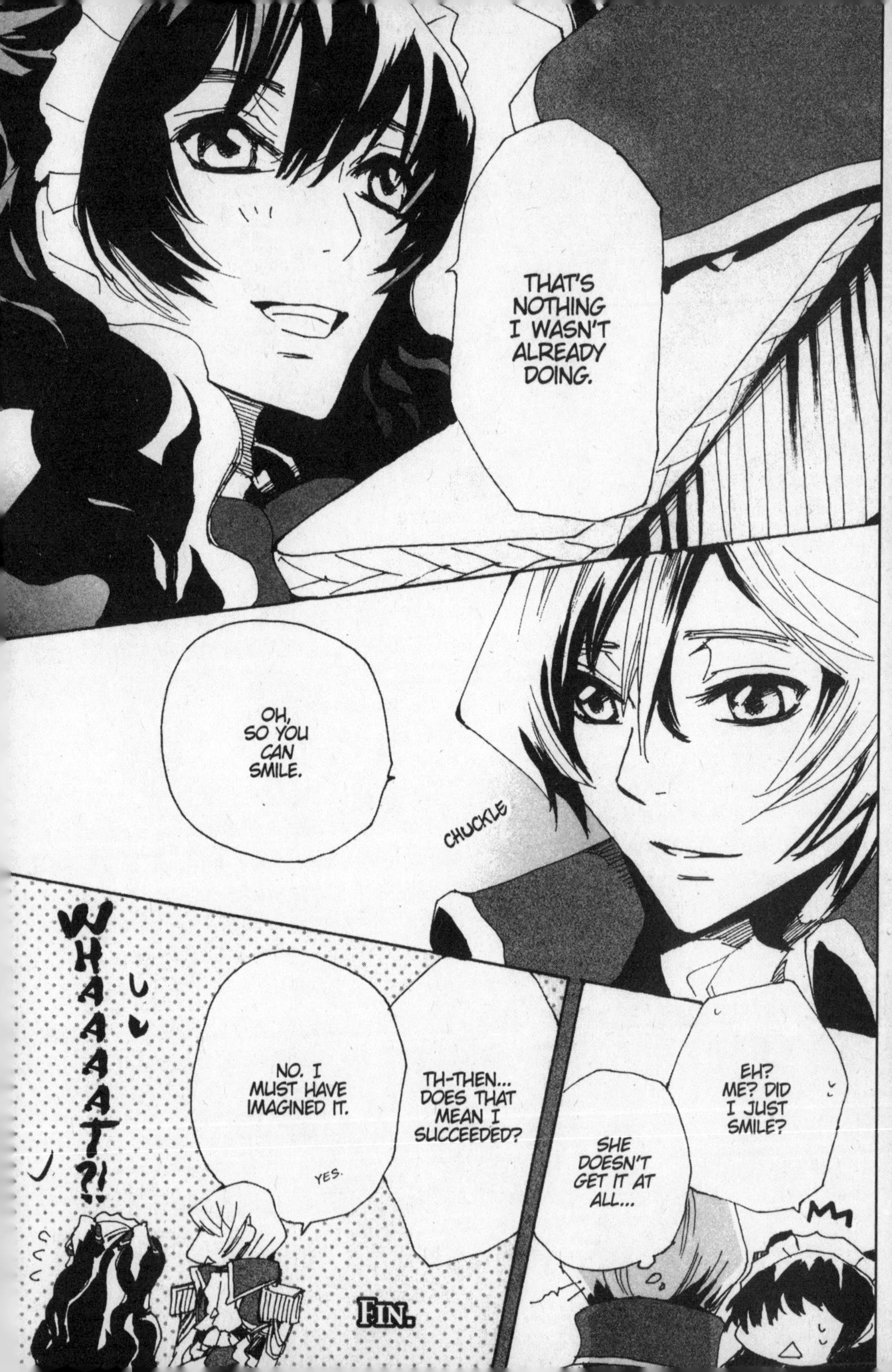
THAT'S NOTHING I WASN'T ALREADY DOING.
OH, SO YOU CAN SMILE.
CHUCKLE
EH? ME? DID I JUST SMILE?
SHE DOESN'T GET IT AT ALL...
TH-THEN... DOES THAT MEAN I SUCCEEDED?
NO. I MUST HAVE IMAGINED IT.
YES.
WHAAAAT?!
FIN.

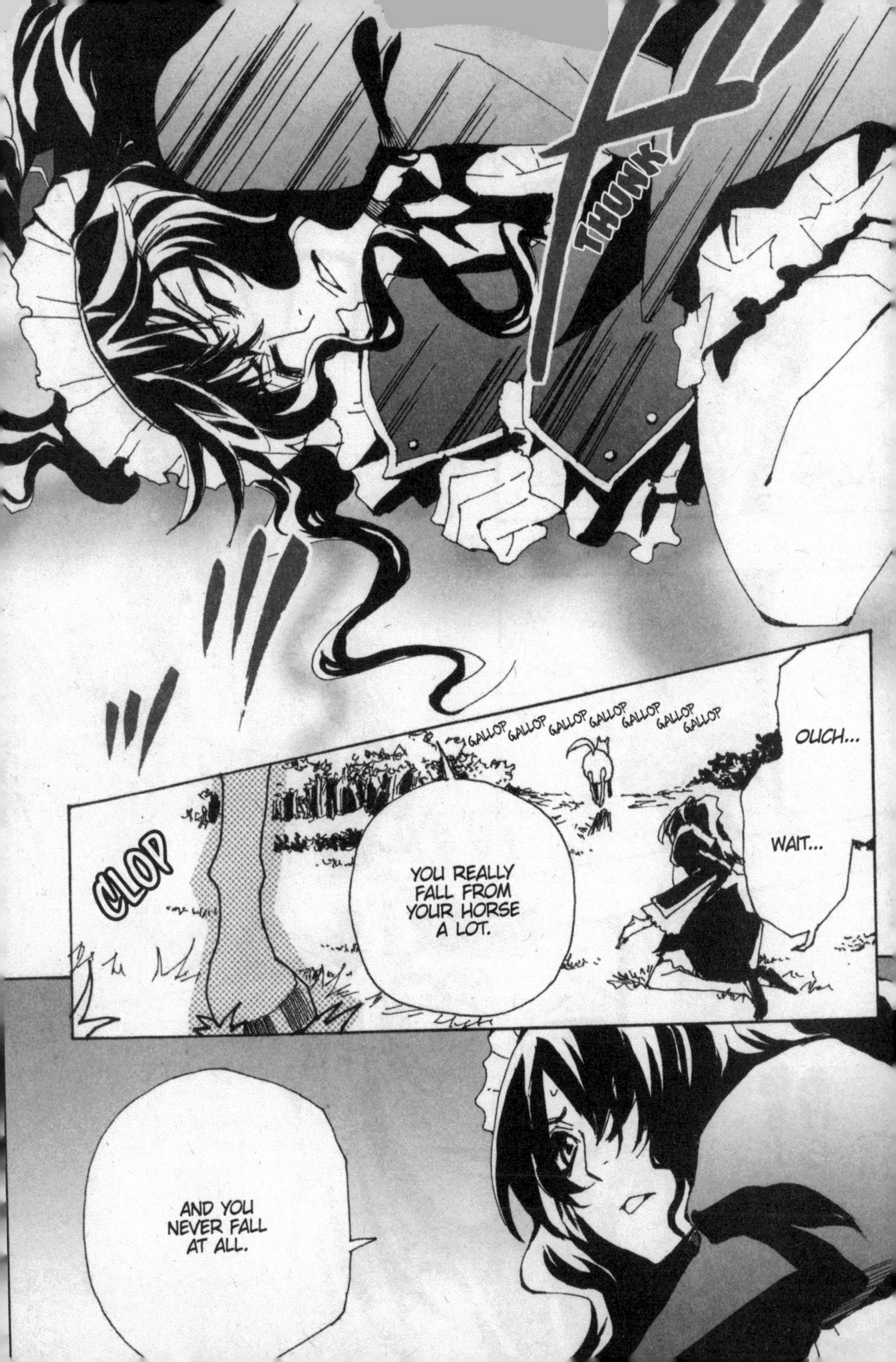
THUNK
OUCH...
GALLOP GALLOP GALLOP GALLOP GALLOP GALLOP GALLOP
WAIT...
YOU REALLY FALL FROM YOUR HORSE A LOT.
CLOP
AND YOU NEVER FALL AT ALL.

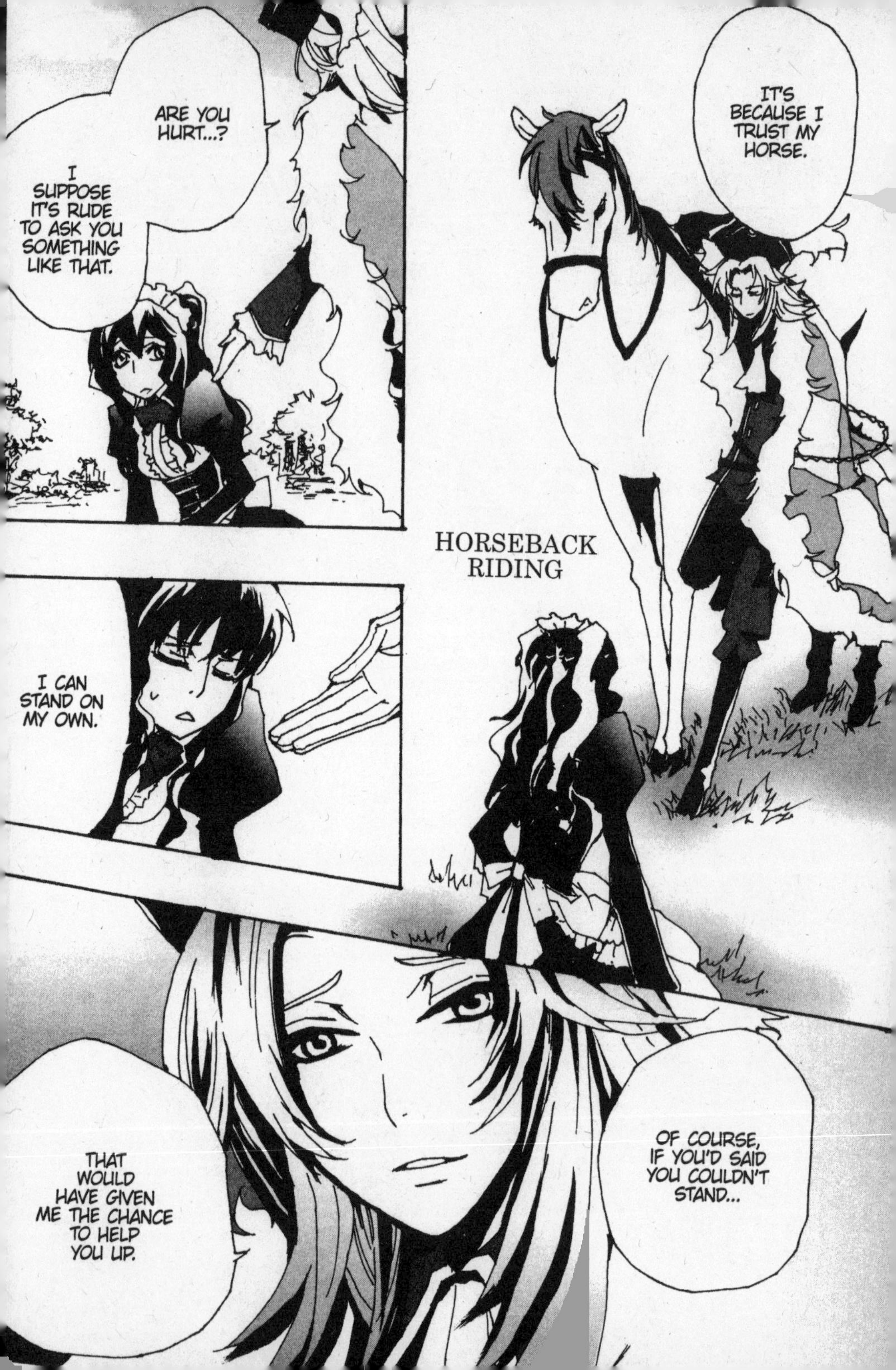
IT'S BECAUSE I TRUST MY HORSE.
HORSEBACK RIDING
ARE YOU HURT...?
I SUPPOSE IT'S RUDE TO ASK YOU SOMETHING LIKE THAT.
I CAN STAND ON MY OWN.
OF COURSE, IF YOU'D SAID YOU COULDN'T STAND...
THAT WOULD HAVE GIVEN ME THE CHANCE TO HELP YOU UP.

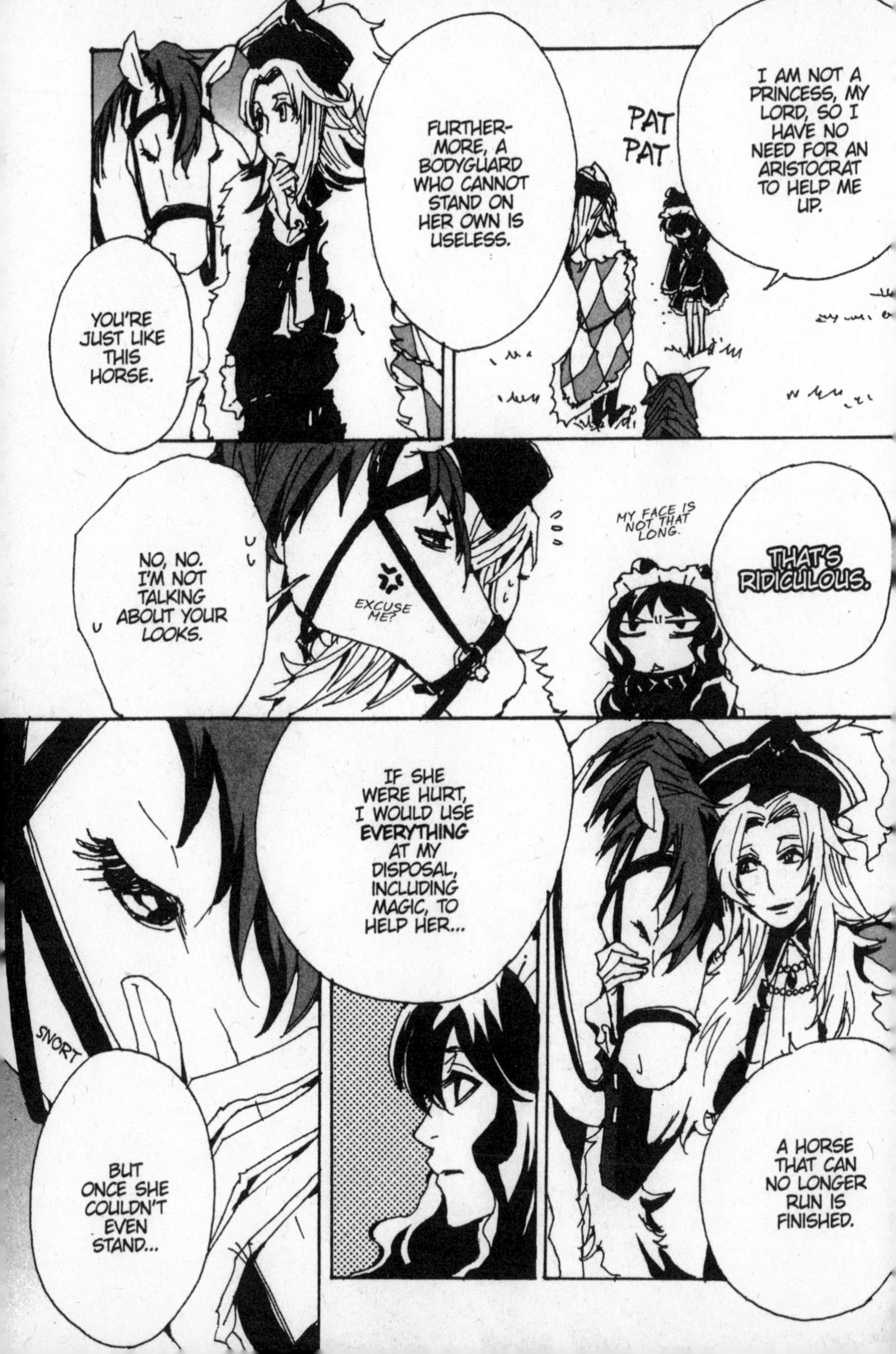
I AM NOT A PRINCESS, MY LORD, SO I HAVE NO NEED FOR AN ARISTOCRAT TO HELP ME UP.
PAT PAT
FURTHER-MORE, A BODYGUARD WHO CANNOT STAND ON HER OWN IS USELESS.
YOU'RE JUST LIKE THIS HORSE.
THAT'S RIDICULOUS.
MY FACE IS NOT THAT LONG.
EXCUSE ME?
NO, NO. I'M NOT TALKING ABOUT YOUR LOOKS.
A HORSE THAT CAN NO LONGER RUN IS FINISHED.
IF SHE WERE HURT, I WOULD USE **EVERYTHING** AT MY DISPOSAL, INCLUDING MAGIC, TO HELP HER...
SNORT
BUT ONCE SHE COULDN'T EVEN STAND...

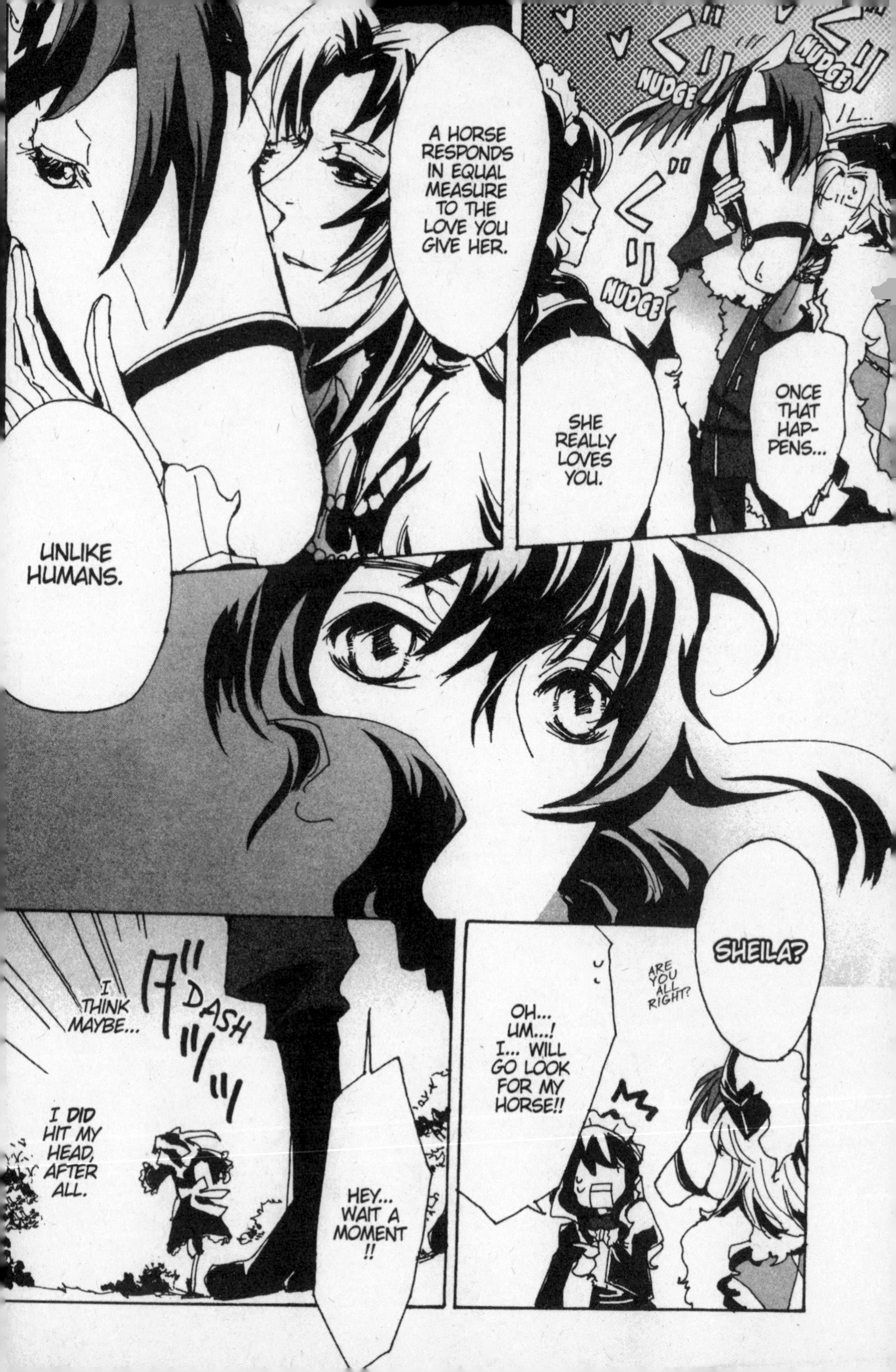

A HORSE RESPONDS IN EQUAL MEASURE TO THE LOVE YOU GIVE HER.
NUDGE
NUDGE
NUDGE
ONCE THAT HAP-PENS...
SHE REALLY LOVES YOU.
UNLIKE HUMANS.
SHEILA?
ARE YOU ALL RIGHT?
OH... UM...! I... WILL GO LOOK FOR MY HORSE!!
HEY... WAIT A MOMENT!!
DASH
I THINK MAYBE...
I DID HIT MY HEAD, AFTER ALL.

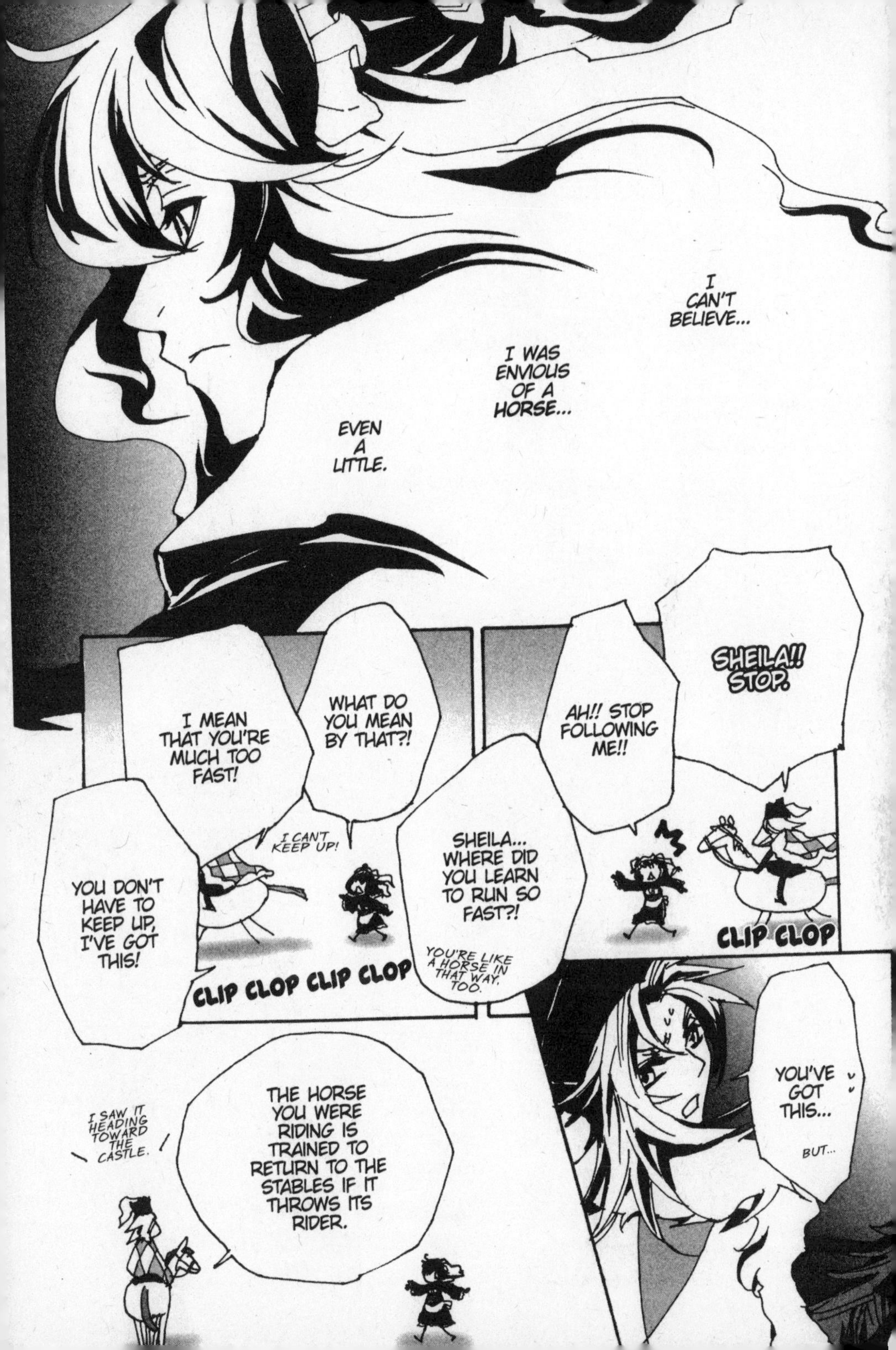
I CAN'T BELIEVE...
I WAS ENVIOUS OF A HORSE...
EVEN A LITTLE.
SHEILA!! STOP.
AH!! STOP FOLLOWING ME!!
CLIP CLOP
SHEILA... WHERE DID YOU LEARN TO RUN SO FAST?!
YOU'RE LIKE A HORSE IN THAT WAY, TOO.
WHAT DO YOU MEAN BY THAT?!
I MEAN THAT YOU'RE MUCH TOO FAST!
I CAN'T KEEP UP!
YOU DON'T HAVE TO KEEP UP, I'VE GOT THIS!
CLIP CLOP CLIP CLOP
YOU'VE GOT THIS...
BUT...
THE HORSE YOU WERE RIDING IS TRAINED TO RETURN TO THE STABLES IF IT THROWS ITS RIDER.
I SAW IT HEADING TOWARD THE CASTLE.

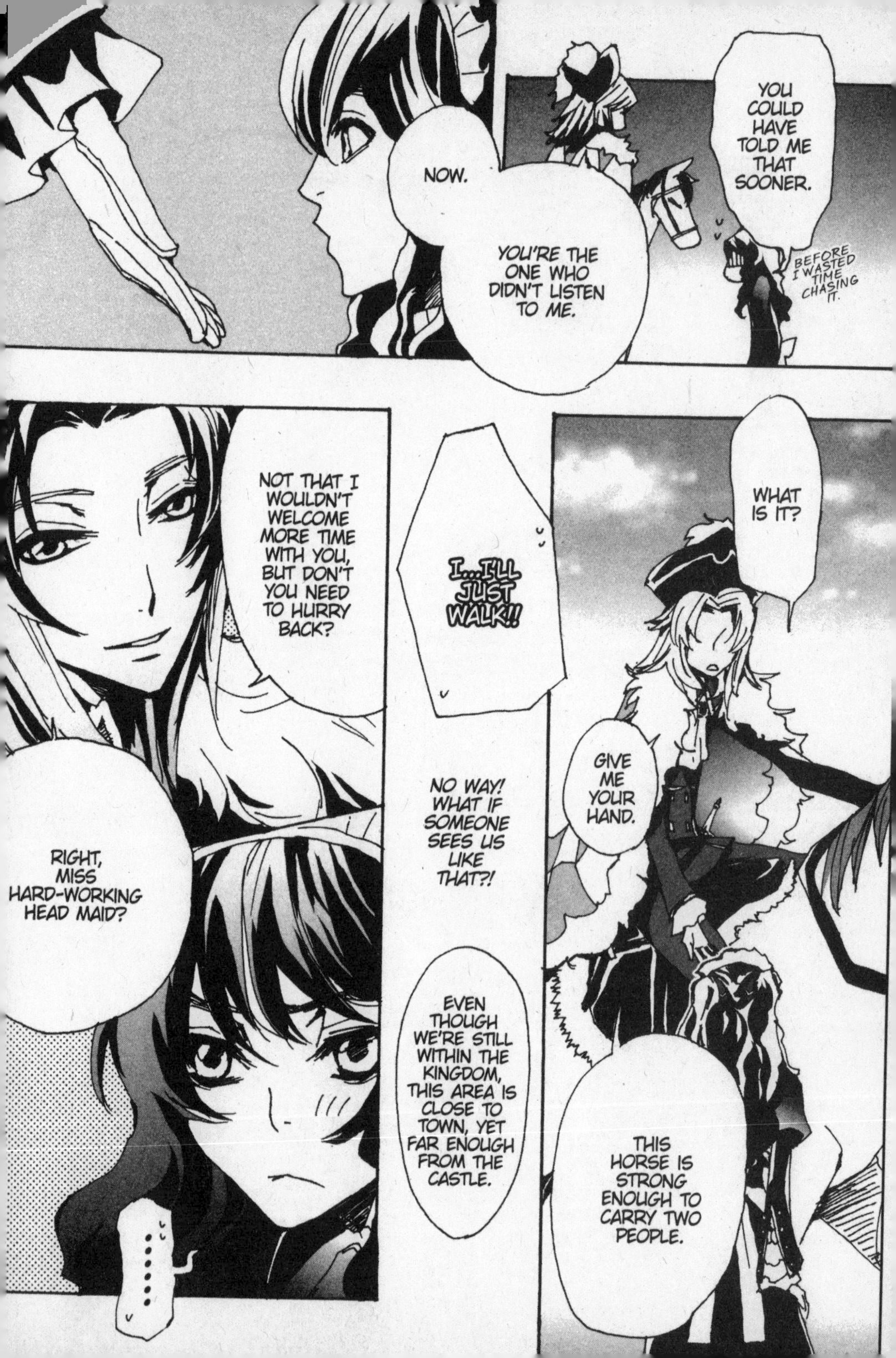
YOU COULD HAVE TOLD ME THAT SOONER.
BEFORE I WASTED TIME CHASING IT.
NOW.
YOU'RE THE ONE WHO DIDN'T LISTEN TO ME.
WHAT IS IT?
GIVE ME YOUR HAND.
THIS HORSE IS STRONG ENOUGH TO CARRY TWO PEOPLE.
I...I'LL JUST WALK!!
NO WAY! WHAT IF SOMEONE SEES US LIKE THAT?!
EVEN THOUGH WE'RE STILL WITHIN THE KINGDOM, THIS AREA IS CLOSE TO TOWN, YET FAR ENOUGH FROM THE CASTLE.
NOT THAT I WOULDN'T WELCOME MORE TIME WITH YOU, BUT DON'T YOU NEED TO HURRY BACK?
RIGHT, MISS HARD-WORKING HEAD MAID?
......

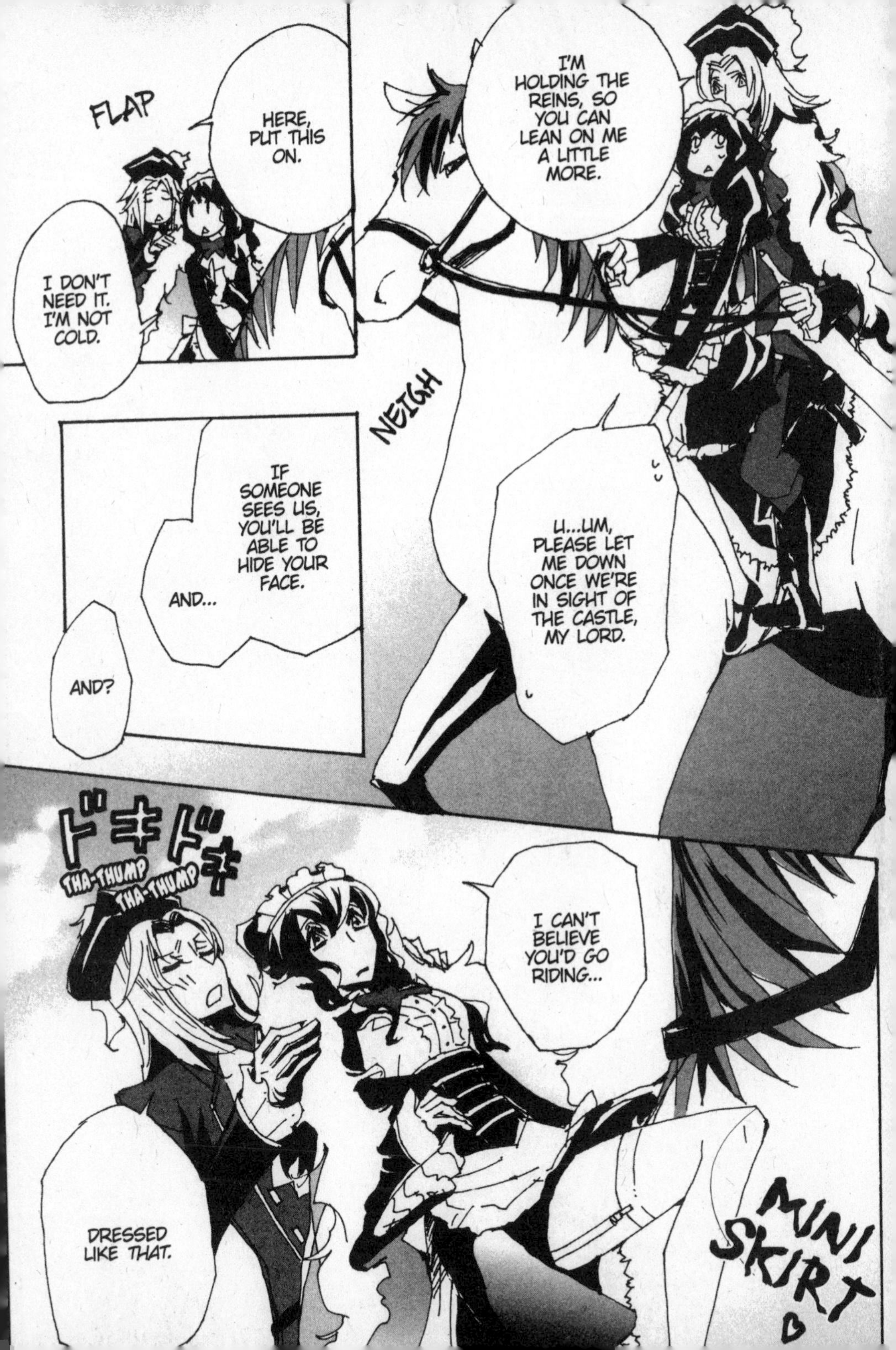
I'M HOLDING THE REINS, SO YOU CAN LEAN ON ME A LITTLE MORE.
NEIGH
U...UM, PLEASE LET ME DOWN ONCE WE'RE IN SIGHT OF THE CASTLE, MY LORD.
HERE, PUT THIS ON.
FLAP
I DON'T NEED IT. I'M NOT COLD.
IF SOMEONE SEES US, YOU'LL BE ABLE TO HIDE YOUR FACE.
AND...
AND?
I CAN'T BELIEVE YOU'D GO RIDING...
ドキドキ
THA-THUMP THA-THUMP
DRESSED LIKE THAT.
MINI SKIRT

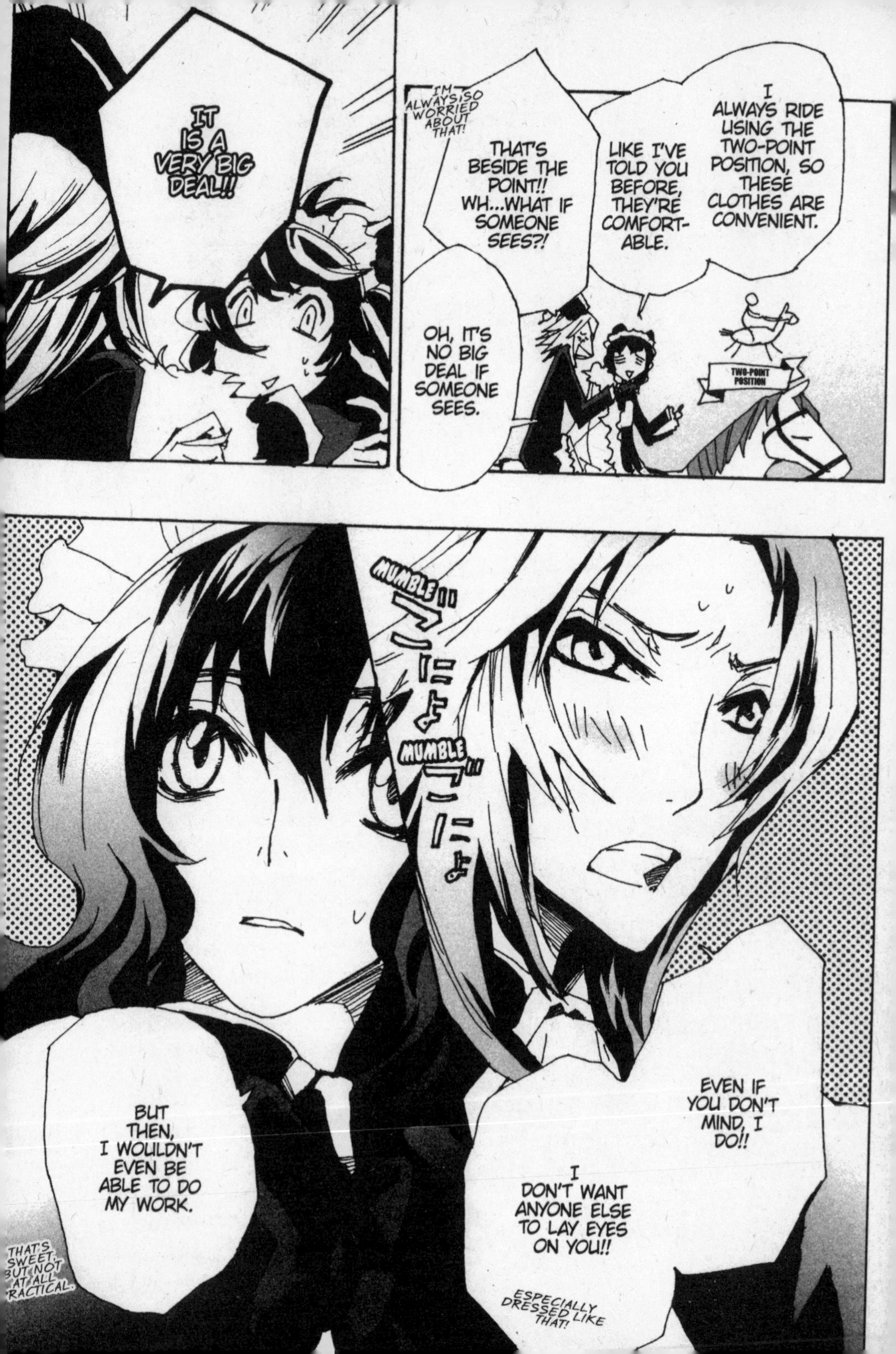
I ALWAYS RIDE USING THE TWO-POINT POSITION, SO THESE CLOTHES ARE CONVENIENT.
LIKE I'VE TOLD YOU BEFORE, THEY'RE COMFORTABLE.
THAT'S BESIDE THE POINT!! WH...WHAT IF SOMEONE SEES?!
I'M ALWAYS SO WORRIED ABOUT THAT!
TWO-POINT POSITION
OH, IT'S NO BIG DEAL IF SOMEONE SEES.
IT IS A VERY BIG DEAL!!
MUMBLE
MUMBLE
EVEN IF YOU DON'T MIND, I DO!!
I DON'T WANT ANYONE ELSE TO LAY EYES ON YOU!!
ESPECIALLY DRESSED LIKE THAT!
BUT THEN, I WOULDN'T EVEN BE ABLE TO DO MY WORK.
THAT'S SWEET, BUT NOT AT ALL RACTICAL.

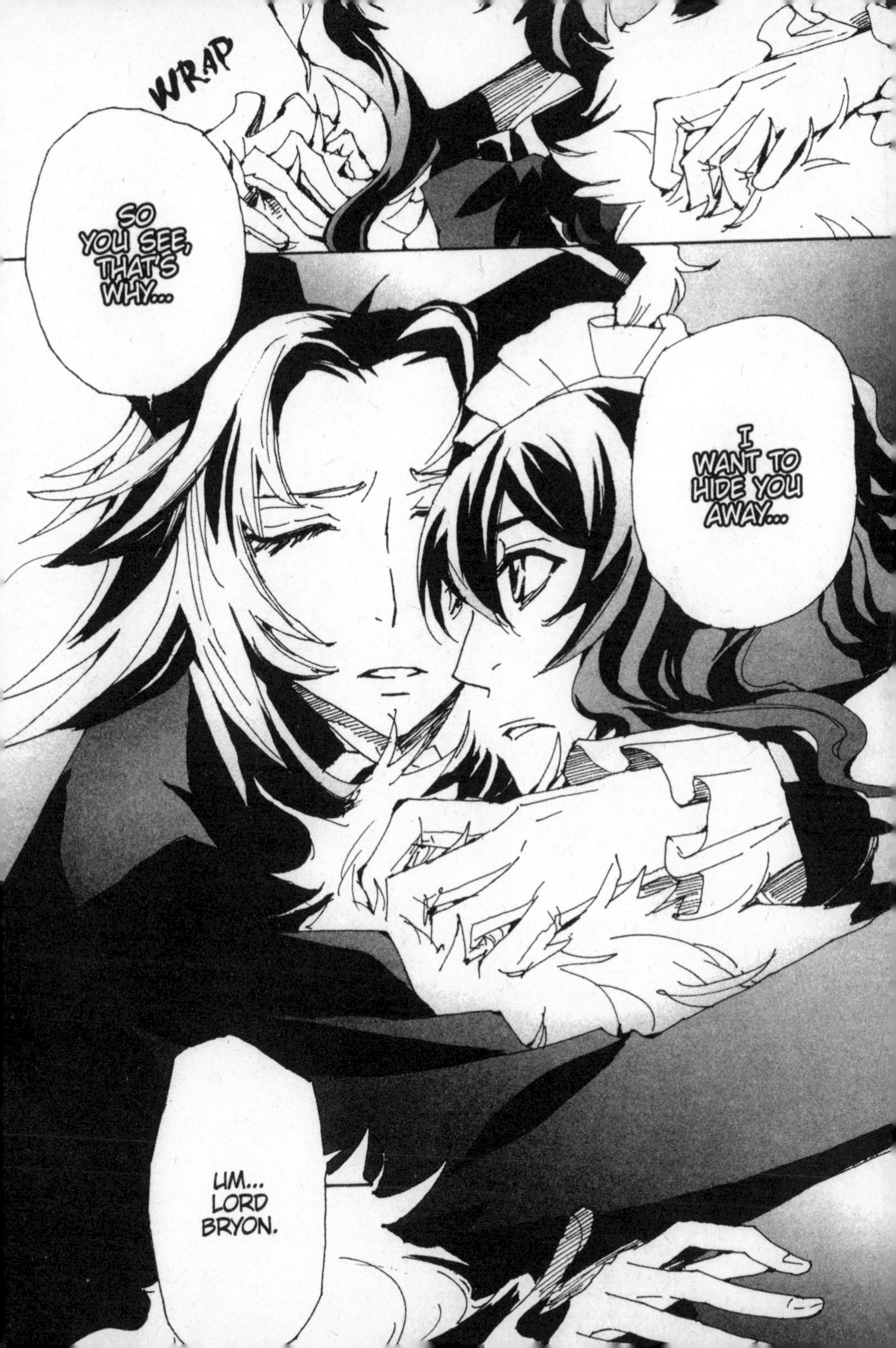
WRAP
SO YOU SEE, THAT'S WHY...
I WANT TO HIDE YOU AWAY...
UM... LORD BRYON.

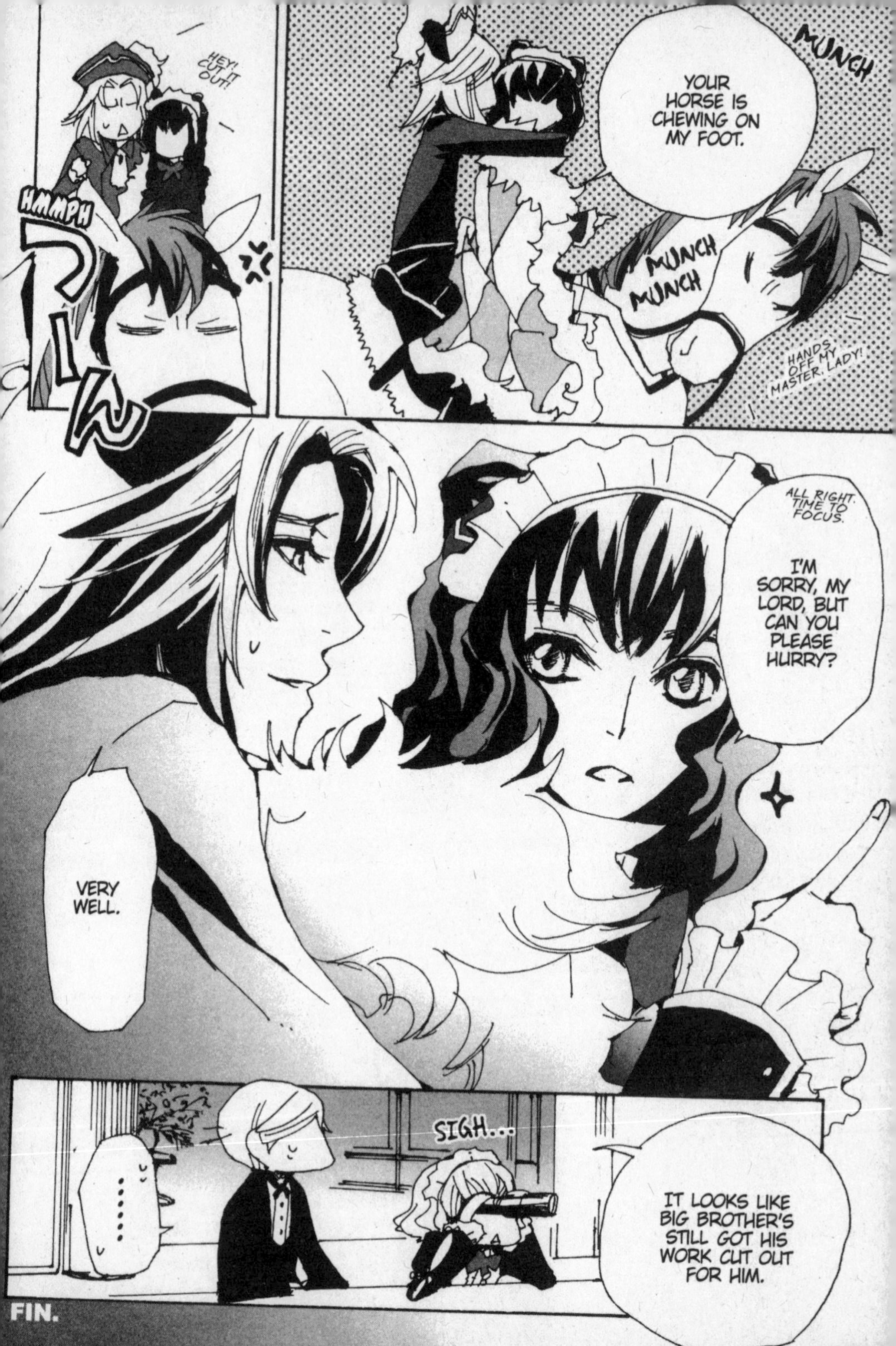
MUNCH
YOUR HORSE IS CHEWING ON MY FOOT.
MUNCH MUNCH
HANDS OFF MY MASTER, LADY!
HEY! CUT IT OUT!
HMMPH
ALL RIGHT. TIME TO FOCUS.
I'M SORRY, MY LORD, BUT CAN YOU PLEASE HURRY?
VERY WELL.
SIGH...
IT LOOKS LIKE BIG BROTHER'S STILL GOT HIS WORK CUT OUT FOR HIM.
......
FIN.

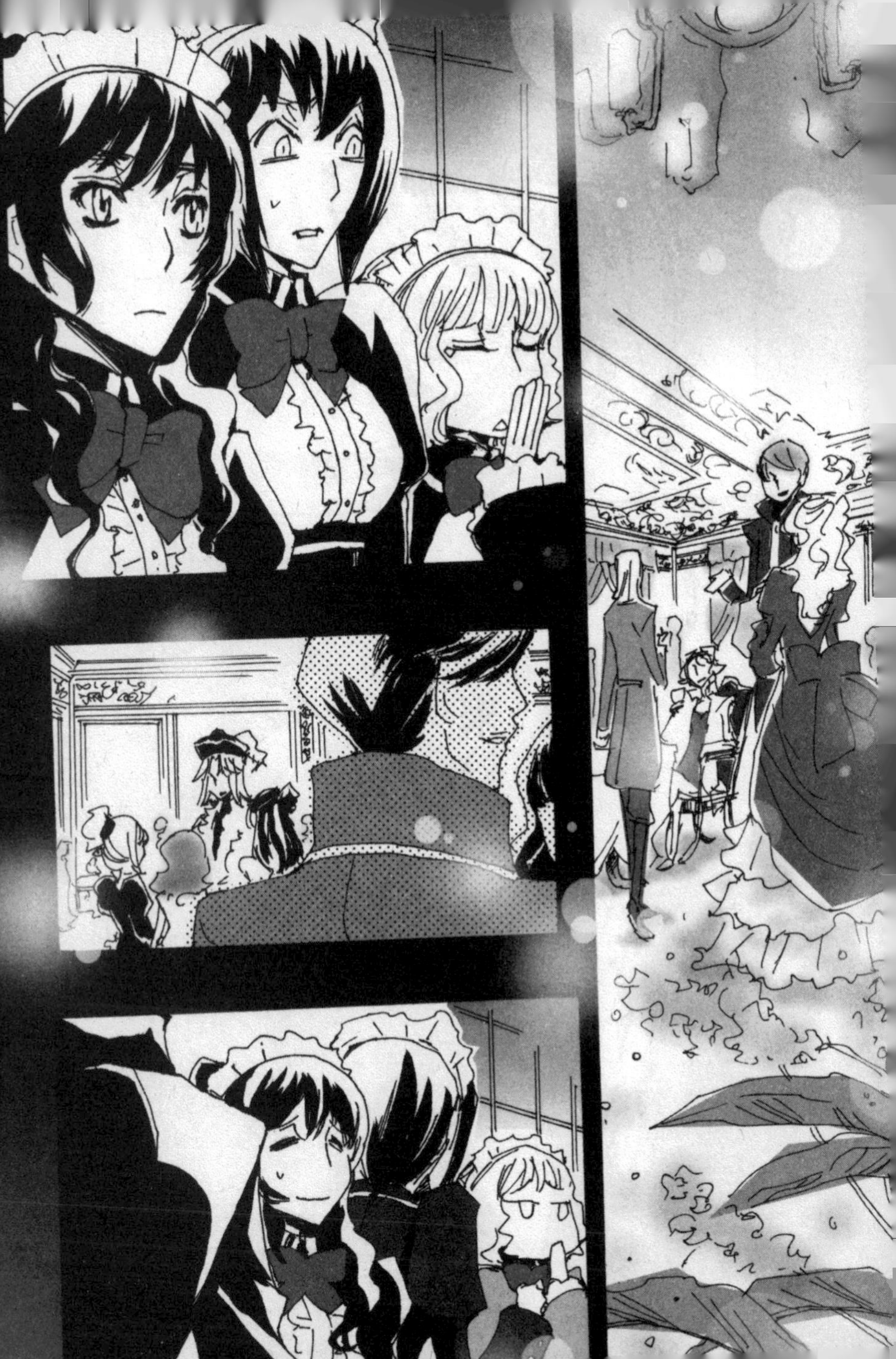

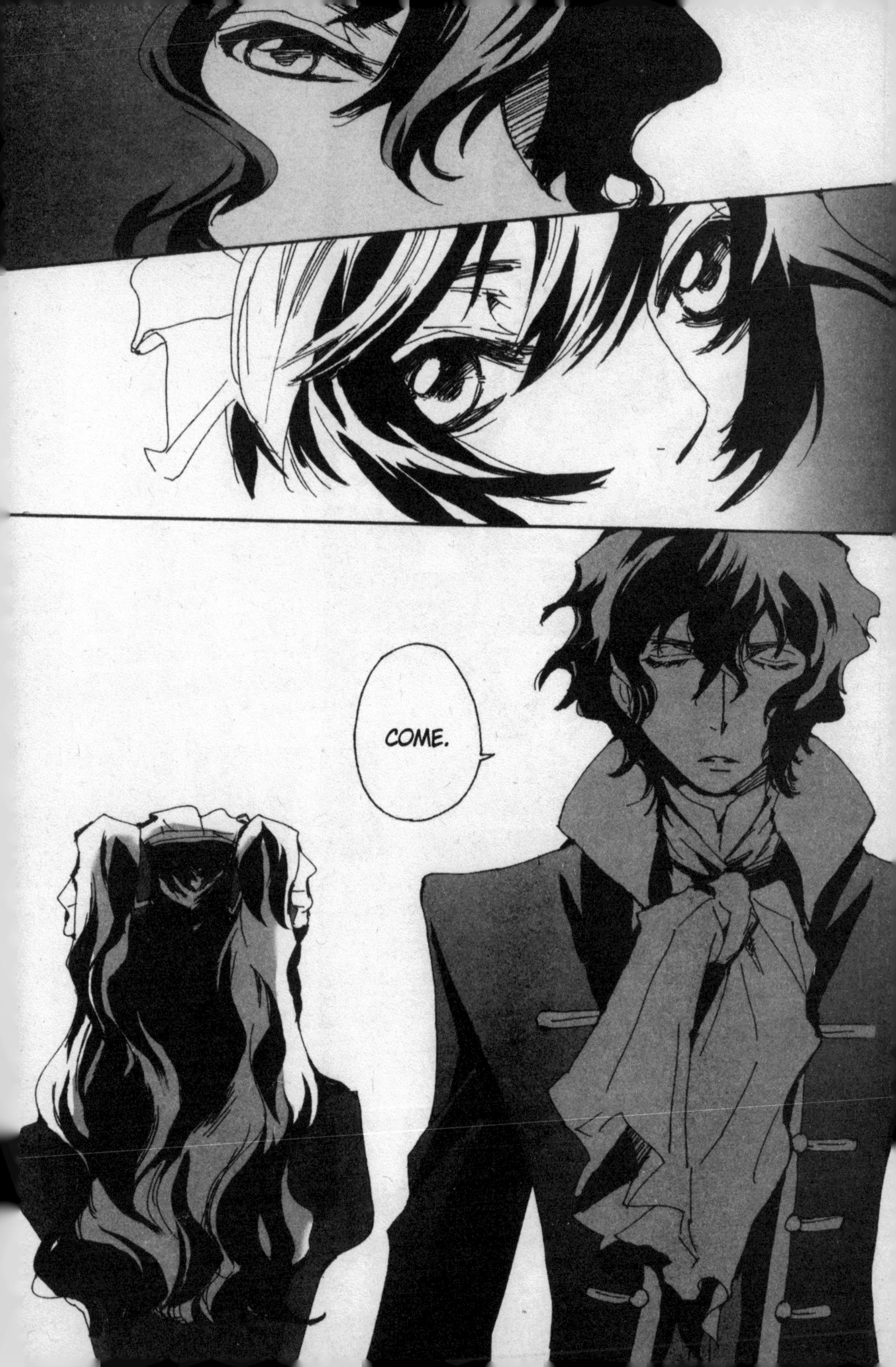
COME.

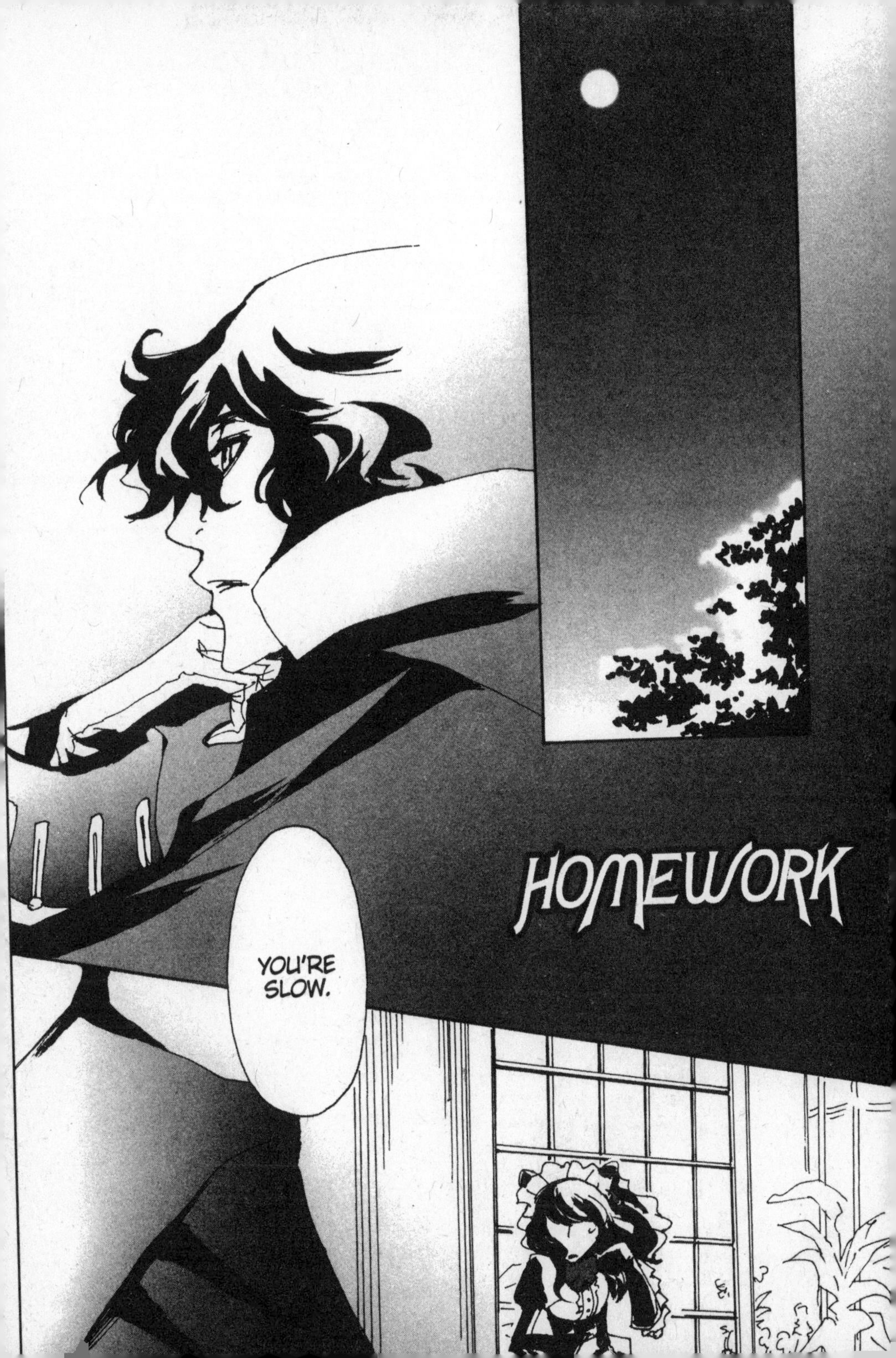
HOMEWORK
YOU'RE SLOW.

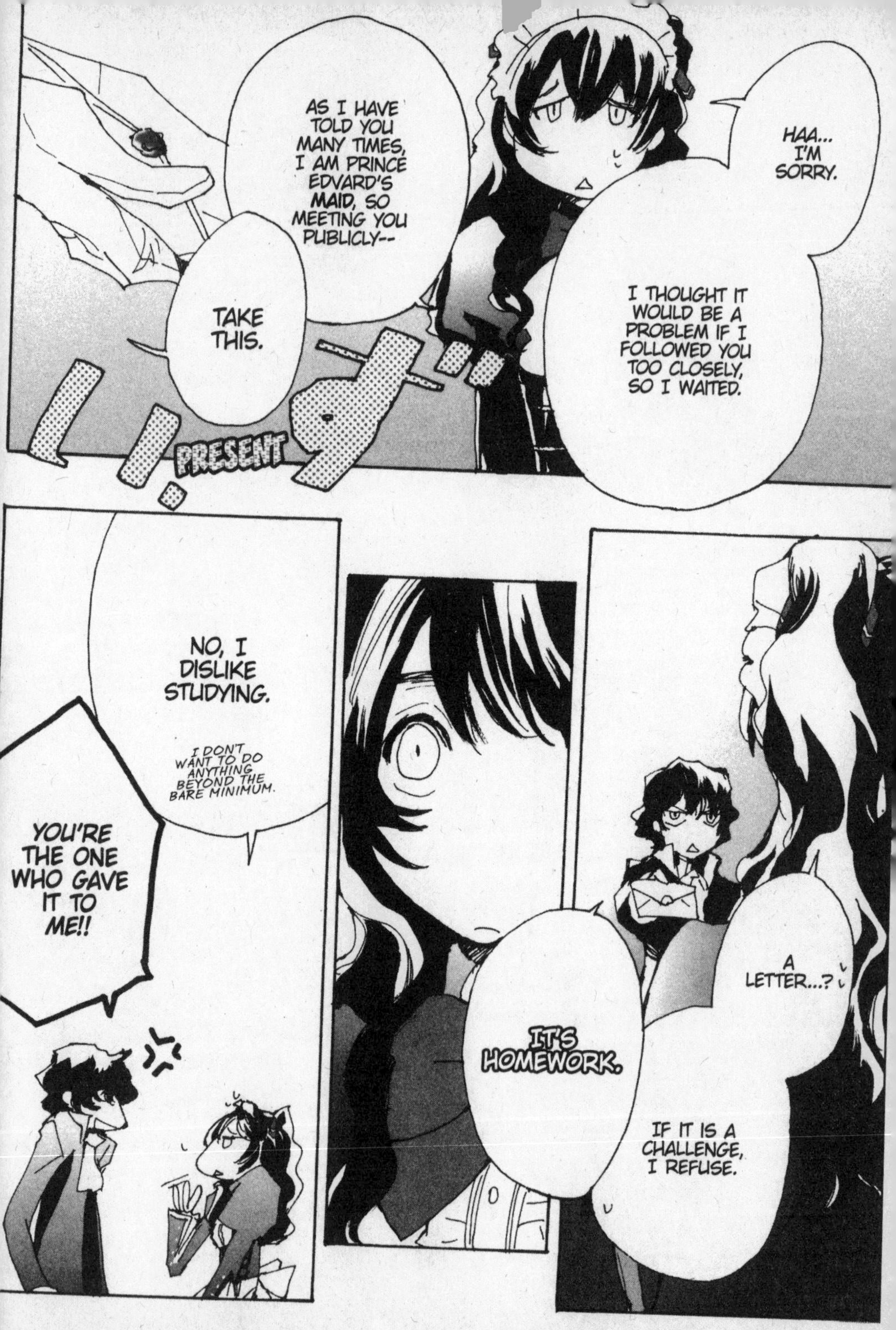
HAA... I'M SORRY.
I THOUGHT IT WOULD BE A PROBLEM IF I FOLLOWED YOU TOO CLOSELY, SO I WAITED.
AS I HAVE TOLD YOU MANY TIMES, I AM PRINCE EDVARD'S MAID, SO MEETING YOU PUBLICLY--
TAKE THIS.
PRESENT
A LETTER...?
IF IT IS A CHALLENGE, I REFUSE.
IT'S HOMEWORK.
NO, I DISLIKE STUDYING.
I DON'T WANT TO DO ANYTHING BEYOND THE BARE MINIMUM.
YOU'RE THE ONE WHO GAVE IT TO ME!!

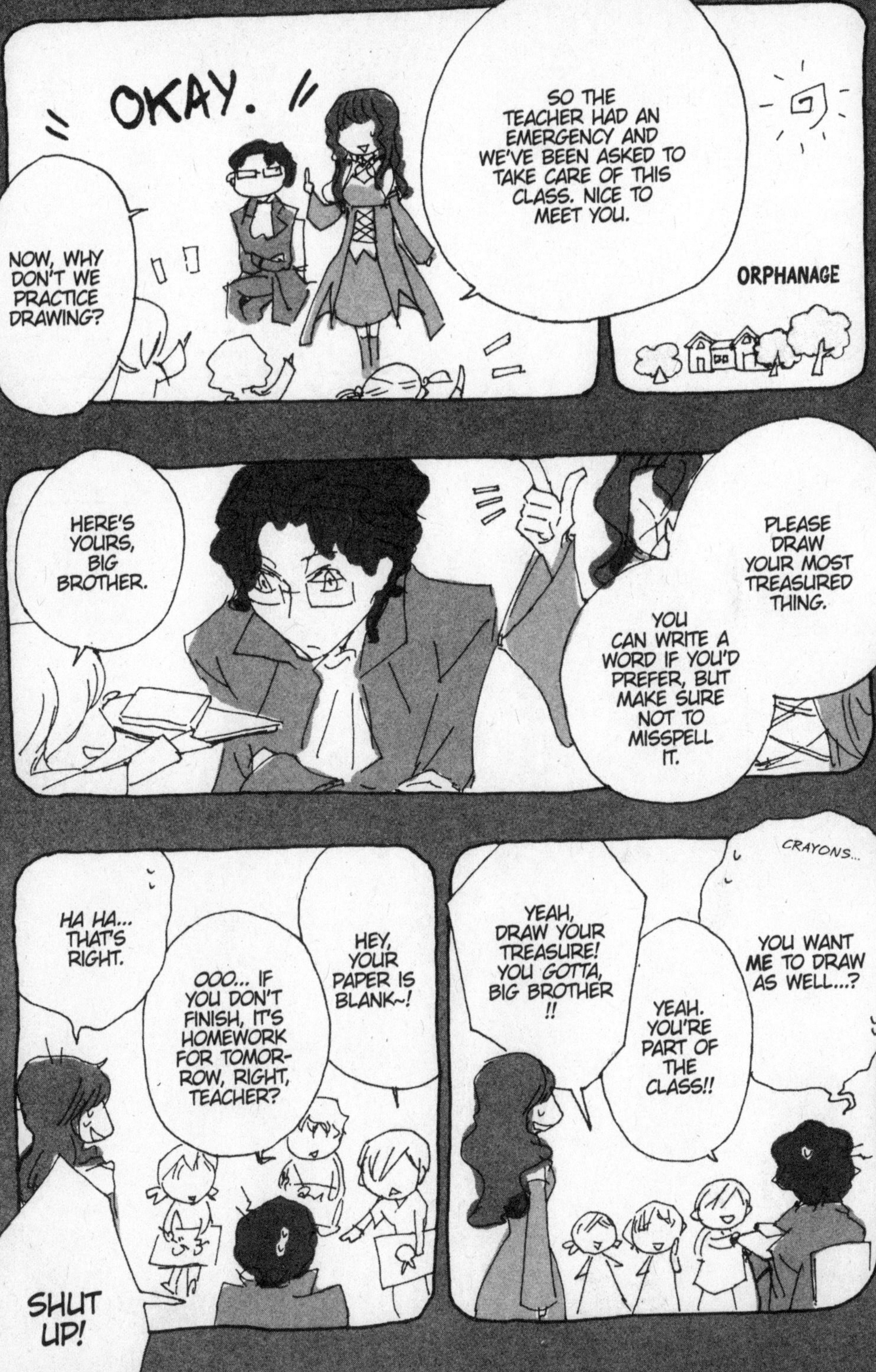

ORPHANAGE
SO THE TEACHER HAD AN EMERGENCY AND WE'VE BEEN ASKED TO TAKE CARE OF THIS CLASS. NICE TO MEET YOU.
OKAY.
NOW, WHY DON'T WE PRACTICE DRAWING?
PLEASE DRAW YOUR MOST TREASURED THING.
YOU CAN WRITE A WORD IF YOU'D PREFER, BUT MAKE SURE NOT TO MISSPELL IT.
HERE'S YOURS, BIG BROTHER.
CRAYONS...
YOU WANT ME TO DRAW AS WELL...?
YEAH, DRAW YOUR TREASURE! YOU GOTTA, BIG BROTHER!!
YEAH. YOU'RE PART OF THE CLASS!!
HEY, YOUR PAPER IS BLANK~!
OOO... IF YOU DON'T FINISH, IT'S HOMEWORK FOR TOMOR-ROW, RIGHT, TEACHER?
HA HA... THAT'S RIGHT.
SHUT UP!

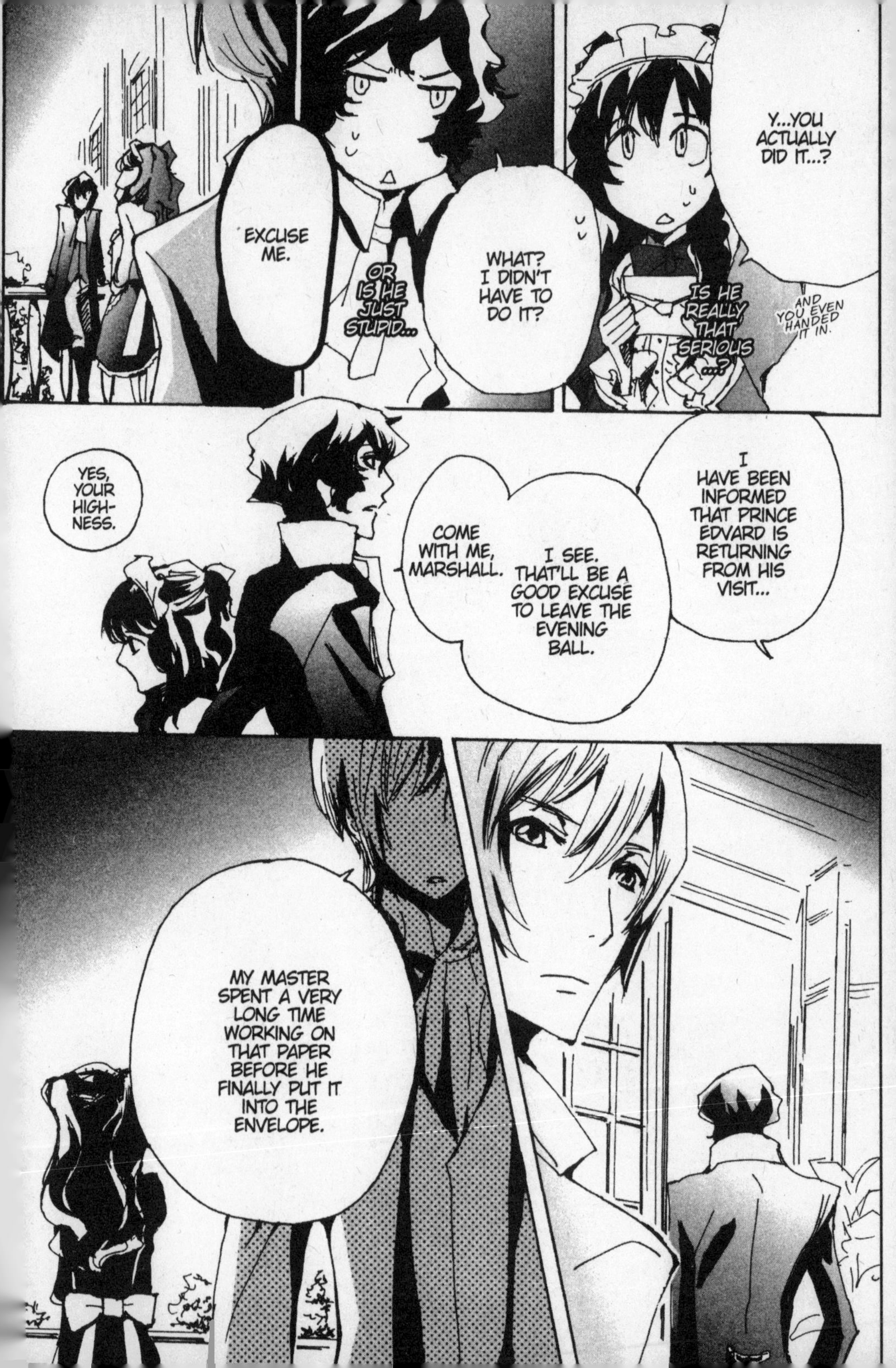

Y...YOU ACTUALLY DID IT...?
AND YOU EVEN HANDED IT IN.
IS HE REALLY THAT SERIOUS ...?
WHAT? I DIDN'T HAVE TO DO IT?
OR IS HE JUST STUPID...
EXCUSE ME.
I HAVE BEEN INFORMED THAT PRINCE EDVARD IS RETURNING FROM HIS VISIT...
I SEE. THAT'LL BE A GOOD EXCUSE TO LEAVE THE EVENING BALL.
COME WITH ME, MARSHALL.
YES, YOUR HIGHNESS.
MY MASTER SPENT A VERY LONG TIME WORKING ON THAT PAPER BEFORE HE FINALLY PUT IT INTO THE ENVELOPE.

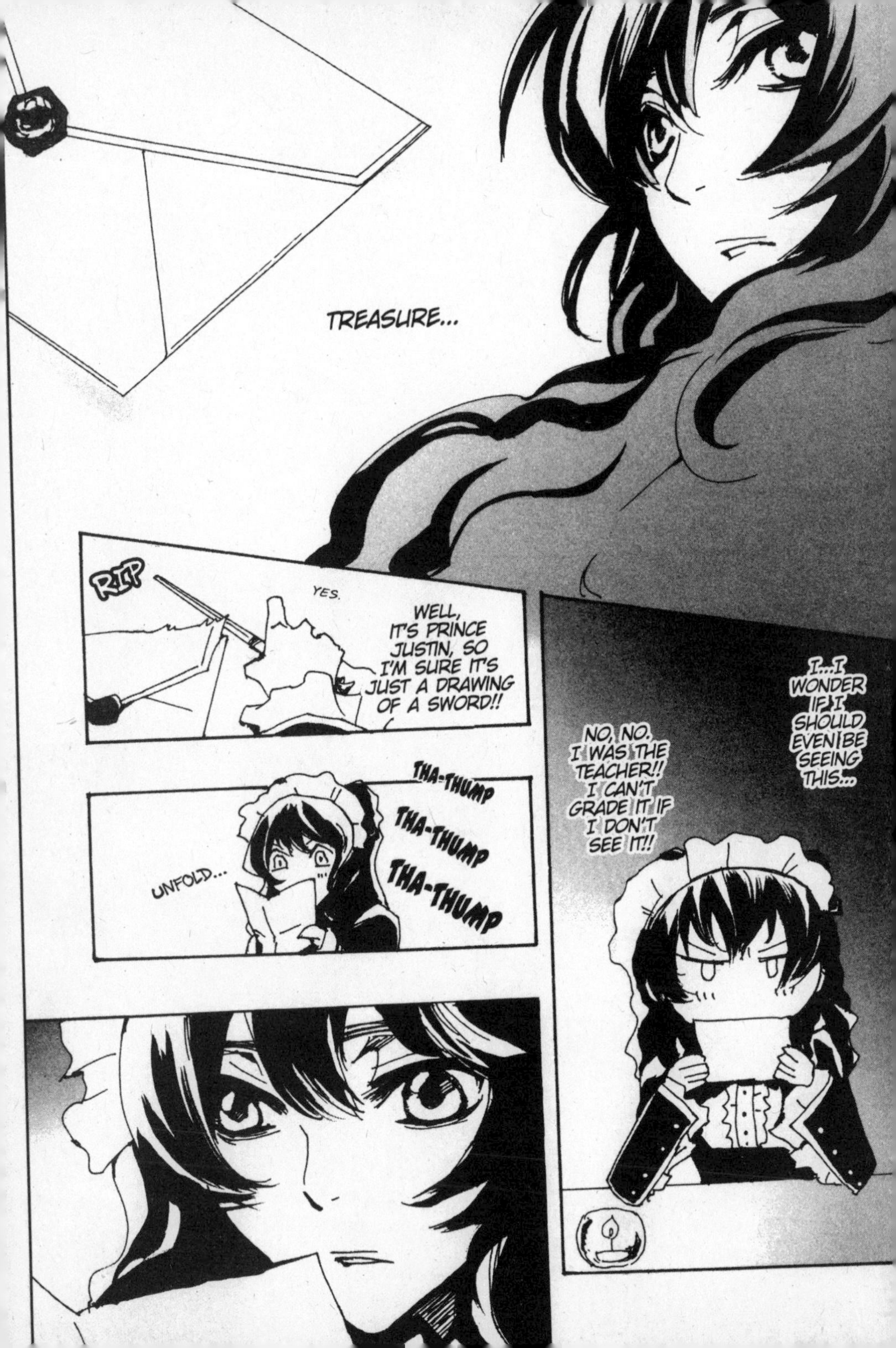
TREASURE...
I...I WONDER IF I SHOULD EVEN BE SEEING THIS...
NO, NO. I WAS THE TEACHER!! I CAN'T GRADE IT IF I DON'T SEE IT!!
YES.
WELL, IT'S PRINCE JUSTIN, SO I'M SURE IT'S JUST A DRAWING OF A SWORD!!
RIP
THA-THUMP
THA-THUMP
THA-THUMP
UNFOLD...

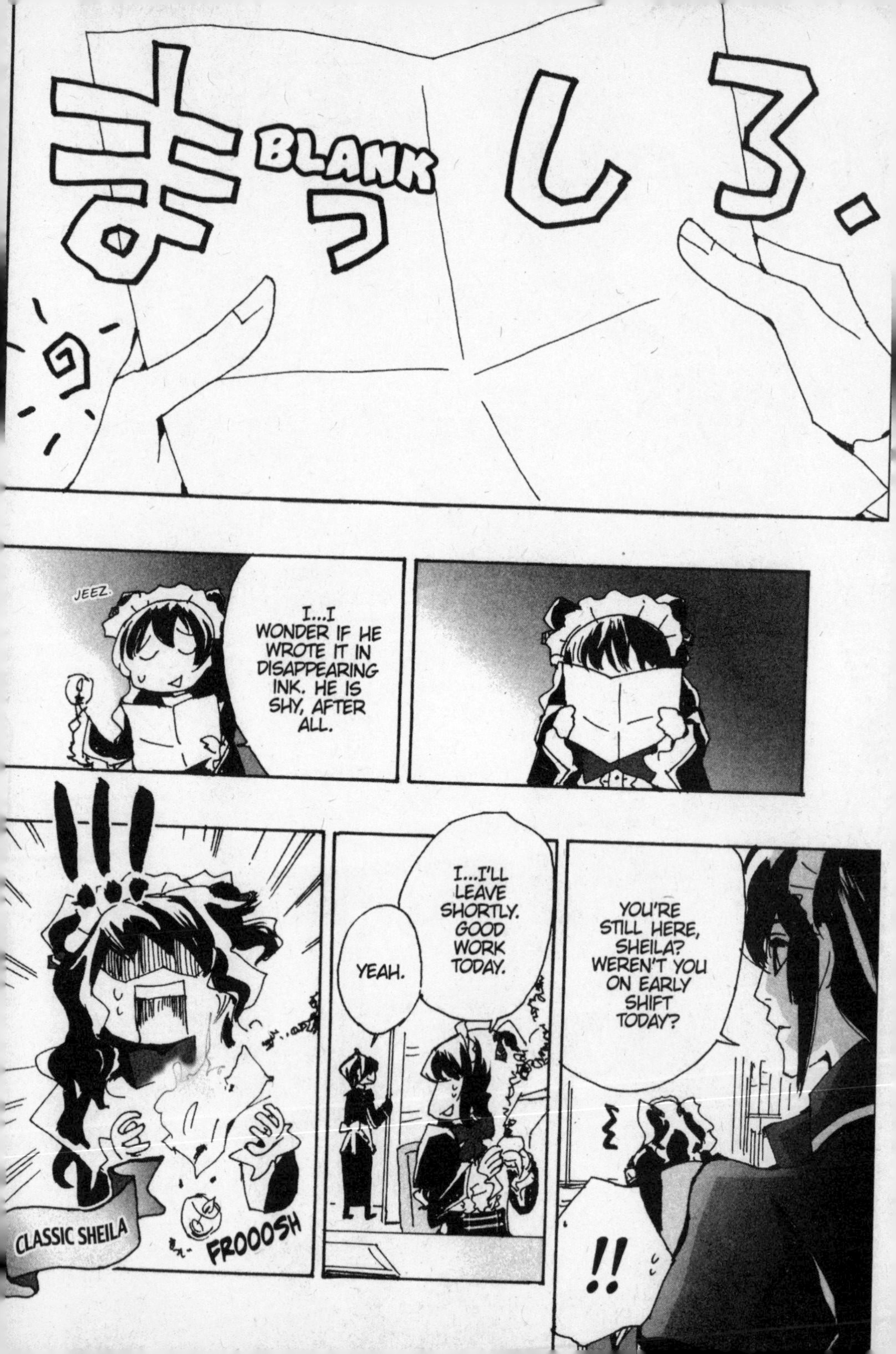
まっしろ。
BLANK
I...I WONDER IF HE WROTE IT IN DISAPPEARING INK. HE IS SHY, AFTER ALL.
JEEZ.
YOU'RE STILL HERE, SHEILA? WEREN'T YOU ON EARLY SHIFT TODAY?
!!
I...I'LL LEAVE SHORTLY. GOOD WORK TODAY.
YEAH.
CLASSIC SHEILA
FROOOSH

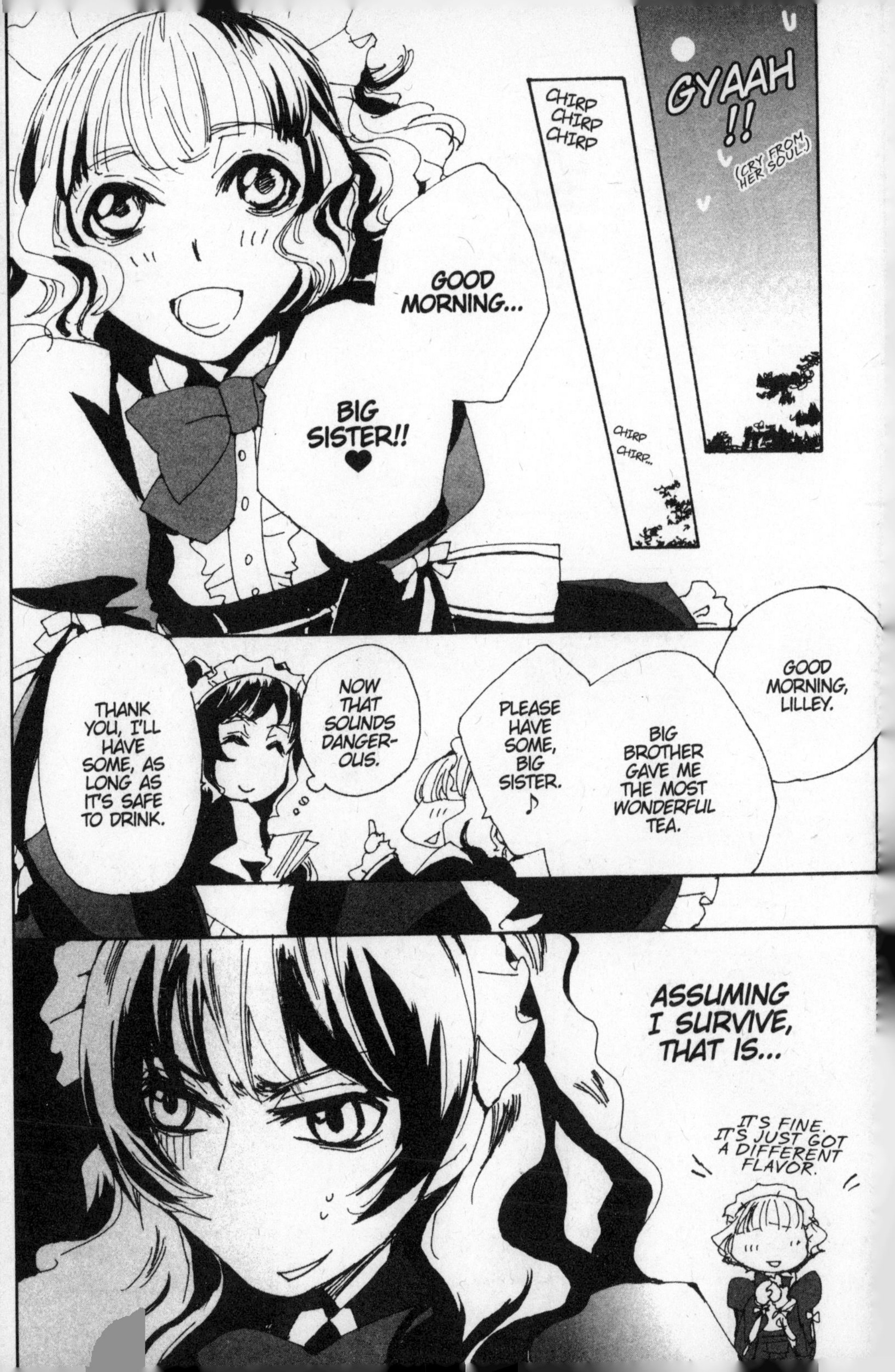
GYAAH!!
(CRY FROM HER SOUL!)
CHIRP CHIRP CHIRP
CHIRP CHIRP...
GOOD MORNING...
BIG SISTER!! ♥
GOOD MORNING, LILLEY.
BIG BROTHER GAVE ME THE MOST WONDERFUL TEA.
PLEASE HAVE SOME, BIG SISTER. ♪
NOW THAT SOUNDS DANGEROUS.
THANK YOU, I'LL HAVE SOME, AS LONG AS IT'S SAFE TO DRINK.
ASSUMING I SURVIVE, THAT IS...
IT'S FINE. IT'S JUST GOT A DIFFERENT FLAVOR.

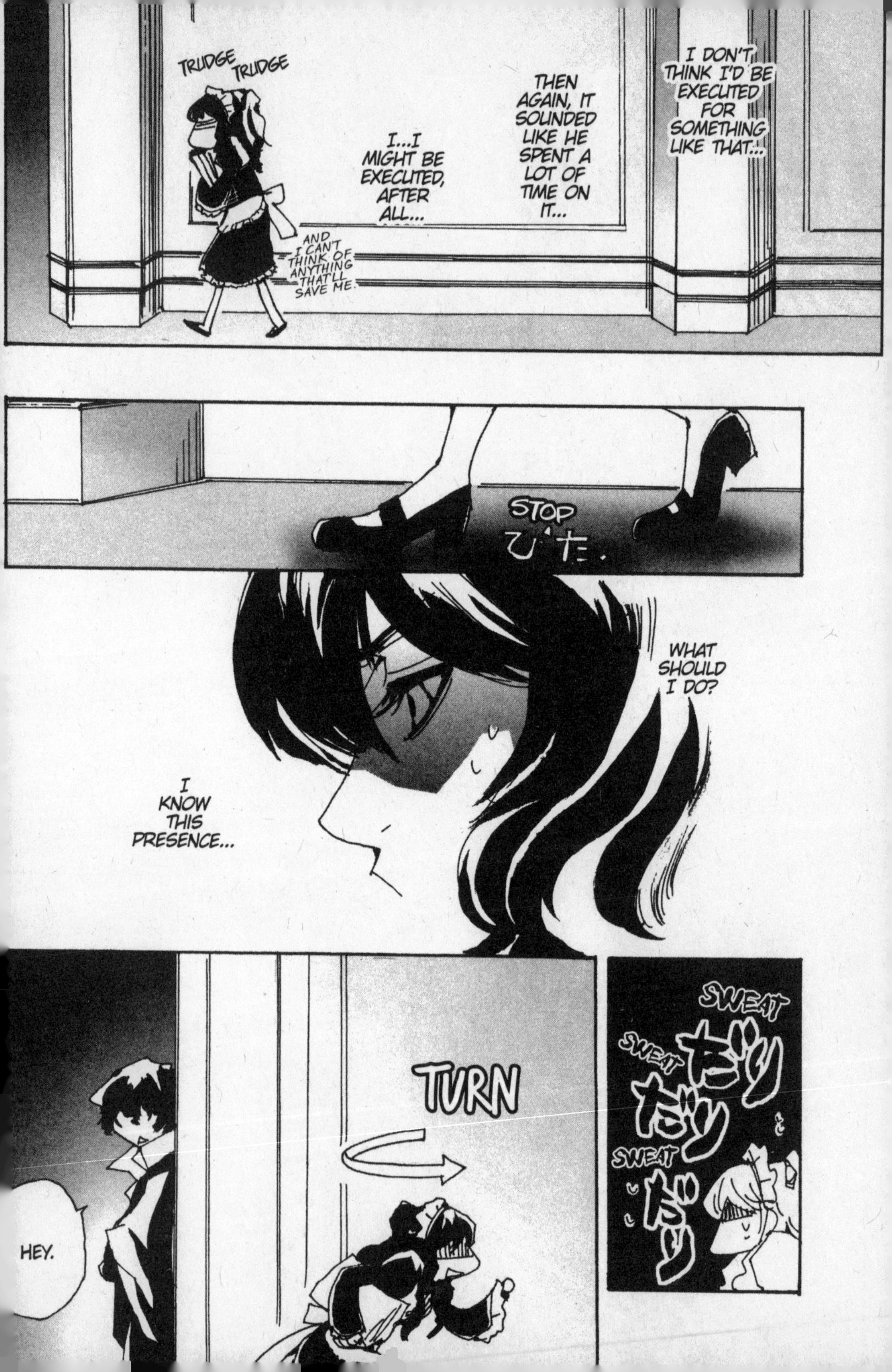
I DON'T THINK I'D BE EXECUTED FOR SOMETHING LIKE THAT...
THEN AGAIN, IT SOUNDED LIKE HE SPENT A LOT OF TIME ON IT...
I...I MIGHT BE EXECUTED, AFTER ALL...
AND I CAN'T THINK OF ANYTHING THAT'LL SAVE ME.
TRUDGE TRUDGE
STOP
WHAT SHOULD I DO?
I KNOW THIS PRESENCE...
SWEAT
SWEAT
SWEAT
TURN
HEY.

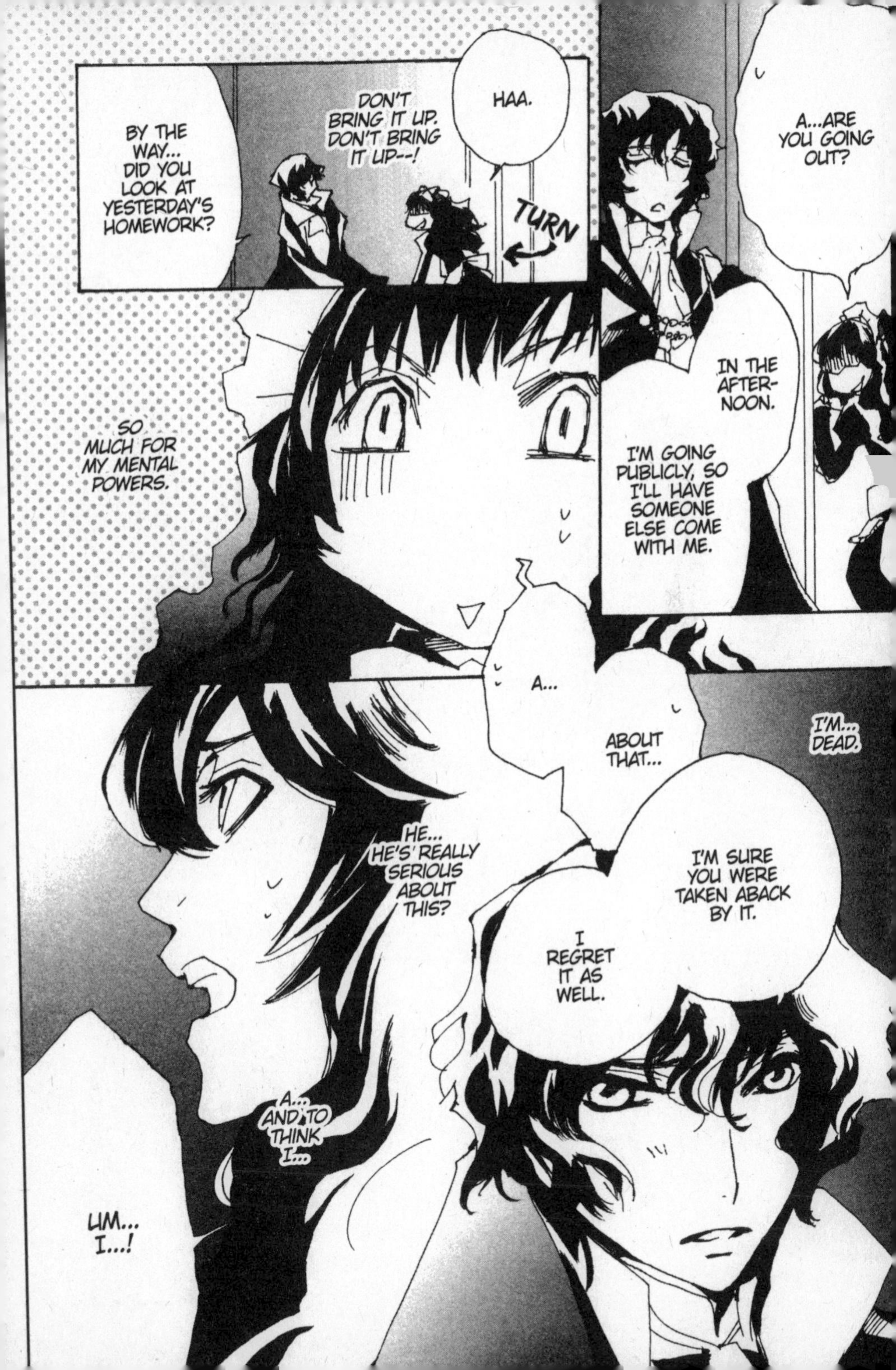
A...ARE YOU GOING OUT?
IN THE AFTER-NOON.
I'M GOING PUBLICLY, SO I'LL HAVE SOMEONE ELSE COME WITH ME.
HAA.
TURN
DON'T BRING IT UP. DON'T BRING IT UP--!
BY THE WAY... DID YOU LOOK AT YESTERDAY'S HOMEWORK?
SO MUCH FOR MY MENTAL POWERS.
A...
ABOUT THAT...
I'M... DEAD.
I'M SURE YOU WERE TAKEN ABACK BY IT.
I REGRET IT AS WELL.
HE... HE'S REALLY SERIOUS ABOUT THIS?
A... AND TO THINK I...
UM... I...!

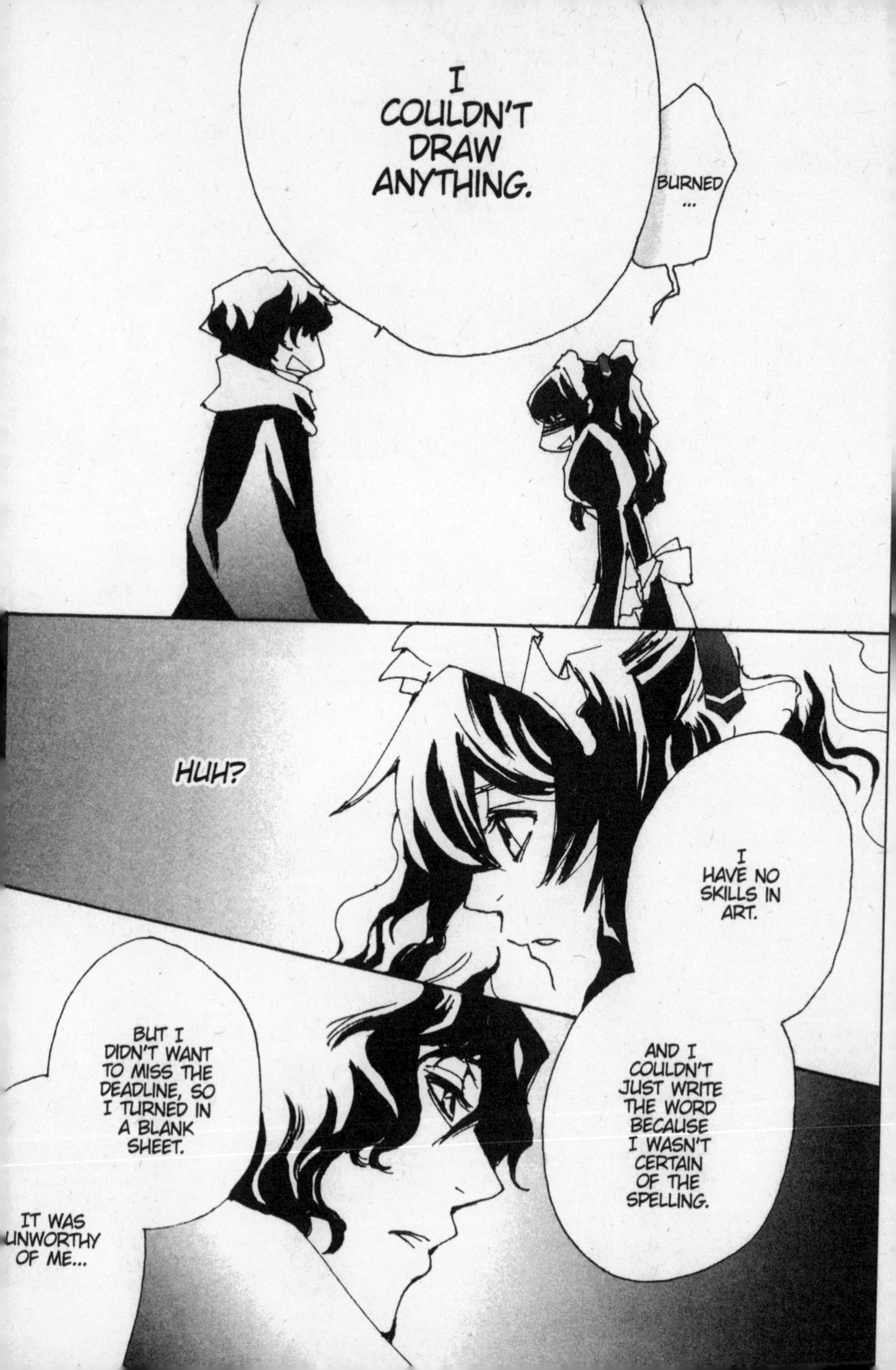
BURNED...
I COULDN'T DRAW ANYTHING.
HUH?
I HAVE NO SKILLS IN ART.
AND I COULDN'T JUST WRITE THE WORD BECAUSE I WASN'T CERTAIN OF THE SPELLING.
BUT I DIDN'T WANT TO MISS THE DEADLINE, SO I TURNED IN A BLANK SHEET.
IT WAS UNWORTHY OF ME...

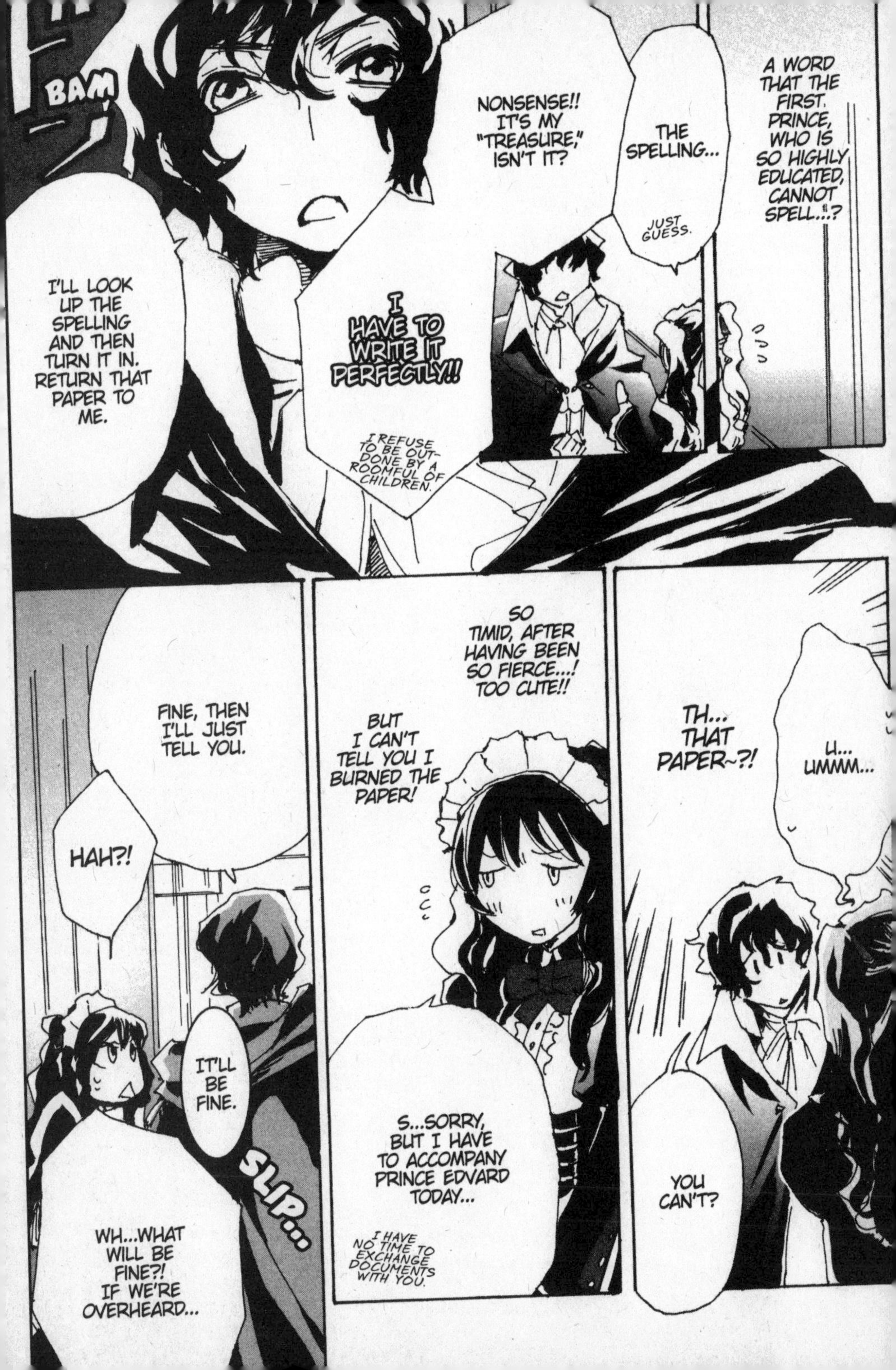
A WORD THAT THE FIRST PRINCE, WHO IS SO HIGHLY EDUCATED, CANNOT SPELL...?
THE SPELLING...
JUST GUESS.
NONSENSE!! IT'S MY "TREASURE," ISN'T IT?
I HAVE TO WRITE IT PERFECTLY!!
I REFUSE TO BE OUT-DONE BY A ROOMFUL OF CHILDREN.
BAM
I'LL LOOK UP THE SPELLING AND THEN TURN IT IN. RETURN THAT PAPER TO ME.
U... UMMM...
TH... THAT PAPER~?!
YOU CAN'T?
SO TIMID, AFTER HAVING BEEN SO FIERCE...! TOO CUTE!!
BUT I CAN'T TELL YOU I BURNED THE PAPER!
S...SORRY, BUT I HAVE TO ACCOMPANY PRINCE EDVARD TODAY...
I HAVE NO TIME TO EXCHANGE DOCUMENTS WITH YOU.
FINE, THEN I'LL JUST TELL YOU.
HAH?!
IT'LL BE FINE.
SLIP...
WH...WHAT WILL BE FINE?! IF WE'RE OVERHEARD...

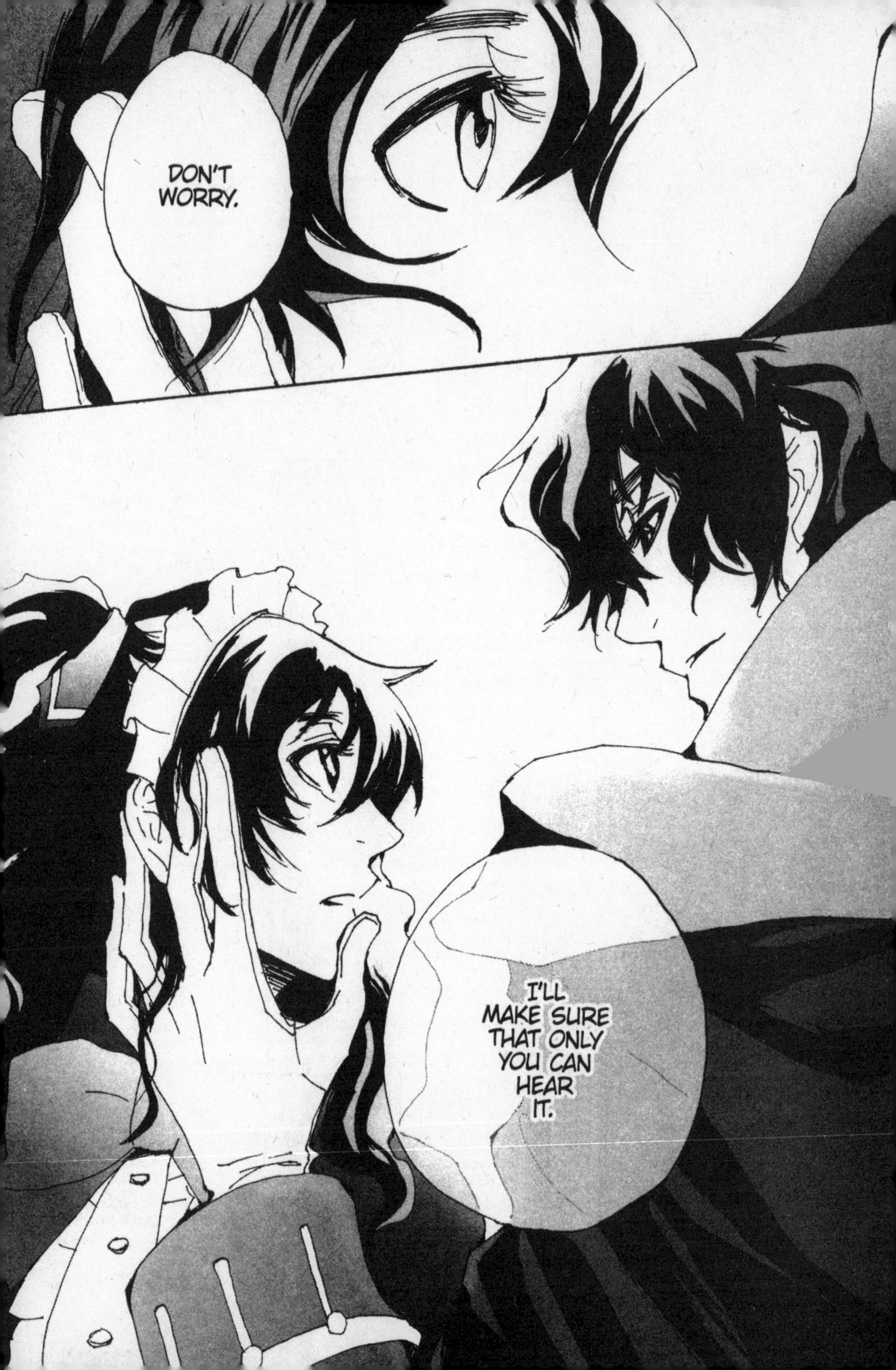
DON'T WORRY.
I'LL MAKE SURE THAT ONLY YOU CAN HEAR IT.

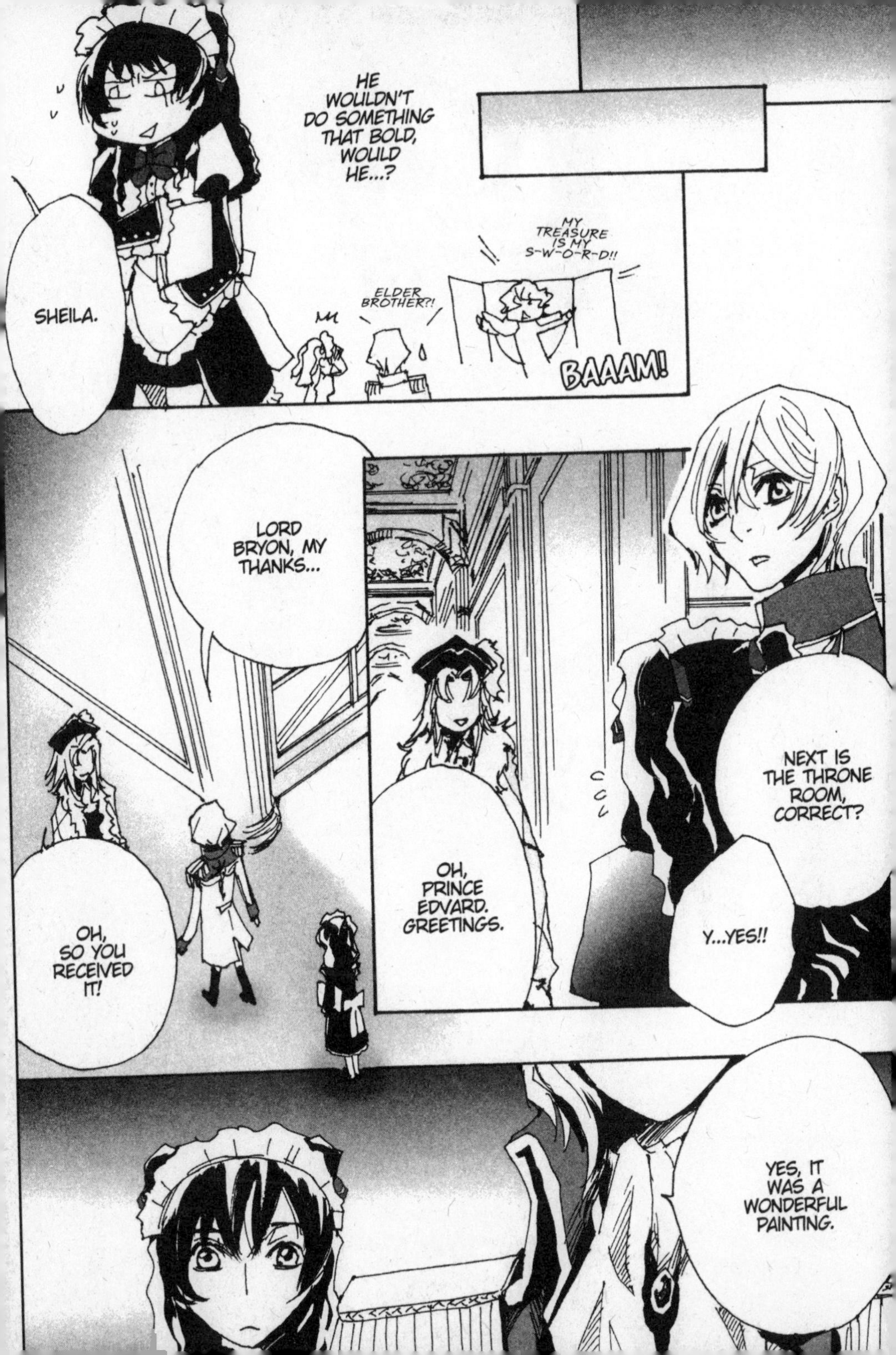

MY TREASURE IS MY S-W-O-R-D!!
ELDER BROTHER?!
BAAAM!
HE WOULDN'T DO SOMETHING THAT BOLD, WOULD HE...?
SHEILA.
NEXT IS THE THRONE ROOM, CORRECT?
Y...YES!!
OH, PRINCE EDVARD. GREETINGS.
LORD BRYON, MY THANKS...
OH, SO YOU RECEIVED IT!
YES, IT WAS A WONDERFUL PAINTING.

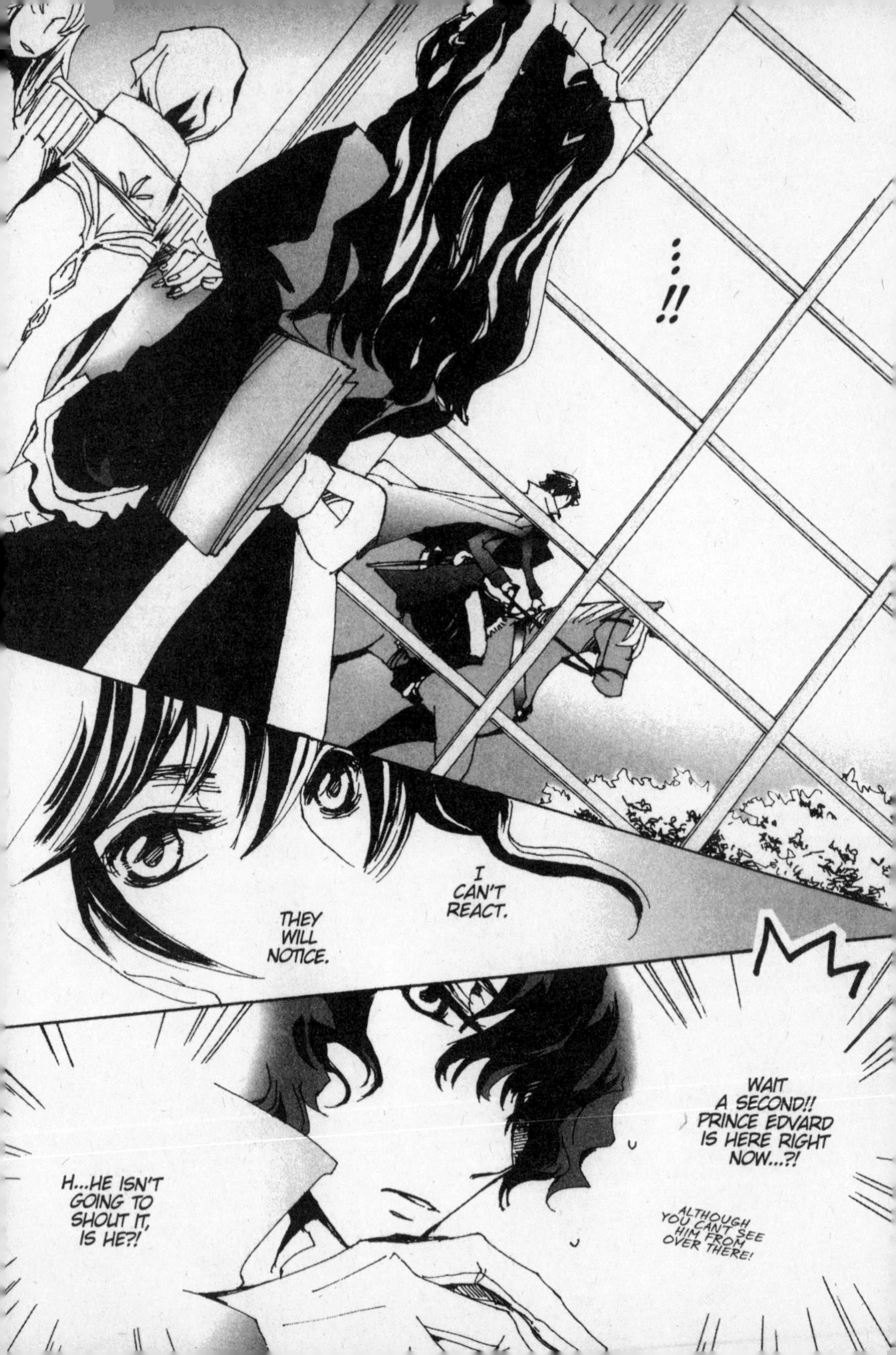
...!!
I CAN'T REACT.
THEY WILL NOTICE.
WAIT A SECOND!! PRINCE EDVARD IS HERE RIGHT NOW...?!
ALTHOUGH YOU CAN'T SEE HIM FROM OVER THERE!
H...HE ISN'T GOING TO SHOUT IT, IS HE?!

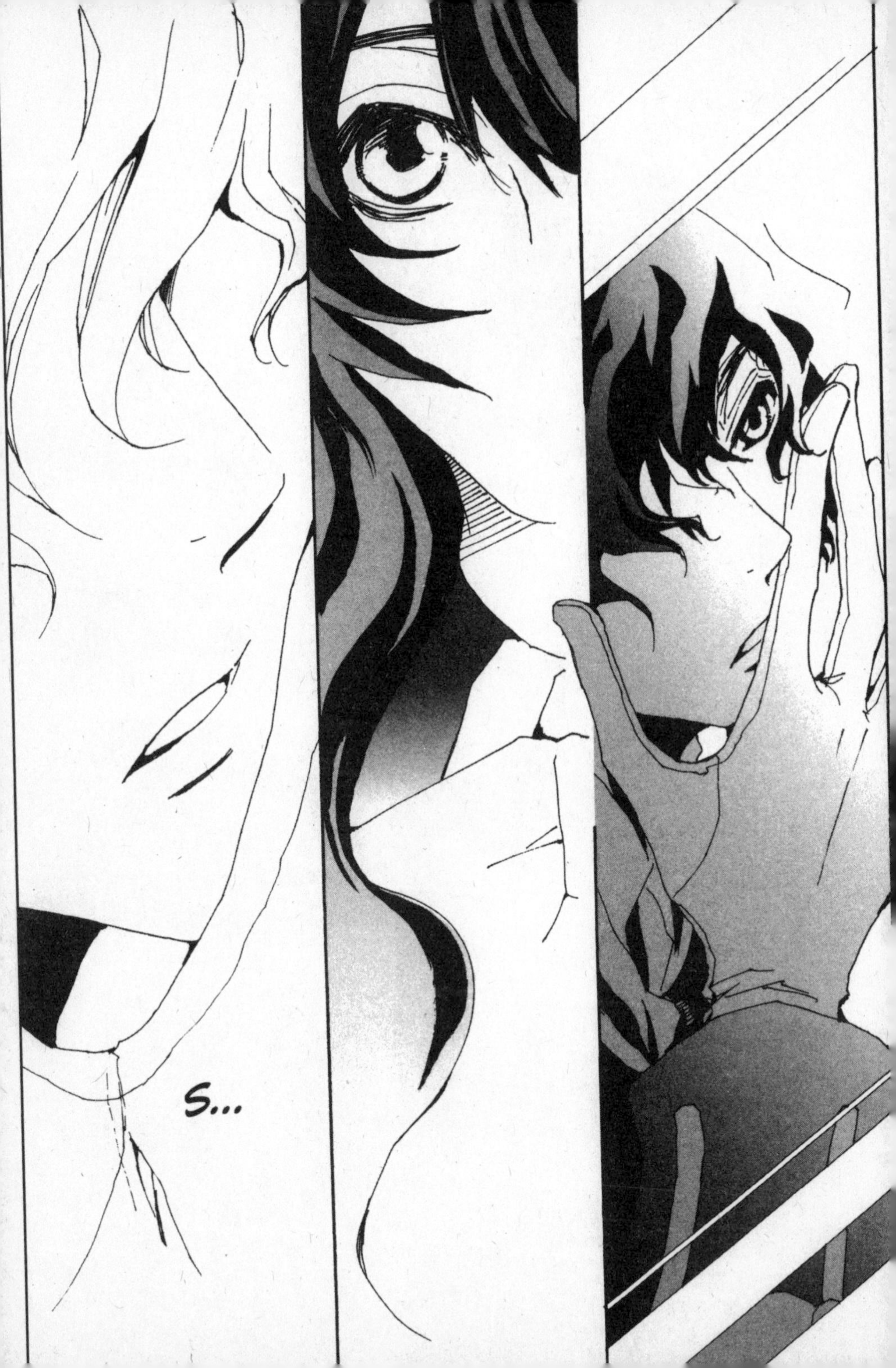
S...

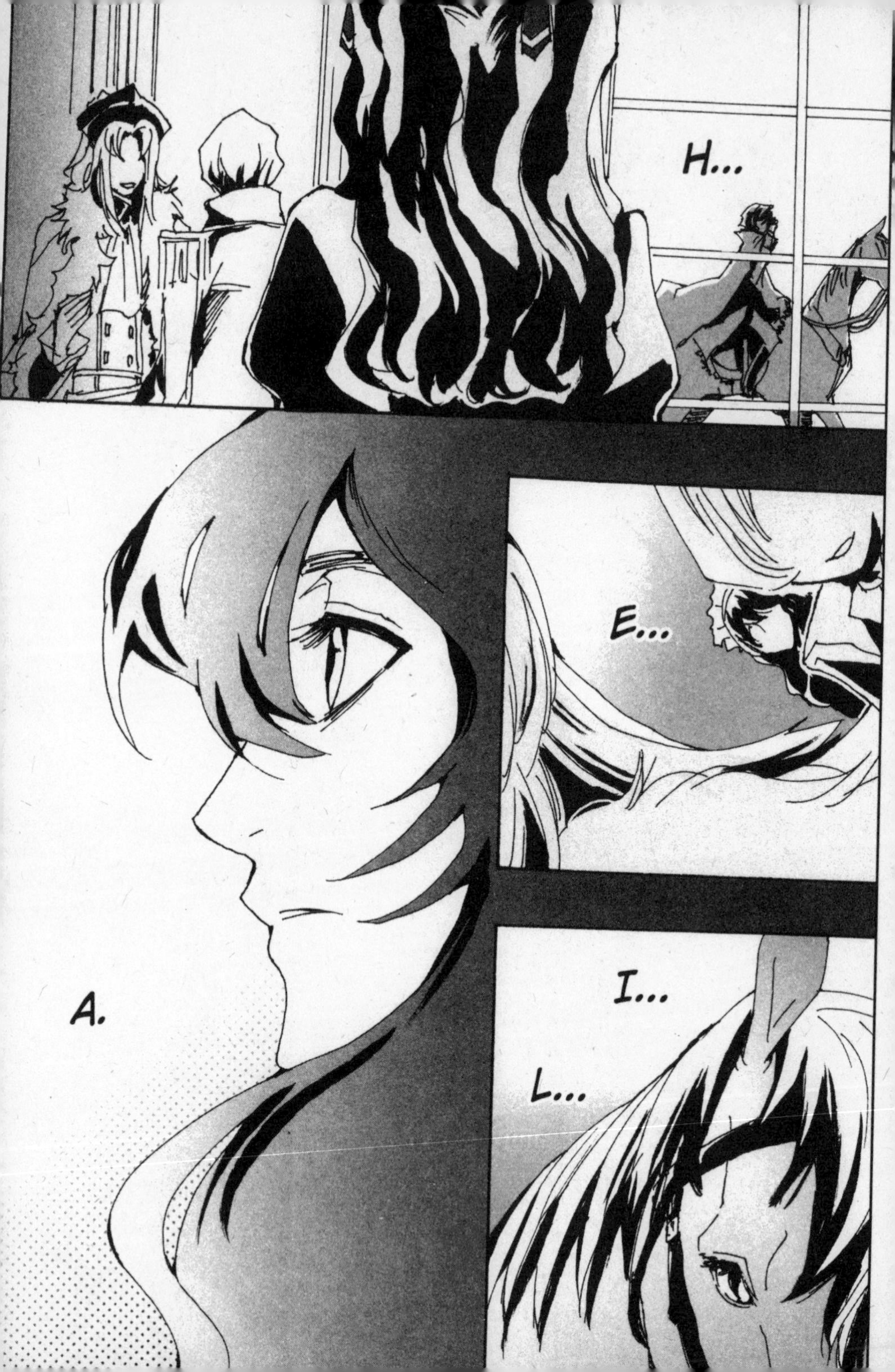
H...
E...
I...
L...
A.

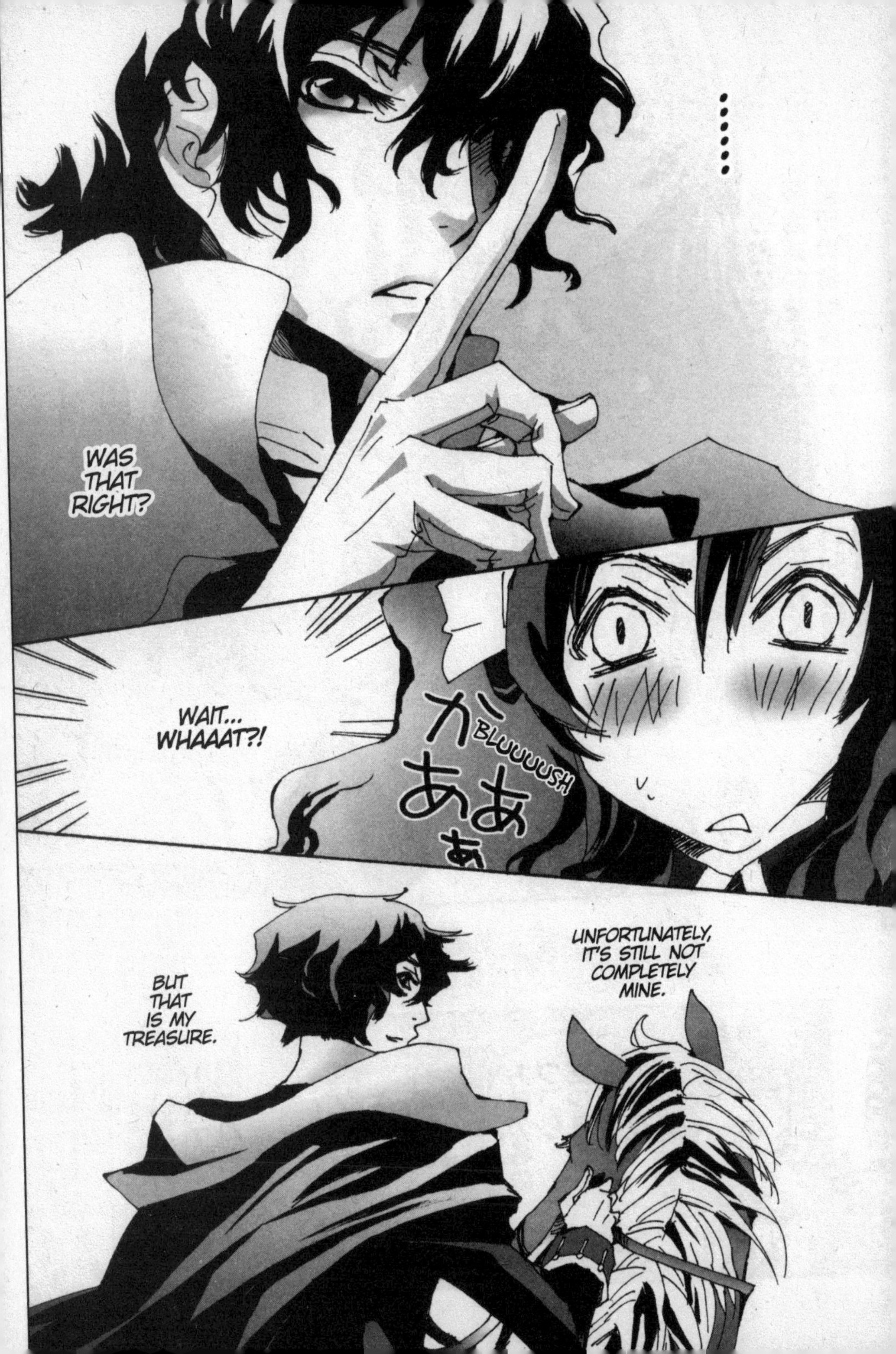
......
WAS THAT RIGHT?
かああ
BLUUUUSH
WAIT... WHAAAT?!
UNFORTUNATELY, IT'S STILL NOT COMPLETELY MINE.
BUT THAT IS MY TREASURE.

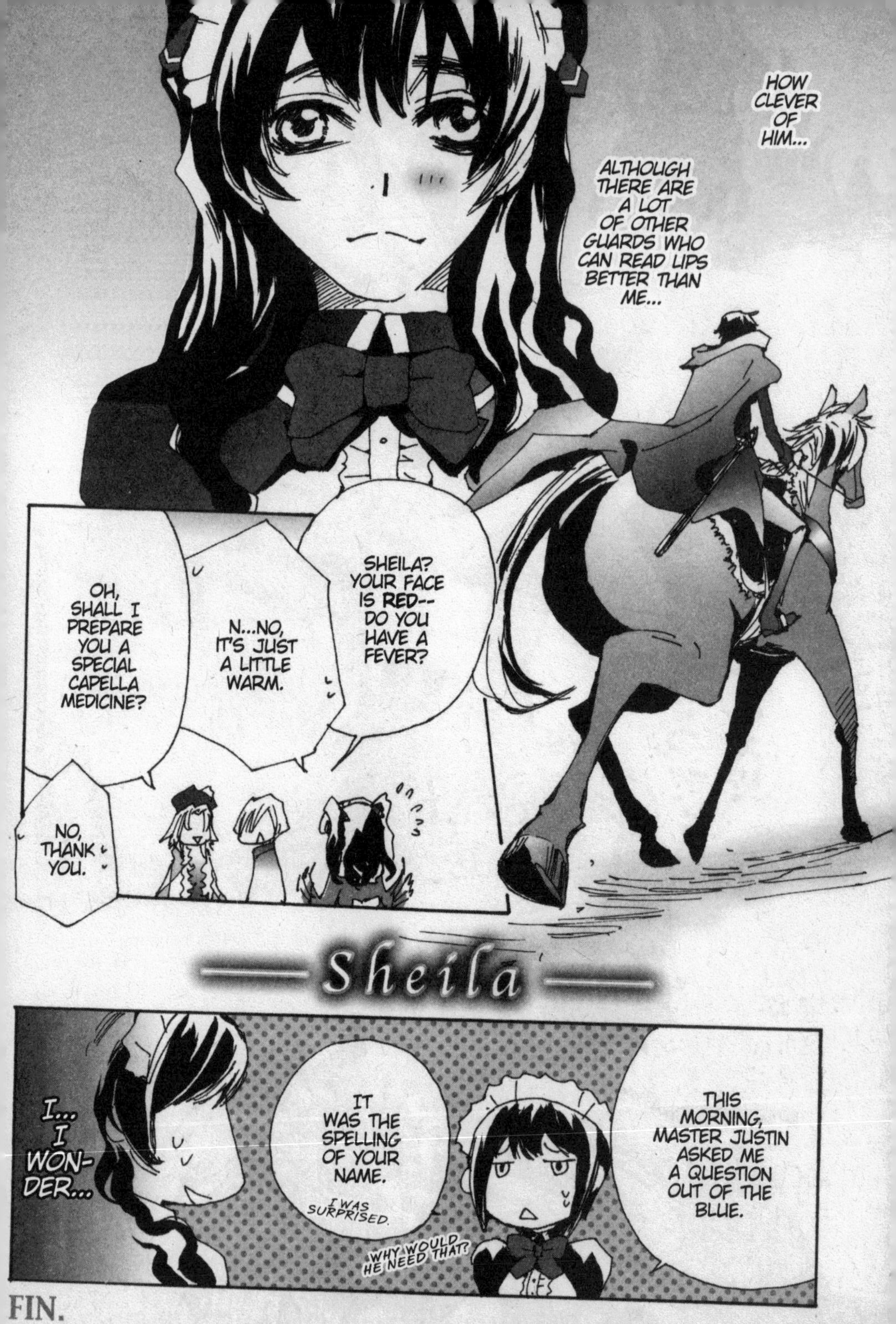
HOW CLEVER OF HIM...
ALTHOUGH THERE ARE A LOT OF OTHER GUARDS WHO CAN READ LIPS BETTER THAN ME...
SHEILA? YOUR FACE IS RED-- DO YOU HAVE A FEVER?
N...NO, IT'S JUST A LITTLE WARM.
OH, SHALL I PREPARE YOU A SPECIAL CAPELLA MEDICINE?
NO, THANK YOU.
—Sheila—
THIS MORNING, MASTER JUSTIN ASKED ME A QUESTION OUT OF THE BLUE.
WHY WOULD HE NEED THAT?
IT WAS THE SPELLING OF YOUR NAME.
I WAS SURPRISED.
I... I WONDER...

FIN.

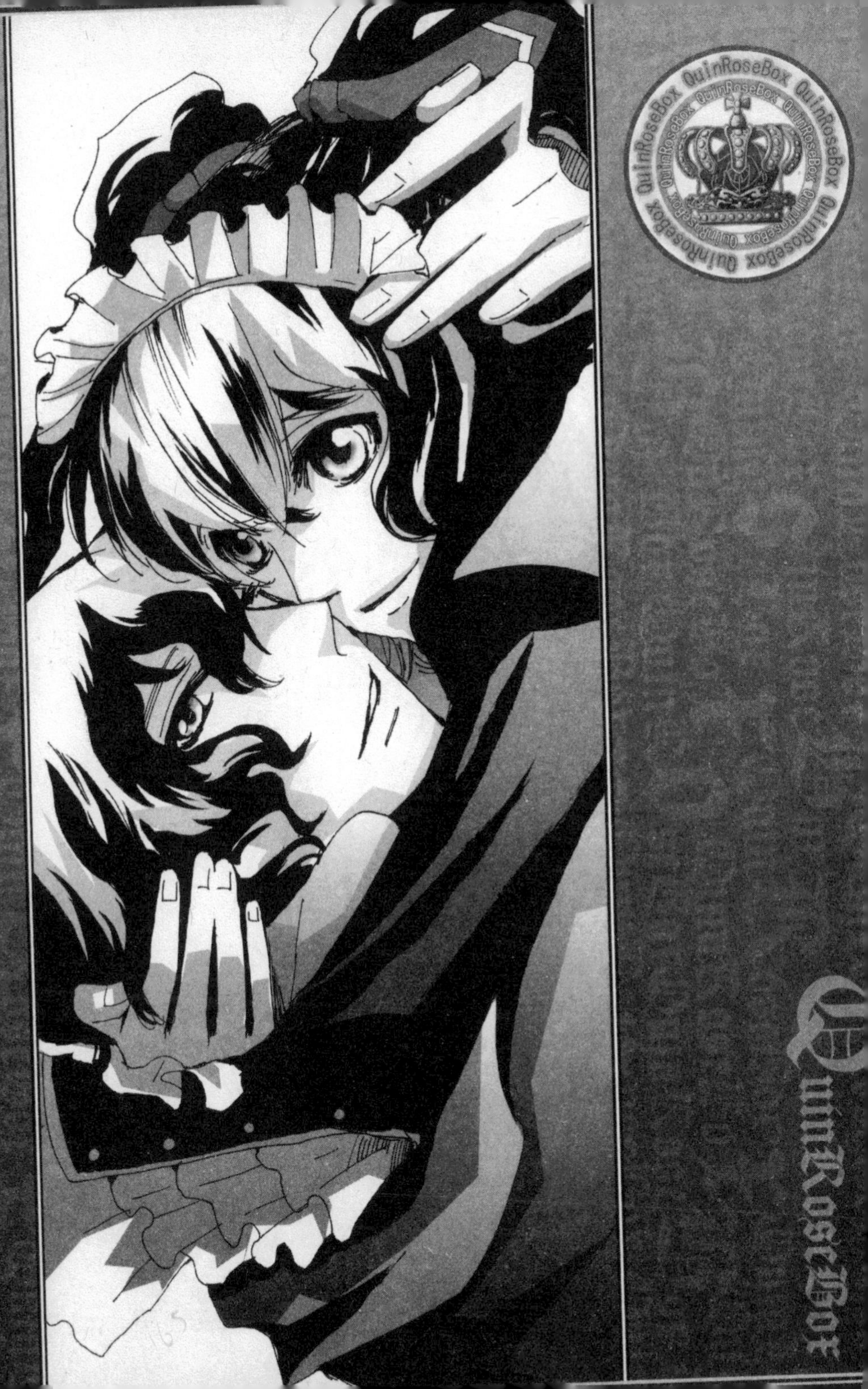

QuinRoseBox

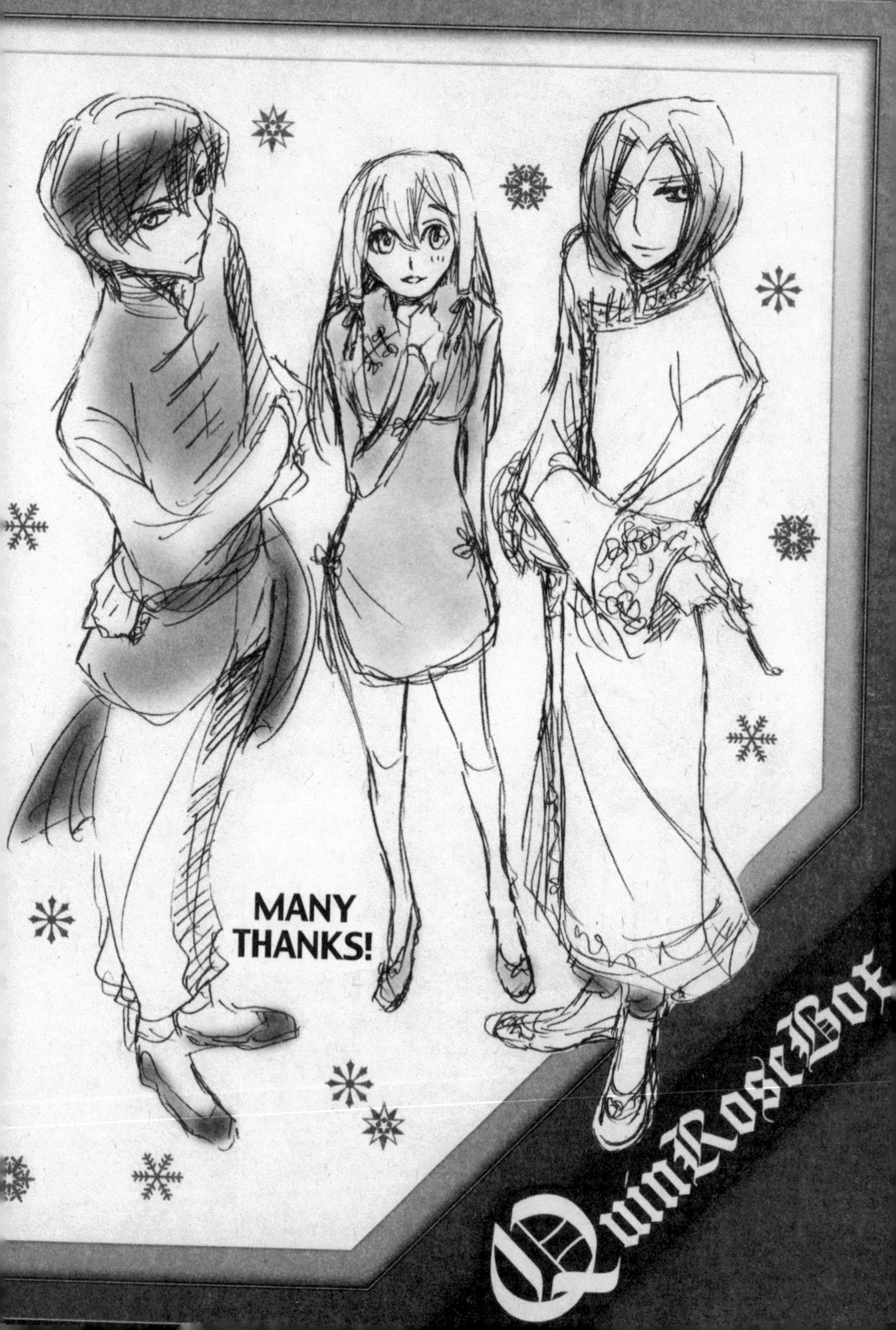
MANY
THANKS!

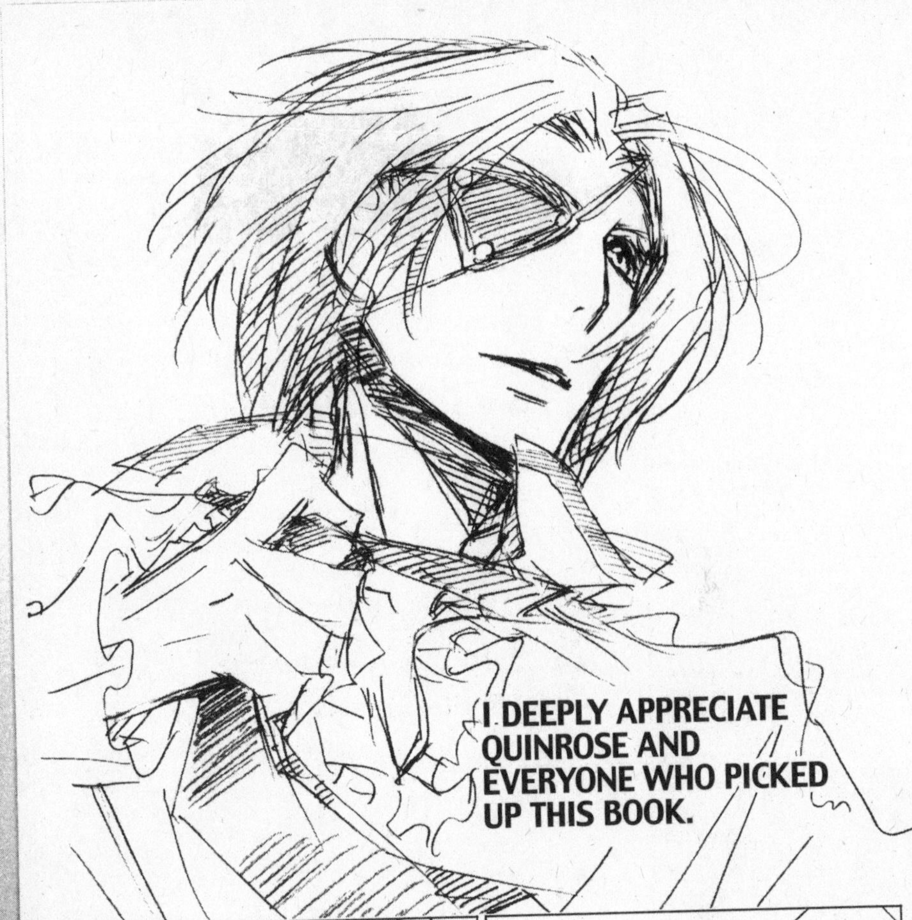
I DEEPLY APPRECIATE QUINROSE AND EVERYONE WHO PICKED UP THIS BOOK.

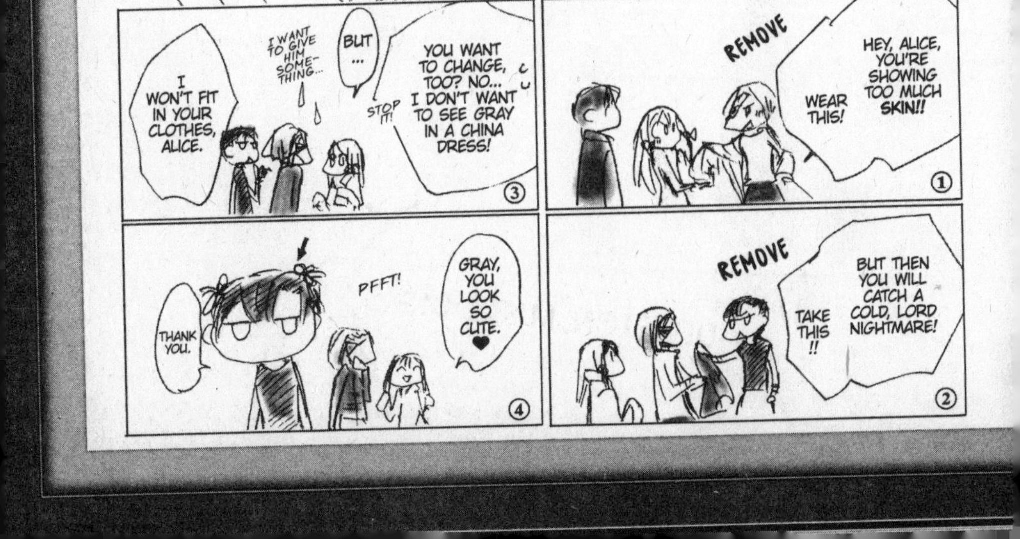
HEY, ALICE, YOU'RE SHOWING TOO MUCH SKIN!!
WEAR THIS!
REMOVE
BUT THEN YOU WILL CATCH A COLD, LORD NIGHTMARE!
TAKE THIS !!
REMOVE
YOU WANT TO CHANGE, TOO? NO... I DON'T WANT TO SEE GRAY IN A CHINA DRESS!
STOP IT!
BUT ...
I WANT TO GIVE HIM SOME-THING...
I WON'T FIT IN YOUR CLOTHES, ALICE.
GRAY, YOU LOOK SO CUTE.
PFFT!
THANK YOU.

COMING SOON

MAY 2014
Alice in the Country of Hearts:
Love Labyrinth of Thorns

JUNE 2014
Alice in the Country of Joker:
Circus and Liar's Game Vol. 5

JULY 2014
Alice in the Country of Clover:
Knight's Knowledge Vol. 1

AUGUST 2014
Alice in the Country of Joker:
The Nighmare Trilogy Vol. 1